THERAPY BEYOND
MODERNITY

THERAPY BEYOND MODERNITY

DECONSTRUCTING AND TRANSCENDING
PROFESSION-CENTRED THERAPY

Richard House

KARNAC

LONDON   NEW YORK

First published in 2003 by
H. Karnac (Books) Ltd.
6 Pembroke Buildings, London NW10 6RE

A subsidiary of Other Press LLC, New York

British Library Cataloguing in Publication Data

A C.I.P. for this book is available from the British Library

ISBN 1 85575 996 9

Edited, designed, and produced by The Studio Publishing Services Ltd,
Exeter EX4 8JN

Printed in Great Britain

10 9 8 7 6 5 4 3 2 1

www.karnacbooks.com

CONTENTS

DEDICATION

I dedicate this book, first, to my daughter, Shanice, in the hope that her generation won't need to resort to the commodified "Therapy Form" for their difficulties of living; to my unconditionally supportive parents—my mother, Rosalie, and my late father, John; to my very special friend, Inga, and her fine son Ludomir; and to "Rosie Alexander", (the late) "Ann France" and "Anna Sands", who have all struggled heroically with the therapy experience, and who have left three magnificent book-length testimonies, transparent in their raw honesty and depth of understanding, to the often unspeakable complexity—and potential abusiveness–of the psychotherapeutic experience.

ACKNOWLEDGEMENTS

First I wish to thank my Independent Practitioner Network practitioner-group colleagues for their support, friendship, and challenge—Tony Donaghy, Irene Galant, Guy Gladstone, Juliet Lamont, Drue Nottage, Denis Postle, Annie Spencer, and most especially Jutta Gassner for her constant and ongoing peer support over a period of years; Richard Mowbray and Juliana Brown for laying bare so painstakingly and thoroughly the ideology of "didactic" professionalization; "Rosie Alexander" and "Anna Sands" for being so helpful in my formulation of Chapters 6 and 8 respectively, and for their invaluable encouragement and support of this book; Professors Ian Parker and Nikolas Rose for their fearless and inspired deconstructions of psychology's many shibboleths; and Yvonne Bates, Jill Brooks, Tim Broughton, Juliana Brown, Cal Cannon, Jean Clark, Lindsay Cooke (thanks for those wonderful conversations!), Benita Cowen, Carol Ferguson, Jill Hall, Sue Hatfield, Steve Hunt, Keith Pearce, Gael Rowan, Fiona Strodder and Brian Thorne for their friendship and much-valued colleagueship.

I am also truly grateful to Professor Ian Parker and David Smail for writing, respectively, the Foreword and Afterword to the book, and to Professors Alvin Mahrer, Ian Parker, Ernesto Spinelli and

Brian Thorne, and Juliana Brown, Cal Cannon, Colin Feltham, John Heron, David Kalisch, Peter Lomas, Richard Mowbray, Denis Postle, and Keith Tudor for finding the time in their enormously busy schedules to offer their summary responses to the original manuscript.

Thanks also to Dr Brien Masters, Editor of *Steiner Education* journal, for permission to reproduce the magnificent painting on the cover, which originally adorned the cover of *Steiner Education*, 33(1), 1999.

I would like to thank Bee Springwood and Malcolm Black for their word-processing pyrotechnics—which were absolutely essential for, and greatly appreciated by, this self-confessed, only recently reconstructed neo-Luddite card-carrying Amstrad-8256 user.

An earlier version of Chapter 8 first appeared in the *European Journal of Psychotherapy, Counselling & Health*, 4(1), 2001, pp. 123–136.

I would also like to thank MacMillan Publishers Ltd for permission to quote extensively from Anna Sands: *Falling for Therapy*, published originally by MacMillan Publishers in 2000, reproduced with permission of Palgrave.

I am grateful to Rosie Alexander for her permission to quote from her book, *Folie à Deux*, originally published by Free Association Books in 1995.

I am grateful to Free Association Books for permission to quote extensively from *Consuming Psychotherapy* by Ann France, first published in 1989 by Free Association Books Ltd of 57 Warren Street, London W1P 5PA.

Finally, my thanks go to my publisher, Karnac Books, for their friendliness and efficiency – qualities so well modelled by my in-house editor, Leena Häkkinen.

FOREWORD

Ian Parker

This book draws together radical critiques of therapy and takes them further, to show how therapists have become all too willing administrators of the mind, and how they then delight in the bureaucratic management of therapeutic practice. Richard House shows how profession-centred, or "professionalized therapy" betrays what should be most genuinely therapeutic about speaking to another about one's self, and he develops an impassioned argument for retrieving some ideas that might help us reflect on the parlous state of the profession.

Some of the important ideas he discusses come from within the broad psychoanalytic tradition, with Georg Groddeck's work getting a good hearing and even Jacques Lacan being treated fairly sympathetically. The psychoanalytic frame for Richard House's polemic might strike a few readers as being a little out of keeping with the spirit of the book, but that frame is in turn embedded in a political agenda that we might in the widest and deepest sense of the word see as "humanist". When we are talking about "therapy", of course, we need to be careful about metaphors of depth, and it is worth emphasising that here we refer to humanism in the best sense of the term, socialist humanism that underpins the book. For all the claims to be "humanist" in present-day therapy, the individualising of experience that House so ably illuminates is itself a betrayal of a form of humanism that looks to human nature as social through and through and as containing within it the potential for collective empowering activity. So, why might we be invited to take psychoanalytic ideas seriously as a way out?

Professionalized therapy has been so successful in recruiting humanism to its own ideal of self-centred insight and social adaptation that psychoanalysis is then positioned as either the epitome of humanism or its diametric opposite. Either way, once this positioning has happened psychoanalysis must then be treated with the same degree of suspicion. There is indeed a tendency for psychoanalysis in the English-speaking world to turn itself into a form of humanist therapy in order to solve the political problems— of collusion with abuse, cultural privilege, elitism—that have beset it. But the flight from psychoanalytic questioning and self-questioning into being the helpmate of psychotherapists (and with the aim of being the "security council" of the psychotherapy registration bodies if the mainstream psycho-analysts can get away with it) will not work. That is, it fails to address the limits of professionalized therapy.

Therapy is professionalized through the limits it draws around itself as a practice, and the bureaucratised procedures by which one can claim the label "psychotherapist" (or "psychoanalyst") are in urgent need of deconstruction. But Richard House knows that this task entails a wider analysis of the way limits are constructed and reconstructed in what he calls "pathologizing *therapese*". I will look briefly at what the dominant therapeutic discourse draws us into, and in this way we will see how psychodynamic notions become part of the ways of speaking about our selves that professionalized therapy then feeds upon and regurgitates.

When therapeutic discourse sets out positions for subjects to adopt so that they can speak and be understood it does not merely lay out empty spaces in language that invite us in. There is something special about therapeutic discourse that draws us all the more tightly into its code, into its network of assumptions about the world, people and the insides of their minds. Therapeutic discourse includes, for example, deliberate attention to cynicism about therapy, and I am sure that hardened therapists well schooled in professionalized therapy will be ready to pathologize Richard House. There is a requirement that there should be a depth of commitment to it as one speaks it that makes it difficult to step back out of it when one has finished speaking. To speak in a position therapeutically, is to perform subjectivity in such a way as to find it difficult to perform any other position again in the same way. It is this that poses such a danger to humanists and to psychoanalysts when they speak therapeutically. Therapeutic discourse also functions within certain apparatuses of care and responsibility that conceal at the very moment that they reproduce patterns of power in the broader domain of the psy-complex. House reviews very well the role of the psy-complex in the professionalization of therapy.

One of the peculiar and entrancing characteristics of therapeutic discourse is that we achieve our position not only, or even not even, by displaying knowledge but by displaying our *interiority*. There are three components of therapeutic identity, that of the "self", "emotions" and "relationships", and the distinctive sense of each of these components lies in how they are interrelated. This interrelationship is crucial, and the therapeutic self only works because there are certain assumptions about the nature of emotions and relationships; that emotions for therapeutic subjects have a crucial role in defining the self and relationships, and that relationships are the necessary medium for elaborating a therapeutic sense of self and emotions.

Let us take the self first. One key therapeutic motif is that the self is treated as something that is deep under the surface. When we hear someone therapeutic say "I don't know if you really *heard* me", there seems to be an image of something inside; as if you can physically hear something, but therapeutic discourse is framing this in such a way as to assume that there is some deeper self inside that could really "hear" or "not hear" what is being said. The notions of "hearing" and "being heard" are talked about as requiring some deeper or behind the surface emotional reception that is more profound than simple acoustic reception.

A second motif is that the self is thought of as being fragile. Now, of course, human beings are quite fragile, but this fragility is much more intense in therapeutic discourse. A third motif is that the self should be a moral example to others. It is noticeable, perhaps, that therapists lead a public life as a moral example. They live in an ambassadorial role. That is why they are sometimes a bit po-faced and humourless. Those who are really drawn deep into their therapeutic identity seem very conscious about being good people who will be a moral example to others. It is then that they become the most unbearable bureaucrats in the registration bodies.

With regard to emotions in therapeutic discourse, what is important here is the way emotions operate in and around the self and through the medium of relationships. There is a notion that emotions can be intuitively grasped, and this is something that a therapeutic training will often promise access to. There is an opposition between thinking and feeling, and a privileging of direct intuitive access to feeling over rationalisation. There is in some arenas, as a consequence, a refusal of theory as a kind of defence. So, to take up a therapeutic identity and to display it to others is to show that we know what other people are feeling. The professionalized therapist is able to say things like "you are angry with me" or even that a group of people might be angry or that they are in some other emotional state.

The emotions are not only treated as inside the self, as deep, but as "between" people in some way. This assumption is made in therapeutic talk, with inside and outside being mapped onto feeling and expression. But emotion here is not simply to do with accumulation and discharge; rather, it is in the seeking of speech and expression.

Further, there seems to be a strong idea that emotions are bound up with morality, with some ways of feeling and showing your feelings being treated as healthy and good. This is brought about in therapeutic discourse through resignification and investment of everyday words with emotional force; words such as "special", "important", "painful", "hard". When these words are said in a therapeutic way they are very much more important, accorded a greater moral weight than in everyday speech.

Let us move on to relationships, which structure the self and operate as a medium for emotions. One aspect of therapeutically framed relationships is the way that the self and emotions are *performed*. There is quite a strong crossover here between therapeutic circles and dramatic circles. It is striking the way that therapeutic talk is often accompanied by a kind of dramatic acting out of what the emotions are that are supposed to be in the talk. There will also often be a certain mode of speech to indicate sensitivity to the reactions of others. It is worth noting that sometimes we see the complete opposite in some hard-line psychoanalysts, for example, who will do their best *not* to act out emotions as they speak. Either way we see the importance attached to the exteriorisation of emotions as part of the performance of therapeutic identity.

A second motif in relationships is the importance given to "boundaries" (cf. House's Chapter 3). We often find in therapeutic identity an oscillation between boundary-mania or boundary-phobia. This is where we will find talk about "containing" emotions and talk about "safe places". It can reach a point, for example, when therapists are so worried about what they call "boundaries" that they cannot be involved in public political activities because their clients might see them or interact with them outside the therapeutic space. This is where we see boundary modelling, and an injunction to clients to respect boundaries. This injunction marks a division between public life and private life, which in the therapeutic space are actually necessarily blurred.

All of these briefly sketched issues are important to grasp what may be so pathologizing about "therapese". This said, it is important not to abstract this kind of analysis from context, as if therapeutic discourse has formal qualities independent of its wider "conditions of possibility". We need to embed this analysis in a broader analysis of the discursive conditions in which therapy operates in Western culture. These conditions are as much cultural as institutional. The question of "culture" here impacts on the analysis not only in the way that psychotherapy exists in a certain "sub-culture" but also in the way that it exists in relation to other cultures and sub-cultures.

Both the cultural and institutional conditions are interwoven with questions of gender. Therapy has been the chosen medium for radical activity for lesbian feminists (and some gay men), who run up against particular forms of pathlogizing discourse and practice in the training organisations. One consequence of this "feminising" of therapeutic discourse has been that the backlash to therapy evident in the activity of the various "false memory" groups has also been a backlash against feminism, perhaps sometimes even a primary motivating force.

The gender composition of therapy has consequences for

developing an analysis and, by implication, a critique of therapeutic discourse and identity. That gender dimension in the increase of therapeutic discourse in Western culture and in its bureaucratization is something that needs further work, and although Richard House does not address this question explicitly in his book, he raises questions aplenty for how a feminist reading of therapy might proceed. As women are recruited into professionalized therapy, and as some feminists find themselves drawn into it at the same time, the role of feminist critique of that process becomes all the more pressing—and there is thus also a political aspect to this kind of analysis.

Deconstruction of the limits of a profession, then, must include deconstruction of the everyday discourse that sustains it, and this book is a marvellous exploration of how it also must include a deconstruction of what we take to be the self. That project might be seen as psychoanalysis allied with social humanist critique. It is certainly a project that professionalized therapy sabotages, a project that Richard House once again puts on the agenda.

ABOUT THE AUTHOR

An Oxford graduate with a PhD in Environmental Sciences, Richard House has worked as a GP counsellor, a WPF group supervisor, and an individual therapist and supervisor in private and voluntary practice. The author of over 100 therapy publications, in 1997 he co-edited the widely acclaimed anthology *Implausible Professions* (PCCS Books). A further co-edited anthology, *Ethically Challenged Professions*, and a collection of his published papers, *With an Independent Voice*, will be published in 2003. Having trained as a Steiner Waldorf class and Kindergarten teacher, Richard currently works as a Steiner early-years teacher. He is Series Editor of Hawthorn Press's "Early Years" series, and has numerous education publications to his name. With Peter Davies, he recently co-founded the W.A.S.T.E. website (**Welfare Action for Surviving Teachers and Ex-teachers—** at **http://www.wasteedu.org**), offering a forum of support for teachers ravaged by the frenetic politicization and deprofessionalization to which mainstream education is currently subject. A collection of his published writings, *The Trouble with Education*, is forthcoming through Education Now Books, Nottingham in 2003.

"Professionalization of helping—which goes hand in hand with scientific detachment—is an unfortunate legacy of the old world-view, and inevitably empowers the professionals rather than the clients"

Gill Edwards, 1992: 199

"I look forward to a society that will have little need for therapists of any sort"

Rollo May, 1987: 219

Introduction

Richard House

"... certain crucial factors exist in therapy that have not been
sufficiently considered by many therapists, [which], in
remaining ill-considered, are likely to increase the likelihood
of negative or abusively-interpreted experiences ... therapists
have incorrectly placed their 'faith' in various principles and
assumptions that are questionable and unnecessary"

Spinelli, 1995: 157, 160

A quarter-century ago now, in the Introduction to his
acclaimed primer *A Complete Guide to Therapy*, the radical
therapist Joel Kovel wrote:

[T]herapeutics necessarily involves ideology ... therapy seems true
to nothing but uncertainty. The proper approach is that of *critique*,
by which I mean an inquiry that reveals the hidden assumptions of
a phenomenon, grounds it in history and does not pretend that the
observer stands separate from the thing observed. [Kovel, 1976: 13–14,
original emphasis]

That the history of therapy since the mid-1970s has notably

failed to follow Kovel's precept is testimony to both the uncritical, non-reflexive stance that ideologies tend to take towards themselves, and also to the *illusion* of reflexiveness and self-interrogation that therapy has been able to perpetrate. The latter feature surely stems, at least in part, from the highly peculiar nature of the therapeutic project, whose very essence is typically that of self-interrogation and awareness—but which typically and uncritically takes the pursuit of that very process itself as an unproblematic given. Thus, only the means by which such awareness is pursued have been open to "critique" and the battle of theoretical ideas (in turn manifested in the proliferation of types of therapy and the enormous growth in the literature of therapy); but the possibility that this very project might itself be suspect is hardly given a passing thought within the ideology of therapy—or what in this book I term therapy's "regime of truth" (borrowing from Nikolas Rose's terminology).

What has tended to happen, then, is that the content of therapy has been subjected to the most stringent interrogation and critique (often stemming from the internal competitive jostling for "market" position of the various approaches), while the very project of therapy *per se* has typically escaped any similar level of problematization (for notable exceptions see Cloud, 1998; Masson, 1988; Smail, 1996).

In this book I attempt to redress this woeful lack of balance by following Kovel's recommendations—that is, by teasing out and laying bare the hidden assumptions of therapy as a modern(ist), increasingly profession-centred healing practice, and the ways in which those assumptions constitute an ideology which, like most if not all ideologies, inevitably takes on a self-serving nature, being surreptitiously more concerned with preserving its own hegemony than with an honest authenticity of procedure and practice.

I write as a "semi-retired" counselling practitioner, having been practising as a therapist since 1990, with 7 years of training, first in Counselling and Groupwork and then in Body-Oriented Psycho-therapy; as a General Practice Counsellor doing strictly time-limited counselling within the NHS; as a former group supervisor for a Westminster Pastoral Foundation affiliate, and experienced individual supervisor; and as a trained Steiner Waldorf class and kindergarten teacher, currently working in Steiner Waldorf early years settings.

I am aware that the content of what follows will challenge in a quite fundamental way the very foundations of the therapy project;

and for that reason it may well be received with affronted hostility in some quarters, and welcome relief in others. Extant critiques of therapy have tended to be pretty long on rhetoric and emotional charge, and, concomitantly, rather light on intellectual rigour and coherence. In this book I attempt to rectify this lack by setting out a fully articulated argument which questions at root the status of some of "professional" therapy's most hallowed and taken-for-granted assumptions.

As will become clear, I believe that as the age of modernity wanes and the flawed and distorting Enlightenment project becomes progressively exposed, we will inevitably begin to enter what I call a *post-professional*, even post-therapy era, soundly rooted in an emancipatory, participative New Paradigm philosophy; and I hope that this book will prove to be just one early harbinger of these momentous historical movements in the evolution of the Western mind (Tarnas, 1991).

Despite initial appearances (particularly in Part II of the book), it is important to stress at the outset that *Therapy Beyond Modernity* is not a Massonian/Eysenckian/Gellneresque wholesale rejection of the very project of therapy—though I do view therapy as just a transient and culturally specific phase in the evolution of the Western mind and human consciousness more generally. But equally, in today's Western culture, therapy both exists and continues to burgeon; and to the extent that it does have a future, I feel passionately committed to influencing that future as far as possible in a "post-professional", "postmodern", participative direction—a direction which, not least, privileges creative "human potential" development and a spiritual, New Paradigm focus over a remedial psychopathologizing and infantilizing ontology (Mowbray, 1995; Parker *et al.*, 1995). If this book succeeds at all in this somewhat ambitious aim, then it will have more than served its purpose in the evolution of ideas—ideas to which we all continually contribute in our different ways in our day-to-day vocational beliefs and healing practices.

Summary of contents

Part I is concerned with those defining features of the therapeutic experience for which I have elsewhere coined the term "Profession-alized Therapy Form" (House, 1999b), and which I refer to in this book variously as "profession-centred therapeutic practice" or discourse, profession-centred therapy's "regime of truth", the "protocol" of profession-centred therapy, and the like. In Chapters 1–4 inclusive, I begin to problematize the very project of therapy *per se*—certainly in the conventional form that it typically takes in mainstream therapy culture.

Following a broad contextualizing introduction to the broad themes addressed in the book in Chapter 1, Chapter 2 draws heavily upon the important work of Ian Parker and Nikolas Rose on discourse and power to show how conventional therapy typically functions as a "regime of truth" which in turn acts as a self-serving and ethically questionable ideology. My central thesis in this book has been greatly influenced by the important work of Nikolas Rose, Professor of Sociology at the London School of Economics and Political Science, and Ian Parker, Professor of Psychology at Manchester Metropolitan University—most particularly, the former's seminal books *Governing the Soul* (1989) and *Inventing Our Selves* (1996), and the latter's masterful multiply-authored deconstruction of the notion of "psychopathology" (Parker *et al.*, 1995), his many works on discourse, power, and social constructionism, and his recent edited volume, *Deconstructing Psychotherapy* (1999), the theme of which I would like wholeheartedly to endorse and be aligned with in the views expressed in this book. The intellectual debt which I owe to Parker and Rose will become especially clear in Chapter 2.

My central argument is that, in its profession-centred, com-modified form, therapy can and sometimes does become routinely and intrinsically abusive to the extent that it self-fulfillingly constructs a framework—profession-centred therapeutic discourse and practice—which serves to guarantee the legitimacy of its own existence within a discursive regime of truth, and outside the confines of which it can become very difficult for clients *and* therapists even to think.

In Chapters 3 and 4, I then examine in detail a number of hallowed concepts from the therapy lexicon—namely, resistance, boundaries and "the frame", holding, confidentiality, safety, abuse and ethics—to illustrate the way in which these arguably *ideological* concepts have far more to do with a therapist-driven self-interest than they do with an authentic and meaningful characterization of the therapeutic experience. My main conclusion is that, in order to avoid these intrinsic abuses, therapy should aim to be ongoingly and processually deconstructive of its professional ideologies and clinical practices—giving an approach to therapy which is post-modern, deconstructive, and unavoidably hermeneutic in both philosophy and practice.

In Chapters 5–8 inclusive, I examine three detailed reports that have appeared in the literature of actual client experiences of therapy, in order to "test out" the propositions developed in the preceding chapters. I focus in particular on the work of "Rosie Alexander", "Ann France", and "Anna Sands", each of whom have written insightfully and in considerable depth about their often extremely harrowing experiences of one-to-one therapy. Chapter 5 includes detailed discussions of why there is such a dearth of studies of actual client/patient experiences of therapy, and of why it is so hard to rely on subjective-report data to assess the efficacy of therapeutic interventions. My principal finding is that there is indeed ample confirming evidence from these experiential data to support the formulations in Chapters 2–4 about therapy's "regime of truth" and the self-serving ideology of profession-centred therapeutic practice.

In Part III I take the argument further still, outlining the features that a New Paradigm, "post-professional" approach to therapy might take. In Chapter 9 I give a detailed account of the pioneering work of the healer–analyst and contemporary of Freud, Georg Groddeck, whose extraordinary therapeutic work can, I maintain, serve as a prototype for the kind of therapeutic approach that will obtain in the postmodern world which is fast supplanting the outmoded positivist legacy of modernity's Enlightenment project. Chapter 10 outlines the case for a "post-therapy era", in which therapy, in its profession-centred commodified form, is system-atically exposed as being part of the problem rather than a solution to the cultural and spiritual malaise of modernity.

Finally, Part IV considers at length the implications of the book's analysis for the praxis of therapy in what I call (following Ivan Illich) a "post-professional era". Chapter 11 summarizes and further discusses the critique of profession-centred therapy developed earlier in the book; and Chapter 12 elaborates upon the possible nature of a mature, viable post-professional framework for therapy, and the specific form that what I call a New Paradigm, "deconstructive therapy" might plausibly take.

Following a brief synthesizing conclusion, entitled "Who would be a therapist?", there is an exhaustive reference section, together with a *Select Bibliography* of the literature on critiques of therapy and therapy professionalization, which I hope the interested reader will find to be a useful "mining" resource for pursuing critical perspectives in and on therapy.

Finally, the Afterword to the book has kindly been contributed by the celebrated writer and clinical psychologist David Smail, whose work I approvingly quote throughout the book, and who has, over several decades, been something of a relentless and inconvenient irritant to those who unquestioningly champion the beneficence of the "therapy" phenomenon in Western culture. Smail originally agreed to write the Foreword to the book, but eventually decided that his position had shifted significantly enough to preclude an unequivocal endorsement of the book's conclusions. In true deconstructive, Trickster-esque spirit, however, we pursued the idea of his contributing a "moderately sympathetic" but not uncritical Afterword—for my overriding wish for this book is that it stimulates an engaged and pluralistic debate, and the evolution of thinking, in and about therapy in modern culture, rather than presenting itself as an "objectively true", unchallengeable commentary on therapy and its professionalizing accoutrements. If the "truth" about therapy is indeed a meaningful notion as we stand on the cusp of modernity and postmodernity, then my hunch is that it lies somewhere along the continuum denoted by David Smail's position at one pole, and my own as outlined in this book, at the other. It might be that the central difference between Smail and myself is more one of timing (i.e. just when will "therapy" have outlived its usefulness as a form of helping?) than of substance; but we happily leave that to the reader to decide ...

A final "editorial" note. The original draft of this book contained an additional part, with three chapters on critical perspectives on therapy professionalization. Length constraints unfortunately meant that they had to be excluded from the current book, so my many critical and sceptical references to the professionalization question that recur throughout this book might appear to need more detailed substantiation. My published writings on this question are many and varied, and are quoted in full in the References and the Select Bibliography at the end of the book. The three chapters in question will appear in my forthcoming collection of critical papers, *With an Independent Voice* (House, forthcoming).

PART I
THE PROFESSION-CENTRED
THERAPY FORM

Consider:

"Regimes of truth govern what can be spoken about, and they also define what will be seen as nonsense or madness"

Parker, 1997a: 7

"... a kind of power that binds us to others, to those to whom we confess and to those who originate the language within which we confess, at the very moment as it binds us to our own identity. So when I use these words—... neurosis, self esteem ...—I am also activating a whole 'regime of truth', an array of authorities who stand behind this language and guarantee it, a complex of practices and procedures"

Rose, 1997

"'You give me a great deal of power', [my therapist] said once ... But it wasn't him who held the power. *It was the situation* ... What is it about sitting in a room, alone, regularly, with one other person and talking about oneself that can unleash such ungovernable emotions? Whatever the answer, it is still one which is far from being understood and until it is, therapists and their patients are liable to find themselves in a similar position to that of children playing with a live bomb"

Alexander, 1995: 86; 1998b: 95, my emphasis

CHAPTER ONE

Therapy in deconstructive perspective

"... is there something specific to therapeutic relationships that tends to dispose them towards unbeneficial consequences? Is there something inherently problematic in the therapeutic encounter?"

Spinelli, 1995: 157

"... therapeutic language, therapeutic techniques, therapeutic scenarios, the proliferation of the therapeutic through our culture, has a role in fabricating us as certain kinds of persons ... the client needs to become a 'good subject of therapy' by representing their problem in a particular psychotherapeutic form ..."

Rose, 1997

This book is not about abuse in therapy, or abusive therapists, but rather, its concern is abuse by therapy itself—by the very form that profession-centred therapy takes in modern culture, with its various technical, theoretical, and "professional" accoutrements. What I have called elsewhere the culturally legitimated "Professionalized Therapy Form" (House, 1999b) can, I maintain, routinely not only of itself be intrinsically abusive, but can actively set up a milieu in which abuse may be to some extent inevitable, irrespective of the conscious intentions of the therapist (which, of course, I hold to be predominantly well-meaning and well-intentioned).

On this view, therapeutic abuse can be said to occur to the extent that an artificial framework (of profession-centred therapeutic practice) is created in which, at the margin, infantilized patients can be thought unable to take responsibility for their own choices or behaviour. On this view, it further follows that at least some "abuse" may be uniquely attributable to, even precipitated by, profession-centred therapy's "regime of truth", with its active (sometimes deliberate) precipitation of power imbalances, transference dependencies, and infantilization experiences. In addition, so-called "abusive therapists" could be seen as being just as much subject to the "regime of truth" that is artificially set up within profession-centred therapeutic discourse as are so-called "abused clients"—albeit, of course, in a different way. I think Ingleby is saying something similar when he writes that, "What the patient submits to is not the rule of the analyst, but the rule of analysis, to which the analyst is every bit as subject. The real authoritarianism of psychoanalysis lies not in the domination of patient by analyst, but in *the domination of both by the analytic doctrine*" (quoted in Lomas, 1987: 102–103, my emphasis).

"Rosie Alexander" (1999) has expressed something similar:

> Many people have the same kind of experience in therapy, principally the invasion of one's emotional space to the exclusion of all else and the suffering of unrequited desire to an incapacitating degree. Doesn't this indicate the existence of some common psychological catalyst in the therapy process rather than a diverse collection of bungling therapists? [*ibid.*]

In this view, then, abuse is seen as being intrinsic to the form taken by therapy and the forces triggered within the therapeutic relationship, rather than being laid at the door of a few aberrant "rogue" therapists. I will have cause to return to this radical proposition in myriad ways throughout this book.

It is interesting to reflect on the way in which, when therapy is seen not to work, it is almost invariably "blamed" on (bad) therapists, rather than the whole project of therapy being called into question. Perhaps this has something to do with the deep "victimhood" dynamics of blaming which are so easily triggered within the framework of profession-centred therapeutic discourse (cf. Hall, 1993), with most therapeutic approaches either explicitly or tacitly embracing the ideological assumption that past experience in large measure *determines* present experience. For, as Alexander puts it, "Perhaps it's more emotionally satisfying to blame a person rather than a methodology—a person, after all, offers a target for all the anger and vengeance which are so often churned up [the raging infant of Jill Hall's 'reluctant adult'—RH] ... but the result of this is that the 'wood' of the problem is obscured by the 'trees' of the individuals involved" (personal communication). This is a central theme to which I will return repeatedly in what follows.

The French Marxist philosopher Louis Althusser talked of "history without a knowing subject"; and in similar vein, I will attempt to show how therapy, as legitimate cultural form, may well entail certain pervasive deleterious effects, the consequences of which typically lie outside the "normal" awareness of both therapists and clients. Very occasionally, the veiled opacity of these effects is momentarily laid bare, only for the lid to be slammed shut again before the field has afforded space for mature and undefended reflection on what is unearthed. Thus, for example, (ex-) therapists (e.g. Jeffrey Masson in *Against Therapy*, 1988) and ex-clients (see Chapters 6–8, below) have dared, either explicitly or implicitly, to point a finger at the "Emperor's-clothes-ness" of therapy, and to suggest or imply that its iatrogenic effects go far wider than the odd "rogue" abusive therapist. Yet such critiques tend to be heavily rooted in the emotional; and while for me this does not in any way compromise their legitimacy or authority (given that there is no logical reason why the rational should necessarily be privileged over the emotional in claims to "truth"), it has enabled the defenders of and apologists for therapy to write off their criticisms as just so much "acted-out" or "unworked-through" neurotic "material" or "psychopathology" (e.g. Holmes, 1992).

As Masson himself has pertinently pointed out (cf. Masson, 1992b: 23, note 3), however, whether or not one's arguments or criticisms are valid is logically quite independent of their possible origins in "neurosis" (Hitler no doubt had many "valid" insights about all kinds of things); so the therapy establishment's deeply personal, *ad hominem* character assassinations that greeted Masson's *Against Therapy* in the late 1980s were not only in many cases deeply distasteful, but constituted a woefully inadequate response to the substance and implications of Masson's critique, however partial and incomplete it may have been (cf. Spinelli, 1995: 153–154). From the client's (or patient's) perspective, Rosie Alexander points to what she calls the "hypersensitive defensiveness" surrounding these debates—a kind of "batten-down-the-hatches" mentality that is at once both antithetical to the openness that therapy enthusiastically urges upon others, yet also hardly surprising, given the very considerable "professional" vested interests that are at stake whenever anyone—therapist, client, or cultural critic—dares to problematize the very project of "therapy".

In what follows I attempt to add decisive ballast to extant critiques of therapy with a sober, relatively unemotional deconstruction of what I call the *form* that profession-centred therapy typically takes—i.e. the specific therapeutic practices that therapy commonly embraces, and the theoretical justifications normally adopted to legitimize those practices. I will attempt to show how therapy, in its modern profession-centred form, increasingly functions as a "regime of truth" whose discourse *actively creates* identity and subjectivity (most centrally, the identities of "therapist" and "client"), and whose accompanying practices self-fulfillingly construct an ideological framework which then reinforces and guarantees the conditions of its own existence. As Nikolas Rose (1997) puts it, "therapies, their languages, techniques and types of authority, have actually played a significant role in making us up as certain kinds of self. The kind of persons that we now take ourselves to be are tied to a kind of project of our own identities ...".

More specifically, the very way in which such therapy is structured (or "framed") continually encourages and threatens to produce client infantilization and dependency through the deep unconscious dynamics triggered within profession-centred therapeutic discourse, and by the assumptive framework typically (and often uncritically) embraced by the therapist. Thus, I want to make it unambiguously clear that my critique of "therapy" refers to what

I call its *profession-centred* form (the full specification of which will become clear later). As I make clear in my concluding chapter, I draw a crucial distinction between such narrowly "profession-centred" therapy, on the one hand, and on the other, the kind of explicitly "deconstructive, post-professional therapy" which I advocate (coinciding quite closely, perhaps, with what others might call "human potential work"—e.g. Mowbray, 1995).

I maintain, then, that the very existence of profession-centred therapy as a culturally legitimate form of "intervention" serves to create a socially and ideologically constructed "regime of truth" which routinely constrains rather than liberates human experience, thereby bringing about the very opposite of therapy's professed intention—i.e. ossification rather than organic growth, change, or transcendence. More widely, furthermore, the ossifying cultural form of profession-centred, individualized therapy also serves to prevent or hold up the emergence of new qualitative shifts in the evolution of human consciousness. Perhaps the commodified form taken by profession-centred therapy has been a necessary stage in the evolution of human consciousness, and has served an important purpose. But what promised to be—and for many no doubt has been—a liberation has increasingly become a fetter which limits that very evolution; and on this view, critiques such as that developed in this book should perhaps be understood as a staging-point on the "human journey"—a harbinger, perhaps, of what I have called (borrowing terminology from Ivan Illich) a "post-therapy, post-professional era".

In similar vein, in his *The Awakening of Intelligence*, the formidable Indian philosopher J. Krishnamurti wrote, "How is one to examine [consciousness], how is one to expose the whole content of it? Is it to be done bit by bit, slowly, gradually?—or is it to be exposed totally and understood instantly, *and thereby the whole analytical process comes to an end?*" (1973: 60, my emphasis). Certainly, I would respond, such a species-wide shift in human consciousness most certainly will not occur while the ideology of therapy's regime of truth holds sway in modern culture. The contrast could hardly be more stark between the Krishnamurti-type view, expressed above, and that of analytic orthodoxy; here, for example, is Patrick Casement: "There are no short-cuts to analytic experience. There is no other path than patience" (1985: 218). The problem with such a view, of course, is that it almost inevitably self-fulfillingly creates precisely what it has assumed to exist in the first place! (cf. McDougall, 1995: 235–236).

Kovel has aptly written that "To state the limits of therapy is also to recognise that the human situation has no closed end, but is rather in a state of continuous historical evolution" (1976: 93). And nowhere is this more starkly observable than in the great historical movement of human consciousness away from modernity and towards postmodernity. I believe that therapy is surely in great danger of becoming an anachronistic irrelevance unless it "post-modernizes" its approach to theory and practice, and its accompanying ideology of professionalization. For Barratt, for example, what he calls the "masterdiscourse" of modernity and the Enlightenment "is now in an irreversible process of collapse" (1993: xi). And though "we cannot yet fully articulate what 'postmodernism' will be, ... we do know that our traditional ways of thinking and speaking, of conducting our lives, are no longer viable" (*ibid*.). Barratt goes on to make the telling point that, "even in its death throes, [the modern masterdiscourse] still constitutes our every moment of thinking, speaking, and acting" (*ibid*.: xii); and hardly could one find a more glaring example of this phenomenon than the world of therapy, caught up as it still is in fighting all the old, outmoded battles of modernity and profession-building, long after the epistemological ship has left port for a very different destination.

Along with a number of colleagues (most notably those involved in the Independent Practitioners Network), I have been challenging the so-called "professionalization" of therapy and counselling for some years (see, for example, the anthology *Implausible Professions*—House & Totton, 1997a,b; House, 1999b); and the current book should be seen as a natural organic development of those critiques. Professionalization can never be a neutral, disinterested process—least of all in the highly peculiar field of therapy, as I will elaborate in detail below.

In what follows I intend to articulate in depth what Jeffrey Masson and other critics have erstwhile failed to address—namely, how abuse is built into the ideological discourse of therapy—into *the very form* that profession-centred therapy takes in modern Western culture. Yet I am concerned not to be hoist by my own petard by replacing one regime of truth with another of my own making: for as will become clear below, the difficulties I outline with profession-centred therapeutic practice lie far more in its very "being" as a regime of truth *per se* than it does in the specific content which that regime actually takes.

Thus, I do not by any means present my arguments as *the* truth about therapy—as somehow being a "better" regime of truth than that which it is replacing; for I sympathize with the Derridean view that it was and is a fundamental error of the Enlightenment project to build systems of "objective" truth which can be assumed to give us reliable, "objective" perceptions of "reality" (cf. Derrida, 1974; Polkinghorne, 1990; see also my Chapter 9 on Georg Groddeck, below). Rather, my truth is inevitably a "local", subjective truth, based as it is upon my own particular and unique experiences of therapy as trainee, client, practitioner, supervisor, trainer, and scholar—and upon my best endeavours to interrogate the phenomenon of therapy as open-mindedly and in as presuppositionless a way as I am able—a state which Krishnamurti called "choiceless awareness". The late physicist Professor David Bohm embraced Krishnamurti's thinking to challenge what both saw as the tyranny and destructiveness of thinking, belief, and theoretical systems of all kinds (e.g. Bohm & Edwards, 1991; Krishnamurti, 1969, 1993)—and the emotional rootedness of that tyranny in a fear-driven experienced need for certainty ... which is in turn surely responsible in large measure for the wilder excesses and obsessions of the scientistic technocratic mentality of modernity (Bohm & Edwards, 1991). These are issues which will repeatedly crop up in the course of what follows.

It will come as no surprise, therefore, that I am an enthusiastic adherent of so-called "New Paradigm" philosophy—represented, *inter alia*, by the ideas informing the Scientific and Medical Network (of which I am a participating member), and by certain strands of postmodernist, deconstructionist, hermeneutic, and even vitalist thinking within Philosophy. The philosopher Henri Bergson, for example, highlighted the inadequacy of the intellect for grasping the full richness of human experience, which he saw as an indivisible continuum better represented by the artistic than by successions of "rational", conceptually demarcated conscious states. Bergson summed up succinctly the inappropriateness of the Enlightenment's hallowed "correspondence theory of truth", thus: "It is understood that fixed concepts can be extracted by our thoughts from the mobile reality, but there is no means whatever of reconstituting the mobility of the real with the fixity of concepts" (quoted in Steiner, 1973: 421; cf. the ontologies of, *inter alia*, Karl Marx, Martin Heidegger, Jacques Derrida, Alfred Korzybski, and Jiddu Krishnamurti—Ollman, 1971; Polkinghorne, 1990; Falconar, 1997).

The great—and criminally neglected—healer-cum-analyst-cum-philosopher and contemporary of Freud, Georg Groddeck, also had great sympathy with vitalist philosophy (Homer, 1988); and in the history of ideas and the evolution of human consciousness it is surely no coincidence that the recent rediscovery of Groddeck (e.g. *ibid.*; House, 1997a; Totton, 1998) temporally coincides with the current resurgence of interest in Henri Bergson's philosophy (Mullarky, 1999), and with the recent renaissance in Goethean science (Bortoft, 1996; Naydler, 1996). And the closely associated "re-enchantment" of science and nature (Berman, 1981; Baruss, 1996; House, 1999a), representing as it does a concomitant retreat from soulless positivism, is yet another manifestation of the paradigmatic sea-change that is threatening the hegemony of the "modern" technocratic world-view.

As will become clear later (in Chapter 9), I view Georg Groddeck as perhaps therapy's earliest proponent of New Paradigm thinking, with his pioneering "clinical" healing and philosophical works providing a wonderful opportunity for those seeking a viable and inspiring bridge between the increasing aridity of profession-centred therapeutic practice and the potential richness of a post-professional, post-therapy world.

While I hold strongly, then, to a non-objectivist approach to "truth", my style is nevertheless born of one who holds his unavoidably parochial truths with conviction and passion—qualities which should not be confused with objectivism or arrogance, though of course I am aware that these two qualities can so easily be mistaken for one another. And following Derrida again, I concur with his view that there is something in the very act of writing itself which evades all theoretical systems and logics—that there is an inevitable "surplus of meaning" which all language unavoidably entails (Polkinghorne, 1990: 104). Discomforts such as these, of course, place a great responsibility on the reader who will, I believe, create their own experience of this text, whatever the intentions of its writer or the ineffable unspokennesses that it contains.

Finally, and in sharp contradistinction to the humanistic, responsibility-taking ideology to which I used strongly to adhere, "I" am increasingly drawn to the Groddeckian view that it may well be an illusion that the I, or ego, is the governor of our thoughts and actions—and our writings! On this view, perhaps what follows has in some sense *written itself*, coming from I know not where—and perhaps I am merely the conduit or "channel" for the expression of these ideas. Of course I cannot completely break with conventional wisdom and say " 'I' am *not* 'responsible' for what follows"! (though such an unheard-of proclamation certainly appeals to the trickster in me!). No doubt I can claim some "credit" for the ideas expressed herein, but equally, I certainly don't claim ownership of them—for they have emerged at least as much from Norwich's wonderful "post-professional" therapy milieu (House, forthcoming) in which I am fortunate enough to live, as they have from my own individual reflection and insight. The arguments set out below will stand or fall on their own internal coherence, and on the extent to which they express a "truth" which resonates with the journey of human consciousness—and this will be so whether or not "I" take responsibility for them.

I don't expect this book to receive a particularly warm welcome from at least parts of the therapy world—and certainly not from those with a professional interest in the legitimacy and continued existence of therapy as an institution of modern culture (which, incidentally, currently includes myself, as I am still practising as a counsellor as I write, albeit in a limited way). In contrast, my hunch is that the book may well receive a far warmer reception from therapy's clientele—current and prospective as well as ex-clients searching for an enabling framework to make sense of their experiences of this peculiar phenomenon called "therapy". It has already received a very enthusiastic response from two of the authors and ex-clients whose work I examine later—Rosie Alexander and Anna Sands. I wish to speculate about the dynamics of the book's likely reception in therapeutic culture, as this will afford me the opportunity to illustrate the core of my argument in a way such that the reader can engage with it at an emotional–experiential level rather than at a narrowly intellectual one.

In a sense, perhaps the didactic professionalization process within the therapy world is just another example of what Barratt (1993, referred to above) calls "the death throes" of the old, increasingly irrelevant world-view of modernity and its hand-maiden, Aristotelian logic (cf. Polkinghorne, 1990; Falconar, 1997). A clue to the possible veracity of this analysis is afforded by the fact that what I call the "didactic" professionalization process has been almost exclusively practitioner-driven rather than client-driven—an attempt by practitioners (whose desperation is, perhaps, unac-knowledged and unconscious) somehow to render *possible* what is intrinsically (as Freud so famously remarked) an *impossible* "profession" (cf. Malcolm, 1980; House & Totton, 1997a,b).

Throughout what follows, I will be referring to what I see as an over-precious boundary- and safety-obsessiveness—and to the abuse-focused, control-obsessed fixations of conventional, profes-sion-centred therapy. I see the "didactic" professionalization process as the "respectable" institutional "public face" of these deep, fear-driven processes; and this process is, I believe, at some level a desperate and essentially unconscious attempt by the nascent "profession" to shore up and make comfortable, non-contradictory, and non-paradoxical that which is intrinsically uncomfortable, contradictory, and paradoxical—and which will remain so no matter how assiduous the attempt to legislate away these uncomfortable realities of human relationship. If my analysis is anything like right, then the covert message we are giving potential clientele through this professionalizing "acting-out" is that we, the purveyors of therapy, simply cannot bear uncertainty, not being in control, paradox, the ineffable ... (there are interesting parallels here with the insightful analysis in Heron, 1990). This in turn constitutes a massive irony for a "profession" whose theoretical formulations *do* typically pay at least some kind of lip-service to notions of "staying with uncertainty", relinquishing the "need for control", and so on!

That these fear-driven processes should become conflated and confused with career-mindedness, material self-interest, and power-infused vested interests (Mowbray, 1995)—important though these latter processes are—threatens to obscure the crucial fundamental point: namely, that the pervasive moves towards professionalization, and their attendant preoccupation with theoretical justification, academic standards, and the over-precious obsession with the "therapeutic frame" (Gray, 1994), are all manifestations of the (typically unwitting) attempt to render safe, manageable, and plausible that which is intrinsically *unsafe*, *un*manageable, and *im*plausible (House & Totton, 1997a,b; Malcolm, 1980). It was the Indian philosopher Krishnamurti who so brilliantly exposed the dynamics of the "control-freak" mentality, showing as he did how the attempt to control (through ego and will) that which is in principle uncontrollable quite inevitably and paradoxically brings about *the very opposite* of one's conscious intention; and I believe that this process is increasingly observable within the therapy field as professionalization and its associated ideological trappings and accoutrements have gathered pace in recent years.

If the foregoing analysis is even remotely accurate, then this book will likely raise considerable anxieties amongst those caught up in the professionalization process, and who would far rather that Therapy as clinical practice and cultural phenomenon was left undisturbed and unproblematized. On this view, my hunch is that what follows will make for quite disturbing reading for many if not most practitioners (from which I do not, incidentally, exclude myself, as it has also been personally disturbing—as well as exhilarating—to write it!).

A central hope I have for the book is that its circulation within culture will contribute towards a stripping away of the attempt institutionally to control the therapeutic healing process, and what I will argue to be the fundamentally wrong-headed attempt to "legislate" good practice into being through what is the largely illusory "policing" of practitioners. I will argue that such policing not only does not work, but is actually deleterious to the net quality of therapeutic help available within culture. Such a "stripping away" of therapy's *institution-itis* (cf. Oakley, 1998) would, I believe, paradoxically bring about a dramatic "leap forward" in human ("client") freedom, growth, and change, as we increasingly dare to embrace New Paradigm epistemologies and practices in the rapidly approaching era of "postmodernity".

Over 70 years ago, as I write, the Indian philosopher Krishnamurti, in a truly memorable speech that for me resounds across the decades, and retains a freshness and a pertinence that is perhaps even more relevant today than in its original context (namely, Krishnamurti's unilaterally dissolving the Order of the Star, the institutional vehicle formed to support his status as the chosen World Teacher), and which doubles as a wonderful statement of postmodern, New Paradigm philosophy decades ahead of its time, said:

> Truth is a pathless land. ... Truth, being limitless, unconditioned, unapproachable by any path whatsoever, cannot be organised; nor should any organisation be formed to lead or coerce people along any particular path. ... If you [organise a belief] it becomes dead, crystallised ..., to be imposed upon others. ... Truth cannot be brought down, rather the individual must make the effort to ascend to it. ... The Truth cannot be organised for you. ... Interest [which is aroused by an organisation] is of no value. The organisation becomes a framework into which its members can conveniently fit. They no longer strive after Truth ..., but rather carve for themselves a convenient niche in which to put themselves, or let the organisation place them, and consider that the organisation will thereby lead them to Truth. ... If an organisation be created for this purpose, it becomes a crutch, a weakness, a bondage, and must cripple the individual, and prevent him from growing, from establishing his uniqueness which lies in the discovery of himself of that absolute, unconditioned Truth. [quoted in Suares, 1953: 111–113 *passim*]

One could scarcely ask for a more clear and moving testimony to the values of pluralism and human potential development which I see as crucial core values of any therapeutic experience.

And what of the book's likely reception from therapy's clientele? I sense that the book may be received with great relief by those clients or ex-clients who get to read it. On reading an early draft of this Introduction, Rosie Alexander (whose testimony to the effects of therapy form a central part of Chapter 6) wrote in a personal communication that, "Reading the first two paragraphs of the Introduction gave me the greatest pleasure because they pretty well sum up my own views on the subject. The idea that the problem lies with thera*py* rather than with individual thera*pists* is generally rejected, even by those who have been at the receiving end". Such relief as the book does evoke will, I think, derive from (ex-)clients being given a framework of understanding with which to comprehend more clearly the ineffable, and above all highly peculiar experience of being a client-in-therapy. In this sense, then, this book is at least as much for therapy's clientele as it is for therapy practitioners themselves, and I sincerely hope that it will reach that "audience" as well.

As I put the finishing touches to the manuscript I felt like the little boy who naïvely wandered into town and dared to point out that the Emperor was stark naked—while everyone else was uncritically praising and eulogizing about his beautiful flowing attire! Of course, "critique" nearly always evokes an emotional response—and most typically a defensive one. I remember all too well my own highly defensive response when, in 1990, I first read Masson's "outrageous" *Against Therapy*, just as I was beginning to practise as a therapist. And I don't recount this anecdote in any "superior" way, implying that I'm somehow further along the "journey of understanding" about therapy than the defensive-feeling therapist who ends up reading this book. Rather, I offer it as an example of how none of us can ever know whether our initial, often reactive response to an argument or criticism will stay the same in the future, as our individual journeys or "destinies" unfold.

All any of us can do, then, is attempt to stay as open as we can be—and all I ask of you the reader is that you monitor and critically interrogate your emotional response to this book's arguments—and, most importantly, dare to stay open long enough to find out whether they find any resonance with your own experience of, or hunches about, the "true nature" of the psychotherapeutic enterprise.

In the next chapter, Chapter 2, I draw on the work of (among others) Ian Parker and Nikolas Rose on discourse and power to argue that conventional therapy typically functions as a "regime of truth" which can, in turn, all too easily function as a self-serving and ethically questionable ideology.

CHAPTER TWO

Therapy's "regime of truth"

"It was maddening to hear such bullshit, to be unable to convince [my therapist] of its wrongness and to know that I was in such a state of emotional slavery to someone whose mind was working along such erroneous lines. ... I was beginning to feel like a political prisoner locked away in a psychiatric hospital; impotent, completely at my captor's mercy, and in danger of being browbeaten into believing anything he wanted to say, no matter how absurd"

Alexander, 1995: 104

Introduction

there exists precious little about therapy that we can say with any certainty ... therapists really don't know what they're doing—even if they insist upon pretending ... they are "experts". [Spinelli, 1996: 56, 59]

I n the mid-1970s Ivan Illich published a seminal book, *Limits to Medicine* (1977b), in which he made a radical counter-intuitive case for the institution of professional medicine actually being deleterious to societal health (even though, of course, many *individual*-level treatment "successes" could no doubt be found). In this chapter I will make the parallel and equally radical claim that the profession-centred institution of "Therapy" as a culturally legitimate form of clinical practice is also in great danger of causing net harm at the societal level, compared with what might plausibly obtain in counterfactual society in which therapy was not a culturally legitimized and regulated healing practice.

Therapists commonly assume that their elegant theoretical formulations about "development", human distress, therapeutic change, and the like, along with their painstakingly encoded "professional" procedures, together constitute the crucial factors that define and deliver effective therapy. Perhaps matters really haven't changed that much since, nearly 20 years ago, David Smail wrote that "Libraries full of published research aimed at establishing the effectiveness of ... psychotherapies ... give no really clear indication of what the important ingredients are or what is the nature of their operation" (1983: 8).

Furthermore, despite decades of research that points to the unifying, so-called "non-specific" or "intangible" factors being what really matters in a therapeutic encounter (Frank & Frank, 1991; Miller *et al.*, 1997; Shepherd & Sartorius, 1989; Smail, 1983), the all-too-common internecine warfare between different therapeutic approaches (e.g. King & Steiner, 1990; Hugill, 1998), and the commonly observed emphasis that specific approaches give to difference rather than to factors of commonality, suggest that such parochial preoccupations have far more to do with practitioners' own insecurity-driven need to self-define and self-justify themselves as a "professionals" than it does with any disinterested, unbiased perspective on what the therapeutic experience consists in.

Nor is this kind of observation particularly new or original; for many years ago, Smail wrote that "a central concern of many writers on psychotherapy has been to defend the theoretical claims of their school against the rival claims of other schools. This has naturally led to an emphasis on the differences rather than the similarities between the ways in which therapists construct their experience" (1983: 13). That such processes seem to go on anyway, willy-nilly, is testimony to the strength of the self-serving institutional dynamics that are driving a field in which a jostling, competitive self-interest in the unholy scramble for clients may be threatening to override clear vision and authenticity.

We should not, therefore, underestimate the influence of economic self-interest in all this: for as Miller *et al.* (1997) point out, in the commodified field of therapy,

> Should a developer [of a therapeutic approach] be unable to distinguish his [*sic*] product from others in the marketplace, sales become driven almost exclusively by differences in cost—something that developers of all types of products want to avoid ... Possessing a special language imbues the treatment model with an aura of difference that, in turn, justifies the claims of uniqueness made by its developer. [pp. 10, 11]

To be blunt, non-specific factors simply aren't very "sexy"— both because they do not "sound unique, special, or intriguingly arcane" (Miller *et al.*, 1997: 17, their emphasis), and because "they do not conform to the kind of technical specification dictated by our [scientific] dogmas" (Smail, 1983: 13).

What if, we may justifiably ask, the "non-specific" healing factors triggered within a therapeutic experience occur *despite* rather than because of any particular distinctive characteristics of the various therapeutic approaches? And what, furthermore, if there were no demonstrable, statistically significant difference in outcome between the therapeutic help offered by highly trained "professionals" and that of very lightly trained "para-professionals", as a great deal of empirical research (well summarized in Bohart & Tallman, 1996) seems to indicate? Perhaps these counter-intuitive findings aren't so outlandish when seen in the context of Smail's typically common-sensical, demystified, and, above all, non-pathologizing view that "we are all highly skilled and experienced psychologists who have spent a lifetime developing ways of living in a world which contains other people, observing the regularities of their conduct, and conducting ourselves in accordance with our observations" (1983: 18). Of course, any "professional" is likely defensively, even desperately, to resist such uncomfortable possibilities (House, 1997c: 104), because their acceptance would, of course, throw into considerable doubt the legitimacy of therapy as a "professional" practice. In short, the whole edifice of "profession-centred" therapy would immediately be thrown into very severe question.

Through lack of space I will not be considering the range of what might be called socio–cultural critiques (Pilgrim, 1997)—for example, the formidable quasi-Marxian claim that therapy as commodity "is part of, and helps sustain, a socio–economic order based on individualism and consumerism" (Bracken & Thomas, 1998: 17). In this and the following chapters, I will be exposing to searching deconstructive examination some of the most taken-for-granted assumptions of the modern therapy world-view. I hope to show that many of therapy's conventional "wisdoms" have the effect of creating a self-serving, self-justificatory, and typically self-deluding ideology.

If indeed the price we are paying in the course of the institutional professionalization of therapy is the loss of therapy's soul, as Edwards (1992) maintains, then some pretty swift footwork (or rather, *heart*work) may well be required if the fundamentally beneficial impulse that underpins "therapy" is to be rescued from the deadening hand of professionalization, and thereby preserved in some organically healthy and culturally enabling form. In this light, then, I will offer some brief thoughts about how we might rescue the "soul" of therapy from the professionalizing juggernaut and the closely associated ideology of modernity, and thereby "re-enchant" or "re-ensoul" the healing experience by reclaiming those essential values and ways-of-being which modernity, materialism, and professionalization are threatening to extinguish (cf. Berman, 1981).

The ideology of professionalization

... it is fear that has, in my experience, characterized the response of psychotherapists to the whole political process of professionaliza-tion. They fear loss of livelihood, loss of status and recognition, loss of legitimacy. And in this fear I detect a strong element of transference itself. [Heron, 1990: 18]

Sussman (1992: 114) quotes Burton (1975) as referring to a persistent feeling on the part of all psychotherapists that "something terribly important is involved in the psychotherapeutic process, and that no one else ... can provide it. The psychotherapist thus feels he is the chosen one". And it is highly sobering to read a prominent therapist writing the following: "perhaps too many therapists have as their *raison d'être* a need to see themselves as extraordinarily powerful, virtually omniscient healers. Consequently, they have a penchant for infantilizing and overpathologizing their patients, viewing them as extraordinarily fragile" (Lazarus, 1994b: 301; cf. Mowbray, 1997)—with consequences for therapeutic practice which, I will argue, can become intrinsically abusive and unethical. That is, I make the strong claim that client/patient abuse can and sometimes does become routinely and intrinsically inscribed into the very profession-centred form increasingly taken by therapy.

A further effect of institutionalized professionalization is the rigidification and rendering legitimate of what some might call the precious, often mystifying language and procedures of the therapy world-view. One important parochial function served by the mystification of the special technical languages of professional therapy is to legitimate the distinctiveness of different approaches without the need for any validating data to justify the alleged distinctions (Coyne, 1982; Miller *et al.*, 1997). In addition, Nicky Hart (1998) cites Habermas's work on communicative distortion (1978, 1982) to make the point that power is often exercised through the manipulation or distortion of communication (cf. Parker's views on discourse and deconstruction, below), and that therapy has become a dominant cultural discourse which threatens to "direct communication towards the achievement of [therapists'] own ends". In what follows I will outline some concrete examples of how power is arguably being abused through profession-centred therapy's "regime of truth". Elsewhere (House, 1999b), I have coined the term "Professionalized Therapy Form" as a convenient short-hand term used to connote the increasingly commodified and professionally boundaried form which psychoanalysis, and the so-called "new professions" of psychotherapy and counselling, have been taking in recent years, as professionalization gathers steam. Much of the remainder of this chapter will be taken up with critically deconstructing the form taken by modern profession-centred therapy, and in the process laying bear the way in which it functions as a self-serving professional ideology.

In an issue of *Counselling* magazine, we read that there are currently no less than 10,000 lawsuits pending against psychotherapists in the USA (Bird, 1998: 235), and that in the UK, litigation in counselling and therapy is definitely becoming more prevalent (*ibid.*).

Now the predictable reaction of the nascent "profession" to this extraordinary situation is to *"professionalize" all the more assiduously*: to "insure" all the more comprehensively ("Without it [practitioners] are acting recklessly", asserts Palmer Barnes, 1998: 67); and to try to legislate all the harder against "bad practice". An alternative response (apparently not considered by the professionalizers) would be to question at root the very project of psychotherapy *per se*, and to wonder whether "10,000 lawsuits" might just be a profound and critical commentary on therapy as a cultural phenomenon, rather than being about "poor quality" therapy alone.

In addition, in books like that of Palmer Barnes's *Complaints and Grievances in Psychotherapy* (1998) (a cultural phenomenon in itself!), authors' apparent lack of awareness of the cultural "victimhood" dynamics (Hall, 1993) with which they are uncritically colluding is little short of breathtaking (cf. Postle, 1999). Brown (1994b: 280) presents an infinitely more realistic perspective on the "cultural madness" which the therapy world is currently embracing:

> our present ethical and legal *Zeitgeist*, which is a concrete, literal-minded, and legalistic one, is destructive to the human, relational qualities of psychotherapy. ... These perspectives will *increase* the likelihood of violations; they encourage therapists to objectify, rather than encounter, the people with whom they work. [her emphasis]

If therapy is about anything then surely it is about the transcending of cultural "madness", and not about its uncritical and collusive reinforcement (cf. House, 1999e; 2001a): yet this is precisely the effect of the fear-driven professionalization process which has unfolded in recent years.

Perhaps it is possible to trace the flawed project of profession-centred commodified psychotherapy right back to the very origins of psychoanalysis itself. For as Frosh points out, Freud was "far less interested in psychoanalysis as a therapeutic system than as an instrument of knowledge [about individual and society]. Freud's project was ... to develop a system of ideas that could make sense of people ... psychotherapy was a secondary project, *undertaken to make a living*" (Frosh, 1987: 211, my emphasis). Kurtz (1989) has similarly pointed to the less than auspicious historical origins of the therapeutic/analytic form: he painstakingly shows how "The narcissistic and psychotic ... layers of Freud's personality entered profoundly into his creation of the psychoanalytic situation and its manifestation in space ... every analyst to some degree recreates that office in the Berggasse" (pp. 28–29).

While I personally have some difficulty with this kind of pathologizing discourse (House, 1997e), it certainly throws a very interesting light on the origins of what is increasingly becoming the taken-for-granted cultural form of profession-centred therapy. And if it is valid to argue that the present-day form taken by profession-centred counselling and psychotherapy is inevitably tainted and contaminated by the way in which the "profession" was originally founded at the start of this century ("to make a living", for example), then this too throws at least some doubt on the whole project of therapy. Not that it is some kind of crime to "make a living"; but the crucial question is whether the values—the heart and soul—of the therapeutic experience can be safeguarded, nourished, and helped to flourish by an endeavour which is delivered within the framework of a commercial commodity. For if that very framework is in principle antithetical to what really matters in a therapeutic experience, then the profession-centred, commodified direction which therapy is increasingly taking, together with the ideological trappings surrounding it, could conceivably be doing a terminal violence to the foundational values from which the healthy and fundamentally good therapeutic impulse no doubt springs (cf. Bracken & Thomas, 1998).

The dubious ethics of psychotherapy and counselling

... psychoanalysts in particular were hypocritical in wanting to protect the public from transference abuse, when their own therapy was riddled with this very phenomenon. They let their clients slip into emotionally regressive attitudes, sustained them there over long periods by manipulative interpretations, and exploited this state of disempowerment to make money by recommending an increase in the number of sessions per week. [John Heron, 1990: 17, describing the behaviourists' response to the Foster Report]

When we put together the commodified form of therapy, the vested commercial interest of those who practise it ("undertaken to make a living"), and the dynamics that are a feature of virtually any therapeutic relationship (not just psychoanalysis), we are surely left with a very dangerous ethical cocktail indeed. Heron (1990) has usefully referred to this situation as therapy's exploitation and abuse of the transference. I contend that the very way in which therapy *as a profession-centred form* is structured actually encourages and *actively produces* client infantilization and dependency through the deep unconscious dynamics triggered within profession-centred therapy's regime of truth, and often buttressed by the assumptive framework typically embraced by the professional therapist (cf. McDougall, 1995). Thus, as I argue below, the protocol of profession-centred therapy can be, and often is, intrinsically abusive to the extent that it self-fulfillingly constructs a framework which then guarantees the conditions of its own existence.

There are a number of ways in which such a process is secured, and at least some of them will be deconstructively examined below. At this juncture I will refer specifically to psychoanalysis—though I maintain that the processes described are more generally observable within the wider therapy field. Hinshelwood (1997), himself a leading psychoanalyst, has bravely outlined some profound ethical dilemmas encountered by the analytic project. Chief among these is "the prior-agreement argument", an unavoidable ethical aspect of which is that

> The patient does not have the capacity to conceive, at the outset, what will befall him [in analysis]. ... The unconscious cannot be explained to the patient to any useful degree. The nature of the [analytic] process ... cannot really be understood prior to treatment at all. We cannot rely on the patient consciously to understand what his unconscious will do. ... [The consent to analysis] is not a fully informed consent. [*ibid.*: 101–102]

It follows from this that the analyst cannot but take up a paternalistic stance in relation to "patients" who necessarily (it is assumed) cannot make informed decisions about entering analysis, and therefore need the analyst to take responsibility for knowing what is in their best interests.

But it gets worse still ... for

> patients become immobilized, as if transfixed, upon the couch until the end of each session ... For periods, the patient in psychoanalysis may subjugate himself ... And this lasts until these unconscious

processes that deplete the patient's personality have been adequately dealt with in the process of the treatment. [p. 103]

In other words, the profession-centred form taken by psycho-analysis actively encourages a particular psychic state within patients, which then requires extensive "treatment" to cure! The self-serving, ethically dubious nature of such an "enterprise" (I use the term advisedly) is relatively clear for all to see—except for the "patient" in analysis, of course! The fierce opposition to the politicization of therapy by those "who regard the clinical as an untouchable, privileged category, on the basis of its contribution to the alleviation of human suffering" (Samuels, 1993: 6) is far more suggestive of a rationalized, therapist-centred professional self-interest than it is of a response that is in clients' best interests. In addition, there are far-reaching ideological assumptions being made here regarding the alleged "spatial location" of distress as residing within individuals—a highly questionable modernist assumption which I will take up later in relation to Ian Parker's important work (e.g. Parker, 1997b). Yet of course, the "individualizing" of distress is in many ways necessary to legitimize psychoanalysis—and much of therapy—as a form of treatment: yet another dimension of the self-serving ideological discourse of profession-centred therapy.

These impressively honest "confessions" of a leading and highly respected psychoanalyst surely throw a very long shadow over the ethical basis of not only psychoanalysis, but over any (and conceivably, every) therapeutic practice in which such relational dynamics are tacitly or explicitly encouraged or allowed to exist, and can be said to operate.

The ethically dubious nature of profession-centred therapy's regime of truth becomes even more pronounced when we consider its various institutionalized procedures, which both create and reinforce clients' disempowered dependent status; just some of these procedures will be examined in Chapters 3 and 4.

The "profession-centred therapy form" and the "professional" society

... the mere existence of experts discourages the use of people's potential to rely on their own resources, and so discourages the full development of human capacities. [Friedson, 1984: 13, on Illich]

I begin this section with some thoughts about the role of expertise and theory in therapy. One of the central trappings associated with, and a *raison d'être* for the existence of, any profession is its pretension to embrace a body of expert knowledge which is assumed to have some kind of privileged exclusivity—a special-status knowledge to which non-professionals are deemed incapable of having easy access.

One of the many difficulties with "the professional society" concerns what Illich calls "the disabling of the citizen through professional dominance" (1978: 34)—the view that the very existence of specialist professional bodies has infantilizing effects to the extent that it actively encourages people to give their own power away to the alleged expertise of culturally designated and legitimated professionals (House, 1995a). As Main has put it, in the helping professions "the helpful will unconsciously require others to be helpless while the helpless will require others to be helpful" (1975, quoted in Hinshelwood, 1997: 136); and "the extreme states of helper and helped that are unconsciously achieved" in many therapeutic encounters "threaten the mental integration and stability of both ... *the patient becomes depleted of his knowledge, power, and agency*, while the helping advisor becomes enhanced in these respects" (*ibid.*, my emphasis). And such a process is only reinforced when "psychotherapists often feel the need to develop a power base in therapy by deliberately fostering and displaying (if not flaunting) their *expert power, connective power, position power* and *reward power*" (Lazarus, 1994b: 301, quoting Howard *et al.*, 1987, his emphases).

If, by contrast, even in more conventionally profession-centred spheres, we believe that "The population which has the problem possesses the best resources for dealing with the problem" (Farson, quoted in Rogers, 1990/1973: 366; cf. Bohart & Tallman's "active client", 1996), then the crucial issue becomes what cultural mechanisms for responding to "the problems of living" might most help to facilitate the process of living—rather than current profession-centred structures which both assume and encourage people's dependency and helplessness.

Following the lead of Illich (1977b), it can be argued that within the field of medicine, it is predominantly through displaced and unowned fear that we have opted for "the medicalization of life" itself, such that social and political ills are routinely and unquestioningly transformed into illnesses—with people thereby losing their very will and ability to cope with indisposition. In the therapy world more specifically, the "anti-expert" view has been most eloquently expressed by Mair (1992): for her,

> Patients and therapists alike are prey to mythical systems ... There are times when people can be served best by being encouraged to have less faith in experts and more in themselves; ... there are dangers in any ideology, whether based on science or frankly magical, that claims to provide solutions to the difficult business of living. [pp. 158, 157]

And this is particularly the case when those same "expert" professionals who are delivering the service have a vested interest in perpetuating the (culturally sanctioned) assumption that their help is somehow necessary and indispensable. Furthermore, there is no need to invoke some crude conspiracy theory here—for these processes are relatively unconsciously and routinely built into the very structure of profession-centred therapeutic discourse itself (cf. Parker's work, discussed below). Spinelli, for example, argues that we need to examine "how our varying theories provide us with assumptions, with values, with attitudes, that may in *themselves* make it more likely for issues of misuse and abuse of power to occur" (Spinelli & Longman, 1998: 181, his emphasis).

There is a highly pertinent stream of thought within the sociology literature more generally which is also highly sceptical of the ideology of "professional expertise" (e.g. Fischer, 1990; Friedson, 1984; Martin, 1996; Perkin, 1996). Fischer refers to "a remarkable loss of confidence in expertise *per se*" (1990: 49), and to "a small but growing number of theorists [who] have begun to rethink the practices of expertise" (p. 347). And Martin's highly sobering critique of six case studies challenging the inadequacy of "establishment" expertise leads to a number of radical conclusions that are highly relevant to the nascent therapy professions.

Theory, need to control, and power

... "theories" about distress masquerade as "Truth" ... that truth is relentlessly forced upon people. ... [Parker *et al.*, 1995: 135]

One of the ways in which professions legitimize their existence is by claiming privileged access to a body of expert (typically theoretical) knowledge or theory, which is seen as being indispensable to their professional practice. As Mowbray (1995: 29) points out, the professional's knowledge base tends to be highly theoretical and academic—and no-one involved in the field will have missed the extraordinary and intemperate stampede into the "academicization" of therapy training and practice which has accompanied professionalization, of which several commentators have been highly critical (House, 2001c; Parker, 2001). Clearly, if an activity is to become sedimented into a legitimate "profession", then it must find a way of claiming that what it has to offer to clients is distinctive, "specialistic", and broadly undeliverable in any other way. Here is Smail again:

> When professional claims are made, expectations established among clients, and money changes hands ..., it becomes important to establish a solid justification for psychotherapy as a discipline ... Ever since the beginnings of psychoanalysis, psychotherapists have been desperately anxious to establish the validity of their credentials ... in order, no doubt, to justify their professional (fee-taking) status. [1983: 7–8]

Schon (1992: 49) has shown how there is a strong tendency for professional education to be "based upon a positivist philosophy which privileges the technical, the testable and the objective and ... fails to train for the real problems of practice". This will sound all too familiar to those practitioners who have been profoundly concerned at recent positivist, technocratic, and efficacy-obsessed trends in what is arguably the quintessentially hermeneutic, meaning-making, even artistic activity of therapy (Messer *et al.*, 1988) rather than an objectively scientific, technical, or medical-model activity, as Erwin (1997) would have us believe. As Smail put it many years ago, "any attempt to standardize or technicize therapy is certain to detract from its proper understanding" (1983: 13).

It is at this juncture where the clash of modernity and postmodern, post-conceptual ontologies and values is most acute (Heron, 1996; Kvale, 1992). At one (modernist) extreme we see Erwin's (1997) claim that

[Psychotherapy] needs to become a science. ... Few would argue that we do not need more empirical work to determine which are the optimal treatments [*really?*—RH] ... the verdict on postmodernist epistemology must be that its positive proposals about validation are both useless and false; the negative arguments given against an objectivist epistemology given by postmodernists are completely lacking in cogency. [pp. 2, 144, 73–74]

Similarly, we find ex-UKCP Chair Emmy van Deurzen arguing that "we have to transform what used to be a craft or an art based on moral or religious principles into a scientifically based accountable professional expertise" (1996: 17).

At the other (postmodern) extreme, we have Lacan, for whom "the noise of theory [could] be as forlorn as the rustle of dry leaves on a dull day"; who saw wit, irony, and ambiguity as being intrinsically constitutive of all theory; and who viewed any therapist who tried to build a permanent conceptual structure with language as a charlatan and a fool (Bowie, 1991: 160, 12). And for Smail, "There is no standard way of being therapeutic, and hence the ideal of the technical handbook, however complex and detailed, is doomed to failure" (1983: 14).

Now if we locate ourselves nearer to Lacan and Smail than to Erwin and van Deurzen (which is certainly my own disposition), then therapy finds itself in a peculiarly problematic position, well summed by the Spinelli epigraph introducing this chapter. And elsewhere Spinelli refers to "the lack of knowledge which is at the heart of any deep human encounter" (Spinelli & Longman, 1998: 184)—which makes it hardly surprising that "in dealing with human beings a certificate does not give much assurance of real qualification" (Rogers, 1990/1973: 365). Look a little further and we discover the disquieting absurdity that "there's a lack of evidence for the things we consider to be most important as therapists, and there's evidence that suggests that what clients find to be important are not those things that we consider to be important"! (Spinelli & Longman, 1998: 182).

In similar vein, just how Wilfred Bion's invitation that therapists enter the consulting room without memory, desire, or understanding can remotely cohere with therapy's burgeoning academic–theoretical preoccupations is far from clear. And for Joan Riviere too, "in analysis it is necessary to keep in mind how strong the not seeing and the not knowing is in us ..." (1987: 148). In the idiom of social constructionist approaches, indeed, a "not-knowing" approach to therapy has been strongly advocated (e.g. Anderson & Goolishian, 1992), with the client being explicitly designated as "expert" within the therapeutic discourse (cf. Bohart & Tallman's notion of the "active client", 1996).

In a quite brilliant but somewhat obscurely published paper dating from 1983, Smail prefigured very clearly and very honestly a personal approach to therapy close to the kinds of postmodern deconstructionist views advocated in this book:

> I have not found that I can rely on techniques ... Over and over again I have to abandon preconceived notions ... I almost never find that I can predict the way a therapeutic interview is going to go, but can only formulate ideas about what has taken place after the event ... it seems to me now beyond question that the view of scientific method conventionally accepted in psychology has not helped us in our attempts to understand psychotherapy. [pp. 9, 10]

In similar spirit, novelist and counsellor Anthony Storey (personal communication) has suggested that therapists take what he calls "disciplined ignorance" into their work.

More generally, it is absurd to argue for a coherent "profession" of therapy when there are quite fundamental theoretical and clinical–practical incompatibilities of view within the "profession" on such existential questions as what it means to be "a person", the origins and maintenance of human distress, the nature of change, the nature of human relationship, and so on. Thus, there is clearly no general agreement about what it is that therapists do (cf. Spinelli's epigraph at the start of this chapter), and the field has recently been described as being in a state of (theoretical) disarray (Erwin, 1997: 2). Not much has really changed since, in the early 1980s, Smail wrote,

> psychotherapists are split into a wide range of different schools, with fundamentally different and often mutually exclusive theoretical ideas ... qualification reflects more often an allegiance to a prejudice than privileged access to established knowledge ... the creation of a scientific mythology ... takes almost no account of our actual experience of psychotherapy. [1983: 10]

More generally still, some commentators have been starting to challenge the epistemological relevance of theory itself (and its associated form of "technical" knowledge) to the healing practice of therapy (Craib, 1987; McDougall, 1995; Riikonen & Smith, 1997), as New Paradigm epistemologies begin to challenge head on the ideology of modernity and its narcissistic preoccupation with ego, control, technocratic science, and the material. Here is George Steiner on what he calls "the drug of truth": "The quality of the obsession is clear from the start. The search for truth is predatory. It is a literal hunt, a conquest" (1978: 42). In the New Paradigm, postmodern world-view of "Chaos", complementarity, and partici-pative consciousness (Skolimowski, 1994), our very foundational notions of "explanation", "understanding", and "truth" are being thrown into question (see Chapters 9 and 10, below)—which situation of course has very profound implications indeed for the practice of any healing art.

Modernity-transcending notions of "truth" privilege postmodern, coherence, participatory, and congruence "theories of truth" (respectively, Lacan, 1965; Alcoff, 1996; Skolimowski, 1994; Heron, 1996) over the aridity of the epistemologically dubious "correspon-dence" theory that has tended to dominate Western analytic philosophy and the modernist world-view of positive science. Here is Krishnamurti: "Truth cannot be exact. *What can be measured is not truth*" (quoted in Lutyens, 1990: 118, my emphasis); and Lacan: "there is no metalanguage ... no language could ever speak the truth about truth, since truth is founded in the fact that it speaks and that it has no other way of achieving this" (1965: 867–868, quoted in Bowie, 1991: 118–119). In the field of therapy, certainly, "effective [psychotherapeutic] treatment involves such non-rational elements as beliefs, rituals, and symbols", far beyond "the application of procedures derived from theoretical knowledge" (Kiev, 1964: cover blurb). Furthermore, Parker's important work on the "discursive complex" (1996, 1997a,b), discussed below, points to how notions of truth within therapeutic discourse can themselves actively structure subjectivity—with the implication that "we must be attentive to the power of the therapist as a ... part of the regime of truth that defines what subjectivity must be like" (1996: 459). And ultimately, "the subject does not know what the truth is; nobody knows, and the most ostensibly open therapeutic dialogue may conceal within it, by virtue of its structure as therapeutic discourse . . ., a position for the client that is disempowering" (*ibid.*).

The professionally driven modernist world-view, by contrast, has recently been making a strong bid for hegemony in the "establishment" world of therapy (e.g. Erwin, 1997)—well illustrated, for example, by the burgeoning preoccupation with so-called "scientific" audit, evaluation, and research (e.g. House, 1996b; 1997d; McMahon, 1998; Roth & Fonagy, 1996). Palmer Barnes's recent book on complaints procedures is a typical example of the ideology of modernity: "The fixing of standards by which to judge competence is a vital part of the establishment of the psychotherapy and counselling professions", she claims (1998: 24). Needless to say, an epistemologically coherent New Paradigm perspective on the phenomena of "competence" and "measurement" leads to very different conclusions (House, 1996b, 1997a). Thankfully, and particularly with the new social constructionist, narrative, and deconstructionist approaches, "we see psychotherapy actually reshaping itself . . ., from following strict rules to enjoying and utilizing the borderland of control and chaos" (Riikonen & Smith, 1997: 13). I return in detail to this perspective in my final chapter; and I certainly see this book as part of this fundamental "reshaping" of psychotherapy.

The question of "theory as abuse" has also been courageously addressed by Spinelli, who argues that therapist reliance on interpretations derived from theory can become "more abusive than anything else. . . . Many of the assumptions we take for granted don't really have any basis to them . . . we might hold [them] because at the very least they keep us employed, or they provide employment for our trainees" (Spinelli & Longman, 1998: 181, 183). Hinshelwood has recently made a valiant attempt to rescue psychoanalysis and therapy from the charge that they impose knowledge upon their clientele. He tries to argue that "the learning that is 'found' in the analysis is the patient's own knowledge" (1997: 167), the revelation of the patient's unconscious. Yet such a view is an inadequate response to the analyst Joyce McDougall's challenge that therapist/analysts' preconceived way of seeing the world, and their theoretical presuppositions about it and about the client, will not only themselves influence the way "patients" can experience themselves (cf. Parker's work on discourse and subjectivity, discussed below), but will also constrain and influence what the therapist *sees* in terms of "knowledge" about the "patient". From this perspective, Hinshelwood's attempt to establish a distinction between a more conventional hierarchical expertise which claims to "[know] the patient better", and an allegedly far less depowering expertise (which he favours) which claims to "promot[e] self-knowledge" (1997: 166), is ultimately unconvincing.

All this, of course, finally leads quite naturally into questions of power—the routinely exercised power of professional orthodoxy and ideology effectively to exploit a highly privileged, culturally legitimated position through client infantilization; a clientele, furthermore, who are assumed to be incapable of dealing with their own difficulties without the (well paid) ministrations of professional experts. It is a sobering and highly revealing fact that, with a few notable exceptions (Guggenbühl-Craig, 1971; Masson, 1988, 1992b; Embleton Tudor & Tudor, 1994; Rose, 1997), the issue of power has been only rarely discussed in the therapy field (N. Hart, 1998). Admittedly, the word "power" does in my experience get trotted out quite frequently in the therapy world (just as with terms like "boundaries", "ambivalence", and the like)—but without the real substance of power ever really being fearlessly and fundamentally addressed. Perhaps we can all convince (delude?) ourselves into complacently and expediently thinking that we've dealt with therapy's thorny power issues simply by repeating the word a few times, like some sort of mantra. Yet as some commentators have either suggested or implied (N. Hart, 1998; Masson, 1988; Sands, 2000), "power" probably constitutes one of therapy's biggest and potentially most embarrassing can of worms.

I will return to the issue of power in the next section (specifically in relation to Parker's important work around discourse and deconstruction), and I cross-refer the reader to that section. Consistent with the position adopted in this discussion and in Parker's work, Nicky Hart (1998) maintains that it is illusory to believe that clients are free to explore their inner worlds in therapy, for "the boundaries and rules, like the vocabulary, are as fixed as they ever were in the psychiatric world of the fifties and sixties": all that has changed is that we now *pretend* that the client has power, and that we as therapists do not use a normalizing and subtly impositional discourse. And as I have argued elsewhere in this chapter, "Therapy can never be value free ... It happens within a context and someone has set the agenda" (*ibid.*).

What might lie in the shadow of the empathic, unconditionally regarding, empowering therapist?—here is Pilgrim in typically provocative style: "Intimacy and empathy can be preconditions of oppression and abuse as well as of helpful interventions. The torturer and the therapist have much in common" (Pilgrim, 1997: 4). I further maintain that the fundamental asymmetry and artificiality of the profession-centred therapy milieu inevitably leads to certain pernicious consequences, just some of which are touched on by Howard: "Such an uneven sharing of confidences makes for an unhealthy, unequal relationship, leaving us (the client) exposed and vulnerable. Knowledge is Power. If I (the client) become transparent while you (the therapist) remain opaque, the empowerment will probably be yours more than mine" (1996: 69, quoted in N. Hart, 1998).

In psychoanalysis (possibly generalizable to therapy in general), Hinshelwood (1997) does concede that the "patient's ... lack of conscious knowledge of his unconscious does put him [*sic*] at some disadvantage. It makes him consciously helpless in the search for his knowledge". Moreover, the extent to which patients operating within a therapeutic milieu (and all that goes with it in terms of both individual and cultural dynamics) are free to exercise full conscious consent may well be significantly compromised (p. 167). All this can routinely lead to a kind of power-imbalanced Laingian "knot" in which the therapist "knows [or thinks he knows—RH] a great deal, but also *knows* that he [*sic*] knows a great deal and *knows* that his client does not know much ..." (p. 168, original emphases). For Hinshelwood, this power imbalance can be carried through "to a degree that distorts both identities. Professional relationships based on this redistribution of knowing will result in the expert enhancing the depletion of the personality of his more vulnerable clients" (*ibid.*).

It seems to me that abuses such as these are ones to which the "professions" of therapy are by their very nature peculiarly and intrinsically susceptible. And in the light of this we would do well to follow family therapist Lynn Hoffman's injunction that "our aim should be a critical stance that favours becoming aware of the power relationships hidden within the assumptions of any social discourse ... therapists of all kinds must now investigate how relations of domination and submission are built into the very assumptions on which their practices are based" (quoted in N. Hart, 1998). Below, I will propose that therapy must routinely and ongoingly embrace a radical deconstruction of its theories and practices (cf. Parker, 1999), paradoxically entailing a continual undermining of its own conditions of existence, if it is to avoid the kinds of abuses which, I contend, can easily be intrinsic to profession-centred therapeutic practice as currently practised and culturally legitimated.

The discourse of therapy and its critical deconstruction

Freud's discoveries ... have gained their significance much more from the way in which they have been assimilated and made manifest in the general culture than from the use to which they have been put by the professional groups of analysts which have tried to make them their own property. [Smail, 1983, 18]

How we reflect upon and define ourselves is determined and constrained by the structures of knowledge available to us ... the practice of psychotherapy is constructed as a kind of practice in which people believe they should speak like that ... any system of therapeutic talk conveys an enigma to the subject, and *positions the subject in a regime of truth*. Then it may not be good to talk. [Parker *et al.*, 1995: 88; Parker, 1999: 1; 1996: 459, my emphases]

Some of the more radical counter-cultural strands of therapy have in recent times begun to embrace the so-called discursive, social constructionist, and deconstructionist approaches to both the theory and practice of therapy (e.g. McNamee & Gergen, 1992; Parker, 1996, 1997a,b, 1999; Parker *et al.*, 1995; Riikonen & Smith, 1997). These approaches typically view language and discourse, and the power relations intrinsic to them, as actively constituting notions of "(psycho)pathology" (Parker *et al.*, 1995), aspects of psychic "reality", and so on; and, by extension, our associated subjective experiences are themselves seen as being deeply structured through the culturally sanctioned discourse which is available to us.

For Riikonen and Smith, "Modernist conceptions of language

tend to lend support to more limited, utilitarian and goal-orientated approaches" (1997: 7). In stark contrast to such a "correspondence theory" approach to truth, it is argued that "Language ... is not a reflection of another world, but *an implement of construction* for the world we now occupy" (Gergen & McNamee, 1997, viii, my emphasis). It follows that words are always far more than merely "labels for objective things" (Riikonen & Smith, 1997: 3). Such a perspective is so crucial to therapy and human relationship more generally because "our conceptions of language and words have a close connection to the kinds of relationships which *can* exist between people" (*ibid*.: 7, original emphasis). Conventional therapeutic approaches typically and unavoidably contain assumptive discourses about what constitutes "a person", "suffering", and "change", and these discourses are typically assumed to cohere into a systematic whole (*ibid*.: 14).

Ian Parker has made a considerable contribution to the discursive deconstructionist line of thinking. Parker makes a radical shift from humanistic assumptions about the subject's being fully responsible for her so-called "inner experience" to the way in which subjects' subjective experience is deeply influenced and constrained in often uncontrollable ways (Parker, 1997b: 480) by the culturally sanctioned discourse to which they have access to think about themselves. Parker therefore explores "the way meaning is transformed and reproduced in culture, rather than trying to find the sources of meanings inside individuals alone" (1997a: 9). More specifically, he maintains that psychoanalytic concepts (particularly around intellectualization, transference, and trauma) have increasingly infiltrated cultural discourse such that it becomes difficult for people to think about their experience outside of this discourse (e.g. Parker, 1997a,b).

On this view, then, Western culture is actively structured by psychoanalytic notions which "saturate and support cultural phenomena" (1997a: 258); and "'regimes of truth' ... make it difficult for participants to challenge the 'realities' [a discourse] refers to ... [and] govern what can be spoken about ..." (*ibid*.: 7). Laplanche expresses a similar view: *"psychoanalysis invades the cultural*, not only as a form of thought or a doctrine, but as a *mode of being"* (1989, quoted in Parker, 1996: 449, original emphases). What Parker calls "discursive complexes" structure subjectivity, "so that when we speak within them they provoke certain types of emotional response, certain notions of what it is to be a self" (1996: 451). For current purposes, what is most relevant is the way in which specifically psychotherapeutic discourse actively "structures the way a person, as therapist or patient, participates in the therapeutic enterprise" (Parker, 1997a: 256; see also Parker, 1996: 458).

There are, of course, very subtle issues here around agency and "victimhood" (Hall, 1993), and whether it is legitimate to see subjects as passive victims of the cultural discourse which is said to constrain or even structure their self-experience. I am sure that Parker would not advocate such a position, for it is perfectly plausible to argue (following Marx) that people make their own history, but not in (discursive) circumstances of their own choosing! As Parker has it, deconstruction seeks "not to devalue the agency of the individual subject, but to *locate* it" (1999: 13, his emphasis). The important point, then, is that discourse does matter, and must inevitably influence, at least in part, the ways in which people can think about themselves and the choices they have in responding to their own self-experience. Thus, for example, it is arguable that the very way in which the notion of "transference" has surreptitiously penetrated cultural discourse makes it more likely that transference dynamics will be created within therapeutic relationships (particularly when the therapist is also expecting to find "transference"!—cf. McDougall, 1995). Perhaps there is also a profound contradiction at the very heart of any therapeutic project that claims an emancipatory goal, for any therapeutic "yield of self-understanding" gained in therapy (and the freedom that goes with that) must simultaneously *"lock the subject into* the systems of talk that comprise the communities in which they live" (Parker, 1997b: 492, my emphasis).

All this clearly has very considerable implications for the ways in which the self-experienced identity of "clients" and "patients" is actively constructed by a psychotherapeutic discourse which is culturally sanctioned, and buttressed by a massively influential ideological framework of professionalization. Thus, people with "personal problems" will tend immediately to think of themselves as potential therapy "clients"—thereby positioning themselves within therapeutic discourse—precisely because that discourse constitutes a dominating set of values and culturally legitimated practices that circulates within the culture and actively creates subjective experience. The fact that profession-centred therapeutic practice typically takes an individualized form is also crucial, for such a form parallels and colludes with the ideological assumption implicit in much therapeutic discourse "that tries to discover what is going on inside the individual ..., as if that [alone] would adequately explain underlying motives and causes for behaviour" (Parker, 1997b: 484). Thus, a psychotherapy which is deconstructive explicitly recognizes this difficulty, and sees conventional therapeutic practices as being embedded in images of the self and others that can systematically mislead us as to the nature of problems (Parker, 1999). By contrast, for Parker, we should celebrate, with Roland Barthes, the "death of the author"—"the end of attempts to trace all meaning to the individual producer" (1997b: 486).

It should be clear, then, that in a very real sense, the psychotherapeutic world-view actively and self-servingly creates the cultural conditions that guarantee its own existence and perpetuation—erecting, as with any ideological apparatus, "a system of defences and discursive operations which guarantee its place in a regime of truth" (*ibid.*: 489). As I will argue later, this situation places an enormous ethical imperative upon therapists continually to deconstruct their own therapeutic practice, such that therapy continually revolutionizes its own theories and practices— actively subverting itself whenever there is any whiff of complacent self-satisfaction—rather than conservatively "keeping things like this" through overly rigid, institutionalized "professional" procedures which arguably have more to do with therapist self-interest than with client well-being.

Parker seems to be saying something quite similar when he writes of "a 'deconstructing psychotherapy' as [being] a practice that is always *in process* rather then something fixed, a movement of reflexive critique rather than a stable set of techniques" (1999: 2, original emphasis); and that

> a ... psychotherapeutic practice that fails to reflect on its culturally and historically specific character ... reproduces [discursive] complexes as enduring characteristics of people's lives when it treats them as necessary to human subjectivity. ... We must be attentive to the power of the therapist as ... part of a regime of truth that defines what subjectivity must be like. [1996: 458]

Parker is certainly not the only commentator to have picked up on these processes. Legg (1998) has written that:

[clients] have to learn their role as the play unfolds, taking their clues from the setting and the other players. One of the jobs of the therapist is to socialise people into the client role ... therapists tend to use a range of conversational ploys to discourage clients from slipping out of client role and use others to reinforce behaviour that is *in* client role. [p. 12, his emphasis]

In similar vein here is Owen: "Clear aims enable counsellors to carry out their role without doubt and *to allot a distinct role to clients*" (1997: 165, my emphasis). Clearly, then, there are crucial issues of power and control at work here:

The issue of control—on a grandiose, omnipotent scale—permeates the analytic situation. It is always the analyst ... who establishes the rules that govern behavior in this primal space. However much these rules may be constructed to enable the patient's cure, the analyst is their maker and enforcer. [Kurtz, 1989: 27–28]

In psychoanalysis (and by extension, in counselling and psychotherapy), it has been recognized how analysis is rendered a viable practice by virtue of its conferring upon clients a position within a discourse, in which they can then exist as subjects (Ingleby, 1984, cited in Frosh, 1987: 220; Sandler *et al.*, 1992). If this is so (and certainly, the comparatively new narrative and social constructionist therapies would concur), one question that is immediately begged is whether there really is anything special and distinctive about the healing properties of profession-centred therapeutic practice *per se*, over and above its coercive ideological and discursive effects on clients/patients, and which could not be found elsewhere in other cultural forms, outside of the confines of the discrete commodified therapy form. On this kind of view, then, perhaps "therapy ... is no more than another ideological stance, an 'as if' way of relating to the world which provides relief from confusion and personal emptiness because it happens to be relatively coherent" (Frosh, 1987: 220).

As already intimated, Parker (*et al.* 1995; Parker, 1997b) has a lot to say about the deleterious effects of professional therapeutic discourse. Thus, in psychiatry, for example, "patients increasingly come to define their experience in relation to professional norms and categories ..." (Parker *et al.*, 1995: 88)—not least the ontologically highly dubious notion of "(ab)normality" itself (House, 2001b). Buck (1992), Knight (2001), and Lowson (1994) have respectively coined the terms "Pervasive Labelling Disorder", "Psychiatric Delusional Disorder", and "Professional Thought Disorder" to describe these alienating diagnostic procedures. And while institutional Psychiatry is of course a rather easy target, the crucial point is that these discursive labelling processes are identity-producing in the wider culture (cf. Harré, 1983), and not just in the exceptional, medical-model arena of clinical psychiatry. And both psychiatrists and therapists surely have a grave responsibility continually to examine and deconstruct the discursive categories which can so easily become the self-perpetuating taken-for-granted shibboleths that actively define, and even constitute, identity within the therapeutic experience—and not least their own!

In the next two chapters I will attempt critically to deconstruct what I see as some of the more pernicious self-serving categories and assumptions of therapeutic discourse: for "structures of language are embodied in clinical institutions and by virtue of that enjoy a certain type of power" (Parker *et al.*, 1995: 15). It is my contention, unpalatable as it will be to many, that there are far more examples of routine client abuse *stemming directly from profession-centred therapeutic practice itself* than there are the kinds of overt abuse against which the therapy institutions so assiduously attempt to legislate.

CHAPTER THREE

Deconstructing profession-centred therapeutic practice:
I. Resistance, boundaries and "frame", holding, "material" generation

"Therapies have an ideology, a certain view of the human world ... whenever a person enters therapy, he is also entering the stream of history and casting his lot with it in one way or another"

Kovel, 1976: 71

Introduction

The raw stuff of human beings ... is *not* individuals; people *become* individuals through discourses and institutions. [Miller & McHoul, 1998: 91, their emphases]

I n this chapter I begin my critical deconstruction of a number of key concepts within the therapy world—terms which have commonly become so taken-for-granted within therapeutic discourse that it is difficult, without considerable effort, to subsist within the therapy world and not be unwittingly dominated by their surreptitious influence on what constitutes legitimate utterances, as part of therapy's "regime of truth" (cf. Chapter 2). My hope is that after reading this and the next chapter, the reader will be far less seduced by therapy's regime of truth, and will naturally adopt a far more critical, even sceptical, attitude to the conventional discourse of therapy and counselling, and its dangerously self-serving effects.

I begin my analysis with the concept of "resistance".

"Resistance" as self-serving profession-centred ideology

Any disagreement with the therapist can be (and often is) interpreted as resistance. [Masson, 1988: 36]

In both classical psychoanalysis and psychotherapy more generally, the notion of "resistance" is seen as being central—as something which has to be "worked through" and "overcome" if therapy is to be successful. Freud in particular focused centrally on resistance: in Frosh's (1987: 75) words, "resistance penetrates throughout the therapeutic encounter". For Freud himself, "all the 'chance events' that occur in a person's life can be made into reasons for interfering with [!—RH] or breaking off the analysis" (*ibid.*). Note the extraordinary use of the notion of "interfering with": the use of "interfere" seems to entail the assumption that the form taken by profession-centred analysis and all its accoutrements is some kind of disinterestedly neutral benchmark, and that any patient/client "resistance" to therapy must then *necessarily* be an "acting-out" of the patient/client's "neurosis" within the relationship created within therapy (the perception of which then, of course, is used to legitimize the therapist's view that the patient/client needs even more therapy!). But what if therapy's profession-centred form itself is far from neutral, and itself imports into the therapeutic relationship an enormously complex (and typically unrecognized) "madness" of its own—both a general cultural "madness" and whatever individual "madnesses" the therapist her/himself is tangled up in? (Sussman, 1992).

From this perspective, then, the phenomenon of resistance takes on a very different hue from that propagated by apologists for profession-centred therapeutic practice; for far from resistance in therapy being a manifestation of the patient/client's "neurotic psychopathology", it is at the very least as plausible that resistance is a *healthy* response (albeit possibly unarticulated) by the patient/client to the self-serving nature of profession-centred therapy into which they have entered and, perhaps, got themselves entangled, via the regression-inducing, infantilizing dynamics which are sometimes generated. (In passing, perhaps we might also understand so-called "negative transference" in a similar light.) Here, of course, we see the "crowning glory" of profession-centred therapeutic practice—namely, the therapist interpreting such healthy resistance (from her/his powerful position of "expert") as the patient/client's *un*healthy "psychopathology", which then, of course, needs more therapy to "cure"!

To reiterate, then, we can see how the procedures and theoretical dogmas of profession-centred therapeutic practice can self-fulfillingly and self-servingly function so as to create, reinforce, and then guarantee the preconditions of its own existence. Nor should we be surprised that when therapy is resisted by patients/clients, this is nearly always interpreted as the client's personal difficulty, rather than as an accurate unconscious commentary on either the therapist her/himself, or on potentially abusive profession-centred therapeutic practice more generally. (The so-called "communicative" approach to therapy does at least acknowledge the reality of the client's unconscious commentary on the therapist's "madnesses"—e.g. Smith, 1991.)

Note also the way in which the preconceived assumptions of the psychodynamic world-view determine the way in which "resistance" is conceptualized: here, for example, is Freud himself (1937, quoted in Frosh, *op. cit.*: 73): "The crux of the matter is that the mechanisms of defence against former dangers recur in the shape of resistance to cure". Thus, it is assumed that present experience is determined by past experience, and that present experience or behaviour is necessarily a compulsive and unwitting re-enactment of historically reified prior experiences: as Frosh (1987: 77) has it, "our earliest relationships ... lay down inside us general tendencies, [which are then] repeated in all our relationships with other people". It is interesting to note in passing that there has indeed been an increasing (postmodern) move in recent years towards challenging the common psychotherapeutic assumption that the past necessarily influences or determines the present (e.g. Hall, 1993; Hillman, 1996).

It is important to re-stress that I am not proposing a conscious conspiracy theory in these arguments: in a sense whether or not there exists a conscious (or an unconscious) conspiracy is far less important than is *the demonstrable effect* that the ideology of profession-centred therapeutic practice has within the therapeutic relationship. And I hope to have shown that there are at the very least a number of causes for severe concern once we dare to begin the process of deconstructing the normally unproblematized regime of therapeutic truth and its assumed neutrality.

Concepts of "boundaries" and "frame" as self-serving profession-centred ideology

> ... everything depends upon the dialectical process between two personalities. ... Under these circumstances any organisation that proposes collective methods seems to me unsuitable, because it would be sawing off the branch on which the psychotherapist sits. [Jung, quoted in Adler, 1976: 534]

Hermansson (1997) has written a very important, thoughtful, and long-overdue paper on the place of boundaries in counselling. He writes,

> there is in some quarters an excessive zeal about boundary control which can lead to stances that seem overly precious and at times even arrogant in relation to clients and to colleagues in the profession. ... What is left can be a pseudo-professional stance that is controlling in its effects and barren in its essence. [p. 140]

I'm sure I cannot be alone in experiencing a certain obsession in the therapy world with "boundary-speak" in recent years (e.g. Heyward, 1994; Katherine, 1991); and I will argue below that this development is by no means a coincidence in terms of the profession-alization and commodification of therapy. The notion of "boundaries" seems to have been seized upon by the emerging profession as an apparently theoretically coherent rationale which can be uncritically used to justify and legitimate institutionalized therapeutic practice. Following a line of argument resembling Parker's (1997a), we can say that as soon as "boundary-mindedness" becomes institution-alized within the "legitimate", taken-for-granted discourse of therapy, it becomes extremely difficult *even to think* in other, non-boundary-obsessed ways about the therapeutic process. This is what makes Hermansson's contribution a particularly important one, and he recognizes this latter issue himself: "... boundary has become a multipurpose term *that influences understanding* of what we do in counselling and how we do it" (p. 134, my emphasis).

Hermansson also suggests that a preoccupation with boundaries tends to entail a conservative stance (cf. Lazarus, 1994a), professionally speaking, thereby "running the risk of undermining aspects of therapeutic effectiveness, ... [with] a concern for risk management and control" driving much of the thinking in this area (pp. 133, 134). Within this complex, substantially fear-driven process, we see "a profession in potential crisis about boundaries": "excessive caution can emerge, rigid rules can come to dominate, and simplistic thinking can prevail" (p. 134). Yet perhaps we should not be in the least surprised by the fear that is intrinsic to the therapeutic encounter, for "When two personalities meet, an emotional storm is created" (Bion, 1979, quoted in Hinshelwood, 1997: 130), and "consciousness is an inconclusive experience, joining in delirious flux with its seeming others" (Ferrell, 1996: 1). And all this is occurring in a discursive context of the "chaotic and complex unconscious network of meanings which pervade language" (Parker, 1997b: 490)! Biologist Brian Goodwin (1997) has said that "Too much order is bad for you! ... Living on the edge of chaos is the best place to be if you want to live a creative life". Nietzsche was surely saying something similar when he said that one must have chaos in oneself in order to give birth to a dancing star. There is much learning to be gained from such a perspective if therapy is to remain an intrinsically creative and transformative experience, rather than becoming an inherently conservative, over-boundaried form of "defensive" therapeutic practice (Mowbray, 1995: 151–154).

Thus, the fear saturating the nascent profession's need to bolster and legitimize its new status as "profession" easily and surreptitiously leads to "a search for a completely safe and protected position from which to operate" (Hermansson, 1997: 134). But if, as Hermansson maintains, effective counselling *necessitates*, albeit in a qualified way, the crossing of boundaries (p. 135), then a fear-induced practitioner rigidity around professional boundaries (often fuelled by fear of litigation and the fury of the "victim"), can in itself produce the very abuse of clients against which boundary-mindedness is alleged to protect (p. 142).

Interestingly, Hermansson alludes, albeit obliquely, to the potential self-serving nature of an over-preciousness with boundaries: "the counsellor, in collaboration with the client, has to determine the most appropriate boundary of operation that will enable a sufficient difference to be made in the person's life without extending so far as to compel her or him to be a lifelong client" (p. 137). The clear implication here is that too rigid a formalization of boundary-mindedness could easily lock clients into a (fee-paying) discursive framework from which it might be very difficult for them to extricate themselves—particularly in the face of the transference and dependency issues that are routinely triggered in any helping relationship, and which processes a professional preciousness with boundaries actually serves to reinforce and actively encourage. The unethical, even abusive dynamics entailed in this process are well drawn out by Parker's poignant observation that "it is vital that the professional boundaries of the relationship be secured *to hold in place* the transferential affects ..." (1998c: 70, my emphasis).

Ethical dubiousness mounts when we acknowledge the quite typical situation where "defining the form of the engagement will be based essentially on what *the practitioner* chooses to provide" (Hermansson, 1997: 137, my emphasis), given a new client's likely lack of awareness of the issues—and not least because of the mystification that can surround them in so much professional therapy (cf. Miller *et al.*, 1997). I hope I am not alone in feeling distinctly uncomfortable when I read statements like the following: "Clients ... cannot readily judge the appropriateness of counselling dynamics for themselves and need additional protection" (Webb, 1997: 177). Yet surely Webb is right when she also suggests that "what counsellors may construe as matters of ethics often turn out to be more those of self-protection" (p. 181).

Following through this logic leads to the unpalatable conclusion that boundary-mindedness can very easily serve the professional needs of the therapist far more than it does the needs of allegedly vulnerable clients (cf. Mowbray, 1997), who, in the profession-centred rhetoric of therapy, are infantilizingly assumed to need clear boundaries so as to protect them from their own vulnerability, and under which there is the professional (and possibly self-deluding) pretence that "the client's needs must be central" (Webb, 1997: 177). Again, then, I am suggesting that there may well be an intrinsic abusiveness in the formalized, professional preciousness with therapeutic boundaries that is so typical of profession-centred therapeutic practice.

Lazarus (1994a,b) also has much of interest to say about boundary-mindedness, and the exchange between him and the various replies to his challenging (1994a) paper are highly revealing. Lazarus summarizes his own position thus, which I quote at length:

> When taken too far, certain well-intentioned ethical guidelines can become transformed into artificial boundaries that serve as destructive prohibitions and thereby undermine clinical effectiveness. Rigid roles and strict codified rules of conduct between therapist and client can obstruct a clinician's artistry ... anxious conformists who ... live in constant fear of malpractice suits are unlikely to prove significantly helpful to a broad array of clients ... one of the worst professional/ethical violations is to permit current risk-management principles to take precedence over humane interventions. [1994a: 255]

What is perhaps most fascinating is the predictable fury and opprobrium that Lazarus's daring paper elicited from a whole group of prominent professional therapists (eight in all), queuing up to vilify Lazarus's views and to re-assert the sanctity of profession-centred therapeutic practice, in an attempt to rescue it from Lazarus's searching critique. (Echoes here of the psychoanalytic establishment's "excommunication" of Lacan for his daring to introduce session-length flexibility as a therapeutic tool.) Needless to say, their arguments are presented in terms of "client protection" and "clinical effectiveness", rather than in terms of their own parochial professional self-interest in defending the profession-centred therapeutic framework as a legitimate form of help for the troubled or distressed. The language of Lazarus's critics is shot through with "professional" pathologizing ideology—"patient", "treatment", "disorders", and so on—and, of course, notably ignores arguments that challenge the ideology of client vulnerability (e.g. Dawes, 1994; Mowbray, 1997). Borys typifies the views of the critics, writing that "... boundaries are critical to protect patients' welfare and thereby promote effective treatment ..." (1994, 267)—to which one might add, "... within the form taken by profession-centred therapy". That is, boundaries only become "critical" when the self-serving ideology of profession-centred therapeutic practice is uncritically accepted as a given, rather than as just one of many possible means for helping the troubled and distressed. I believe that Lazarus deserves great admiration for his brave public challenge to the Holy Writ of profession-centred therapeutic practice.

In addition, as Lazarus points out in his rejoinder, his critics "dwell mostly on potential costs and dangers, I focus mainly on the advantages that may accrue when certain boundaries are transcended" (1994b: 299). The language here is crucial, in that Lazarus talks of "transcending" rather than "crossing" boundaries—which in turn implies finding a creative, New Paradigm way-of-being which moves beyond boundary-mindedness, rather than staying stuck in a self-limiting ideological framework which privileges old-paradigm categorical thinking, driven by an unedifying cocktail of professional defensiveness, theoretical preciousness, and economic self-interest.

Hermansson agrees with Lazarus:

> Setting on fixed-boundary positions that set up and maintain a protective distance may well serve the safety factor admirably, but is likely to be deleterious to therapeutic involvement and outcome ... [Counselling] must not develop in the direction of creating protective positions which counsellors rely on to maintain safety. [1997: 142, 144]

Perhaps the modernist obsession with boundaries and their control is substantially fed by the fear-driven desire of the therapist (and the "profession") to somehow render safe and predictable that which in principle never can be so. Profession-centred therapeutic practice inevitably entails the fixing of crucial aspects of the therapeutic experience—for if it didn't do this then the profession-centred therapeutic regime would, of course, be untenable as a professional framework for delivering therapy as a commodity.

In addition, the ontological status of "boundary" as a concept should by no means be taken for granted, for:

> The term boundary ... does not ... sufficiently describe the relationship between two or more people ... [the term] is

insufficient when it is used for describing the qualities of being-together, of face-to-face co-empathy, of the felt sense of what lies between ourselves and others, because it refers to a ... demarcation between people ... it cannot by itself adequately portray the dynamic quality of a relationship. [Owen, 1997: 171, 172]

Boundary-mindedness is firmly rooted within the conventional modernist paradigm of Aristotelian categorical thinking, rather than in the New Paradigm dialectical thinking that privileges inter-subjectivity (see Chapter 10) and non-conceptual being-values—associated with, for example, Korzybski and Krishnamurti (Crossley, 1996; Falconar, 1997; Heron, 1996; Natterson & Friedman, 1995; Owen, 1997) over dualistic either/or, me/you thinking. For Hinshelwood, the erosion of the notion of the discrete person leads quite naturally into the social–relational world: "The intra-psychic world of the individual exists within an interpersonal context of other intra-psychic worlds, which dismantle and re-constitute the individual person. The worlds of social relationships and of the individual are mutually constitutive" (1997: 199).

Indeed, perhaps the term "intersubjective" itself implies too great an emphasis on individuality and ego, as the prefix "inter" necessarily assumes, in some sense, discrete individualities which *then* interact to produce co-created relational experience. But what if, for example, discrete individuality is a delusion of the psyche (albeit, perhaps, an evolutionarily necessary one) at this point in the evolution of human consciousness (cf. Lacan, Krishnamurti, and Zen philosophy), and "consciousness" is a universal, transpersonal phenomenon in which "individualities" merely in some way inscribe themselves? (see, for example, Sardello's notion of "the soul of the world"—1992: 15). These are deep ontological questions with which New Paradigm thinking is forging new and exciting insights; I return to some of these issues later in this book. Suffice to say at this point that these kinds of radical New Paradigm views quite decisively undermine the modernist philosophical foundations that underlie and legitimize conventional therapy both as a body of "expert" knowledge and as a clinical practice.

A more "intersubjective" viewpoint sees boundary-mindedness as a sort of fear-driven wishful thinking, for perhaps "we ... culturally defend against feeling divided, spread out on the social domain, a locus with inconsistent character. Our perceived discreteness and independence is wishful and, in the nature of the human world, wishes can easily come to constitute reality" (Hinshelwood, 1997: 198). Perhaps this points to another reason why the concept of "boundaries" has been so assiduously seized upon as a "valid" ontological reality with which to structure, and allay the primitive anxieties that inevitably accompany, the therapeutic encounter. Just as boundary-mindedness seems to parallel the recent professionalization of therapy, so we can predict that New Paradigm, intersubjective approaches can be expected to cohere well with the "post-professional" (Illich with others, 1977a), post-conceptual (Heron, 1996) values which will surely organically emerge in a new "post-therapy era" (e.g. House, 1997a; see also Chapter 12).

Carl Rogers himself had a great deal to say about both the place of boundaries within counselling, and about the professionalization of counselling more generally (House, 2002a; Owen, 1997: 167). My strong hunch is that he would have been very uneasy about, and profoundly critical of, current professionalizing developments. As Owen points out, Rogers was committed to "a natural and ordinary way of relating to clients" (*ibid.*) which eschewed over-professionalism, obscurantism, and authoritarianism in the counselling relationship. The typical lack of overly fixed and rigid boundaries within the Person-Centred approach, with its overt and self-conscious attempt to demystify the "therapeutic process", is in many ways consistent with the spirit of my own "post-professional" position . . .—as are Rogers' robust views on professionalization: "the urge toward professionalism builds up a rigid bureaucracy . . . if we did away with the 'expert', 'the certified professional' . . ., we might open our profession to a breeze of fresh air, a surge of creativity, such as has not been known for years . . . In every area . . . certification has tended to freeze and narrow the profession" (Rogers, 1990/1973: 364, 366). Owen well encapsulates the humanistic approach to boundaries—a position which is becoming increasingly difficult to maintain in the face of the march of the profession-centred therapeutic juggernaut: "The use of strict boundaries may even be seen as part of an authoritarian and potentially exploitative mystification which invents artificial concepts that are discriminatory, judgemental and dehumanising" (Owen, 1997: 168).

I have spent a lot of space on the concepts of boundary and

frame, as they together hold a most influential and prominent—and typically unproblematized—discursive position within therapy's regime of truth. The conventional view of boundaries within therapy, essentially derived and uncritically adopted from psychoanalytic ideology, is that boundaries constitute "the most influential core conditions leading to ethical and successful counselling" (Owen, 1997: 169), and that "clarity about practice gives clients a sense of 'being held' (*ibid.*, 165). Perhaps clients are being "held" (on to) by such an approach in more ways than therapy's (no doubt well intentioned) client-protecting rhetoric would have us believe ... which elegantly leads me on to the notion of "holding".

"Holding" as self-serving ideology of profession-centred therapeutic practice

The function of holding in psychological terms is to provide ego-support, in particular at the stage of absolute dependence before integration of the ego has become established. [Davis & Wallbridge, 1987: 98]

"Holding" is another term which has achieved a kind of hallowed status within the therapy lexicon, and it is very revealing to consider the origins of the term "holding" within therapy. According to Davis and Smallbridge, "the 'holding phase' in Winnicott's theory is equivalent to the stage of being merged or of absolute dependence ..." (1987: 99). Similarly, in the somewhat grotesquely titled text, *Tactics and Techniques in Psychoanalytic Therapy* (ed. P. L. Giovacchini), we read that "Winnicott ... felt that the creation of a comfortable holding environment involved the acceptance of the patient's dependence, a crucial aspect of the treatment of patients" (Giovacchini: 1990, 233). Thus, as Lomas (1987: 85) describes it (referring to Winnicott's theory of holding), "If holding fails there is a threat of annihilation, a loss of continuity of being ...; In therapy the patient will attempt to ward off a repetition of the original breakdown by all the means at her disposal".

Now as the psychoanalyst Joyce McDougall has recently pointed out, the grave danger of making assumptions such as this is that the therapist ends up actively and self-fulfillingly creating that which s/he is expecting to find: "We discover only what our theories permit us to find. ... Our cherished concepts appear to be continually self-confirming" (1995: 235–236; cf. Kivlighan, 1989). Hinshelwood also concedes that "Any communication an analyst makes must come from a loaded framework of words and concepts derived from his [sic] social position ..." (1997: 165). Now if McDougall is right that clients are profoundly influenced and constrained by the way their therapists think about them, then clearly the notion of "holding" (taken as it is from Winnicott's notion of maternal holding) cannot but tend to encourage an infantilizing dependency in the therapeutic relationship—which in turn, of course, means that the therapist's assumptive world-view has tended actively to create the conditions in which their client then feels in "need" of them! Here is another way, then, in which the self-serving discourse of profession-centred therapy's regime of truth creates the conditions and *raison d'être* for its own existence.

For current purposes, of course, it is highly germane that Winnicott extended the meaning of "holding" to cover the total care of the child (Lomas, 1987: 84–85)—quoting Winnicott, "[Holding] includes the whole routine of care throughout the day and night ... it follows the minute day-to-day change belonging to the infant's growth and development, both physical and psychological" (quoted in *ibid.*). In his important chapter on the misuse of psychotherapeutic power, Lomas (1987: 99) points out that "The danger of Winnicott's notion of 'holding' ... is that it may imply an ideal relationship in which the mother and the baby [try substituting 'therapist' and 'patient' here! ...—RH] are locked in a mutual narcissistic identification ..., [ignoring] the fact that they exist in the world, not in a sterile test-tube". (The implicit analogy here between a "test-tube" and the therapeutic setting is, perhaps, not nearly as far-fetched as it might initially sound.) In a critique with which I have much sympathy, Lomas goes on to criticize psychoanalytic child development theory, for "it encourages the therapist to cushion her patient from reality by cultivating a milieu in which the latter ... can experience the illusion of omnipotent care" (*ibid.*: 101). Lomas goes on to discuss the dangers of a *folie à deux* developing in such a setting (*ibid.*)—an issue I will return to at length in Chapter 6, below.

A critically well received text by Lemma-Wright (1995)

illustrates very clearly the infantilizing effects of this aspect of therapy's ideological discourse. For Lemma-Wright, the holding environment "is an expression which highlights [the therapeutic frame's] containing function—just as mothers provide the baby with such an environment which maximises the opportunities of physical and psychic survival and growth" (p. 191—note the analogy with the mothering of a baby). A bit later, we read that "The analyst's function to an extent mirrors the early parental function ..." (p. 192); and again, Lemma-Wright draws attention to "a parallel between the mother's containing functions ... and the analyst's function of receiving, containing and transforming the patient's communications ... *[this] lend[s] to the analytic relationship a regressive, infantile quality*" (*ibid.*, my emphasis). Clearly, the infantilizing assumptions about the therapeutic process here are legion; and in this light Lemma-Wright is singularly unconvincing in her claim that this (psychodynamic) therapeutic approach leaves the patient to find their own way "without any pressure to conform" (p. 191). Yet clearly one crucial function which such a self-deluding belief serves is to disguise the self-serving, self-fulfilling nature of profession-centred therapeutic practice, which it routinely succeeds in doing—until, that is, its discourse is exposed to the searching light of discursive deconstruction.

"Holding" is in itself a fascinating term, a closer examination of which is most revealing of the hidden, tacit ideological discourse of profession-centred therapeutic practice. Thus, the *Concise Oxford Dictionary* defines "(to) hold" variously, as: "keep fast, grasp, keep (thing) in particular position ...; grasp *so as to control, keep in particular attitude or condition*"; and also "*to possess* ..., be the owner or holder ... of, have in one's hand ..., engross (person, his attention), *dominate*", and "*to keep (person etc.) in a specified place, condition, make (person) adhere to*", and "remain unbroken, not give away" (my various emphases)—as well as meaning to "contain or be able to do so". Now our choice of words is never a random event: the ideological process through which any given term becomes a culturally legitimate concept in discourse entails an infinitely complex condensation and distillation into tangible form of the ineffable, of the beyond-words-ness of human experience. The therapy world could have embraced and made legitimate a variety of alternative terms to convey the idea of "containment", but the fact is that it has sedimented a term, "holding", whose dictionary meaning has demonstrably far more to do with control, grasping, and *"keeping things like this"* (to quote Ted Hughes' hawk in his poem "Hawk Roosting"—Alvarez, 1962: 179) than it has to do with an appropriately facilitative way of being with clients in the therapeutic encounter.

What I am suggesting, then, is that in reality, therapy's legitimation of "holding" as an allegedly key aspect of the therapeutic process for the client has more to do with *the therapist's* "professional" holding needs than it does with facilitating the client's therapeutic process. Dartington is surely approaching a similar conclusion when she writes that

> There is a tendency in all of us, as therapists and counsellors, to become necessary to our clients, and like parents of adolescents we sometimes do not want our "children" to leave home until we decide they are ready. This is due not only to our concern but also perhaps to *our own needs to become dependent on their dependency*. [1995: 266, my emphasis]

Rutter too makes a similar point, which again should make highly uncomfortable reading for the professional therapist: "We rarely acknowledge the degree to which we are co-dependent with our clients. But we do depend on them: for money, for company, for inspiration, for psychological growth, for sexual fantasy, and to some degree for self-validation" (1989: 74). Certainly, on reading closely the very apposite and sobering book *A Curious Calling: Unconscious Motivations for Practicing Psychotherapy* (Sussman, 1992)—a book which lays bare in painstaking rawness the myriad unconscious reasons why therapists choose to be therapists—I am left wandering just who is *really* holding whom in the therapeutic dyad ...

The origin of the term "holding" in analytic discourse, then, stems from the infantilization that analytic practice typically entails and actively encourages. The uncritical adoption of the term in the wider therapeutic lexicon perhaps constitutes yet another example of the way in which therapeutic discourse (including, sadly, much of humanistic praxis) has been surreptitiously colonized by the infantilizing ideology of analytic thinking, which was typically formulated in working with severely disturbed, so-called "borderline" or psychotic "patients".

Finally, I want to be clear that I am not criticizing the therapist's insecurity and vulnerability within the therapeutic encounter; but I *am* criticizing both the way in which that vulnerability is systematically denied and disguised through erecting an ideological façade emphasizing *the client's* vulnerability and need for "holding", and also the way in which holding-mindedness is then made into a self-serving professional ideology within therapeutic discourse. And if this analysis is anything like correct, then it also follows that professional therapists are typically taking a highly distorting influence into their work (for example, by denying *their own* vulnerability and projecting it on to their clients), which further contaminates and renders "neurotic" what is already a highly peculiar, artificial relationship.

Conclusion

If ... the psychotherapist overvalues her thought and method, assuming that she has the right to control the conditions and content of the dialogue, she makes the tragic error of the politician. [Lomas, 1987: 103]

Existing forms of professionalization have predominantly been developed within the assumptive base and ideological discourse of modernity and a predominantly technocratic world-view (House, 1997a), and are inevitably contaminated by "the tendency of helpers of all kinds to objectify people, words and experiences" (Riikonen & Smith, 1997: 12). As Bracken and Thomas have it, "Personal distress and sorrow are no longer the concern of the 'soul' and its journey through life ... Suffering and healing are increasingly framed in a technical idiom" (1998: 17). And if it is the very cultural "madnesses" (not least, the "materialist" denial of spirit and soul) that are at the root of so much of the emotional and spiritual malaise that many clients bring into therapy, then it follows that we may well be *reinforcing* rather than healing societal malaise if we "deliver" therapy in a profession-centred framework that privileges the underlying values and practices of modernity. For as Riikonen and Smith have it, "Narrowly referential views of language have impoverished our ways of understanding human life" (1997: 6).

In this chapter I have offered a critical deconstruction of three key concepts that have come to inhabit professional therapeutic discourse—namely, resistance, boundaries, and holding—in an attempt to show how both the definitions of these terms, and the ways in which they are used theoretically to think about clients and about the therapeutic process, contribute towards a regime of truth whose ideology is both professionally self-serving and limiting for clients as *their very subjectivity* is shaped by their position within this ideological discourse. Chapters 6–8 will provide copious evidence supporting these radical propositions from the detailed documented experiences of actual clients.

In the next chapter I continue this analysis by critically deconstructing the therapeutic notions of confidentiality, safety, abuse and ethics.

Coda: The "material"-generating nature of profession-centred therapeutic practice

... psychotherapy is a self-generating phenomenon; the more it is done the more illness is created. [Sardello, 1990: 10]

... therapeutic situations are like laboratories, they force certain things into existence. And ... *they force those things into reality which have already been dreamed up in the minds of the therapists.* [Rose, 1997, my emphasis]

Both in this chapter and in the next chapter (in the section on safety), I refer to the way in which profession-centred therapeutic practice actively and routinely *creates subjectivity* such that client "material" is triggered by the form itself, working upon which "material" then becomes the rationale and *raison d'être* for the therapy's continuation.

I can hardly do better than cite examples of this phenomenon from three of the foremost contributors to our understanding of the client experience of profession-centred therapeutic practice—Rosie Alexander, Ann France, and Anna Sands (whose work I examine in detail in Chapters 6–8, below). First, France (1988: 122) writes: "this desirable and potentially constructive luxury [to know that this one hour is devoted to oneself] also sets up guilt feelings, which can be quite considerable, at devoting so much attention to oneself and ignoring the other person's needs". In other words, the form taken by profession-centred therapy *itself* generates the "material" of guilt, which then (in the thrall of therapy's normally unspoken "regime of truth"), has to be "worked on". At points throughout her book France refers to the artificiality of the therapy framework (e.g. pp. 51, 60, 85)—the implication being, again, that this artificiality actually creates subjectivity within the relationship. As she rather graphically puts it, "Psychotherapy ... can merely be the replay of past traumata ... which leads to nothing ...; It creates an artificial situation ... *which could lead to ... the artificial creation of [problems]*" (1988: 32, 1, my emphasis).

I also want to repeat here two quotations from Rosie Alexander which I have used elsewhere in the book, to illustrate this potentially abusive process of profession-centred therapeutic practice. First, she writes thus: "The personal difficulties that led me to therapy were dwarfed into insignificance by what was happening within the therapy itself ... Therapy induced an obsession with self and therapist which precluded normal human intercourse" (Alexander, 1998a: 91). And second,

> It was maddening ... to know that I was in such a state of emotional slavery to someone whose mind was working along such erroneous lines. ... I was beginning to feel like a political prisoner locked away in a psychiatric hospital; impotent, completely at my captor's mercy, and in danger of being browbeaten into believing anything he wanted to say, no matter how absurd. [Alexander, 1995: 104]

In Chapter 8 I also examine at some length Anna Sands' penetrating insights into material generation. At this juncture, one selected quotation will suffice—viz. when she poignantly asks, "[D]oesn't therapy sometimes reveal, sometimes replicate, and sometimes create the feelings and behaviour that arise there?" (2000: 133).

These quotations also illustrate graphically the point I am making here with regard to the way in which *therapy itself* can become the problem (to which it then posits itself as the solution!), rather than the means of solving *pre-existing* problems.

I call this process the unethical, *"material"-generating* nature of the form taken by profession-centred therapy (I am grateful to my friend and colleague Lindsay Cooke for helping me to articulate this concept). And to the extent that this process is intrinsic to profession-centred therapeutic practice itself—certainly under conditions in which the unreflective therapist is unaware of it—then it follows that practitioners have a grave ethical responsibility to do everything they can to minimize this dynamic (I return to this in Chapter 12, where I specify the characteristics of what a non-abusive "deconstructive therapy" might look like).

The following analogy is illuminating. If, when you took your car in to the local garage for a service, the garage mechanic trashed the engine in the process of checking it over (= "neurosis" generated by profession-centred therapeutic practice) and then charged you for the privilege of fixing it, you probably wouldn't be very happy—and this kind of behaviour no doubt happens in *all* "professions" where clients/customers "give away" their power within a "regime of expertise", couched in turn within a (so-called) "efficient" division of labour. What makes the highly peculiar nature of profession-centred therapy different, however, is that such an "abusive" professional process can routinely occur as a *natural by-product* of profession-centred therapeutic practice itself, without any conscious or intended dishonesty on the therapist's part, and outside of the awareness of the protagonists in the therapeutic dyad.

This discussion highlights one of the central contradictions of the whole private-therapeutic enterprise, where the therapist relies upon and needs his or her clients to come back, in order to "pay their mortgage", so to speak. In a personal communication Keith Tudor (1999) has made the point that for therapy practice to be scrupulously ethical, it is crucial that the therapist does not need the client's fee to "pay the (proverbial) mortgage". There is a strong case to be made for the argument, then, that any profession which needs its clientele to come for regular "professional" service or "treatment" cannot but have an unethical dimension. And dare I suggest that the overt, high-profile concern expressed by the therapy bureaucracies about ethics and abuse-prevention may well *at some level* be an unconscious attempt to distract attention from the unethical nature of profession-centred therapeutic practice.

In sum—and this is a central theme which recurs throughout this book which I cannot emphasize sufficiently strongly—therapy as a profession-centred therapeutic practice can *actively precipitate* and *create* "psychopathology", which it then "treats" in order to justify the need for its own existence. In other words, profession-centred therapy's "regime of truth" first generates and creates "client material" by the very nature of its form, therapeutic practices, and ideologies—and then both therapist and client collusively (and no doubt genuinely) believe that this regime-generated subjectivity is somehow "true" rather than being merely an artefact of profession-centred therapeutic practice itself (either through the deep dynamics triggered by that practice, or else because the therapist has unconsciously [and self-fulfillingly] "planted" in the client's subjective experience precisely what, through her preconceptive framework, she was expecting to find "in" the client in the first place; cf. McDougall, 1995).

That such a process is quite explicitly recognized within psychoanalysis has at least been acknowledged by Kendall and Crossley (1996: 178, 180, 181, 186), themselves by no means hostile critics of psychoanalysis:

> The psychoanalytic setting and method incites (transference) "love" in the patient and (countertransference) "love" in the analyst, feelings which are then subjected to a variety of governmental procedures so as to transform abnormal "love" into healthier "love" ... the network of love governance ... constitutes the ever-growing psychoanalytic establishment, linking practitioners and their patients to each other and to an ancestry that traces back to Freud. ... Analysands ... usually pay for [analysis]; but once in the relation [or "regime of truth"—RH], that consensual element is superseded by the asymmetrical relations of analyst (governor) and analysand (governed) ... *The analyst needs the analysand to resist, with love, in order that he has something to work with and upon.* [my emphasis; cf. my discussion of Hinshelwood (1997) in Chapter 2]

And Freud himself made no secret of what he saw as the central aim of analysis: in 1913 he revealingly wrote that, "it remains the first aim of the treatment *to attach [the patient] to [the treatment]* and to the person of the doctor" (quoted in Kendall & Crossley, 1996: 185, my emphasis). It is crucial to my argument that these "material-generating" features of profession-centred therapeutic practice are not confined to psychoanalysis and the more "pure" analytic psychotherapies; rather, they are far more ubiquitous across the therapy modalities, whether the therapist consciously intends it or not—with the possible exception of those approaches which adopt the kind of explicitly deconstructive, post-professional values and practices which I outline below in Chapter 12. To repeat again a quotation from one of the "recovering" ex-clients in Alexander's *Folie à Deux*: "This business about dependence; it doesn't seem to matter whether the therapist encourages it or discourages it. It's just there, like the weather" (1995: 145).

In such a way, then, does profession-centred therapeutic practice become a self-fulfilling and self-generating ideology—and all the more effectively when it is normally outside the conscious awareness of both clients and therapists—which is probably the case in many forms of therapy other than pure psychoanalysis and psychoanalytic psychotherapy. And if my analysis is anything like right, then these are sobering insights indeed for those who are uncritically committed to the profession-centred therapeutic framework—not to mention "professionally wedded" to and financially reliant upon it for their "bread and butter" and next mortgage payment ...

Chapters 6–8 will provide dramatic examples of the material-generating nature of profession-centred therapeutic practice, and ex-clients' experiences of it.

CHAPTER FOUR

Deconstructing profession-centred therapeutic practice:
II. Confidentiality, safety, abuse, ethics

The ideology of confidentiality

One of the functions of confidentiality is to create for clients a sense of psychological safety, necessary to fruitful and therapeutic relationships ... [Charles-Edwards *et al.*, 1989: 411]

P erhaps the most seemingly invulnerable ethic of profession-centred therapeutic practice is that of client confidentiality, a conventional wisdom well captured in the above epigraph. As Heather has pointed out, however, positivist psychology entails an ontology which views "human beings as isolated individuals, abstracted from the world of social and economic forces which bear upon their lives" (Heather, 1976: 51); and the confidentiality criterion can be seen as colluding with and effectively reproducing such an individualizing ideology.

Institutional therapy's codes of ethics, then, typically make a big issue of client confidentiality; yet there is a great danger in this of both reflecting and actively creating an obsession with the private, with "the privatization of distress" within the framework of the isolated, asocial self of late modernity (cf., for example, Cloud, 1998; Cushman, 1995; Henriques *et al.*, 1984; Smail, 1996). We may well ask whether therapy should be colluding with such an ideology—particularly if that very ideology happens to be at the root of so much of the emotional and spiritual malaise that afflicts people, and arguably determines many of the difficulties they take into therapy! On this view, then, and with massive irony, the privatizing therapeutic form may actually serve as an ideological framework which itself actively reinforces the very difficulties for which it aspires to offer help.

In addition, I would argue that while the rhetoric of confidentiality is very much client-focused, in reality "confidentiality" is at least as much to do with protecting the therapist—both in terms of a close investigation of her or his therapeutic practice, and more generally in terms of protecting the precious sanctity of profession-centred therapeutic practice from critical deconstructive gaze. On this view, then, "confidentiality" is, certainly at one level, a highly convenient "professional" ruse—albeit a normally unconscious and unacknowledged one—that further serves to buttress the self-serving ideology of profession-centred therapeutic practice and its regime of truth.

Moreover, not only does the solemn confidentiality criterion guarantee that privatized profession-centred therapy can never be the subject of external deconstructive scrutiny, but the criterion also conveys, often tacitly or surreptitiously, a strong privatizing message to clients—that the stylized therapeutic encounter is impenetrably private and (artificially) isolated from the outside world. Quite apart from the subjectivity-creating dynamics that this process entails (see Chapter 2), the confidentiality ethic is, of course, at least as much for the protection of the therapist and the unproblematic reproduction of profession-centred therapeutic practice, as it is for the client. In my own experience as a practitioner, the very occasional client does make a special point of stressing the importance of confidentiality; but for the most part it never gets mentioned at all by the client—only by the (regime-setting) therapist. Do we really know, or have we ever taken the trouble to find out, just how important confidentiality is to the generality of clients? Certainly, I believe that we ("the Profession") make massive (regime-reinforcing) assumptions in our ethical codes; and the confidentiality criterion is just one of them.

I want to make it unambiguously clear that I am not minimizing the importance of confidentiality for some, and perhaps many, or even most, clients; and I am equally not suggesting that therapists cease to respect and treat with appropriate sensitivity, and some-times reverence, the issues which their clients bring to therapy. But I am suggesting that an over-precious, unproblematized approach to confidentiality may well be far more therapist-centred than we may care to acknowledge. A colleague (Lindsay Cooke, personal com-munication) once said to me that it is *the spirit* of confidentiality, and the way in which we carry it in our very being, that really matters, not the letter of some automatic, robotic adherence to a didactic ethical injunction. Cooke's remark certainly captures the spirit of what I am arguing here.

On client "safety"

The work of psychological healing begins in a safe place. [Havens, 1989: vii]

The notion of "safety"—like "boundaries", the "frame", and so on—is yet another example of the mantric *therapese* that trips so easily—and often unreflectively—off the tongues of those initiated in therapy's regime of truth—the above epigraph from Havens being a typical example. (Havens's book is in fact entitled *A Safe Place: Laying the Groundwork for Psychotherapy.*) The rhetoric of therapy is supersaturated with references to "safety", presented (or dressed up?) as a professional concern for the client's safety, which is no doubt a consciously and genuinely held concern on the part of practitioners. But what are the unarticulated assumptions and the effects of this preoccupation if we analyse it more closely and critically? First, there are the implicit assumptions that, first, it is in principle possible to legislate for, or create, "safety"; and second (given that the latter *is* indeed feasible), that it is appropriate so to do. In my view, certainly the first of these assumptions (possibility) does not stand up to even cursory deconstructive scrutiny; and the second (appropriateness) is also far less clear-cut than it at first appears. And worse still, what we then have is an *illusion* of safety—which is, paradoxically, far more dangerous than is a situation where we at least acknowledge that it is in principle impossible to "legislate safety into existence" in the therapeutic (or any other human-relational) domain. Again, then—and this is a theme which recurs repeatedly throughout this book—we see another dramatic example of the way in which the deliberate attempt to plan and legislate for a specific therapeutic effect actually tends to bring about the very opposite of its professed intention. I am reminded of the old joke that just oozes with perennial wisdom:

> Someone once asked a friend, "Do you know how to make God laugh?" "No, how do you?", came the reply. "Tell him *your plans!* ...".

Lindsay Cooke (personal communication, 1999) makes a useful distinction between safety *from* ... and safety *for* ...: the former, which has been my focus in this section to date, has essentially "negative" connotations, tending to focus around potential or actual abuse; whereas, it might be argued, the creation of an enabling, "growthful" kind of safety can be seen in a positive, growth-oriented way rather than in a preventive or pathology-focused way. On this view, "safety" could be argued to be not only achievable, but a positive, "healthy" aspect of profession-centred therapeutic practice. Yet a closer, deconstructive scrutiny reveals just as many difficulties with this more positive view as there are with the abuse-prevention approach to safety.

The nub of the problem is that not only is it no easier to create a "safety-for" than it is a "safety-from" therapeutic milieu, but the very act of the therapist taking responsibility for "safety" *per se* can be intrinsically infantilizing, to the extent that the provision of something provided from the outside, external to the client (e.g. the so-called "secure therapeutic frame" of Robert Langs—see Gray, 1994) will almost inevitably trigger dependency issues for the client.

The foregoing discussion of "safety" leads quite naturally into the related question of abuse.

On client abuse

> I have very rarely been able to get a clear open discussion going on the subject [of sexual passion in therapy] because most therapists retreat behind defensive words such as "transference" and "projection" as if naming is a sufficient understanding ... [Jayran, 1992: 18]

The issue of "safety" leads quite naturally into a consideration of the question of abuse in therapy. We may justifiably ask, is it possible to prevent abuse in therapy? All extant evidence suggests that there is at least as much abuse by registered practitioners as there is by the unregistered or the unregulated (Mowbray, 1995; Howard, 1996). And there are very compelling arguments for the view that, far from making client abuse less likely, an institutional form of "policing" and sanctions might actually increase the likelihood of abuse (House, 1996c; Mowbray, 1995).

First, there is a complacency factor involved, whereby practitioners can be lulled into a misplaced sense of security about the work and their safe practising in it because of the illusion of protection afforded by legislative sanction. Moreover, as practitioners must ultimately rely upon their own ethical judgement about moral issues rather than some external authority, given the inherent uniqueness of each and every relational experience, they are actually far more likely to reach an ethically appropriate and fully embodied position or decision if their moral sense is fully owned, internalized, and intrinsically authoritative (House, 1997b; as Gale has put it in typically robust fashion, "I don't need a code of ethics to tell me whether or not to have sex with my clients"—1996: 16). Furthermore, and leading on quite naturally from Gale's point, just what quality of therapeutic work is a practitioner going to be doing when s/he requires an external code of conduct to tell him or her how they should or should not behave within the therapeutic relationship?

In my view, then, the infantilizing "thou-shalt-not" mentality (Brown, 1989, 1997) simply doesn't work: it fails to deliver what it is intending to deliver, and not because the legislation isn't tight enough, or the "rules" not sufficiently thorough or comprehensive, but because the very attempt to bring it about is fundamentally misplaced. And the paradox is that the very act of relying on external rules in order to make practitioners "safe" may actually render them unsafe!—not least because our own intrinsic authority tends to be usurped in that very process (House, 1997b).

There is also the phenomenon of "defensive psychotherapy" (Clarkson, 1995; Mowbray, 1995: 151–154; House, 1997b: 327–328), and the argument that the very existence of a fear-saturated environment that attempts to render safe what is intrinsically un-make-safe-able (i.e. human relationship) will have the effect of reducing the effectiveness of therapeutic work by limiting risk-taking and the depth of intimate work that therapists will be prepared or be able to do with their clients (cf. House, 1995b).

Even if it were sustainable that preventing abuse is possible (which, for the reasons just given, I don't believe it is), would such prevention be appropriate? It is of course completely under-standable that people should want to prevent abuse—the calculus appears to be very simple: *A is being abused; if I do B, then A's abuse will stop, ergo if I do B, it is to A's benefit that I do it, and an overall improvement in well-being will be the net result of my intervention.* Within the simple, highly controlled, and artificial situation just described, this simple cause-and-effect logic of "appropriate" prevention is perhaps unchallengeable. Unfortunately, in the real world, matters are, of course, infinitely more complex than this; for ultimately, there is no way of knowing definitively, first, whether overt attempts to prevent abuse might simply *redistribute* abuse to other, less visible and less easily policed parts of the work rather than eradicating it; and second, whether the very attempt to prevent abuse might have such wide-ranging side-effects in terms of the overall quality of therapeutic work that the "cure" might do more, overall damage than the "disease" it is attempting to expunge.

I make these points not to argue against the appropriateness of prevention, but merely to make the point that in such highly complex "systems" like these we can never know whether we might not be bringing about the very opposite of our professed intention (and history is, of course, littered with such examples). But such arguments are not only speculative, they are essentially spurious—for if it is not possible to prevent abuse and render therapy safe (as I argued above), then the question as to whether it is appropriate to try to effect this prevention arguably does not arise.

The conventional view on (sexual) abuse in therapy is well summed up by Pokorny: "Sexual abuse is a very serious matter and it must be tackled" (1998: 265). Now being "against abuse" can degenerate into little more than a "mom and apple pie"-type argument—of course we are all "against abuse"; and not least for this reason, I am acutely aware of how dangerous it is to dare even to think about deconstructing the notion of "abuse", and challenging the taken-for-granted assumptions that surround it—for it quite understandably arouses extremely strong emotions. And yet I believe that such a fearless deconstruction is very long overdue. This process was in fact started by Jill Hall (1993) in her courageous and very important book *The Reluctant Adult* (see also Hall, 1988).

In *The Reluctant Adult*, Hall explores the debilitating impact of what she calls "the victimhood archetype" operating at an unconscious level within our culture. She challenges the mechanistically causal thinking which has held sway since Descartes, arguing that the cause-and-effect approach to explaining psychic reality inevitably leads to a deterministic conception of the person with its associated traits of blaming and victimhood. Thus, if I am "caused", then *ipso facto* I must be *an effect* of others or my environment, rather than a unique self-determining being in my own right, with my own volition, destiny, and sense of responsibility.

Hall, then, challenges the prevailing "wounded-child" orthodoxy which dominates the discourse of abuse: the assumption—which either explicitly (as in psychoanalytic theory) or tacitly dominates much of psychotherapeutic ideology—that children are essentially passive victims of their histories, and are largely "determined" by what is done to them (for examples of this view, for example, see the work of Alice Miller—e.g. 1987, and Guidano, 1987; Perris & Arrindell, 1994). Thus, their wounds are seen as sculpting their destinies, with choice rendered vacuous, and people not being creative in any meaningful sense. That such an ideology is so culturally all-pervasive, and that the therapy world colludes so uncritically with it (notwithstanding a significant and growing literature which challenges the "victimhood" perspective—e.g. Caplan & Hall-McCorquodale, 1985; Clarke & Clarke, 1976; Corsaro, 1997; Eyer, 1992; Gladwell, 1998; Hawkins & Dollahite, 1997; Hillman, 1996; Horner, 1985; Katz, 1997; Lerner, 1986; Walsch, 1995) is entirely consistent with and testimony to Hall's invocation of the "victimhood archetype" to throw light upon this phenomenon, and to locate it more generally within the evolution of human consciousness (cf. Hillman, 1996).

The therapy field should surely, in my view, be at the very forefront of challenging and deconstructing notions of abuse, victimhood, and environmental determinism in child development—and yet instead, the calcification and rigidifying institutionalization that tends to accompany didactic, career-focused professionalization (e.g. House, 1999f) is actually moving, if anything, in the opposite direction. For those with a personal, material interest in the perpetuation of an individualized therapeutic ideology are not very likely to wish to deconstruct it, and will therefore tend to embrace and collude with those cultural norms that buttress and reinforce the old world-view. And thus do ideologies become reproduced and ossified, constituting a fetter on the evolution of human consciousness rather than a facilitator and enabler of it. Not that I am naïvely implying here that a full and open embracing of the implications of the "victimhood archetype" perspective would necessarily make the practice of individualized psychotherapy redundant; but I certainly feel that it would make it into a qualitatively very different "animal" which might conceivably bear little resemblance to the profession-centred therapeutic practice that currently holds such hegemonic sway in our culture.

I believe it is implicit, then, in Hall's argument that the process of abuse is an extremely complex intersubjective experience; and simplistically to focus on "blaming" and punishing the "abuser" diminishes the abused yet further. Yet this is precisely the culture that exists within conventional therapy, with its punitive, legalistic complaints procedures. In my view it is naïve, and reveals a quite fundamental misunderstanding of the nature and dynamics of abuse, to assume that one can somehow "legislate it away" by a kind of Code-of-Ethics definitional fiat. Moreover, and as I have written elsewhere, the not inconsiderable danger is that "didactic codes of ethics can have the effect of simply *redistributing abusive behaviour to a different part of the work* rather than removing it; that the ideology of didactic codes of ethics can actually collude with abuse by giving the erroneous impression that their existence somehow magically expunges abusive behaviour from therapeutic work" (House, 1997b: 325).

In sum, and in a proposition which I think may be received with something approaching outrage by some in the field, I maintain that the determined erecting of institutional structures to prevent abuse has unintended side-effects that, as a generality, may well have a net detrimental effect on the field and for the overall quality of therapeutic work, doing greater net harm than the malpractice these very structures are endeavouring (with inevitable lack of demonstrable success) to prevent: what I have called elsewhere "an illusion of policing" (House, 1996–7).

Now the danger in what I am writing here—and I am only too aware of it—is that it could be seized upon as a kind of "abuser's charter" and used to justify abusive behaviour. I want to make it absolutely and unambiguously clear that I do believe that there is such a phenomenon as "abuse"; and in citing the foregoing examples I am most certainly *not* saying that I would condone what would conventionally be deemed to be abuse. But I am saying that I think it very important to remain open-minded about what precisely constitutes harmful abuse. I believe that the simplistic assumptions and knee-jerk reactions around the subject of abuse so prevalent in the therapy world, and in our culture more generally, tend to obscure more than they reveal about abuse, thus severely inhibiting our capacity to understand such interaction in anything more than a superficial and abuse-perpetuating way. (There are of course exceptions—not least the excellent study by de Zulueta, 1993.) That is, the very fact that our conventional response to abuse is so oversimplified, and swamped by understandable emotional outrage, has the effect of perpetuating the abusive culture which those responding to it in this way are, understandably, so keen to eradicate.

Returning to the issue of the profession-centred response to abuse: it is highly revealing that those mainstream practitioners who have responded in print to the challenges to professionalization seem to assume that by merely asserting the mantra "We must protect clients from abuse", that this somehow completely short-circuits and makes redundant all of the highly detailed and sophisticated challenges to "regulation-mindedness" articulated by Richard Mowbray (1995) and others. Elsewhere I have spent some time deconstructing and exposing the lack veracity in this argument (e.g. House, 1997f); here, I simply wish to add that as soon as we begin to challenge and problematize conventional, accepted notions of and attitudes towards abuse, as I am doing here, then the whole rationale for didactic professionalization being a valid strategy for the field threatens to collapse and sink without trace.

A very good example of this is afforded by ex-UKCP Chair Michael Pokorny's extraordinary response to Denis Postle's important and substantial (30-page) paper "Gold into lead" (Postle, 1998a). In what masquerades as an "article" (of less than 500 words, and with an Abstract of 40 words!), Pokorny is contemptuously dismissive, attempting to short-circuit the whole anti-professionalization case simply by invoking the spurious "client-protection-from-sexual-abuse" argument. For Pokorny the importance of eradicating practitioner sexual abuse seemingly overrides all other considerations (not least whether institutional strivings to eradicate abuse might well throw out the therapeutic baby with the abusive bathwater, by precipitating far-reaching and unintended detrimental effects upon the whole field of therapy; cf. my earlier argument). But given the ease with which the "client-protection" argument can be refuted, the flimsy Emperor's-clothes-ness of the "anti" anti-professionalization argument is starkly exposed for all to see.

It is, in addition, a telling irony that Pokorny's use of the "client-abuse" argument to reject out of hand any conceivable case against didactic professionalization *itself* borders on being abusive—not only in its loftily cavalier dismissal *per se*, but also in the very style of the dismissal. Thus, for example, we are told that "Postle laments that Mowbray's book [1995] has been largely ignored but does not seem to consider that it may have got the level of attention it deserves" (p. 265). Then there is his extraordinary *ex cathedra* assertion that "the Independent Practitioners Network ... is neither effective, nor is it in the public interest" (*ibid.*). It is scarcely believable that figures so prominent in the field can throw around phrases like "the public interest" with apparently not the slightest sense of their ideological, ontologically suspect nature.

I have had several personal experiences of what happens when one dares to challenge accepted shibboleths about abuse. First, in 1994 I submitted a paper to a journal (House, 1995b) which was initially rejected in a most cursory *and abusive* manner. In that paper I argued that we should proceed with caution before attempting to legislate against abuse in therapy. Once a colleague and I had successfully challenged the dynamics of this rejection, I had received an editorial apology from the journal in question, and the paper finally appeared in print, a significant number of practitioners told me how pleased they were that I had written and had the courage to publish it—not least because it dared to say the kinds of things about abuse that many reflective practitioners think to themselves in private, but would never dare to say in public. I quote below from a letter (dated 14/9/94) I wrote to the journal's editors (if writing it today I would certainly avoid much of the pathologizing *therapese* it contains):

> the only conceivable way in which I can account [for the referee's offhand rejection of my paper] is that [the referee] is acting out unconsciously from a completely disowned and denied abuser in himself. My paper has clearly touched some deep, highly defended material in [the referee]. And of course, to someone who has totally denied and split off the potential abuser in himself, my paper would indeed appear to "say nothing" [which was, in fact, the sum total of the referee's "report"!—RH], because such a person would be rigidly defended against and quite incapable of "hearing" what I was saying in the paper ... [the huge irony is that] your response to my article is actually confirming the very arguments I was making in the paper. ... The fear and anxiety around the area of abuse is such that it is virtually impossible to get any real and open debate going on the issue—and your rejection of my paper only serves to confirm this.

I cringe somewhat in reproducing this text, written over 7 years ago as I write; for while its analysis might well have some accuracy, my whole approach, if a comparable situation were to arise today, would no doubt be very different. But in reproducing it here I hope to throw light on the very considerable complexities and archetypal ineffabilities of the abuse question—and the very great difficulty in attaining anything approaching reliable "emotional competence" (to use a fashionable term) in this area—even for experienced therapists.

(For the record I do wish to add that the difficulty around this paper's rejection and subsequent acceptance for publication was handled by the editors of the journal in question in an exemplary and very sensitive way.)

The other example I will quote illustrating the therapy world's inability to deconstruct the notion of abuse occurred at a one-day workshop I attended in London in September 1996, led by Peter Rutter (of *Sex in the Forbidden Zone* fame). In the workshop I experienced at first hand the lack of openness to even beginning to challenge accepted norms on abuse. (It is perhaps a telling irony that those who do dare to make such a challenge are subjected to considerable abuse by those who claim to champion its eradication. I came away from the workshop thinking that perhaps the massive indignation with which people often attempt to stop the abuse of others is being driven, at least in part, by a need to deny and project out on to "the other", or the culture, one's own internal abuser and/ or "abused".)

In his workshop, Rutter argued that we require what he called a "psycho–social archaeology" fully to understand the continuing existence of abuse in our culture, yet in my view his analysis fell woefully short of providing anything like a plausible and complete explanation of the pervasive nature of abuse. At no point, for example, did he suggest that perhaps the common cultural denial of trauma and abuse is rooted in species-wide, all pervading (even archetypal) "imprints" of abuse, possibly stemming from the "normal" traumata of pre- and peri-natal experience (the work of David Wasdell is seminal in this area—e.g. Wasdell, 1990; echoes here of Bollas when he writes of "the universality of child abuse, if by this we mean that each human subject is anguished by some of the products of his or her mind"—Bollas, 1992: 240–241). On this view, then, Rutter's celebration of the DSM's recognition since 1979–80 of the clinical category of "Post-Traumatic Stress Disorder" (PTSD) seemed at the least naïve; for the way in which the PTSD diagnostic category has been seized upon and reified in both clinical and cultural discourse tends to make PTSD into an objectified "abnormal" condition that happens to the unfortunate other, rather than a species-wide, commonly held, possibly archetypal experience lodged deep in the unconscious of all of us.

In the course of the seminar Rutter expressed quite unequivocal support for the statutory registration of the therapy field in order to protect clients from abuse, and he strongly criticized the open, unregulated system we had (and thankfully still have) in Britain. It was at this point that I challenged Rutter on what seemed to me to be an uncritical and unreflective position; drew his attention to some of the central arguments in Mowbray's *Case Against Psychotherapy Registration* (1995); and argued that by trying to legislate into existence a copper-bottomed guarantee of client safety, we were in great danger of throwing out the healing "baby" with the "bathwater" of potential or actual practitioner abuse.

The venom unleashed within the group when I dared to challenge Rutter's expressed views about regulation was awesome —and those who protested quite quickly demonstrated that they had either largely misheard, or grossly distorted, what I had said. Such is the barely containable strength of the emotional response to issues around abuse that the faculty of perceptual accuracy is, in my experience, one of the first to go. And all this merely reinforces the veracity of Jayran's quotation which serves as an epigraph to this section. Again, however, it was fascinating that at the end of the seminar, several participants approached me to say how much they agreed with and appreciated what I had said—but they clearly hadn't felt able to express their support within the seminar itself.

I close this section with a quotation from Jill Hall's *Reluctant Adult*. Referring to the Medicine Wheel teachings of the Native American teachings, she writes,

> Clearness of thought is important in the American Indian teachings ... but fixed thought is seen as a great danger. ... Once something has become clarified it can not only become set but can also be mistaken for reality itself. In this way we misuse the ability of the rational mind to define and make distinctions by allowing whatever we make precise to harden into fixed definitions and categories which we then impose upon reality. ... The enemies of the wise and receptive mind are set conceptual frameworks. ... With short-sighted conviction of this kind our modes of thinking solidify into rigid dogmas. ... We can no longer receive new knowledge nor allow our ideas to grow and develop. We are then bound to be involved in merely defending the status quo. [Hall, 1993: 103]

For me, this statement, when set alongside Krishnamurti's "Truth is a pathless land" speech (quoted on p. 22) and Brown and Mowbray's argument that "Where there is a genuine need for structures, we should develop structures that foster our values rather than betray them" (Brown & Mowbray, 1990, quoted in Mowbray, 1995: 225), points resoundingly to the following conclusion: that *any frameworks (institutional or otherwise) which we create to facilitate and encourage successful therapeutic work should surely reflect the core values of what is most enabling and healing in the activity of therapy*; and I submit that the didactic institutionalizing of "professional" therapy may well constitute a move in entirely the opposite direction to that which would enable therapy organically to grow, evolve, and, if necessary, transcend itself as its existing profession-centred form increasingly becomes a dead-weight upon, rather than a facilitator of, human development at both individual and cultural levels.

The question of ethics—authoritarian, humanistic, post-professional

[The counsellor] is personally responsible, and there is no substitute for his [*sic*] considered judgement. This irreducibility of personal responsibility is why the simplicity of an ethical code is likely to be a snare and a delusion. [Blackham, 1974: 8]

The foregoing consideration of safety and abuse leads quite naturally on to the centrally important issue of ethics, and in what follows I will attempt to deconstruct the conventional approach to ethics within profession-centred therapy. I have written elsewhere about what I call "participatory ethics" (in contradistinction to didactic ethics), and the form they might "healthily" take in a self-generating practitioner community (Heron, 1997; House, 1997b).

The conventional approach to ethics is well represented in a number of studies (Austin *et al.*, 1990; Bond, 1993; Owens, 1987; Palmer Barnes, 1998; Pope & Vasquez, 1991), and it is of course no coincidence that the literature on ethics has burgeoned as the professionalization process has gathered pace ... for just as any formal profession needs a "body of expert theoretical knowledge" in order to legitimize its existence (Mowbray, 1995), so too must it be an activity about which reasonably clear, coherent, and consensually accepted ethical precepts can be devised and encoded.

What, then, are the main characteristics of conventional ethical codes in therapy, in terms of both content and process formation? And—perhaps more important for current purposes—what are the (often tacit) assumptions that they entail? I have written about this elsewhere at some length (House, 1997b). Owens sums up the conventional, modernist view of ethics succinctly:

professional bodies should be ... in a position to control the actions of their members ... those in such positions *should be required* to subscribe to an explicit and public code of conduct. Therapists should be *subject to strict external control* of their activities. ... Simply appealing to the personal characteristics of the therapist is not enough. [Owens, 1987: 107, 112, my emphases]

The modernist assumptive epistemology of this statement (note, for example, its stringent control orientation), along with its essentially authoritarian tone, will surely strike chords with those who are familiar with the ethical codes of the psycho-institutions. (And no doubt it is not surprising that this statement emanates from a "radical behaviourist" standpoint, with behaviourism arguably being the very acme of modernity within the therapy field— Woolfolk & Richardson, 1984.)

What I am most concerned with and want to problematize here is the subjectivity-creating, attitude-formational influence of conventional "code-of-ethics-mindedness". For such an "institutional" mentality entails a whole host of crucial (and normally tacit) assumptions—for example:

- that practitioners can't be trusted to be, or are incapable of being, responsible for their own authentic ethical decision-making;
- that the therapeutic process is sufficiently programmatic and articulable that it is in principle possible to devise universal statements about what does and what does not constitute ethical practice, regardless of the living uniqueness of the context;
- that we should be preoccupied with things not going wrong in therapeutic work—a kind of "Thou-Shalt-Not ..." mentality ..., rather than working openly and congruently with whatever emerges in the work. [House, 1997b: 323]

Now the crucial point here is the effect upon the subjectivity and the belief system of practitioners (and by "osmosis", their clients) who uncritically embrace the modernist, hierarchical ideology implicit in this institutional, top-down approach to ethics. I submit that such practitioners will tend *unavoidably* to take modernist (often medical-model) assumptions into their "clinical" work with clients, and that their work cannot but then be significantly limited and circumscribed by that assumptive framework.

Without actually mentioning a postmodern epistemology by name, Tennyson & Strom, (1986) point to what is an embryonic postmodern approach to ethics in therapy:

Given the extraordinary complexity of practical problems encountered in counseling ..., it is not enough merely to use professional standards in making decisions. Two processes, critical reflection and dialogue, working together in continuing development of professional responsibleness, ... heighten ethical sensitivity and enhance moral judgment making. [p. 298]

There certainly do exist approaches to ethics within the therapy world that quite deliberately attempt to free themselves from the constraints of modernity and tacit authoritarian patriarchy. There is, first, a thriving feminist literature on ethics in therapy (e.g. Brown, 1989, 1994a,c, 1997; Gartrell, 1994; Lerman & Porter, 1990; Payton, 1994; Rave & Larsen, 1995), which has already very effectively deconstructed many of the prevailing conventional assumptions of institutional codes (which, in their terms, are often termed "hierarchical" and "patriarchal"—e.g. Brown, 1994c). Laura Brown has recently written, for example, that "Hierarchy is not only permissible in [dominant] ethical standards, it is valued and reified ... we must continue to search for *the hidden hand of dominance in each line that is written*" (1997: 60, 66, my emphasis). For Brown, ethical standards can and should be truly emancipatory, rather than merely setting out to protect clients from abuse or therapists from persecution (p. 61).

One interesting, highly relevant, and frequently discussed strand in the feminist ethics literature concerns what they term "overlapping relationships" (cf. my section on boundaries in Chapter 3). Far from being regarded as professional abominations that should be avoided at all costs (due as much to self-servingly protecting the sanctity of profession-centred therapy's regime of truth, as to altruistically "protecting the client"? ...), such overlapping relationships

are potentially beneficial to both parties by bringing another level of meaning to the therapeutic exchange. ... [The feminist therapist] and her client must arrive together at a solution that honours their uniquenesses, their connection, their social and political context, and the framework of the therapeutic relationship in which they have engaged. [Brown, 1994c: 210–211]

And most importantly, such relationships can subvert and transcend the ideology of hierarchy and the alienating dynamics of expertise (Brown's book is actually titled *Subversive Dialogues*, 1994c): "because they have struggled together, their discourse does subvert the patriarchal assumptions of a hierarchy of knowledge and value in which the therapist, as the only expert, imposes the [ethical] solution on the client" (p. 211). (Incidentally—and this is very important—Brown is most certainly not advocating that therapists actively seek out overlapping relationships—merely that they do not immediately run for the cover of their didactic ethical code whenever they encounter them.)

There is also a growing literature in the field of postmodern ethics (e.g. LaFountain, 1995; Hart, 1995), which constitutes an important starting-point for anyone seeking a viable and coherent post-professional approach to ethics in therapy (see Bates & House, in preparation). In his recent article "The postmodern counsellor", Lowenthal argues that ethical codes may well protect the professional rather than the client (notwithstanding the surface rhetoric about client protection): for "an ethical code is a contradiction in terms if this code comes first rather than the other for whom it is meant to be intended" (1996: 379). More generally, existing institutional codes can be problematized not only politically (as with the feminist critiques mentioned above), but epistemologically—and this is where the (to my mind) devastating postmodern critique of modernity becomes of central import (cf. Chapters 9 and 10). For LaFountain, postmodern thought "confronts us anew with the enigma, irony and vexation, indeed the very impossibility of figuring the unfigurable" (1995: 6). As I have written elsewhere, "It is a telling indictment of the field of therapy that the *epistemology* of ethics tends to receive so little coverage ..." (1997b: 322, original emphasis): as Holmes and Lindley have it, "Practitioners would on the whole rather think about technique than ethics" (quoted in *ibid.*).

The problem is, of course, that existing institutional codes are a quintessentially modernist endeavour, both in terms of their procedural formation and their assumptive content. Thus, for example, there is no grappling with the seeming imponderables of intersubjectivity (cf. Chapter 10); and there are more or less implicit assumptions about, for example, the "centred", knowing subject of modernity (in contrast to the decentred subjectivity of the postmodern "self"), the assumed conscious knowability (and even potential *controllability*) of the therapeutic process, and the "universalizability" of behavioural norms within the therapeutic encounter. These are all, of course, massive assumptions which have major determining effects upon therapy's ethical discourse, and the very way (in processual and content terms) in which practitioners (and clients) think about the ethics of the therapeutic experience.

I do not have the space here to even begin to articulate what a postmodern therapy ethics ("which is not one") might look like (see, for example, Tobin Hart's important work on the deconstructive force of the transpersonal—Hart, 1995—for a very useful beginning; and Bates & House, in preparation); but certainly, the approaches to ethics being embraced by the Feminist Therapy Institute in the USA and the Independent Practitioners Network in Britain (House, 1997b: 328–331; see also Chapter 12) are much closer to an authentically participative, local/"communitarian" (Heron, 1997), hierarchy-transcending epistemology than are the modernity-mimicking, implicitly patriarchal institutional codes that still tend to dominate the therapy field in Western culture world-wide.

I have referred elsewhere in this chapter to Hall's important work on the "victimhood archetype". It seems to me that the conventional approach to ethics and the policing of "the profession" is shot through with victimhood dynamics and the regressive culture of "blaming", which it should surely be a central task of a progressive and mature approach to therapy to transcend (Hall, 1993). Thus, as litigation-mindedness (a natural hand-maiden of institutional professionalization) increasingly takes hold, a fear- and defensiveness-inducing atmosphere of punitive sanction and potential litigation, shaming, and humiliation threatens to pervade the field—one which is surely quite antithetical to the values of openness and full engagement that underpin therapy at its best.

In the USA, for example, we read that "The list of 'thou-shalt-nots' grows exponentially over time; the list of 'thou shalts', meanwhile, is whittled away by the advice from lawyers that one should not imply a promise to do good by including aspirational statements in official ethical documents ... [for warnings from legal counsel are that] a statement of desired virtue will lay the group open to legal action" (Brown, 1994c: 205). And all the signs are that the UK seems to be headed in the same direction (see, for example, Palmer Barnes, 1998). The kind of participative ethics proffered by the FTI (USA) and the IPN (UK) certainly offers a viable and creative alternative to the reactionary and punitive "blame and punish" complaints procedures of the psycho-bureaucracies.

The Truth Commission in post-apartheid South Africa, while

not without its difficulties and contradictions, has provided a wonderful model of the way such a system can work in practice, promoting healing rather than revenge, blaming, and punishment. Totton (1997b) has outlined one approach to "complaint" which appeals to such values, eschewing and transcending the legalistic blame-and-shame procedures of institutional complaints procedures. And "wronged" clients are actually far more likely to obtain satisfaction from such a procedure than from a punitive procedure that merely serves to reinforce and confirm the client's "victimhood" status.

Not only is a litigious culture of "blame-and-shame" likely to promote what has been termed lowest-common denominator "defensive therapy" (Clarkson, 1995; House, 1997b; Mowbray, 1995), but there is the problem that attempting to legislate abuse away might simply have the effect of redistributing it to a less visible part of the work (cf. earlier, and House, 1997b), or, worse, even ossifying abuse within the institutionalized structure of therapy. Here is Fairbairn: "... [with] the tendency to construe the accountability of practitioners mainly in terms of the possibility of being blamed when things go wrong ..., practice is likely to become more conservative, with emphasis being placed on avoiding the possibility of accusations of lack of care than on enhancing client welfare" (1987: 264).

Certainly it cannot be uncritically assumed as some commentators do (e.g. Pokorny, 1998) that increased professionalization will necessarily reduce the incidence of abuse: Pope (1990), for example, suggests that level of training does not seem to reduce either its likelihood or incidence.

It should not be assumed that the kind of radical, feminist, postmodern, post-professional views on ethics adumbrated in this section to date are necessarily particularly new. As long ago as 1915, for example, we find E. B. Holt writing what could easily be a tailor-made epigraph for the present discussion: "In nearly all these philosophic discussions of ethics one has somehow the haunting sense of a wrongness of direction. Virtue is somehow imposed from above ... it has to descend very low indeed before it reaches us; and when there, it has lost the buoyancy wherewith to lift us up" (Holt, 1915: 149). On reading this I was reminded of both the deadening experience of ploughing through a "thou-shalt-not"-imbued institutional code of ethics, and the title of a feminist book on ethics in therapy, *Bringing Ethics Alive* (Gartrell, 1994).

Over 50 years ago we find Erich Fromm (1949) expressing some very interesting humanistic views on ethics, which again echo closely many of the foregoing arguments. Fromm makes a distinction between what he calls humanistic and authoritarian ethics. It is worth quoting Fromm at some length: for him, "In authoritarian ethics an authority states what is good for man [*sic*] and lays down the laws and norms of conduct; in humanistic ethics man himself is both the norm giver and the subject of the norms ..." (pp. 8–9). And later,

> The position taken by humanistic ethics that man is able to know what is good and act accordingly on the strength of his natural potentialities and of his reason would be untenable if the dogma of man's innate evilness were true (pp. 210–211). ... The aim of humanistic ethics is not the repression of man's evilness (which is fostered by the crippling effect of the authoritarian spirit) but the productive use of man's inherent primary potentialities (p. 229). Humanistic ethics takes the position that *if man is alive he knows what is allowed*. ... As long as anyone believes that his ideal and purpose is outside him ... he will look for solutions and answers at every point except the one where they can be found—within himself. [pp. 248–249, his emphasis]

Fromm also has pertinent things to say about the place of conscience in ethical conduct:

> Conscience is a more effective regulator of conduct than fear of external authorities; for while one can run away from the latter, one cannot escape from oneself ... (p. 144). ... the prescriptions of authoritarian conscience are not determined by one's own value judgment but exclusively by the fact that its commands and tabus are pronounced by authorities (pp. 144–145). The strength [of the authoritarian conscience] is rooted in the emotions of fear of, and admiration of, authority. [p. 146]

The humanistic conscience, by contrast,

> is our own voice, present in every human being and independent of external sanctions and rewards ... it is ... *knowledge within oneself*, knowledge of our respective success or failure in the art of living

(p. 158). .... I do not believe that ... the authoritarian conscience has
to exist as a precondition for the formation of humanistic conscience
... [p. 167; his emphasis]

Fromm would no doubt have agreed with Erikson (1964: 242)
that "Ethics cannot be fabricated. They can only emerge from an
informed and inspired search for an inclusive human identity". And
Fromm concludes with what could be read as a resounding
condemnation of the way we deny our own intrinsic power and
authority: "Since we do not trust in our own power, we have no
faith in man, no faith in ourselves or in what our own powers can
create. We have no conscience in the humanistic sense, since we do
not dare to trust our judgment" (p. 24). By contrast, "Every increase
in joy a culture can provide for will do more for the ethical
education of its members than all the warnings of punishment or
preachings of virtue could do" (p. 230).

I submit that the kind of institutional arrangements and
practices that typically accompany didactic professionalization are
quite stifling of, and antithetical to, the kind of flourishing "joy" to
which Fromm is referring here; whereas the creativity, joy, and
freshness that lie at the core of the Independent Practitioners
Network effectively create an atmosphere in which an organic,
"local" ethics is born from the living deliberations of each and every
practitioner group, taking full responsibility for thinking about and
devising the ethical framework in which they work. As Brown puts
it, "Ethical behavior is a process, not a static outcome" (1997: 65). (I
discuss the IPN in more detail in Chapter 12.) In House (1997b) I
refer to this approach as "participatory"—as Skolimowski (1994:
373, 382) puts it, "In the very idea of participation ... are contained
ethical signposts concerning how we should treat all other forms of
life. ... To participate is to be responsible. The larger the reach of our
participation the larger the scope of our responsibility."

I will close this section with several quotations from a different
occupational field—journalism—which capture very well the spirit
of my case for a post-professional approach to ethical conduct in the
therapy field. In a fascinatingly titled article, "Journalism: art, craft
or profession?", Kimball asks, "Can there be a science to something
so perversely unpredictable?" (1988: 137); and later he writes, "A
professional ethic can take form without formal machinery or an

elaborate code. Professionalization is a human process, a feeling that comes over a person when he [*sic*] behaves in concert with his own conscience" (*ibid*.: 145). Words could hardly be chosen that more accurately describe the principle underlying the approach to ethics found in the US Feminist Therapy Institute and the UK Independent Practitioners Network, described earlier (see also Chapter 12).

Conclusion

... far more subtle, and devastating, abuses are provoked when therapists are not sufficiently cautious and critical of the theories or models they espouse. [Spinelli, 1995: 158]

As we move away from the naïve certainties of modernity and into a postmodern era (Barratt, 1993), a central deconstructive task is surely to "develop and practice [*sic*] 'undisciplined theories' which constantly question the limits of the canon and expose the porous character of boundaries" (Genosko, 1998: dust jacket). In this and the previous chapter I have attempted to deconstruct a series of therapy's most hallowed and taken-for-granted theoretical and clinical assumptions, which, when unproblematized, in my view contribute to securing therapy's hegemonic "regime of truth" which I posited in Chapter 2.

There are of course a number of other key concepts which I have not had the space to interrogate: to take just a few of the more obvious examples—there is the question of "dependency". Critics of therapy commonly refer to the creation (whether deliberate or circumstantial) of dependency—to which most therapists retort that, variously, "regression to dependency" is necessary for change (e.g. van Sweden, 1995), and that such criticisms are rooted in a fear of dependency, which they perhaps equate with weakness (Kovel, 1976: 293) or helplessness. In other words, in order to reassert its ideological hegemony, the bearers of profession-centred therapeutic practice psychopathologize, from an alleged superior perception of "truth", people's criticisms of therapy's dependency culture. Only very rarely is it considered that the profession-centred regime's circumstantial creation of dependency might, in fact, be damaging, therapeutically superfluous, and unnecessary, and above all self-serving to the ideology of profession-centred therapy, and its need to justify and provide a confirming theoretical rationale for its own existence.

Another "regime of truth" shibboleth I could have unpacked is that of the ideology of therapist "expertise". Mair (1992) has already done an excellent job at so doing, and I refer the interested reader to that seminal source. A number of other prominent therapy practitioners have openly challenged the ideology of expertise—most notably David Smail, Ernesto Spinelli, and Nick Totton. What is clear is the way in which the ideology of professional expertise, carefully built up and mystified as it is by "the profession", is absolutely necessary to guarantee the unquestioned acceptance of profession-centred therapeutic practice as a legitimate form of healing assistance. It might also be that it serves to defend therapists from the uncomfortable reality that they do not know what they're doing (Spinelli, 1996)—in which circumstances a self-deluding expertise serves to render the practice of "profession-centred" therapy possible, bearable, and justifiable.

In Part II of the book, I now recount and comment upon some harrowing personal experiences of one-to-one therapy, in order to throw some experiential light upon the rather abstract discussions of the previous three chapters. My aim is to illustrate how profession-centred therapy's "regime of truth" severely affected the therapeutic experiences of several real-life clients who have had the courage to "go public" on those experiences.

PART II
"CONSUMER" EXPERIENCES OF PROFESSION-CENTRED THERAPEUTIC PRACTICE

Consider:

"I'm in a dreadful mess, as if you'd picked me up, smashed me on the floor and hadn't bothered to put me together again. It makes me wonder if you can have any conception of the emotional maelstrom stirred up by 'therapy'"

Alexander, 1995: 17

"There seems to me to be an element of double-bind in the conventions governing therapy. On the one hand, the overt aims are the creation of a more autonomous, critically perceptive person, confident enough … to throw off the shackles of blind conformity to others' expectations. On the other hand, most therapists expect unquestioning obedience to the laws [of the therapeutic frame]"

France, 1988: 52

"The potential for damage should always be borne in mind … Therapy can play havoc with one's equilibrium and sense of reality … a kind of game which can become a maddening experience, in both senses of the word … For me it felt, for a short time, as if I had gone permanently crazy … The internal chaos I was caught up in bore little identifiable or obvious resemblance to anything that had happened to me before … For the first time in my life I experienced panic attacks, constant nights of sleepless confusion and an eerie loss of self-confidence"

Sands, 2000: 5, 82, 135, 142, 143

CHAPTER FIVE

Experiences of profession-centred therapeutic practice:
I. Background issues

"Our field has tended to shy away from looking at negative outcome. It is seldom reported, perhaps due to fear that the institution or researcher will be stigmatized, perhaps due to embarrassment, perhaps due to a failure to look at individual cases. . . . Yet is not our reluctance to examine failures for fear of some perceived danger in itself neurotic?"

Mohr, 1995: 23–24

Introduction

The personal difficulties that led me to therapy were dwarfed into insignificance by what was happening within the therapy itself. . . . Therapy induced an obsession with self and therapist which precluded normal human intercourse. [Alexander, 1998a: 91]

Chapters 6–8, below, are centrally concerned with *listening carefully* to three former clients' detailed documentations of personal therapy experiences, from which analyses I attempt to illuminate the nature of the profession-centred therapeutic discourse through which therapy is predominantly offered in

Western culture. Chapters 2 through 4 offered an essentially abstract commentary on what I allege to be the machinations of profession-centred therapy; but what "clinical" evidence is there for the kinds of arguments I have presented to date? Difficulties immediately present themselves when posing such a question: for as Alexander writes, for those who have had therapy, the subject is "the ultimate taboo"—something "unmentionable" (1995: 75).

In this chapter I examine in depth the dearth of reported client experiences of therapy—the extent of the dearth, some plausible reasons for it, and its effects on the legitimacy of the cultural project of therapy. I then examine the thorny question of the efficacy of therapy, and the associated difficulty of saying anything either "objective" (set in quotation marks to denote the highly problematic ontological status of the term) or reliably subjective about the therapeutic experience, from either the client's or the therapist's standpoint.

The substantive personal testimonies in the literature are those of "Rosie Alexander" (1995), "Ann France" (1988), and "Anna Sands" (2000), detailed "readings" of which will form the basis of Chapters 6–8 respectively. The quotation marks, denoting pseudonymity as they do, are of course very telling; for they pay stark testimony to the power of the "privatizing", sometimes shame-inducing influence of profession-centred therapeutic ideology, and the way in which it surreptitiously militates against client openness in the "outside world". In the course of the analyses I will attempt to draw out the way in which these three authors' (often extremely harrowing) experiences of therapy are consistent with and significantly substantiate the arguments about the self-serving form taken by profession-centred therapy and its associated "regime of truth" which I developed in Chapters 2–4.

The studies of Alexander, France, and Sands are very complementary one to another: Alexander offers a raw, invariably gripping, and sometimes breathless autobiographical narrative (reminiscent at times of Sylvia Plath's autobiographical novel *The Bell Jar*), relatively unencumbered by (though by no means lacking in) theoretical deliberation; France's book is written from a more academic standpoint, with her highly perceptive personal experience being liberally interlaced throughout with a sophisticated understanding of the underlying theoretical rationale of therapy; and Sands' book possesses the strengths of both these qualities.

France's study is perhaps limited by being subject to the subjectivity-producing influence of therapy's "culturally legitimate" regime of truth (Parker, 1997a); while Alexander's book, while lacking the explicit theoretical sophistication of France's book, offers us a rawness of direct experience which is less (e)(a)ffected by therapy's regime of truth. In this sense, these two studies give us a wonderfully complementary insight into the experience of therapy from the client's perspective.

It is worth reiterating that my concern here is not with overt client abuse *qua* abuse, but with the arguably intrinsic iatrogenic "abusiveness" which is, I believe, substantially inscribed into the form taken by profession-centred therapeutic practice. It is worth noting at this point that in neither Chapter 3 nor 4 did I deconstruct the notion of "transference"—mainly because it is too easy a target and has been adequately challenged by others (e.g. Szasz, 1963; Spinelli, 1994; Handley, 1995), and also because the difficulties with the concept will be more than adequately considered in the remainder of this and the next chapter. (I pass over in this study—with some reluctance—its problematic ontological status—see, for example, Shlien's "counter-theory", 1984; and Spinelli, 1994, 1995.)

It is highly significant that in writing this book it was somewhat of a last minute decision to write Chapters 6–8; and the evidence which they therefore provide in effect serves as some kind of "independent" corroboration of my analysis, rather than being the data base from which I then developed it.

I hope that by the end of Chapter 6 it might be slightly easier to respond to Spinelli's highly pertinent and searching question, "... why did [Rosie Alexander] continue in therapy? ... why do these [therapeutic] encounters continue to maintain such a powerful hold upon her?" (Spinelli, 1995: 162).

The dearth of real client evidence

... the vast mass of literature on the subject presents the problem only from the point of view of the analyst (therapist, counsellor) ... there is rarely any attempt to complete our knowledge by telling us how the experience of therapy felt to the person undergoing it. [France, 1988: 2]

Several writers have referred to the notable lack of published client experiences of therapy (Alexander, 1995; France, 1988, Chapter 1; Howe, 1993: 5–6)—a situation which, as I argue below, the therapy field should be extremely concerned about, not least because of the commentary this notable omission is arguably offering on the very nature of profession-centred therapy, with its ideology of "privatized" individualism and the procedural trappings that go with it.

That the subject of one's own personal therapy seems to be such a taboo subject is, then, entirely consistent with the arguments developed in this book about the precious artificiality and fetishization inherent in profession-centred therapeutic practice. The number of studies devoted predominantly or exclusively to client experiences of therapy is meagre (see, for example, Alexander, 1995; Bates & Sands, 2002; Dinnage, 1988; Dreier, 1998; France, 1988; Howe, 1993; Kassan, 1999; Llewelyn, 1988; McLeod, 1990; Mayer & Timms, 1970; Oldfield, 1983; Sands, 2000; Strupp et al., 1969). Objectively, the paucity of detailed public statements about clients' therapeutic experiences is quite extraordinary, given the enormous amount of literature in the therapy field (for example, the published Karnac Books catalogue for 1998 contained well over 5000 entries— and this is only books in print)—and when, every year, possibly hundreds of thousands of individuals end up seeking therapy of one kind or another (Howe, 1993: 1).

That precisely one-half of the protagonists in the therapeutic dyad (or rather, far more than half, given that at any one time, total clients-in-therapy no doubt greatly outnumber total therapists) has contributed such a minuscule proportion to the literature on experiences of therapy is, perhaps, a telling testimony to the distorted one-sidedness and, arguably, relatively exclusive clubishness of this "profession which is not one"—and perhaps even to the "disabling" nature of a "profession" (Illich, 1977a) which does little or nothing to create an enabling facilitative space in which public statements about real client experience could more easily be shared. (The Ipnosis journal provides one notable and welcome exception.) Furthermore, when such statements do from time to time appear in the media, there is a tendency for them to be self-servingly "pathologized away" by the profession and its apologists (cf. Spinelli, 1995: 153–154, and my discussion of Folie à Deux's published reviews, below).

There do exist a number of analysts and therapists who have "gone public" about their "training" therapeutic experiences (e.g. Guntrip, 1975; Herman, 1985; Little, 1985, 1990; Masson, 1992a; Moser, 1977; Rudnytsky, 1991: Chap. 7)—but such reports cannot validly count as authentic, reliable client *qua* client commentaries precisely because of the schooling and "initiation" (or even brain-washing—Hinshelwood, 1997) into the ideology of profession-centred therapy that a personal "training" analysis or therapy typically represents (Masson, 1992a), and the inevitable biasing effect thus introduced. Here is Masson on his analytic training:

> As I look back on my training, I can see that much of it was an indoctrination process, a means of socializing me in a certain direction. ... The guild mattered more than anything else. If this process was successful, *it became impossible to question* any of the major ideas within the parent organization. [1992a: 210–211, my emphasis]

And for Frosh, a training analysis "ensures the perpetuation of the values and the words of the high priests of analytic doctrine. ... The demand for commitment made by psychoanalysis can drift near to exploitation" (Frosh, 1987; 226). Now I am not claiming that the whole therapy world fits such a description; but I do believe that the process described is not somehow confined to the rarefied world of psychoanalysis alone, but is a function of institutions and self-reproducing ideologies more generally (of which "therapy" and its discursive regime of truth is just one example).

Because of the very fact that there is something about the therapeutic experience which renders clients very reluctant to share their experiences of it with others (reasons for which I explore below), it could well be that there is a significant degree of harm (or, in the jargon, "iatrogenic effects") taking place in the therapy world that we not only never hear about, but which we in principle never could hear about precisely because the very form taken by profession-centred therapeutic practice, and the influence on clients of its pervasive, sometimes mesmerizing ideology, renders them unlikely even to talk about their experience—either with their therapist or their friends and acquaintances. In his recent extensive literature review of deterioration effects in psychotherapy, Mohr (1995) stresses that we still possess "a minimal understanding of the risk factors involved" in client deterioration (1995: 23). Moreover, there is by no means a consensus on whether psychotherapy actually causes client deterioration, or merely fails to forestall it (*ibid.*). Mohr concludes that "psychotherapy may not be the treatment of choice for some people ... We should not be so presumptuous as to assume [it] can help with every emotional problem" (*ibid.*). Certainly, the research literature on deterioration effects in therapy is by no means extensive (for exceptions see Buckley *et al.*, 1981; Crisp, 1966; Hadley & Strupp, 1976; Mays & Franks, 1985; Mohr, 1995; Sachs, 1983; Strupp *et al.*, 1977; Sutherland, 1987, 1992).

The question of why it is that ex-clients/patients seem so very reluctant to "go public" about their therapeutic experiences repays some attention—particularly as the discussion will throw further light on the (often unintended) effects of profession-centred therapeutic discourse and its accompanying ideology. My discussion of the ideology of confidentiality (Chapter 4) is, I think, relevant here. In a personal communication, Rosie Alexander (who has a strong personal interest in this field and has been active in discussing therapy experiences with ex-clients) has written that "One of the difficulties I've come across is that many people who have had bad experiences of therapy are still so emotionally bound up in the experience that they tend to focus all their energy on the individual therapist concerned"—rather than upon therapy *per se* as a form of help.

First, then, we have the question of how clients can be so emotionally bound up in (or *by*?) the therapeutic experience that it becomes extremely difficult if not impossible to challenge what is happening in anything approaching a clear, self-assured way. And when, in addition, we consider the pervasive dynamics of "expertise" that tend to dominate the helping relationship (e.g. Mair, 1992; Rose, 1997; Spinelli & Longman, 1998), the concomitant relatively "inexpert", unequal position that the therapy client typically experiences within profession-centred therapy, and the fact that any challenge that the client does manage to express is often met with a pathologizing response from the therapist, then it is clear that we have here what can indeed become a highly poisonous cocktail whose effect will typically be to forestall any challenge by the client to what is happening in their therapy, whether directly to the therapist or more publicly. And I must emphasize again that this typically occurs *without any conscious or deliberately conspiratorial intention on the part of therapists*: rather, it is an effect which lies latent within, and can even be a largely *inevitable* product of, the form typically taken by profession-centred therapy and its accompanying ideology and practices.

Referring to her own often harrowing experience of therapy (1995), Alexander goes on to write that

> the experience is a very difficult one to put into words. I felt as if I would need a whole new vocabulary to describe my emotional and psychological condition. ... I think many people would hesitate to expose these feelings and the associated behaviour to public view for fear of being considered totally mad. ... I've spoken with a number of ex-clients who have expressed overwhelming gratitude to me for expressing something they themselves had felt inexpressible. [Personal communication, 1999]

In this telling quotation we see all too clearly how the often ineffable nature of the experience also makes it extremely difficult for (ex-) clients even to speak *to themselves* about their experience—let alone coherently, and in a way that will be taken seriously by any (personal or institutional) listener.

Shame is also surely a very strong factor in the deafening silence around client experiences of therapy. For many clients feel (sometimes acute) shame at having or needing to seek therapy; and to reveal this fact to anyone can to many feel unbearably painful—in which case any suffering that is experienced will tend to be born in silence.

For current purposes, the relative dearth of direct client evidence actually makes it extremely difficult to achieve anything approaching "objective" or reliable research evidence on the efficacy or otherwise of therapy as a culturally pervasive healing practice.

Difficulties with "research" evidence on client experience

> A considerable amount of research has been done on the topic, without any hard and fast conclusions being reached, because *there can never be true control experiments*. [Ann France 1988: 239, my emphasis]

The research evidence which does exist has been argued to be quite fundamentally flawed, given its typically aggregative, "ecological" nature (Epstein, 1995)—which fact might well in turn hide a significant amount of iatrogenic or deleterious effects of therapy, which such aggregative research and its associated "averaging effects" can by definition never pick up. And as argued above, this problem is reinforced by the fact that due to the highly peculiar nature of therapy and the forces (transference, dependency, infantilization, shame ...) routinely triggered within a profession-centred therapeutic experience, by far the majority of therapy's casualties very possibly remain silent—perhaps tacitly encouraged into a state of "self-blame" ("it's my fault my therapy has failed") by the pathologizing ideology that surreptitiously circulates within cultural therapeutic discourse. (If you felt yourself to be an "expert" on human emotional difficulty or distress, you'd be far less likely to seek help from one; and it is very difficult to challenge a culturally sanctioned "expert" from a position of relative, experienced "inexpertise"—as many a non-mechanically-minded car owner would no doubt testify!)

There are many further difficulties with research evidence in the therapy field. First, there is the obvious problem of "transference" (discussed in depth in this and the following chapters), both positive and negative, and its distorting, even disabling effects upon human perception and experience. Furthermore, quite apart from the fact that the subjective evidence from introspective experience is a far from reliable means of eliciting reliable evidence about human experience (cf. Dixon, 1981; Nisbett & Ross, 1980; Taylor & Brown, 1988), there exists the fundamental and unresolvable methodological problem that *the very act* of asking clients about their experiences of therapy inevitably contaminates the data provided, quite possibly distorting unacceptably the results obtained through such a process. (And worse still, there is also no methodological means of objectively ascertaining the extent of any such distortion!) All such research can ever give us, then, is information on what clients report when asked about their therapeutic experience, rather than about the therapy experience itself.

In any attempt at measurement, the first question must surely be to specify what one is trying to measure; and in therapy efficacy research it is by no means clear about either what one should be attempting to measure, and whether one actually is then measuring what one thinks one is trying to measure! (and these difficulties are in addition to the problem, just mentioned, that the very act of measurement changes what would have obtained without measurement having been done—whether so-called "double-blind" procedures are operating or not: cf. Heron, 1996: 191, 198–200).

It will be recalled that in the "Coda" to Chapter 3 I discussed what I call the "material generation" that occurs as a direct by-product of the form taken by profession-centred therapeutic practice. This phenomenon introduces yet another profound complication for any attempt to measure the efficacy of therapy— one which tends to be ignored in the research literature. Now in any attempt at so-called "objective" outcome research there is the insurmountable difficulty that it is impossible objectively to separate out the difficulties *within* therapy which the client brought to begin with, on the one hand, and the difficulties *of* therapy which arise from the material-generation phenomenon I described in Chapter 3, on the other. If this analysis is anything like right, then the compelling conclusion is that *we have little choice but to turn to the subjective reports of clients* for our research evidence on efficacy. Unfortunately, as we will see there are also profound difficulties with this kind of "evidence". (It is worth noting in passing that the difficulty of analytically separating out profession-centred therapy's generation effects from other factors operating in therapy has the convenient effect of insulating and protecting profession-centred therapeutic practice from critical gaze—though Alexander, France, and Sands *do* do an excellent job in this regard, as we will see below.)

In the therapy literature there is, of course, a great deal of reported evidence of clients' positive subjective experiences of therapy; and if such evidence were to be taken at face value, then it might be thought decisively to undermine the arguments in this book. Unfortunately for therapy's advocates, such evidence is extremely problematic, and most certainly cannot be used to support the beneficence of therapy *qua* therapy as a healing practice. (Of course, that this evidence does not and cannot in principle prove therapy's beneficence does not prove that therapy *is* not broadly beneficent.) Thus, Ann France makes the telling point that "consumers" of therapy have a powerful vested interest in making it into a positive experience (cf. Bohart & Tallman's "active client", 1996), whether in a tangibly authentic or a self-deluding way: "one does not want to have spent all that time and money for nothing" (France, 1988: 27). There may well also be some kind of "conditioning" or "schooling" process brought into the ideological discourse of therapy—an almost "born again", quasi-religious, even mesmerizing process which could have comparatively little to do with the specific content of therapy ... rather like Tubby Passmore in David Lodge's fictional book *Therapy*, with the ideological discourse of therapy's regime of truth surreptitiously blending into every aspect of life (cf. Parker, 1997a).

I will quote just one example of an ex-client, evangelizing about her therapy in a way which shows signs of having been "schooled" into therapy's subjectivity-creating discourse. I am quoting from the chapter by "Carmel" from Dinnage's book *One to One* (1988: 41–50)—with apologies to "Carmel" for artificially breaking up her seamless narrative. (I have italicized points at which such "subjectivity-generation" might be visible.)

> The pain *all came from inside* ... immediately, within a week *I developed transference* and all those things I didn't know about. ... I wasn't even aware that I was depressed. ... If there had been no analysis, it would have been a mess. A mess. Knowing myself now, I would have *acted out*. ... Of course *I had resistances*, of course I fought against analysis. ... My first commitment in life, my analysis. Yes, more than my marriage or my children—absolutely! ... I think that some people have a breakdown when they don't feel there is anyone around who can actually *contain* them. ... But, as *I was regressing* ..., I was like a little girl. ... But the analyst *contained* whatever I put out ... Finding them, your fantasies, your *inner world* of needs. ... [My parents] *impinged* ..., they oppressed ... the more you start *owning things*, the more the emptiness and *the sense of self fills up*. ... Someone is *containing* whatever you are bringing. Then *the transference, through which we see our needs and fantasies, our ambivalence, our confusions* ..., *our emotional, internal, mental world*. ... I did get angry with my analyst *in the transference*. ... *I internalized him*. ... Both of us decided that I could leave in six months [!!—RH]. ... I thought I needed him, like a crutch, but then to discover that *he is there inside me*. ... Self-destructiveness ... was a total denial of *my true self*. ... And *I was terribly greedy* ... really it's an expression of *deprivation*, a sense of emptiness, a sense of *envy*, and once you deal with it you can *contain your envy and destructiveness*. ... I know when

I was entertaining him. . . . *It was projection*, but it was almost real. . . .
I do love my analyst as a person. . . . He gave birth to me. [pp. 41–50
passim, my emphases]

Of course, and as Parker (1997a) points out, these subjectivity-
creating therapeutic notions are circulating within culture more
generally as well as within therapy itself (cf. Rose, 1996, 1997); but
my point here is that such "data" are clearly very problematic if
used to specify the efficacy of therapy *qua* therapy as a form of
healing practice.

More generally, and in addition to the foregoing difficulties,
there is a whole range of problems with "subjective" efficacy
evidence. First, it typically ignores the "natural history" aspect of
emotional/psychological difficulties, and the very real possibility
that in many cases the client might have "got better" with *or without*
a therapeutic intervention. Of course a client might well make the
assumption that it was the therapy *per se* that helped them; but not
only is this by no means necessarily the case, but there is no way to
discover objectively whether or not this was the case through
subjective introspection. Another way of expressing this difficulty is
that we can never know what would have happened to a given
person had they not "had therapy" (cf. France, 1988, discussed
under "Efficacy" in Chapter 7).

A further problem is that perhaps many clients who "find
therapy" do so precisely because they are ready to make a personal
shift or change, which would have happened anyway, either
naturally, or through some other culturally legitimate form of help
that was available (cf. Frank, 1973; and my Chapter 9 on Groddeck);
and to the extent that this is so, then it is clearly the client's capacity
to use *whatever* help is available to them that is decisive, rather than
the nature of the help *per se* (cf. Bohart & Tallman, 1996; Frank &
Frank, 1991).

Next, returning to the potentially "distorting" effects of
"positive transference" on subjective client experience and the
evaluation of therapy, it would be truly extraordinary if the vast
majority of people who had experienced a therapeutic "helper",
attentively, "unconditionally", and exclusively listening and trying
to understand them within the artificial milieu of a therapeutic
relationship, were *not* to find this to be a positive experience

(cf. Spinelli, 1995: 163)—from which position it would then be entirely natural and understandable to attribute such a positive experience occurring *within* therapy, *to* "therapy" itself. It should be clear that the two (i.e. an experience had *within* a therapeutic milieu, and therapy *per se*) can very easily be conflated in subjective experience—with potentially highly distorting effects in any efficacy research that relies upon such "evidence".

Even more complicating for the would-be researcher is that one can also not assume that a client's subjectively *negative* experience of therapy necessarily means that therapy was not a therapeutic, facilitative, or enabling experience for her or him. Thus, perhaps clients sometimes need, and unconsciously draw to themselves, "negative" experiences because that is their "journey", their growing point. (A world-view which embraced, for example, notions of Karma and destiny would certainly be consistent with such a view—e.g. Hillman, 1996.) Indeed, perhaps human relationship (therapeutic or otherwise), and experience and existence in general, are in principle beyond the ambit of rational or theoretical human understanding (cf. my Chapter 9 on Groddeck)—in which case, again, the whole theoretical project of therapy is surely called into considerable question.

I have no wish to replace one "regime of truth" with another in this discussion; rather, I merely make the crucial point that the specification and reliable measurement of efficacy in the therapy field is fraught with epistemological and methodological difficulties—and to such an extent that there is, at the very least, severe doubt as to whether we can say anything "scientifically" meaningful or accurate about it. One could hardly do better than end this section with a quotation from a "recovering" ex-client (quoted in Alexander, 1995):

> Well, I did feel slightly depressed after nine years with George [her therapist], and I did feel slightly less dependent at the end of the twenty years [!!—RH], but who's to say that I wouldn't have experienced the same differences without therapy? ... *I've no idea how things would have been otherwise*. I might have got married, had children, had a proper career. ... As regards the efficacy of therapy in general, I suppose I have to remain agnostic, but all I can say is that it's no way to spend a life. [p. 146, my emphasis]

In my view this insightful statement speaks more eloquently to therapy's efficacy than any number of "empirical" research studies, with their insurmountable methodological difficulties, ever could.

With these very many formidable provisos firmly in mind I will closely examine the limited available evidence on client experiences in so far as they touch on the issues raised in this book. Apart from the studies referred to directly in the next three chapters I know of only one other major study of clients' reported experience of therapy—Dominique Frischer's *Les Analyses Parlent*, of which (as I write) there does not seem to be an English translation.[1] There are also a number of studies which give autobiographical accounts of an analytic experience—see, for example, Guntrip, 1975; Masson, 1992a; Sutherland, 1987; and France's Introduction to *Consuming Psychotherapy*, 1988: 9–10.

The books by Alexander (1995), Dinnage (1988), France (1988), and Sands (2000) in particular provide a welcome antidote to the highly unbalanced, predominantly therapist-centred literature that exists on experiences of therapy. (France quotes Murray Cox thus: "Books on psychotherapy tend to describe patients as ... experimental objects, to be 'worked on' and studied"—p. 3.) In the course of the following "readings", I will also include some personal evidence from my own subjective experience of being a client-in-therapy.

Note

1. At proofs stage I came across another client "memoir" by Emily Fox Gordon, entitled *Mockingbird Years: A Life In and Out of Therapy* (Basic Books, New York, 2000), quoted in Spinelli, 2001, pp. 161–172.

CHAPTER SIX

Rosie Alexander's *Folie à Deux*

"Some years ago I started taking drugs. ... I imbibed them, unwittingly at first, through some kind of emotional osmosis in the course of therapeutic encounters ... these drugs (administered by a process known as transference) turned out to be intoxicating, addictive, hallucinogenic and destructive. My dealers were respectable, middle-class professionals who meant me no harm"

Alexander, 1995: 1

So begins Alexander's dramatic and disturbing narrative of her therapeutic experiences. In what follows I will draw extensively on Alexander's text to elaborate upon the arguments about therapy's regime of truth developed in Chapters 2–4. I hope Alexander will forgive me for subjecting her relatively seamless narrative to what is a somewhat systematizing analysis.

In brief, Alexander's book offers us an experiential journey through three therapeutic relationships, with "Marion", "Dr Weissmann", and "Luc"—the relationship with Luc taking up by far the majority of the book (pp. 19–123). On the dust jacket we read that the book "recounts harrowing details of a therapy which brought [Alexander] to total despair and to the very edge of her being. It bears witness to the terrible suffering which can be engendered when things go wrong in therapy".

Informed consent?

> But you're so caught up in this emotional state that your reason is suspended at the moment. [*Folie*, p. 91]

In Chapter 2, I discussed, in relation to Hinshelwood's (1997) work, the extent to which clients entering therapy are in a position to make an informed and rational choice about whether therapy is the appropriate form of help for them. This issue emerges at several points in Alexander's study. With her therapist Luc, Alexander reports how she "had no idea" she had become so dependent on him (p. 23—she was seeing him every other day), which is a theme echoed by Ann France—namely, that deep processes can be triggered within a therapeutic milieu, the full reality of which only becomes apparent some time later, long after the client has been drawn into the infantilizing, even addictive thrall that a profession-centred therapeutic experience can inculcate. Just how a client can be expected to exercise informed consent to "treatment" in such circumstances is again very difficult to comprehend (cf. Chapter 2).

In her Epilogue, Alexander quotes one of the therapy "survivors" from the self-help group of which she was herself a member:

> What's so amazing is that I found myself having therapy *without realising what was going on*. ... We just used to have these sessions, about the family situation. And *before I knew it* I was addicted. I was in a fully-fledged state of transference. ... I became totally dependent very quickly and I was in such pain all the time ... But I couldn't leave him any more than a child could leave its mother. I had to keep on going back to get these pains healed, but they never did get healed. It just seemed to get worse and worse. [*Folie*, p. 147, my emphases]

Again, it seems highly plausible that the processes triggered within profession-centred therapy led to a kind of emotional entrapment which occurred before the client was in a position to make any balanced, rational judgement about the kind of help she was receiving. I would tend to call this an "abuse of the transference" that can arguably be *intrinsic to* the form taken by profession-centred therapy, and need by no means be deliberately intended by the therapist. Sometimes the abuse is more overt, as in psycho-analysis, which erects a self-justifying theoretical rationale that clinically legitimizes the invoking of a "transference neurosis" in the "patient"; and sometimes it is covert, when it occurs irrespective of the particular orientation of the therapist. As I argued in Chapter 2, this raises very profound ethical questions about the very project of profession-centred therapy itself—questions which, strangely, don't seem to figure with any degree of prominence in the otherwise exhaustive codes of ethics of the therapy world's professional institutions (cf. Chapter 4).

I will end this section with an important statement which I found on the relatively new Internet web site, "Emotional and verbal abuse in psychotherapy and psychoanalysis" (web site address quoted in the References in Alexander, 1999; my thanks to Rosie Alexander for drawing this important source to my attention):

> If I had been told at the start of the therapy that there was a strong probability that I would form an emotional bond with the therapist that would take away much of my enjoyment and efficiency, and I had been able to appreciate what this meant, I do not think I would have consented to this kind of therapy. . . . [My therapist] could have told me before the start of therapy what might happen but he did not. . . . *The principle of informed consent does not seem to be carried across [from medicine] to psychotherapy* . . .
>
> It may be impossible for anyone who has not experienced transference to fully believe in it or appreciate it. *If this is the case, then it means that informed consent can never be obtained in psychotherapy.* [Natalie Simpson, "Emotional and verbal abuse . . ." web site, 1999, my emphases]

These are sobering words indeed for anyone in the therapy field with a concern for the ethics of their practice—which, I am sure, is virtually all practitioners.

Transference

> When you are transported into the other world of transference there
> are no *real* people. On good days the rest of your life—family,
> friends, work, domestic and other concerns—is on the back-burner.
> On bad days it simply doesn't exist. [*Folie*, p. 142, original emphasis]

One of the most significant features to emerge from *Folie* is how
extremely powerful transference dynamics can be triggered almost
immediately in the work, and don't necessarily need any length of
time gradually to build up. I have occasionally experienced this
with clients in my own work—even in very short-term GP
counselling settings in the NHS. It would be far too simplistic, of
course, to "blame" the machinations of profession-centred therapy
alone for this phenomenon—for people have similar experiences in
non-therapeutic situations (for example, the experience of "falling in
love at first sight"); but I would argue that the typical *form* and
accompanying ideological assumptions of profession-centred therapeutic practice, as outlined in this book, do make such a response
more likely, especially, perhaps, in the analytically inclined
therapies.

Alexander describes her first therapeutic encounter, with
Marion, thus:

> A very dynamic, and for me highly-charged, relationship was
> quickly established. Strong transferential bonds had already been
> formed ... Within a matter of weeks I had been sucked into an
> emotional whirlpool with Marion—an experience which was all the
> more bewildering as, given my initial impression of her and my
> subsequent objective perceptions, it was a singularly unlikely thing
> to occur. ... I was by now welded to her by a visceral bond which I
> couldn't understand or identify and which had no parallel in my
> conscious experience. She became the emotional centre of gravity of
> my life. All my emotional energy was poured into my relationship
> with her. [*Folie*, pp. 4–5 *passim*]

Alexander's Prologue (quoted in the epigraph, above) refers to a
parallel with drug addiction, which crops up at several points; and
France (1988) draws a similar analogy between addiction and
therapy (see Chapter 7). Alexander writes (talking to Dr Weissmann),
"I think you're an arsehole, but I need you, I'm addicted to you, I

can't do without you" (p. 12). This passage is also illustrative of the impossible double-binds (discussed below) that can be precipitated within a profession-centred therapy milieu, and which Ann France also refers to extensively (see Chapter 7).

Alexander describes with great clarity the kind of subjective experiences she was having in the course of the therapy. Thus, in terms of what, in the jargon of therapy, we would call idealization and fantasy, she writes:

[Luc] was sex incarnate. His physical presence dazzled me. I would look at him sitting opposite me, unable to believe that such masculine perfection could exist. ... I was living increasingly in a world of sexual fantasy, but fantasies of such clarity and intensity that the word "fantasy" no longer seemed appropriate. ... This whole business with Luc was largely based on fantasy; illusions which I wove around his character, rejecting those things which didn't correspond to the person I wanted him to be and magnifying those which did. [*Folie*, pp. 32, 37, 63]

There are also signs in *Folie* of pre- and peri-natal dynamics possibly having been triggered (even though of course Alexander was not working with Primal Integration therapists—cf. Brown & Mowbray, 1994). She writes,

I had been in the process of travelling back in time, going back into the womb. I was already there, and then I was brutally expelled, no longer able to regress in this manner, but now rendered so vulnerable, so dependent on the environment of the "uterus", that I could no longer exist outside it. ... It was as if I was an embryo. I had been aborted and the bed was my incubator. [*Folie*, pp. 51, 92]

It was Otto Rank in his much neglected *Trauma of Birth* who argued that the process of analysis replicates the client's own actual birth process (see also the work of David Wasdell—e.g. 1990). In her Epilogue, Alexander indeed refers to this possibility herself, as a peri-natal perspective would account for much of what occurred in her therapies:

the feeling of being welded to Luc, bound together in a state of ecstatic communion with him, unable to have a separate existence. The feeling of being in another universe with him, a universe occupied by him and me alone. The need to seek out enclosed,

cocoon-like places. The fantasy that my bed was an incubator. The
fantasy of being cut away from a Siamese twin. . . . [*Folie*, pp. 149–150]

Again, these may well be deep processes triggered within the
profession-centred therapy milieu which neither therapist nor client
were remotely in a position to understand, handle, or respond to
facilitatively. And I am not just arguing here that these particular
therapists weren't sufficiently competent to handle what was
happening, but that the profession-centred therapy milieu *itself* can
trigger "material" that no therapist, no matter what her orientation or
competence, would know how to respond to in a facilitative,
enabling way. Alexander sensed something similar herself:

I felt very insecure with all these psychotherapists. They didn't
seem to have much idea of what they were doing. I had the
impression that in the "psy" domain, knowledge was about as far
advanced as medicine at the time of Hippocrates: a minimum of
facts, a number of wild theories, and a great deal of groping around
in the dark, doing far more harm than good. [*Folie*, p. 98]

It comes across very powerfully how much Alexander wanted to
re-enter the real world:

"All I want is to get back into the real universe", I burst out
desperately. "You took me into another universe and abandoned
me there [this sounds like an accurate perception of Luc's—and
possibly anyone's—inability to respond to what was being
triggered within the profession-centred therapy milieu—RH]. It's
like a parallel universe . . . there's no means of communication
between one and the other [a Langsian 'derivative'?—RH]. And
there's no way for me to get back. . . ." [*Folie*, pp. 81–82]

There are even times when Alexander seemed very conscious of
the process that was happening to her, and yet was *still* quite unable
to do anything about it:

I now seemed to be getting very heavily involved in some kind of
infantile thing . . . but I couldn't see what good could come of
experiencing it. . . . But whenever I considered how I might bring
things to a conclusion my mind refused to countenance the idea. My
life was wholly impregnated with Luc and an independent
existence was no longer possible. [*Folie*, p. 116]

I have referred elsewhere to the abuse of the transference, and on the Internet web site referred to above, Liz Green (1999) makes the following observation:

> What frightens me is when a therapist says to a client (without the client raising the issue) that they need to come twice or more each week. Thus is abuse I believe. ... I am aware of therapists who simply advise their clients that they still need to come because they have X, Y and Z to deal with, but really it is because the therapist is so dependent on the client for their income. ... We are all insecure and frightened, and therapists can prey on this with their "greater knowledge".

And here is "Natalie Simpson" again (web site, *op. cit*.): "Typically therapists will tell patients that the intensity of the transference is a sign of resistance, which means the therapy is close to finding the truth, and therefore the last thing the patient should do is leave".

On the same web site we read Margo Phillips (1998) writing that "I am at a loss to know how to not get automatically tangled in the transference. As aware and well oriented as I am, I wonder how less aware, former abuse clients can not have a problem with this also. ..."

I close this section with another quotation from Natalie Simpson, from the web site referred to earlier:

> Before I ever thought about entering therapy I would not have believed that something similar might happen to me. If my therapist had told me about transference before I started therapy, I would have told him not to worry ..., that I was far too independent to become trapped by him or the therapy. It seems that transference can only be fully appreciated by those who have experienced it. ... [Natalie Simpson, "Emotional and verbal abuse ..." web site, 1999]

The peculiar "personal–professional" relationship

> it was a relationship riddled with cancer. ... He'd done wrong, both professionally and at a personal level. In a way it was under-standable, the kind of thing that happens all the time in non-therapy situations. [*Folie*, p. 30]

I have referred elsewhere to the highly peculiar, and deeply contradictory, nature of a therapeutic relationship which is somehow expected to be both profoundly intimate (often triggering deep wishes, fantasies, and even erotic desires) and yet professional and scrupulously "abstinent" (to use Freud's term) at the same time—which the profession-centred therapy discourse quite deliberately sets up. At times the inevitable tension of this peculiar relationship comes to the surface in Alexander's account. Thus she recounts saying to Luc: "It's completely unrealistic for a therapist to expect his patients to have transferential feelings about him, often extremely powerful ones, and at the same time to make a complete distinction between the professional person sitting opposite them in the consulting room and the person who has a personal life ..." (*Folie*, p. 57). Interestingly, Luc "made no reply to this, instead changing tack" (*ibid.*).

Elsewhere Alexander refers to

> the strangeness of the situation, most of all ... its terrible disparity which rendered it grotesquely absurd. We were conducting a professional relationship in a position of physical familiarity. We were talking about the crux of my being ... almost the acme of intimacy. To him I was just a client between the one before and the one after ... [*Folie*, p. 79]

And Alexander captures well (talking to Luc) what is perhaps the impossible complexity of the "personal–professional" position within therapeutic relationship:

> It's unhealthy the way you carry on, with all these games of hide and seek. Why make such a big secret about what's just a perfectly normal domestic life. You tie yourself in knots trying to hide all trace of that person. Of course if something is hidden people want to know what it's all about. It's enough to drive people insane even if they're not crazy already. [*Folie*, p. 87]

At one point Dr Paget is revealingly quoted as saying to her, "There's too much confusion between the professional person and the private individual. You don't know what you're dealing with" (p. 83).

Now there seem to me to be two main responses to this situation: the conventional response of "the profession", which amounts to a fear-driven tightening of the professional boundaries (see Chapter 2), ever more "comprehensive" codes of ethics (see Chapter 4), and the like—which response can only serve to compound and *reinforce* that to which it is attempting to respond; or else look for a viable *post-professional* way of being in therapy work (see my Part III) which obviates the need for an obsessive (and self-defeating) professionalization. I return to this crucial question in Chapter 12, where I offer suggestions as to what a viable post-professional, deconstructive therapy might look like.

Dependency, pathologizing, and infantilization

> So often with therapists the patient has the impression that his opinions and reactions are only valid as indicators of his state of mind or symptoms of his neurosis. [*Folie*, p. 58]

The related issue of dependency recurs throughout *Folie*. At one point Alexander tells us that "I wanted to be a baby, [Luc's] baby" (p. 85); and "often I felt like a tetraplegic, utterly helpless, and *totally dependent* but with no one to be dependent on—a state which induced panic. My 'self' seemed to be continually hovering on the brink of disintegration; a slight nudge and it would shatter into myriad pieces" (*Folie*, p. 86, my emphasis).

There is one classic example in *Folie* of the pathologizing profession-centred therapy regime that is, in my view, all too common in the therapy world. Thus, a neuropsychiatrist "Dr Paget", who was consulted for help for her difficulties with Luc and possible medication, is quoted as saying to Alexander, "You obviously have a problem of excessive dependence and it's been highlighted by this incident with Dr Landau [Luc]" (p. 51). Note the assumptions that, first, the "problem" is one that the client has, rather than it being either an artefact of profession-centred therapeutic practice, or some interaction between the therapy milieu and the client; and second, that Luc has made no active contribution to the problem. The first assumption is, of course, a crucial and necessary one that must hold if the legitimacy of profession-centred therapy's regime of truth is to be preserved from critical scrutiny—a protection which most all professional therapists clearly have a major vested interest in asserting.

At one point Alexander recounts how she brought up the dependency issue herself:

> The way I feel, total dependence on a therapist, it's a well-known syndrome. How is it that therapists can encourage this state of affairs to come about without having any means of clearing up the mess when things go wrong ...? Why isn't there any advice that can be given to the patient in these circumstances? [*Folie*, pp. 97–98]

And on being advised to stop the therapy, Alexander again illustrates the double bind she was in—"What about ... when you just can't stop because you know that you'll die if you do?" (p. 98).

Despite clear and repeated signs that the therapists were not equipped to handle what was happening in Alexander's therapy, the "one-track" analytical infantilization continued apace: "I felt let down. It was as if my attempt to behave like an adult and take the whole business seriously had been ignored" (p. 111).

Iatrogenic effects of therapy

> The experience laid waste my life. ... Had I been in a relationship it would have been totally destroyed. [Alexander, 1998a: 91]

> I had to keep on going back to get these pains healed, but they never did get healed. It just seemed to get worse and worse. [ex-client quoted in Alexander, 1995: 147]

I have already described at some length the incapacitating effects of the transference dynamics triggered in (or by?) the work. At a number of points in Alexander's narrative there are additional signs of deleterious effects which, at the very least circumstantially, seem attributable to her therapy itself. To take a few examples: there are many unambiguous signs that her personal, extra-therapeutic life was profoundly affected—and for the worse—during her therapy. Thus,

> ... Gilles, my lover, ... found that he could no longer kindle any spark of sexual desire in me. ... All I knew was that these strange and indistinct feelings triggered off by the therapist precluded sexual attraction to any other man. [*Folie*, p. 13];

> I would only go to films which I thought he would be unlikely to be interested in and in areas I didn't expect him to frequent. ... All my mental and emotional energies were monopolised by the relationship.

[This is just one illustration of how terrified she was of setting foot out of the door for fear of bumping into her therapist Luc somewhere—RH.] [*Folie*, p. 36];

My activities in the real world had almost come to a halt. I was so perturbed by the experiences I was going through that it was virtually impossible for me to communicate socially. I reduced personal contact to a minimum. [*Folie*, p. 55];

"What about your social life?", I asked. "I didn't have one. I'd no money, of course, to do anything. ... And anyway all my mental energy was absorbed by the therapy. My whole life revolved around the sessions. My whole being was devoted to the relationship with George." [A therapy "survivor", quoted in *Folie*, p. 144];

And of course, it had a terribly damaging effect on my social life. I couldn't ever make any plans to do anything, for example, because I never knew how I would be feeling. I just couldn't function socially. [A therapy "survivor", quoted in *Folie*, p. 147]

When Alexander tried to challenge Luc about what was happening to her, she received the predictable professionally defensive response which illustrates a self-serving inability—or unwillingness —to even consider that the problem might lie within the conventions of profession-centred therapy itself rather than with the client's "psychopathology":

[RA]: "Two years ago, before I started seeing you, I didn't have any need to go into a clinic. It's because of you that I'm in this terrible mess". [Luc]: "That's not quite true. You had problems then which were difficult to live with, but it's only now that you're beginning to realise the extent of their emotional impact on you." [*Folie*, p. 95]

And of course, the professional's typical response to this would be, "You obviously need more therapy"! ...

Signs of "material generation" within the regime of profession-centred therapy

"You give me a great deal of power", he said once, when I spoke of these things. But it wasn't him who held the power. *It was the situation*. [*Folie*, p. 86, my emphasis]

"Resistance!" The word was shouted out triumphantly, the battle cry of the therapist. [*Folie*, p. 102]

"Therapy. You need therapy to find out why you are so dependent on [your therapist]". [*Folie*, p. 136]

Quite apart from the examples of material generation given above in the "Transference" section, Alexander's text is littered with further examples. As already quoted, she refers to "the emotional maelstrom stirred up by 'therapy'" (p. 17); to feeling "insane with grief, but I didn't know what the grief was about" (p. 75); and later, "The feeling of grief had no identifiable object, and I therefore had nothing to mourn" (p. 131).

Therapists often take great pains to ensure that their clients never see one another—the manifest rationale being to preserve confidentiality. I submit that another, far less conscious motivation might be *the preservation of the preciousness of profession-centred therapy's regime of truth*—with all the accompanying effects on the client's experience (cf. Chapter 4). This comes out clearly in the text, when Alexander writes, for example, that: "He showed out the previous client. It was strange to think of him in that room with someone else. So far it had been as if I was the only one ..." (*Folie*, p. 21). This suggests that the intensely privatized world of one-to-one therapy—the sometimes stark regime of profession-centred therapeutic practice—*actively sets up* such feelings of exclusive specialness, which in turn cannot but tend to generate all manner of so-called "regressive material".

I have already referred to the question of the therapist's private life, and the inevitable tensions that the personal–professional identity creates. Alexander's account (e.g. p. 34 *et seq.*) shows how a client can become "obsessed" (the quotation marks indicate that I am not using the term clinically) with the therapist's personal life. Rather than such a response being a symptom of the client's so-called "psychopathology" which needs to be worked with in therapy, however, perhaps it is at least as much *a quite natural and understandable response to the peculiarity of the profession-centred therapeutic relationship*. In my own practice I have in recent years started openly to discuss the peculiarity of the milieu in which therapy occurs, and the possible effects it has on their experience (and, if appropriate, on mine too)—thereby (I hope) actively demystifying and defetishizing the experience as far as possible in an empowering way, rather than pathologizing their discomfort and making it into just more grist for the therapeutic mill to chew over (and collect the fees for).

At times in *Folie* there emerges a clear sense of the entanglements that can routinely be triggered within (or *by*?) the regime of profession-centred therapy: "As so often before when talking with Luc, I had the impression that our conversations only complicated matters. Even the simplest things took on a complexity which was impossible to unravel" (*Folie*, p. 91). And a bit later, "As so often we seemed to be communicating in riddles and talking at cross-purposes" (p. 94)—perhaps because the therapist was endeavouring to impose his "regime of truth" on the client.

At one point Alexander does even consider whether she might be a "victim" of the subjectivity-generating effects of therapeutic discourse circulating in culture (Parker, 1997a), and to which she was aware she had exposed herself. Thus she writes, "I told myself that these fantasies had simply arisen out of notions which had been put into my head by everything that I'd been reading about psychoanalysis and theories of infant sexuality, and that none of it had anything to do with my emotional reality or childhood experience" (*Folie*, p. 100).

It clearly became very difficult for Alexander to differentiate "truth" from fantasy for much of the time—which again I see as predominantly an artefact of the profession-centred therapy protocol, rather than the client's natural, pre-existing "psychopathology" manifesting itself in the presence of a "sane" therapist. Certainly, at one point she poignantly questions the sanity of the whole therapy world: "And how many people were there in the world worked up into this kind of state about some therapist or other. It was a collective madness" (*Folie*, p. 118). She continues,

> I was beginning to think that [my self] was the least knowable thing of all. I had been plunged into a state of total confusion. All I could do was hypothesise and surmise, and no single theory about myself seemed to have any more validity than a number of other ones. I was equally perplexed about therapy itself. Was I undergoing a psychological mugging? [*Folie, ibid.*]

One of the main ways in which the profession-centred therapy regime generates material is through double-binds (an issue which will also crop up in Chapters 7 and 8). Thus, she writes, "The fury I felt [with Luc] was inexpressible in that it seemed that the only way

I could fully express it was by rupturing my relationship with him. I wanted to be able to scream at him ... 'I don't want you!'. But I couldn't do this because I was indissolubly bonded to him" (*Folie*, p. 31). And a bit later, "Whichever way I looked at it, there was no solution. I couldn't leave him and yet I couldn't develop my relationship with him along any therapeutic lines because ... I didn't trust him. I discussed it, analysed it, dissected it from all angles and got nowhere" (*Folie*, p. 32).

Alexander again: "I was unable to stop because, no matter how much I was suffering with the therapist, without him it would have been even worse. Without him I would have died. Not physically ..., but in some other way that I could not define" (1998a: 91). Finally, when Alexander *did* try to extricate herself from the entangling thrall of profession-centred therapy's regime of truth, she received the predictable response: [RA]: " 'But it's just not working. Nothing is any clearer. Things are only getting worse. I want to stop.' [Luc]: 'You're not ready to stop yet. If you stop now you'll only have more problems to cope with'" (*Folie*, p. 92). And "each time I spoke of quitting, [the therapist] would threaten that if I did so my suffering would only increase" (1998a: 91).

Again, then, the therapist battens down the professional hatches, and fails for even a moment to consider that *it might be the regime of profession-centred therapy itself which "isn't working"*, rather than the patient's "pathological" psyche. Furthermore, Alexander is repeatedly told by "psy" professionals that she should stay with the present therapist and work the difficulties through with that therapist rather than looking for another one (e.g. p. 99). This seems to me to be another classic example of the massive, self-serving assumption that problems occurring *in* therapy are not problems *of* therapy itself—so never once in Alexander's account do we see a psy-professional openly considering whether it might be a problem of profession-centred therapy's framework *per se*, rather than a patient "neurosis" to be "worked through".

Epilogue, afterword—and aftermath to Folie à Deux

... for people who have had therapy, the subject remains the ultimate taboo, much more intimate than sex, money or any other of the things which were once unmentionable. [*Folie*, p. 71]

Alexander's extraordinary account of her experiences of individual therapy cannot simply be "pathologized" away and dismissed by "the profession" as the intemperate ravings of one isolated client: for much of what she describes bears significant resemblances to the accounts of Ann France and Anna Sands (see Chapters 7 and 8). In her Epilogue she recounts at some length the very similar experiences of a self-help peer group of therapy "survivors" of which she was a member; and the Internet web site (quoted earlier) also provides rich and disturbing accounts from ex-clients world-wide of the havoc that "transference" can wreak in client's lives.

Even if it were to be argued that Alexander's experiences were more a function of her own "psychopathology" than of the machinations of profession-centred therapy's regime of truth, there is still a profound difficulty for defenders of profession-centred therapy: namely, the very fact that such experiences can be triggered within (if not *by*) therapy, and that we have no way of predicting beforehand whether they will be so triggered, simply reinforces the view that perhaps therapists don't ultimately know what they are dabbling with (or doing—Howarth, 1989; Spinelli, 1996) in their work with clients.

Just how, in such circumstances, it can be argued that therapy should become an established "profession" along quasi-conventional lines is, to say the very least, highly problematic. And even if it could be sustained that the constraining frame of profession-centred therapy bears no responsibility for these deleterious experiences (which I don't believe it can), it would still be the case that therapists have a major responsibility for the relational dynamics which can obtain in a setting in which they themselves "freely" choose to work and make a living. (I place quotation marks around "freely" because I believe it to be very much an open question as to whether those caught up in the culturally fashionable, subjectivity-influencing thrall of therapeutic discourse can be said to be choosing fully and freely—be they client or therapist: see Parker, 1997a and my Chapter 2.)

At the close of his perceptive and impressively open Afterword to Alexander's *Folie à Deux*, Spinelli wrote, "I ... hope that her account will [challenge] therapists to address the issues raised in an honest and non-defensive manner" (1995: 164). To what extent has Spinelli's hope been realized in practice? Certainly, the publication of *Folie*, and the therapy world's response to it, is a crucial "test-case" for my critique of the form typically taken by profession-centred therapy. For a full, open, and non-defensive engagement with this book by the "profession" might well significantly undermine my challenges to profession-centred therapy's regime of truth.

It is both fascinating and highly revealing that there has been virtual silence from the therapy world in (*non*)response to Alexander's book (amazingly, to my knowledge the book has only been reviewed in two therapy journals). There have been a few responses to Alexander's experience of therapy—ranging from the broadly sympathetic and positive views of Spinelli (1995) and Sivyer (1997), to the little-short-of dismissive and contemptuous (Davis, 1996; Dixon, 1998). According to Alexander (personal communication), "therapy professionals tend to react like scalded cats when dissatisfied clients speak up"—and she is certainly in a very privileged position to know! For "therapists are often accused of being totally resistant to any criticism of their practices, generally passing it off as a symptom of psychological disorder rather than an indication that the practices themselves need scrutiny" (1996: 16).

In relation to the arguments in this book, such reactions are indeed telling. Typical is Seligman's (1998a,b) response, which uses Alexander's revelations as an opportunity to exhort would-be clients to frequent members of her own professional "trade association", the United Kingdom Council for Psychotherapy (UKCP), with the naïve claim—which completely misses the point of Alexander's story—that "Therapists registered with the UKCP uphold codes of ethics which should prevent the outcome Ms Alexander suffered" (1998a, 103; for a contrary view see House, 1997b). Certainly no opportunity is missed to "sell" the UKCP to aspiring clients! (see Seligman, 1998b). And more pertinently, that Alexander's experience might conceivably be a resounding commentary on *the whole project* of therapy as a helping activity is not even considered by Seligman. Dixon's (1998: 103) response is even more vituperative: "I found [Alexander's 1998] article self-seeking and distasteful, with flashes of crude, topical sensationalism for which she should be ashamed"! (We are not told, incidentally, what interest or personal stake Dixon might have in the debate.)

The web site correspondent "Natalie Simpson" (referred to

earlier) also makes an interesting observation about Freud—that he talked almost exclusively about the difficulties of transference *for the analyst*—"and made hardly any reference to the suffering of the patient who was enduring the transference". In our brazenly therapist-centred self-serving "profession", perhaps this phenomenon is still alive and kicking today, and explains why Alexander's brave testimony has received so little attention in the "professional" therapy literature (after all, if, for example, bridges suddenly started falling down, one might expect professional engineers to take some notice of the fact and do something about it ...).

I hope I have gone some way to remedying this neglect of *Folie à Deux* in this chapter, following on as it does from Spinelli's constructive and engaging Afterword to the book.

Conclusion

> I did not suffer from the aberrant condition described in the book before encountering the therapist and have not done so since recovering from the experience. [Alexander, 1996a: 17]

In this chapter I have drawn at length on Rosie Alexander's experiences of one-to-one therapy. I have quoted verbatim in order to represent the experience in her own words, as an antidote to the conventional dominance of therapists' descriptions and interpretations of their clients' therapeutic processes. My selection of what to quote has, of course, been informed by my quest for "clinical" data which will add experiential ballast to the arguments developed in Chapters 2–4. In my view the foregoing analysis does indeed succeed in adding practical substance to those formulations.

Of course the data I have drawn upon is that of subjective experience, and does not cohere with the canons of "objective" empirical science: as Mohr (1995: 22) puts it, "an individual study cannot confidently make any conclusions" about the efficacy of therapy. But drawing on my methodological discussion in the previous chapter, I believe that any "objective" empirical research is in principle impossible in this highly peculiar field—in which case subjective, impressionistic data is at least as reliable as is any other. As Mohr puts it, "anecdotal information ... can be much richer than objective data" (*ibid*.)—and no-one could surely gainsay the richness of the data of Rosie Alexander, Ann France, and Anna Sands which I describe in Chapters 6–8.

It seems to me that we (the therapy field) must begin to take seriously what looks increasingly like abuse which can be *intrinsic* to profession-centred therapy's constraining regime of truth. I agree with Alexander that "Many people have the same kind of experience in therapy. ... Doesn't this indicate some common psychological catalyst in the therapy process rather than a diverse collection of bungling therapists?" (Internet web site, *op. cit.* 1999; cf. my Introduction); that "strong, even excessive, attachments to therapists is a regular phenomenon" (1996: 17); that as she has argued repeatedly, the problem of excessive dependency and unresolved transference is crying out for attention.

Finally, Alexander leaves us with what is to my mind an absolutely crucial ethical question—and one which still goes largely unaddressed by "the profession": "What precautions should therapists take to minimise the risk of severe psychological reactions occurring [in therapy]?" (1998c: 113). Mohr is surely right when he writes that "it cannot be too much to ask that we [the therapy "profession"] do what we ask of our clients—to examine our failings with an open mind and with a view toward change" (1995: 24). Just what direction such "healthy" change might take is the subject of the final chapter of this book.

I move on in Chapter 7 to a similar detailed analysis of Ann France's *Consuming Psychotherapy*.

CHAPTER SEVEN

Ann France's *Consuming Psychotherapy*

"... that a non-professional ... should presume to give a long, cool look at the sacred cows of psychotherapy is bound to arouse cries of 'resistance' and 'intellectualisation'"

France, 1988: 16

Introduction

In *Consuming Psychotherapy* Ann France has left us a wonderfully open, detailed, and analytically sophisticated study of her own personal experiences of therapy, and in my view it should be obligatory reading for every trainee and working practitioner in the field. France's stated aim is to give a personal view of what it feels like to be in therapy, and "to look at the underlying assumptions governing psychotherapy" (p. 7). (Her choice of the term "governing" is interesting, incidentally, in the light of my discussion of therapy's "regime of truth" in Chapter 2.)

France begins her book with a telling dedication—to three friends "whose friendship was more therapeutic than any professional counselling" (1988: v). Following a wide-ranging Introduction (which usefully summarizes the limited published literature then [and still] available on client experiences of therapy), in Part I France discusses the expectations she took into therapy, the decision-making process involved in her choice of therapists (three therapists are extensively referred to in the book), and "frame" issues (time, place, and cost). In Part II, "Experiencing Psychotherapy", she systematically examines a series of key therapeutic issues—for example, the transference phenomenon, the personhood of the therapist, interpretation, silence, holding, absence and loss, and separation. As in the previous chapter, I will radically restructure France's long text with a "reading" that illuminates my arguments about therapy's regime of truth and its accompanying profession-centred practice, as set out in Chapters 2–4.

What I found so impressive and useful about France's book is that the author clearly had a highly perceptive and wide-ranging theoretical understanding of the therapy process, and was able to be analytically critical without being either outright condemnatory or uncritically evangelical about therapy ("I am not trying either to advocate therapy or to attack it"—p. 2). Her three therapists also read the script and "offered helpful comments" (p. ix). Altogether the book is a model of insight and balance, and a mine of information for anyone—practitioner or client—looking for a theoretically informed taste of what a therapeutic experience can be like, with all the complexities, paradoxes and ambivalences that perhaps inevitably accompany the therapeutic experience.

Consuming Psychotherapy is to some degree limited by being saturated with the tacit ideological assumptions of therapeutic discourse, drawing heavily upon that discourse in its descriptions of the therapy process (cf. Parker, 1997a; my Chapter 2). Thus, for example, we see uncritically slipping into her text the dominant cultural (deterministic) belief that "the past has determined the present": e.g. "*On account of my own experience ... in childhood*, each experience of silence in therapy was to me painful" (p. 182); and "The intensity of the pain, then, *was due to my past*" (p. 220, my emphases). But despite this, France possesses an admirable critical faculty which inspires some confidence that few of therapy's "conventional wisdoms" will slip through the net without being deeply thought about and problematized. In the dust cover "testimonial", the well-known analyst Patrick Casement describes

the book as "diligently unsentimental and uncompromising ...,
[raising] many questions that challenge the established norms of
psychoanalytic technique"; and analyst Peter Lomas writes of "a
lucid account [which] makes a thoughtful critique of the nature of
the relationship between the two people involved [in therapy] and
the theory which informs the practice".

My analysis of *Consuming Psychotherapy* is significantly longer
than those of the books by either Alexander or Sands because Ann
France's book has sadly been out of print for some years, and is
therefore quite difficult to get hold of.

General context

At the start of her Introduction, France states her aim as being to
explore how "certain features of the [therapy] transaction appear
beneficial or frustrating to the consumer, and to see to what extent
these are inherent in the exercise" (p. 1). In her very first paragraph
she refreshingly questions the assumptive framework of therapy (or
what I call its regime of truth): "psychotherapy ... not infrequently
seems to achieve its therapeutic aims more in spite of its conceptual
framework than because of it". She is clear that she didn't have
much idea about what therapy would involve before she entered it
(p. 24)—which of course touches on my discussion of the ethics of
"informed consent", to which I return below (see also Chapter 4).

France refers at several points to the fundamentally contradictory nature of therapy. Thus, for example (and as already quoted
epigraphically):

> There seems to me to be an element of double-bind in the
> conventions governing therapy. On the one hand, the overt aims
> are the creation of a more autonomous, critically perceptive person,
> confident enough ... to throw off the shackles of blind conformity to
> others' expectations. On the other hand, most therapists expect
> unquestioning obedience to the laws [of the therapeutic frame].
> [p. 52]

Near the end of the book she writes of "the inherent difficulties
of combining a professional framework with a personal relationship. Some of the problems arise because the traditional concepts

governing the professional framework are interpreted too rigidly, and inhibit the expression of the personal relationship" (p. 240).

At several points France draws attention to what I am calling the "material-generating" nature of profession-centred therapeutic practice, echoing many of the arguments I developed in Chapter 4: for example,

> By encouraging the child/parent relationship therapy fosters selfish demands and an inability or refusal to acknowledge the needs of the therapist. Moreover, *the set-up* is designed by therapists, who are therefore *able to tailor it to suit their needs* ... It may be *called* the consulter's therapy, but the extent to which this operates is, to say the least, variable. [p. 231, my emphases]

The question of profession-centred therapy's propensity for material generation (see Chapter 3) will recur throughout the following discussion, as France's account provides many clear examples of it.

It is noteworthy that it was when she was most busy in her professional life that France did not miss going to her therapy sessions, and rarely even thought about her then therapist(s) at those times (*ibid.*: 233). France saw her first therapist weekly for three and a half years, and then another therapist twice weekly for nearly five years (during the final year of which she concurrently saw a third therapist once weekly) (p. 13).

Possible iatrogenic effects of therapy

> ... my experience suggests that there are some very real dangers in psychotherapy. *Some ... are inherent in the exercise.* The danger of addiction is, I think, considerable. *It is fostered by most therapists' [behaviour]* ... [p. 235, my emphases]

During her second period of (twice-weekly) therapy, France "sank into the longest and most painful depression of my life" ... and it seemed to her to have "much to do with the transference neurosis, and with the loss of my previous defences; *both phenomena were attributable to psychotherapy itself.* The force of the negative feelings in the transference became unbearable" (p. 29, my emphasis). She describes this harrowing period at some length:

I became abjectly dependent on my second therapist. Increasingly I felt that "reality" concerned my sessions of psychotherapy, while *"real life" became merely an intrusion*. ... There seemed to be an increasing conflict between the regressed self ... and the demands of the outside world that I should be responsible and efficient. I became prey to a continual feeling of panic; a sensation of overwhelming dread at some unspecified disaster. ... I became much less able to cope with things which ... [had] never before proved unmanageable ... I became unable to enjoy any of the activities I have previously taken pleasure in, unable to eat, unable to do anything creative ... [p. 30, my emphasis]

The culmination of this period was that France became acutely suicidal and had to be hospitalized in a nursing home (*ibid*.). For me the crucial question in all this, of course, is to what extent France's "breakdown" was a necessary aspect of her "healing process", or an iatrogenic artefact of the therapy process itself. The reader will not be surprised by my hunch that it might well have been *at least* as much to do with the latter as the former. Certainly, it comes as little surprise that this experience

made me seriously doubt the value, or at least the wisdom, of psychotherapy. ... It is difficult to say whether. ... I would have fared better without psychotherapy ... during therapy I became worse than I had ever been before ... therapy ... seemed to be doing more harm than good. ... At times I felt it was creating more problems than it solved. [pp. 30, 31]

And later in the book, she writes of how, during this phase of therapy, she "constantly muttered that I was going to abandon the entire exercise, that it had been the most damaging and non-therapeutic experience in my life" (pp. 93–94).

Yet simply quitting or taking a break from therapy was not an option either, for in what was for her an excruciating double-bind,

Rationally, I felt I should stop therapy ...; Emotionally, I couldn't bear to abandon this one hope of security and improvement. ... I had invested too much energy in the process and become too attached to my therapist to quit. And the more I hung on, the more incapable I seemed to become of leading a normal life. ... I only know that I had got into a dangerous and stagnant situation in, and partly because of, psychotherapy. ... [p. 31; cf. also her p. 155]

It is not even possible for someone who is relatively detached from such a situation to assess with any degree of confidence whether therapy was the very problem it itself was trying to solve—let alone for someone caught up in the thrall of such a double-bound cauldron of emotional turmoil. Just how many other therapy clients have been caught in such an impossible double-bind, enmeshed in and mesmerized by the milieu of profession-centred therapy and the processes triggered in it, and unable even to talk about the experience, can only be guessed at.

France reached interesting conclusions after this experience:

> I am now not at all sure that vulnerable people should be exposed to psychotherapy. This implies that ... most of those who need it may not be sufficiently resilient to benefit from it, given the strain it actually causes ... psychotherapy ... can be harmful, *without there being any very clear way of knowing in advance whether this will happen. ... It can merely be the replay of past traumata* ... which leads to nothing. ... The dangers in such a perilous undertaking ... provided the genesis of this book ... it works best with the healthy. [p. 32, my emphases]

And of her second therapy she writes, "the transference became damagingly negative without my realizing it ..." (p. 42).

It is also worth noting that before this harrowing experience France had always been very self-reliant in her life. She writes:

> It was only during therapy with Harriet that this lifetime of independence had crumbled, *because* of the relationship with the therapist, and largely because of the element of non-fulfilment within it. I did not therefore simply grow out of dependency, but rediscovered some measure of a self I had once had, which to my mind had been as badly bruised by "therapy" as by other relationships. [p. 234, her emphasis]

I am reminded of Winnicott's oft-stated view that therapy must always, at some level, be a "failure"—and can never, perhaps, satisfy those needs or desires that its framework almost inevitably stirs up (and is sometimes *designed* to precipitate) in the client. At one point France does write of "my feeling of betrayal when the therapist proved less than totally reliable" (p. 241) (which in turn again raises fundamental questions about whether the "betrayal" feelings might have been triggered more by the therapeutic regime itself, and whether any human being can ever be "totally reliable"— even though that "fantasy" might be being actively encouraged by the very nature of profession-centred therapeutic practice ...).

This discussion leads in turn into a much neglected and highly complex question about the extent to which it is appropriate (or therapeutically necessary) to "stir up" possible early developmental traumata, and whether such a "waking up of sleeping dogs" might not do more harm than good. In France's case I think a strong case can be made that it did indeed do her more harm than good; that is, that therapy had an iatrogenic effect—or in my terms, therapy became a material-generating process that largely caused that which it then struggled (and largely failed) to "rectify".

This is not necessarily to argue, of course, against self-awareness and insight in principle; but it is to highlight the (to my mind) intractable problem that it is quite impossible to predict beforehand (whether by client, therapist, or independent "judge") whether therapy is going to have such an iatrogenic effect or not. If I am anything like right in this analysis, then it clearly raises profound ethical questions about the very project of therapy, particularly when seen in the light of the other deconstructive arguments developed in this book. And yet a further twist is given to these difficulties when we consider the "illusion as health" research from the Social Psychology field, which I discuss later in this section.

France also helpfully draws attention to a much-neglected issue—namely, the possible iatrogenic effects of therapy *for the therapist*. In my Introduction, it will be remembered, I dared to suggest that therapists might well be just as much subject to the thrall of regimes of profession-centred therapeutic practice and their accompanying ideology as are abused clients—caught up in and profoundly (e)(a)ffected, as they are, by the compelling logic of therapy's ideological discourse (cf. Parker, 1997a). Thus, for France, "Therapists are dissimulating the emotions which they feel. This would seem to be putting considerable strain on the therapist ..." (p. 119). And a bit later she refers to "the unreality of the situation in psychotherapy, when the therapist tries to be invariably tolerant *in a way real people never are*" (*ibid.*, my emphasis). And taking the argument further still: "There is some doubt in my mind as to whether it is right to expect inhuman standards of forbearance, stoicism and invulnerability from therapists, whether indeed the insistence on these does not operate detrimentally on the relationship" (p. 127).

These considerations lead on quite naturally to the important question of therapists' (unconscious) motivations for choosing such a peculiar occupation—an issue thoroughly and revealingly explored in Sussman's important book *A Curious Calling* (1992).

France devotes two chapters (Chapters 12 and 13) to absence and loss, and separation. In her second therapy she found the therapist's absences profoundly traumatizing (p. 210), "unbearably painful" feelings that were intensified by the powerful transference created with this therapist. Perhaps her distress "was due to the different nature of this second therapy, involving a closer relationship, more frequent sessions and more of a re-enaction of past traumata" (p. 215)—or, using my own language, a significant, material-generating function of the particular regime of truth taken by this therapy. There are other seeming examples of such material generation (p. 217)—for example, with France suffering intense anxiety and "inconsolable" grief before her second therapist was about to leave for several months holiday. In this case the therapist's response was actually to *increase* her sessions to three per week! (a classic case, perhaps, of the profession-centred therapeutic ideology overriding any sense of what was therapeutically appropriate). And of course, yet more "material" was then generated to "work on", with France feeling "guilt at not being glad the therapist was having ... a rest, and resentment at my minding the absence of someone who was not even part of my life when present"! (p. 218).

As far as separation anxiety is concerned, again France sees this as an artefact generated by profession-centred therapeutic practice (though of course she does not use this terminology), and one which needs far more consideration than it has received (p. 220). For her, far from separation anxiety declining with time as her therapy progressed, it actually got worse: "I became less able to bear it. It reinforced, in present reality, something which had been unbearable in the past" (*ibid.*). For France (and rather caustically), "it is illogical to expect people to throw themselves unreservedly into therapy, and then switch off when it does not suit the therapist to be around". The scarcely concealed anger which from time to time erupts to the surface in France's account would no doubt be "interpreted" pathologizingly by some therapy commentators; whereas it makes far more sense to me to see it as an appropriate and quite natural, *healthy* response to the nature of profession-centred therapy's regime of truth.

In what appears to be yet another classic case of profession-centred therapy's material generation, France describes how, having gone on holiday herself during one of her therapist's holiday breaks,

> I had become unable to get any enjoyment out of the travel, and felt unbearably lonely. Before entering psychotherapy with Harriet I had often travelled alone to distant parts and never felt lonely. I cut short the holiday and returned home. ... The day she was due to return I became prey to acute anguish. ... Until this point, sixteen months after the inception of therapy with Harriet, I had not minded her absences. [p. 223]

In trying to work with these feelings in therapy,

> I felt I was going round in vicious circles, [Harriet] seemed unable to help me rephrase the despair or surmount it. Sessions seemed to become increasingly full of silences and I felt worse after each one than before. ... The systematic frustration in the professional encounter seems to me the most untherapeutic thing about psychotherapy. My only answer ... was to cease psychotherapy, and go away myself. [pp. 224, 229]

France also refers to being traumatized by the use of silence in her therapy: "I reckon I can take an unnatural amount of silence in real life, but was traumatized by it in therapy, in part due to the transferential nature of the experience" (pp. 184–185). In other words, what she is suggesting is that, again, acute anxiety stemming from a silent therapist is likely to be at least as much an artefact of the profession-centred therapy frame itself as it is a "neurotic" throwback to the client's earlier life (cf. my discussion of "material generation" in Chapter 3).

In her penultimate chapter France touches on the important issue of the effects that individual therapy has on one's "extra-therapeutic" personal relationships. There does exist some research pointing to the (sometimes deleterious) effects of being a therapist on one's personal intimate relationships (Guy, 1987); and it would be surprising if the same were not true for clients-in-therapy as well.

The well-known case of Fay Weldon offers interesting anecdotal evidence; and France also offers some suggestive observations: "The danger of not being able to make, or keep, close relationships with others while in therapy is, I suspect, a not uncommon problem ... new friendships ... were not being given a chance to blossom while psychopractice engaged so much of my time and energy" (pp. 232, 233).

Finally, France touches interestingly on a grossly neglected issue in therapy—the possibility that self-awareness and insight might actually be injurious to mental health. In discussing her realization that she had never been shown affection until her adulthood, far from this leading to growth,

> all it did was reveal a lack of something important in my childhood which had not been remedied by adult life. Knowledge of this need did not appease it, but on the contrary made it obsessive and destructive, since I no longer seemed to be able to function efficiently in other spheres because of my crippling sense of emotional deprivation. [p. 199]

There is an important body of Social Psychology literature which supports an "ignorance-is-bliss"-type view that some level of self-delusion, cognitive distortion, and so on, is actually a "normal" attribute of mental health. As Taylor & Brown (1988: 204) write, for example, "the mentally healthy person appears to have the enviable capacity to distort reality in a direction that enhances self-esteem, maintains beliefs in personal efficacy, and promotes an optimistic view of the future. These three illusions ... foster traditional criteria of mental health ...".

Although I certainly think that such research warrants a healthy dose of deconstructive scepticism, it nonetheless clearly raises some profound questions about the assumptive base of any insight-oriented therapy (which I assume most are), questions which surely cannot be ignored. For if illusions *are* in some sense integral to "mental health" (however that might be conceptualized and measured), then this could well constitute a significant source of iatrogeneity arising from psychotherapeutic experience. At several points France hints at this possibility herself: first, she downplays the importance of insight in concluding that, for her, "the positive effects [of therapy] came about less through greater self-knowledge than through the gradual development of a warm and trusting relationship" (p. 241). And more substantially, she writes:

> The accepted opinion would be that the demolition of false self in the interests of truth can only be good. I am not so sure, from the experiencing end, of the validity of this statement to which I subscribe theoretically. My previous defences had worked; I did not dwell on my problems, but got on with living, and this was beneficial to others as well as myself. [p. 237]

Note, incidentally, the phrase "to which I subscribe theoretically", which, I suggest, is a classic case of the subjectivity-determining influence of therapy's ideological regime of truth—cf. Chapter 2 and Parker, 1997a). And more revealingly still, France goes on to add that she felt more positive "*before* I had seen through my own strategies" (*ibid.*, her emphasis).

While of course these views cannot positively verify the "illusion as mental health" viewpoint, they certainly suggest that there may be something very important for the therapy world to consider in it.

I will close this section by reporting France's own conclusions about the dangers of therapy, which she bases on both her own experiences as reported in her own book, and also the observations of friends (pp. 239–240). While she is confident that short-term counselling "usually does help" specific problems (239; cf. my Chapter 12), she identifies three dangers of more long-term, in-depth therapy. (Note that she adds "... of a more analytic nature"; whereas I have suggested elsewhere [e.g. in Chapter 1] that these kinds of dangers are in fact triggered more by the nature of profession-centred therapeutic practice in general, of which the therapist's particular orientation is only one feature, than by the particular [analytic] approach *per se*). France writes:

> I would suggest that the dangers are threefold: firstly, that the breaking down of defences during therapy temporarily makes the person unable to cope with life; secondly, that there is a distortion of reality (which becomes seen as only the unreality of the consulting room); and thirdly, that addiction to the practice makes it very difficult to terminate. [p. 240]

And she adds further that

only those with a fair amount of emotional resilience, and support in the outside world, between sessions, should embark on such a perilous enterprise. ... I am not at all convinced that those who are very much alone in the world can be expected to weather the crisis engendered by psychotherapy itself, although *these are precisely the people who need it most.* [pp. 243, 240, my emphasis]

Therapeutic efficacy

therapy had restored a sufficient sense of self in me for this gesture of independence to be possible. ... I remain uncertain, however, as to the extent this was due to therapy, or due to other circumstances in life which had fostered my sense of worth. [p. 234]

In her book France struggles at several points with the intractable efficacy issue (discussed in Chapter 5). Thus, she notes that there was a "marked improvement" in her degree of trust and levels of depression for about 6 years after the first therapy, "although it is difficult to say with certainty how much was due to therapy" (p. 22). For France, "The process is ... difficult to define, with such wide-ranging or nebulous aims ... that success is difficult to determine" (p. 25). Elsewhere she writes that "there is no firm assurance that [therapy] will help" (p. 27); and while many who have had therapy do testify, often enthusiastically, to its benefit, "of course those who have undergone it have as much vested interest as therapists in declaring that this is so. One does not want to have spent all that time and money for nothing" (*ibid.*).

In terms of negative feelings within the therapy itself, "There is no easy answer to the dilemma of whether negative feelings are a reliable sign that this is the wrong person or situation, or whether they are a transitory stage to be battled with ..." (p. 48).

At several points she makes the crucial observation that in trying dispassionately to assess therapy efficacy, there can never be a valid control experiment (pp. 27, 196, 239; cf. my Chapter 5 discussion). In her Conclusion, for example, she writes that "it is not always possible to know, even with hindsight, whether a particular procedure was the best at the time, or even 'good enough'" (p. 241). Overall, then, France's analysis only reinforces the conclusion reached in Chapter 5 about the impossibility of any controlled, "objective" research on efficacy in the therapy field.

Flexibility

> my own experience of psychotherapy ... suggested that there was
> room for far more flexibility in practice, and that this did not prove
> harmful. [p. 241]

From the start of her book France expresses the explicit hope that
her book might lead practitioners to consider greater flexibility in
their practices (1988: 1; cf. House, 1999c, and my Chapter 12, below).
She expresses a strong preference for a "general exchange of ideas
with which I wanted to replace a one-sided analysis" (p. 132). She
writes further, "... my own experiences ... suggest [therapy] can be
effective without following traditional guidelines" (p. 2). Such a
view sits very comfortably with the position I take in this book; yet
in order to preserve the ideological sanctity of profession-centred
therapeutic discourse, "the profession" would be expected to attempt
(and does so) to limit such flexibility—and, of course, to provide a
coherent theoretical, self-justifying rationale within its own discourse for such a view (cf. my deconstructive analysis of specific
features of profession-centred therapeutic practice in Chapters 3
and 4).

A major example of flexibility in France's therapy experiences
was the unorthodoxy of her third therapist agreeing to see her
concurrently with her second, "co-operating with her while
operating entirely independently" (p. 41), which "deviant frame",
she says, worked very well for her (e.g. pp. 159, 232–233). In
addition, she found her meetings with a male psychiatrist very
helpful with regard to his flexible attitude: "[My psychiatrist] did
not insist on any regular contact when a crisis had been weathered.
This response to my needs as and when they occurred felt to me far
more natural than the rather mechanical regularity of psychotherapy"
(p. 196).

In her Chapter 3 France refers to "the dogma of the fifty-minute
hour" (p. 50)—a key feature of profession-centred therapeutic
practice, of course. For France the 50-minute frame highlights the
artificiality of the therapeutic relationship, for the relationship "is
only real within strict time-limits and in a space divorced from
everyday reality. ... The fixed intervals and hours of psychotherapy
have always seemed to me unsatisfactory because unrelated to real
need" (pp. 51, 213). Furthermore, "people function at different

rhythms, a truism not much allowed for by psychotherapy ... fifty-minute spurts do not occur as and when mood takes one [and] the time-limit does not correspond to emotional need or the demand of the discourse" (pp. 51, 50). And much later she writes, "It is very difficult for most people to shift gear from their daily preoccupations and delve into their inner world at set hours on particular days" (p. 155). And there were even times "when I dried up and felt I had nothing to say ... usually it was because I was fed up with having to find the time for a session when I felt I had better things to do" (p. 154). Later still she writes that "The ability and permission temporarily to stop consulting the person when the need no longer arose seemed to me to obviate the likelihood of emotional dependency or addiction which I think psychotherapy fosters" (p. 196). And of course it works the other way too: for "People do not just have nine-to-five problems, or distress that can be shelved for long periods, at the therapist's convenience" (p. 220).

Of course there is a precedent within the therapy world for varying or flexible session lengths—notably in the innovative work of Ferenczi, Lacan, and Winnicott (France, 1988: 51–52, 54, 57; cf. House, 1999c; Spinelli, 2001: 163). For France, such flexibility can be part of the system of help offered (e.g. as with the Samaritans), and "does not seem to have harmful results for either party" (p. 57). It is certainly fascinating how a whole self-justificatory theoretical edifice has been built within the therapy world attempting to justify why clear, regular time boundaries are crucial for creating "safety", putatively for the client (cf. my discussion of safety in Chapter 4). On closer deconstructive inspection, however, it really does look as if the time boundary has *at least* as much to do with practitioner convenience ("the therapist could not function without it"—p. 52), for which client-safety arguments are largely invoked as an effectively obfuscating pretext and rationalization.

There certainly do exist precedents for radical forms of unstructured psychological help (p. 54). The "renegade" psychoanalyst Jacques Lacan experimented with variable session lengths (no doubt being a factor in his expulsion from the orthodox psychoanalytic movement, who, no doubt, could not brook for one moment such a subversion of the sanctity of orthodox practice). Lacan's sessions were designed as far as possible to suit the subject matter presented; and one of his analysands wrote that "The gesture of breaking the session off [early] was a way of telling people to move forwards, not to get stuck or fascinated by the aesthetics of the experience" (Schneiderman, quoted in France, p. 58). (It would also seem to me, incidentally, to be a very effective way of subverting the transference-dependency dynamics triggered within the milieu of profession-centred therapeutic practice itself, and to challenge the associated addictive nature of therapy—cf. France, p. 240.)

In her chapter on holding (Chapter 11), France argues for a much freer and less precious attitude on the part of therapeutic helpers towards physical contact (in stark contrast, for example, with Casement's celebrated, lengthy analytical discussion of a similar issue —1985: Chapter 7). Thus, France describes how her local Samaritan did all the things that a ("'frame"'-preoccupied) therapist is not supposed to do—things like ringing her up every day during bad patches and "above all holding me sometimes while I cried" (pp. 196–197). Yet France is clear that these gestures not only did not, for her, generate any "morbid dependency", but they even helped to generate analytic insight (p. 197). She goes on to quote Peter Lomas' critique of the Freudian doctrine of abstinence, which, Lomas argues, can re-create in therapy the traumatic conditions responsible for the "neurosis", accompanied by the therapist's persistent refusal to alleviate the trauma by offering contact or comfort (p. 204): "one does ... wonder what sort of human being it is who can watch pain and neither say nor do anything to show their concern" (France, p. 205).

The general issue of therapeutic flexibility is not unrelated to those of "demystification" and "ordinariness". France approvingly quotes Hobson's (1985) statement that "We should spell out as far as possible what psychotherapy is about" (quoted on p. 151). I discuss "ordinariness" in a separate section, later in this chapter.

In her concluding statement on the benefits or otherwise of therapy, France writes that its positive aspects "are somewhat undermined ... by only being available in a strictly circumscribed framework, limited to specific hours which are subject to the apparently arbitrary withdrawal through the therapist's holidays and other absences" (p. 244).

Finally, she has no illusions about the limits of therapy when it comes to flexibility, for "even the more flexible ones not unnaturally believe in the importance of whatever they do, and collude with consulter-dependency up to a point" (p. 235).

Thoughts on transference and interpretation

> When therefore [the patient] confronts the analyst, he inevitably tends to treat him as he has treated others in the past. [Anthony Storr, quoted on p. 110]

> The concept of transference ... [protects] the analyst from too intense affective and real-life involvement with the patient. For the idea of transference implies denial and repudiation of the patient's *experience qua experience*; in its place is substituted the more manageable construct of a transference experience. [Szasz, 1963: 432, original emphasis]

One of the consequences of the kinds of flexibility just discussed, of course, would be that it would significantly lessen the likelihood of transference dynamics being triggered in the therapeutic work. Yet for the dynamically inclined therapies at least, the encouragement, development, and so-called "resolution" of the so-called "transference neurosis" is typically regarded as being an essential requisite for a successful and complete therapeutic experience. France devotes a whole chapter to the experience of transference from the client's perspective (Chapter 4), which again should surely be required reading for all therapy practitioners. (In what follows I am making the assumption that "transference" is a valid ontological category of human experience. I am very aware of, and have some sympathy with, arguments against this view [e.g. Spinelli, 1994], but that deep philosophical debate is alas beyond the scope of the present discussion.)

France has major misgivings about the concept, particularly with regard to its tendency towards the infantilization of clients. For her, the invoking of transference "is responsible for the excessive focus on the past and on fantasy, to the detriment of present reality" (p. 78); and she approvingly quotes Jung's view that a fixation with transference "destroys the patient's attempts to build up a normal human relationship" (*ibid.*). Not only does transference devalue the possible accuracy of the client's perceptions of the therapist, but—and this is crucial to the arguments in this book—what is referred to as "transference" is often an "artifact [*sic*] *caused by the therapeutic setting*, rather than a pure manifestation of childhood experience" (Peter Lomas, quoted in France, p. 75, my emphasis). France agrees:

for her, "[The] realistic appraisal of the therapeutic situation, by an autonomous adult, . . . obviates the necessity for a long working-out of a painful and degrading situation *which has been artificially created by the therapy itself*' (p. 101, my emphasis).

In terms of my argument in Chapter 2, France also makes the important point that "transference . . . will happen anyway, whether or not the therapist facilitates it by offering the consulter a blank screen on which to project fantasies" (p. 81). In other words, transference dynamics are triggered and created by the very nature of profession-centred therapeutic practice itself, and are not confined to the rarefied realms of psychoanalysis and analytic therapy; and for France, "[transference] is inevitable, once therapy has reached a certain depth" (p. 85). In addition, for her a conscious defence against (say) dependency "would not have been sufficient to have countered strong unconscious forces if they had been at work" (p. 98).

For Lomas (writing very much from the "humanistic" pole of psychoanalysis), "transference must be given second place to a mutual exploration of each other's stance" (1981, quoted in France, p. 77). France certainly agrees: for her, "an actual exchange in the present . . . was . . . more therapeutic than any transference. . . . I am . . . sceptical that an intense transference has to exist; or that, if it does, it is therapeutic" (pp. 84, 85). She goes on to describe (in ways reminiscent of Rosie Alexander—see Chapter 6) that during powerful transference experience she suffered "total disorientation" (p. 85). Overall, France felt that her "cooler" therapeutic relationships were more therapeutic for her than was the intense transference she underwent with her second therapist (p. 86). Certainly, the labyrinthine entanglements, and even quasi-psychotic disturbances, that the transference-induced emotional cauldron generated within the profession-centred therapeutic frame can precipitate come across very clearly in France's discussion (particularly pp. 89–90, 220; cf. the dramatic experiences of Rosie Alexander described in Chapter 6).

In sum, France is more drawn to the Rogerian, client-centred notion of retaining the client's adult dignity, entailing a "shift of focus from past and fantasy, to the present and reality" (p. 101) than she is to the analytic/dynamic preoccupation with transference: for her,

There must be more room for the reality of the present situation, and for respect towards the adult who is still present in the regressed child. Maybe it is by building on this, on an exchange related to real-life situations, and not a highly artificial and angst-making dependency, that there is most chance for growth and re-education. [p. 100]

A few words too about interpretation. France devotes a chapter to it (Chapter 9); and while it might appear that its relevance is quite narrowly confined to the more analytic therapies, in fact "interpretation" is in my view merely a special case of the more general principle that *it is therapeutically legitimate for therapists to import preconceived theoretical templates or specific techniques into their client work*. Such an assumption goes far wider in the therapy field then merely the analytic/dynamic therapies, of course; and unsurprisingly, France is very critical of it. Thus she approvingly quotes, respectively, Peter Lomas' view that "non-technical qualities are central to healing" (quoted on p. 49), and R. F. Hobson's that "A psychotherapist should never even imply 'You don't mean that, you *really* mean this'" (quoted on p. 163, original emphasis). Contrast this with the (to my mind) extraordinarily arrogant and power-abusing (but fairly orthodox analytic) view of Fromm-Reichmann, that "If a patient gets upset or angry about an interpretation, this is usually indicative of its being correct"! (quoted on p. 169). It is therefore refreshing to find Patrick Casement expressing the view that "There are ... times when a patient has to stand firm with the therapist, in the name of his or her own truth" (quoted on p. 175).

Ordinariness

"How can I talk to you?", I expostulated one day ...; "I don't even know if you like spinach". [France, p. 110]

Perhaps the best antidote to a fixation on transference dynamics is what Lomas (1981) refers to as ordinariness in the therapeutic relationship; and perhaps it is the forces of professionalization that have moulded profession-centred discourse and its accompanying ideology such that it is now "very difficult for two people to meet each other and discuss, in a natural and ordinary way, the problems of one of them. ... The psychotherapist ... needs to free himself ...

from the sense of distance which his professional training may have given him" (Lomas, quoted in France, pp. 1, 190).

For France "the crux of the whole psychotherapeutic endeavour" is expressed by the question, *"does one want a therapist, or a friend?"* (p. 105, her emphasis); and "To what extent is it desirable that a therapist ... should approximate their behaviour to that of a friend?" (p. 106). On one occasion France plucked up the courage to ask her second therapist for a cup of coffee—and for her "It did more to eradicate a lifetime of feeling too unworthy to ask for anything than any analytic interpretation could have done"! (p. 108). Such ordinariness contrasts sharply with what she calls the "rationalized defensiveness" of "professional doctrines and technical procedures" (p. 111).

France discusses Carl Rogers' notion of "unconditional positive regard" to illustrate what she means by ordinariness (pp. 109–119). For her, the core of the therapeutic process is "a friendly acceptance by the therapist" (p. 111). Further, for her "At certain stages in the relationship ... it might be appropriate to introduce an element of sharing and mutuality" [into the relationship] (p. 128). And she strongly supports what she acknowledges to be a very unorthodox view, that the therapist "must be an ordinary human being; he must not conceal his frailties" (Peter Lomas, quoted on p. 129). Lomas, then, advocates "an atmosphere of ordinariness"—"a relationship in which the patient feels valued for his ordinary human qualities, those which he shares with the rest of humankind" (pp. 128–129). Yet for France an emphasis on ordinariness does not mean analytical mundaneness: for "there are some essentially poetic experiences which should not be subjected to the scrutiny of logical analysis" (pp. 137–138); and (following Winnicott), "Psychotherapy has to do with two people playing together" (p. 144). In her own case, however, there was disappointment; for her playfulness and creativity "were present at the beginning of my therapy with Harriet. It took some years of 'therapy' ... to kill this ability in me" (*ibid.*).

Encountering therapy's regime of truth

It is the one place in the world where your *function* is to be inadequate, at least in the early stages of the therapy. [p. 118, her emphasis]

The so-called "informed consent" problem is of crucial ethical importance for the practice of therapy. When, at the beginning of her first therapy, France had misgivings about it, "I didn't verbalise them to myself at the time because I had nothing else to go by [and] knew little about psychotherapy" (p. 34). And some time into her first therapy, France became aware of her therapist's neo-Freudian "rigidity", but at the beginning "I did not consider her approach doctrinaire; I only did so in retrospect" (p. 39). Later she reports the experience of a friend who, when asked by her therapist after a trial period whether she wanted to continue in therapy, said "how difficult it was ... to reply that actually it felt dreadful ... [but] she could not ... bear the thought of starting again at zero" (p. 47).

France states quite unambiguously that in her first therapy she often thought she was getting nowhere (pp. 25–26). She quotes her first therapist, who responded to her own expressed surprise at the lack of progress, as saying to her: "You can't expect to undo in three years the mess it took thirty to make" (p. 26). There could hardly be a clearer example of the self-fulfilling assumptive framework that profession-centred therapeutic practice assumes in order to provide a self-justifying *raison d'être* for its existence and legitimacy.

The question of termination is also very important in any discussion of therapy's regime of truth. France (p. 46) quotes analyst Nini Herman (1985) thus: "It can be easier to transplant oneself across whole worlds than to find the courage it requires to terminate a therapy". And here is France herself : "... it is sometimes difficult to know at what stage in the proceedings the contract should be terminated ... many people are reluctant to get out of a bad match" (p. 33—perhaps by "people" France means both clients and therapists ...). This could be seen as a real trap, in that those very people who enter therapy may tend to be those most susceptible to encountering difficulty in terminating it—not only because of the regressive dependency attachments triggered within profession-centred therapeutic practice but because of the "pathologizing" interpretations which an expressed decision to end can evoke from the therapist.

I had a personal experience of this myself during 2 years of psychoanalytic psychotherapy (twice-weekly and then weekly). Despite being a "highly experienced" client with hundreds of hours of personal and group therapy behind me, and being an experienced practitioner, I found it enormously difficult even to voice my wish to end the therapy—and my difficulty only became compounded when my therapist proceeded to make what appeared to me to be "pathologizing" interpretations about my decision to leave! And what does a client stuck in the mesmerizing thrall of therapy think that her or his friends might say if they were to share their experienced inability to quit their therapy? Ann France actually lost many friends during such a period of her therapy—1988: 30; for very few (if any) people would even begin to understand what such an experience was like unless they had experienced it for themselves—in which case they too would probably never talk about it. ... (cf. Alexander, 1995).

In this way, then, the closed circle of secrecy is complete, and the difficult-to-challenge sanctity of profession-centred therapy's regime of truth is effectively and self-servingly insulated from the critical gaze of its clientele. And this unchallengeability is, I submit, a direct result of the very form that the therapeutic "regime of truth" takes, with its associated ideological assumptions and their subjectivity-producing effects (cf. Chapter 2). Certainly, practitioners who are ideologically wedded to, and have a major personal-identity investment in, profession-centred therapeutic discourse (cf. Masson, 1992a,b) will of course be likely to pathologize a client's expressed wish to end, as such a wish will often represent a direct challenge to the hegemony of profession-centred therapeutic practice itself.

More generally, France calls into question the whole basis of the pathologizing role of the professional therapist (cf. Lowson, 1994; Parker *et al.*, 1995)—a role in which "a professional ... would pounce on particular aspects of the admission, dissect them and toss them back with labels attached—labels, moreover, which tended to dispute my presentation of the object and rename it" (pp. 159–160).

France had a similar experience to myself with her third therapist. She refers (tellingly) to "my becoming gradually able to leave the womb-room of the therapist, confident that I could survive alone", and had negotiated a more flexible therapy arrangement with therapist Harriet which allowed her to "explore the limits of my independence, with the security of a safety net there" (p. 235). She continues,

> Harriet ... was far more willing to let me go ... than Simon. ... It took me about six months of muttering that I was ready to abandon the exercise for him to remove his ear muffs sufficiently to answer, and then it was with a guarded negative. When I finally wrote saying that I wanted to put him on the back burner for three months, in order to get on with some urgent work and to see how I survived alone, *he made me feel that I did not have the right to declare unilateral independence*. [pp. 235–236, my emphasis]

I found myself in total agreement with France's observation that "Whenever the consulter thus decides not to pursue the consultations it would be disingenuous to declare that this represents *only* a failure on his or her part; it is also a failure of efficacity [*sic*] of therapy" (p. 233, her emphasis).

I need hardly point to the highly dubious ethics entailed by such a response from a therapist around the issue of termination. It was Freud himself who (according to Sandor Ferenczi) "said that patients are only riffraff. The only thing patients were good for is to help the analyst make a living and provide material for theory" (quoted in Rowe, 1990: 19); and as Rowe herself points out, the abuse of power and authoritarianism are quite central here, for in dynamic therapy,

> The psychotherapist is superior, the patient inferior. ... The psychotherapist's truths have a higher truth value than the patient's truths. The psychotherapist interprets the patient's truths and tells him what they *really* mean. ... All authoritarian systems instil obedience, conformity and acceptance of the authority's version of the truth by undermining the self-confidence of their ... patients. [1990: 13, 14, her emphasis]

Just how, in such circumstances, clients can make a healthy and own-best-interest decision about when to end therapy is very difficult to imagine. Certainly, France found it "very difficult to leave the therapy when I felt it had become destructive" (p. 35).

France returns to the question of "endings" in her chapter on separation (Chapter 13). If Hobson (1985: 257, quoted on p. 230) is anything like right when he writes that "A personal relationship never ends", perhaps the term "ending" is indeed a misnomer—which would also help to make sense of why endings are so notoriously difficult in therapy ... not, perhaps, primarily because of the "neurotic material" the client possesses around previous unworked-through endings (though of course those dynamics might be present as well), but because *the very nature* of profession-centred therapeutic practice tends to make the co-construction of a "natural", even healthy ending intrinsically well nigh impossible. For the relationship that is being "ended" is not the ending of a love partnership, a friendship, a bereavement through family loss, a pet dying ..., but the ending of a highly peculiar, idiosyncratic relationship for which no other comparable templates exist in human experience.

On this view, then, the arguably over-precious preoccupation with "endings" in the therapy field can be seen as yet another aspect of therapy's self-serving regime of truth, whereby great amounts of "material" are generated within profession-centred therapeutic discourse itself, and then worked with at great length— commonly to the financial benefit of the practitioner, of course. Certainly, France "began to feel that there was no way I could bring myself to separate" after four and a half years in therapy with Harriet (pp. 231–232). (Of course, I am aware that the foregoing analysis might be seized upon by some critics, wishing to "psychopathologize" my argument as indicating *my own* "un-worked-through material" around endings—a critique which [as Karl Popper would say] is not only unfalsifiable, but which could in some circumstances be quite "mad-making" for at least some people exposed to such a personalized critique.)

France interestingly builds into the picture the well known phenomenon of therapy clients going on to become professional therapists themselves. In my view it is almost as if a kind of ideological "indoctrination" takes place whereby the hegemony of the profession-centred regime's discourse is transmitted and reproduced through a lineage that ultimately traces back to Freud and the origins of psychoanalysis (cf. House, 1999b). I can certainly relate to some kind of process like this having (pretty much unconsciously) gripped me in my own practitioner development process (House, forthcoming). In one sense, clients-becoming-therapists might be a manifestation of their therapy never being brought to an end—rendering them into "eternal clients", perhaps—and reflecting in turn the aforementioned impossibility of ending in this highly peculiar sphere. Certainly, I can think of no other "professional" field in which such a large proportion of clients/customers decide to become practitioners themselves—and some kind of explanation is clearly required to account for this extraordinary phenomenon.

France recounts an amusing anecdote which speaks to the foregoing analysis:

> After four years of therapy a friend announced to me that she felt much happier about herself and her life ..., and thoroughly recommended the experience, which she now felt ready to end. ... Four years later the friend was still in therapy, with the same person, but now training to be a therapist herself. I became slightly sceptical about the lasting benefits or general validity of *a situation from which one could not escape, even when it had fulfilled its apparent function* ... therapy has not returned [such clients] to a natural existence ... [p. 231, my emphasis]

I close this section with a composite quotation (some of it repeated from elsewhere in this chapter), which for me captures very well the feel of a client comprehensively caught up in the thrall of profession-centred therapy's regime of truth:

> I did have misgivings ... [but] I didn't verbalize them to myself at the time, because I had nothing else to go by [and] knew little about psychotherapy. ... Rationally I thought I should stop therapy since it seemed to be doing more harm than good. Emotionally, I couldn't bear to abandon this one hope of security or improvement. ... I had invested too much energy in the process and become too attached to my therapist to quit. And the more I hung on, the more incapable I seemed to become of leading a normal life. ... I only know now that I had got into a dangerous and stagnant situation in, and partly because of, psychotherapy, which could not have been solved with the same therapist. ... [The good rapport I had with my therapist] made it very difficult to leave the therapy when I felt it had become destructive. [France, 1988: 34; 31, 35 respectively]

Concluding remarks

Does it only heal, or can it also be harmful? The latter question I am still asking myself, after eight years of psychotherapy. ... [France, 1988: 21]

I want to reiterate, first, that *Consuming Therapy* is by no means a "therapy-bashing" book written by a bitter, "blaming" ex-client—for as France herself writes, "I am not trying either to advocate therapy or to attack it" (p. 2). In this chapter I have devoted a significant amount of space to Ann France's testimony, not least because (as implied earlier) I see it as an important and neglected document in the history of psychotherapy—a book which is now difficult to get hold of (being out of print), yet one which therapy practitioners of any and every orientation would do well to study closely.

France's massive ambivalence about therapy comes across at numerous points in the book: for example, "While occasionally I wish I had never heard of the word psychotherapy, and at times I think the practice came near to destroying me, yet it was also very worthwhile" (p. 238). As will be clear from my earlier discussions of efficacy, both in this and the previous chapter, I believe such ambivalence is pretty much inevitable, given the methodological and experiential impossibility of specifying with any reliability the extent to which any therapy experience *qua* therapy experience is being, or has been, effective in bringing about personal change—whether such an assessment be based upon so-called "objective" empirical research or upon subjective experience. This is indeed a highly sobering conclusion for both practitioners and clients alike—although it does not, of course, necessarily amount to an argument against therapy as a generality (although, equally, it might do!—the "truth" is that *we really don't know*, and never can "know", certainly not in any narrow "scientific" sense).

In a review of France's book, Rowan wrote that "I think anyone reading this book and trying to decide whether to go for therapy would stay away, would run a mile if they had any sense" (1988: 276). Rowan surely deserves great credit for such an honest appraisal, which is notably lacking in other reviews of France's book by therapists. What I find most fascinating, however, is that the book (writes Rowan)

> made me angry (276): [for all of her therapists] failed her in the end. ... My own best guess is that none of them went far enough back into the origins of the depression ... they did a bad job and did not succeed with this particular person ... it seems crystal clear from

this book that authenticity and genuineness are not enough ... none of the people she consulted had enough knowledge to deal with her deep problems. [Rowan, 1988: 276, 277; 1996: 12]

Thus, rather than problematizing the very project of therapy itself (which France does herself several times in her book—barely mentioned in Rowan's review), the legitimacy of profession-centred therapeutic practice is rescued by the argument that it was shortcomings of the thera*pists* rather than of therapy *per se* that was the problem (cf. my Introduction). (After years of intermittent bouts of severe depression and suicidal tendencies, Ann France tragically took her own life six months after the publication of *Consuming Psychotherapy*—Rowan, 1996b.)

I would like to conclude on an optimistic note for those wishing to salvage something positive about therapy from France's book. She writes of her third therapist, "It felt like an encounter between equals, of equal reality and intelligence, despite the artificiality of the framework" (p. 85)—a tantalizing intimation that it is perhaps possible to create an empowering therapeutic experience notwith-standing the machinations of the profession-centred therapy form. I strongly agree with France's point that, for better or worse, therapy does exist within our culture, and is likely to do so for the foreseeable future; and given that reality, "The question is not whether to ignore it, but how to conduct it so that it really is therapeutic, and does not exacerbate problems, or merely fail to relieve them" (p. 240). Anti-therapy arguments like those of Jeffrey Masson, Raj Persaud, and Fay Weldon, which verge on the destructive, do little to help us specify what such an enabling, "post-professional" therapeutic practice might look like. France does give us a few clues for answering this crucial question (cf. the section on flexibility, above): for example, she is in favour of "short-term counselling for specific problems" (p. 239), and the discussion in her "Holding" chapter (especially pp. 195–197) offers a useful insight into how "ordinary" caring (cf. Lomas, 1981; Smail, 1987) can be far more therapeutic for a person than the rarefied encounters of an overly rigid and obsessively over-boundaried profession-centred therapeutic practice.

Near the end of her admirable book France offers us a resounding statement, forged in the fiery emotional furnace of hundreds of hours of encounter with profession-centred therapy's regime of truth, and which I would like to repeat here in full:

> The stress in psychotherapeutic theory and practice needs, I think, to shift from the idea that this is a treatment meted out by a specialist to a sick person, who has no right to question it, to the attitude that this is a co-operative venture between two equals, with the same goal of effectively enhancing the life of the consulter, and freeing him or her from the temporary bond created with the therapist. [p. 243]

Perhaps it would make a very fitting epitaph to Ann France's troubled life if the therapy "profession" were to take deep heed of this passionate offering to us; for while I think most practitioners would consciously, and in principle, adhere to the sentiment and the substance of France's plea, I believe that the way in which much professional therapy is *actually practised* is a long way from meeting her precepts, as my analysis in Chapters 2–4 attempts to demonstrate.

I return at length to the question of a viable post-professional, deconstructive therapy in my concluding Chapter 12.

Coda

> One is driven to the simple conclusion that psychotherapists do not know what they are doing and cannot train others to do it, whatever it is. [Howarth, 1989: 150]

> . . . therapists really don't know what they are doing—even if they insist upon pretending to themselves and to the world at large that they are experts. [Spinelli, 1996: 59]

Perhaps the radically uncomfortable conclusion reached by Spinelli and Howarth, among others (see also Mair, 1992), should not really surprise us, given Haley's (if anything conservative) observation that "Every minute *hundreds of thousands* of bits of information are exchanged in words and with body movements and vocal intonation. Both client and therapist may be conscious of only small amounts of so complex an interaction" (Haley, 1976: 200, my emphasis).

David Mohr concludes his literature review of deterioration in therapy thus: "it cannot be too much to ask that we do what we ask our patients to do—to examine our failings with an open mind and with a view toward change" (1995: 24). Needless to say, I agree wholeheartedly with this sentiment; and of course, on the basis of the analysis in Part I of this book, I invite therapists to extend such open-mindedness to *the very form* that profession-centred therapy now takes in modern culture, and the unconscious, subjectivity-creating effects that an uncritical embracing of that form might be having on all those with a stake in the therapeutic project.

In Chapter 8 I turn to the latest published client commentary on the therapy experience—Anna Sands' formidable book *Falling for Therapy*.

CHAPTER EIGHT

Anna Sands' *Falling for Therapy*[1]

Introduction

Who needs who in psychotherapy? ... [B]eing the sole focus of someone else's interest is a double-edged sword. [Sands, 2000: 121]

As I hope the previous two chapters have illustrated, the potential benefit for therapy stemming from client perspectives is considerable; for no matter how much personal therapy is experienced by trainees and practising therapists, the very fact that they *are* trainees or practitioners means that their client experience can rarely if ever be that of a client *qua* client, uncontaminated by therapy's regime of truth. For as "Anna Sands" (another pseudonym) points out in her recent and impressive book *Falling for Therapy* (hereafter, *FfT*), "Most of us [clients] stumble into therapy knowing little about it" (p. 3).

Therapists really need to know just what struggles are entailed in being a client, and the effects that our therapeutic structures have upon client subjectivity and "being possibilities"—for we might just then have a chance of creating a therapy culture which is consistently and reliably humane, openly reflexive, and enabling. I return to this central question in Chapter 12.

Ann France and Rosie Alexander bravely began the process of clients *talking back* to therapy, and this important tradition has been greatly enriched by Sands in her engagingly intelligent book. The themes which I will highlight and develop in this chapter will echo many of those seen in earlier chapters, and draw heavily on the results of my own struggles with deconstructing therapy's regime of truth.

Scene-setting

The "therapeutic" relationship can harm and hurt as well as help and heal. [p. 5]

In Chapter 1 Sands pinpoints some highly uncomfortable questions for practitioners: "Are problems more likely to arise in therapy when a propensity on both sides to perceive a hidden agenda is a driving force of the work?"; "What happens ... when dealing with feelings becomes a profession?"; "[D]o therapists, at times, help to create new problems—problems which stem primarily from the nature of some psychotherapeutic practice?"; "What part do the system and the environment of therapy play, and what part is played by the individual psyches of those who create that environment?". And all this in the first two pages! ... *FfT* was clearly to be no easy read for therapists wedded to any degree of profession-centred complacency.

Sands describes two extensive experiences of therapy: the first being analytically inclined (with a male therapist–analyst), which Sands believed to have precipitated a major breakdown; and a second, humanistically/transpersonally inclined therapy (female therapist), which she found helpful and humane.

Psychodynamics and transference

[T]he concept of the unconscious means that nothing is irrefutable. ... Once someone suggests that something is unconscious, any-thing—in theory—is possible. This gives the therapist tremendous power. [pp. 136–137, 63]

Throughout *FfT*, there are recurrent references to the ways in which a psychodynamic approach can "tie us up in knots rather than straighten us out" (p. 7). Not least is the way in which it can fetishize thinking and analysis, and, concomitantly, serve to distance both therapist and client from direct emotional experiencing (p. 20). For Sands it is *holistic experiencing* that is necessary for an authentic experience of realness and participative aliveness— while in her experience "a psychoanalytic approach can weaken our sense of connection with the world and our faith in the validity of all our judgements and perceptions" (p. 34).

Sands' first therapeutic experience led to her reality becoming "less, rather than more, sharply defined ..." (p. 87); and for her, at its worst, the act of analysing can become a defensive substitute for engaged compassion for the client's suffering: "[W]e need to be seen in our wholeness *before* we are fragmented into analysable chunks" (p. 189, my emphasis).

In a chapter on transference, she raises the poignant question of just "who is trying to recreate what?" in any re-enactment that might occur within therapy (p. 124). Psychodynamic therapy commonly tends to accentuate and fetishize the "negative" aspects of the past, making it "doubly hard for [the client] to free herself from their effect" (p. 65). As Ernesto Spinelli among others has shown, it is in fact pure surmise (and *deterministic* surmise at that) to assume that the past *causally* influences or determines the present; and if, indeed, such a worldview is erroneous, then an approach which deliberately seeks to activate "transference issues" can all too easily unleash a causal-deterministic wild goose chase. Little surprise, then, that "the problems that arise in psychotherapy ... might ... also be caused by the confused nature of the relationship" (p. 25) as much as by the client's alleged "psychopathology" or "re-enactments".

It's not just that "transference allows therapists to distance themselves" (p. 72, quoting Spinelli). Overall, the accurate distinguishing between "inappropriate transference from the past" and a valid response to the current relationship "is a minefield" (p. 71); and there are surely profound and well rehearsed ethical question-marks accompanying any therapeutic approach in which "transference is artificially [and deliberately—RH] provoked" (p. 118) by the therapist's behaviour.

At one point Sands turns the psychodynamic approach back upon itself, with potentially devastating effect. Thus, she asks,

"What if ... *the client* ... soaks up what the therapist is unable to deal with in himself? ... If the work is coloured by the therapist's unresolved issues, and this is not clarified, then *the nature of the problems and their exact location get lost*" (p. 140, my emphases). And who can *ever* claim to have worked through all of their own "material"?—as the work of Jeffrey Masson and Professor Bob Young, among others, has conclusively shown, some of the most "neurotic acting-out" behaviour imaginable is routinely perpetrated by psychoanalytic organizations run by practitioners who have been psychoanalyzed or "therapized" many times weekly for years on end!

If this analysis is anything like right, then Sands' assertion that therapists in general are "playing with fire" (p. 143)—not least because of sheer (and unavoidable) ignorance about what they're actually doing—is uncomfortably close to the mark. For she is surely right in asserting that we do not (yet?) possess "a sufficiently clear and common understanding of what we mean by mental and emotional health ..." (p. 158) because of "the unfathomability of the human mind and, therefore, of what therapy is about" (p. 183).

In sum, some of the dangers of a psychodynamic approach are that "We become mesmerised by conjecture and hypothesis about what things mean, disappear up blind alleys and lose sight of the target" (p. 60); and "the psychodynamic approach actually encourages the therapist to re-enact parts of the damaging aspects of the parent/child relationship" (p. 120). And can any therapist *ever* guarantee that re-traumatization will not be the result of therapy?—for "How confident can practitioners be that their clients will always work through, rather than simply relive, early emotions and experience?" (p. 131).

Pathologization and iatrogenic e(a)ffects

> Is there a sense in which "analysis" can pathologise our human-ness? ... Therapy can play havoc with one's equilibrium and sense of reality ... a kind of game which can become a maddening experience, in both senses of the word. [pp. 2, 82, 135]

Pathologization must necessarily invoke some notion of "healthy normality" which then becomes a normalizing benchmark against which "*ab*normality" or "psychopathology" is relationally defined (cf. House, 1997e, 2001b). Such a worldview on human experience has all kinds of e(a)ffects—not least of which is the creation of a legitimate "object" for the therapeutic enterprise to work upon—and to give it its very *raison d'être*.

For Sands, "Therapy cannot feel healthy if the therapist fails to employ the language of health. . . . Isn't it primarily the language of psychological disturbance which informs the concepts framing the work . . .?" (p. 43); and the wish for "a supportive, natural and open relationship where the client is treated as an equal can be pathologised in therapy" (p. 37). Sands is challenging the very foundations of a widespread therapeutic worldview that accentuates the "negative" and the "abnormal" and, concomitantly, plays down (or even pathologizes) the healthy (cf. the analytic notion of "flight into health".

Freud's essentially pessimistic view of "human nature" (Postle, 1998a) seems to have surreptitiously influenced generations of analysts and therapists in this regard—and continues to do so, notwithstanding the strong recent growth of the humanistic and transpersonal therapies. Thus, "Are practitioners inadvertently [or even "advertently"—RH] encouraged to stick unhelpful and unfitting labels on their clients, pathologising rather then improving their self-image?" (p. 44). There is also the neglected question of whether and, if so, how, the discourse of "psychopathology" can *actively create* what happens in therapy.

Worse still, the constraining discourse of "psychopathology" can even create *the very way that clients think about themselves*: "I began to wonder if I was riddled with unusual psychological deformities which somehow set me apart. Was I in some undesirable way different from other people?" (p. 87). At its worst, Sands "began to feel that whatever I said to my analyst would be taken as yet another illustration of what was wrong with me"—leading in turn to "the loss of a sense of my own identity" (p. 90). In sum, for Sands "Therapy may . . . overemphasise difficulties, giving them a significance which is disproportionate" (p. 54); and therapy should not be about experiencing oneself "as a case, a patient" (p. 86).

The imposed discourse of psychopathology, then, in tandem with the assumed expertise of the therapist, can easily destabilize one's sense of coherent identity, creating rather than alleviating the kind of "madnesses" that therapy is alleged to "treat" (cf. p. 38). Sands is referring here in particular to the analyst/therapist declining to give any feedback to the patient/client about what the former is experiencing. Most damning of all, "Knowing whether or not my perceptions are correct is fundamental to my sense of my own sanity. Leaving the client in the dark in this respect can promote feelings of confusion and helplessness, whilst preserving the power that the practitioner's distance gives him" (p. 93). Finally, and not least, as Hillman and Ventura have suggested, there is a danger that "the very focus on oneself ... is, *per se*, a depressive move because we concentrate on 'What's wrong with me?'" (quoted on p. 139).

Therapy's regime of truth

> Whose truths do we investigate during therapy? The client's, or that of the therapist, or of the particular school of thought which the therapist follows? [p. 51]

Therapy can, as I have argued earlier, routinely construct a "regime of truth" which self-fulfillingly creates a framework which serves to guarantee its own legitimacy, and outside the confines of which it is often exceedingly difficult for clients *or* therapists to think. Throughout *FfT*, Sands repeatedly alludes to such dangers. She refers to therapy's "*way of thinking* to which the client will become particularly susceptible" (p. 3, my emphasis), and the way in which "the characteristics of the [therapeutic] interaction will, in great measure, be defined by [the therapist's] professional training" (*ibid.*). Sands offers a devastating counterintuitive insight that, "[in] training someone to respond in a certain way", this may paradoxically render that person *less* able to be (spontaneously) responsive (p. 151). Training might even "sometimes make practitioners less rather than better able to communicate with their clients" (p. 42). At its self-fulfilling worst, "Could [the therapist's] reality even help to *create* what his training has told him to look for?" (*ibid.*, my emphasis). Certainly, "Attachment to a particular theory can restrict and restrain, engendering ... a dangerous narrow-mindedness" (p. 128)—with conventional procedural guidelines "tak[ing] precedence over the ground rules about decent human behaviour" (p. 25).

Moreover, therapy's regime of truth can only be reinforced in a situation in which "what procedures the therapist propounds, the patient is predisposed to accept" (quoting Mark Aveline, 1990: 30). In her first therapy, Sands describes the experience of feeling that she had done something wrong "because I was not doing what I thought analysands were 'supposed to do'" (p. 96). And in a neat table-turning exercise on analytic orthodoxy, Sands asks whether the client might sometimes enter therapy as "a blank wall for *the therapist's* projections"! (p. 58, my emphasis)—for "Therapists make their clients the object of their negative projections, as well as the other way around" (*ibid.*).

A therapeutic regime of truth has a whole range of determinate effects, of course—and some of them potentially "mad-making". For Sands, for example, what is so crucial is the fundamentally disrespectful stance taken by some practitioners, and the client's experience of not being believed, which can be so devastatingly undermining (personal communication). And the regime of truth is certainly exerting its hold when it leads practitioners to make the extraordinary assumption that a client's anger at a given therapist interpretation simply proves the correctness of the interpretation! (cf. her p. 55): for when a therapist is wedded to a questionable and inherently disrespectful form of logic, "his client can feel trapped by the notion that any objection proves that the therapist's suggestion is correct. Her objection might be to the fact that her feelings ... have been so peremptorily dismissed" (p. 56). Clearly, to the extent that clients are discouraged from challenging the regime of truth precisely because they fear the pathologizing response of the therapist, so is the regime of therapeutic truth insulated from challenge, and is thereby tacitly perpetuated *irrespective of whether such perpetuation is deserved or not*. Therapist complacency, not to mention sheer ignorance of the self-fulfilling consequences of their regime of truth, could so easily be—and, I submit, often is—the result of this state of affairs.

In sum, then, an unproblematized regime of therapeutic truth can lead a therapist to "unconsciously expect the client to encompass their reality" (p. 13), and inculcate "a way of thinking ..." (p. 3). The implication of this, as I have written elsewhere (House, 1999b), is that in order to avoid imposing a subjectivity-constructing straightjacket of therapeutic orthodoxy, therapy at its best should be *ongoingly and processually deconstructive* of its professional ideologies and clinical practices if the kinds of dangers so ably highlighted in *FfT* are to be as far as possible avoided.

"Material generation"

[D]oesn't therapy sometimes reveal, sometimes replicate, and sometimes *create* the feelings and behaviour that arise there? [p. 133, my emphasis]

As discussed in Chapter 3 and elsewhere in this book, "material generation" refers to the disturbing insight that therapy can, *in and of itself*, create difficulties—which then provide "material" which gives therapy much of its *raison d'être*—or in other words, therapy can quite surreptitiously and self-fulfillingly generate the difficulties to which it *then* offers a solution! Thus, it is by no means necessarily true that problems that arise in therapy can always be ascribed to what is being imported from "outside"—e.g. from the client's past (p. 133); and therapy can "reinforce fear and pain" when it "recreates and amplifies ... old problems" (p. 137). For "so-called solutions ... may even perpetuate the problem" (p. 144), with the emphasizing of difficulties "simply mak[ing] us feel more imprisoned by them" (p. 152).

New clients typically enter a therapy relationship in a position of far inferior knowledge about what to expect, and in such circumstances, "Therapy then becomes, in part, a process of learning how to deal with an environment which is ... singular and unknown" (p. 29)—one which can itself become "an additional source of disturbance" (*ibid.*). There can be little doubt that the orthodox analytic "blank screen" stance *is* material-generating: thus, "An absence of response can ... become, in itself, a diversion away from what the client is trying to sort out" (p. 86).

It could be countered that it is not therapy (or analytic therapy) *per se*, as a generality, that "generates material", but (for example) the (previously hidden or dormant?) "issues" the client brings into therapy, or the personality of the therapist, or the particular therapeutic approach followed. I return at length to this critical question in my "Discussion" section (this chapter). Sands herself offers one clear argument for therapy *qua therapy* being a culprit, when she writes that *"Because the focus is always on the client*, the system becomes pernicious, feeding the problems it highlights and leaving the client carrying the burden of responsibility" (p. 153, my emphasis). There might well be considerable mileage in this insight for sorting out precisely how it can be that therapy *qua* therapy can be a self-fulfilling material-generating enterprise.

Perhaps there can all too easily be something very seductive about therapy which can then very easily precipitate counter-therapeutic effects. Certainly, Rosie Alexander (see Chapter 6) repeatedly describes the kind of hypnotic, mesmerizing thrall into which she felt drawn, and from which she found it quite impossible to withdraw. Similarly, Sands revealingly writes that although some of her first analyst's comments were "irrelevant, far-fetched or illogical" ..., at the same time *I was seduced*. I had fallen for therapy and, as a result, my truth ... often took a back seat. Instead of rejecting ideas that felt out of place, I tried to find meaning in them" (p. 57, my emphasis)—material generation *par excellence*. Perhaps an ethical, responsible psychotherapy should do all it can to minimize such effects, in order to neutralize the possibly pernicious counter-therapeutic effects that can be precipitated in such an interpersonally intense, rarefied, and individualized framework.

The thorny problem of informed consent

How do I, the client—or how, in the end, can anyone—distinguish with any certainty between those things which are caused by the flaws of the system, or by therapist error, and those things which are caused by transference and which, with persistence, might be resolved? [p. 166]

The issue of informed consent arguably constitutes one of the most complex and under-recognized problems of the whole therapy experience. Thus, although "most of us assume it will be beneficial" (p. 3), "I had no idea what I was letting myself in for" (p. 4); "no one tells the client the rules of the psychotherapy game" (p. 22); and "Going into any kind of potentially healing relationship is, inevitably, an act of faith" (p. 26). Certainly, *how to be* in a relationship that is "a hazardous journey to an unknown destination in which we are each dependent on our travelling companion" (p. 48) will, for many, be highly problematic. Perhaps the most a client can expect is to "consent" to there being no way of knowing what will subsequently unfold in the therapy encounter—except that the therapist will be working within the bounds of a clear and published set of ethical guidelines.

The difficulties are only compounded when "doubts about a certain therapist or style of therapy may only become manifest when it is too late" (p. 144). And unless mistakes along the way are glaringly obvious, it is often only when the work is finished that we can properly judge the outcome. At what point in therapy do we evaluate the outcome? ... How long does one wait? How many times does one try? ... Perhaps it's a bit like fruit machines—the more you put in, the greater can be the desire to keep on going until you get something back (pp. 164, 165, 121, 122). Moreover, to what extent is a client in therapy able to make a relatively dispassionate assessment of her therapy when she is in the middle of the process?

What possible responses might there be to the inevitable asymmetry of knowledge about what therapy entails? For Sands, "Professional practitioners cannot afford to play down the dangers involved in the potency of the cocktail they offer" (p. 90)—for "How many clients are aware of the ... huge emotional investment and upheaval therapy involves? Most of us are not" (p. 131). Might practitioners be open from the outset, at initial meeting stage, that it is *in principle* impossible for either party to know what will happen in a particular therapy relationship, and therefore impossible for the client to give informed consent to the content of their future therapy experience? Yet how many practitioners would dare to be so honest at the outset, for fear of putting off at least some, and possibly many, new potential clients?—difficult questions indeed ...

In sum, it is surely every practitioner's responsibility to be fully aware of the "impossible" position in which new clients routinely find themselves on entering therapy, and that they actively inform new clients about what they might subsequently experience in therapy—or in other words, a conscious and deliberate attempt to *demystify* therapy and its associated regime of truth; and that *such an ongoing demystification process should be explicitly built in to the therapeutic process from beginning to end*. Therapists will then at least be doing their level best to minimize the possibility that a mesmerizing or self-fulfilling regime of truth is being imposed upon suggestible clients.

Questions of accountability

[T]here is no other profession in which the practitioner is so well equipped to attribute a lack of success to the client's problems rather than his own. And there is no other situation in which the client would so easily allow herself to be dumfounded by this assertion. [p. 160]

Sands makes it absolutely clear, first, that she did *not* want to make any formal complaint against her first therapist (p. 175): all she wanted was for him "to acknowledge that he was partly responsible for what had been a terrifying disintegration" (*ibid.*). But the confusion, shame, and hurt she had experienced "was never addressed either by my analyst or his colleagues" (*ibid.*). The reticence she discovered hardly inspired Sands' confidence in the "profession" of psychotherapy: "When things go wrong in therapy, and no one is prepared to talk about why, the general public is right to question the integrity of the profession" (p. 178). And such reticence can precipitate yet more traumatization, with clients being left "feeling alienated and further disempowered" (p. 180).

All this is very sobering for those who would professionalize the therapy field along the lines of the conventional professions. For "Some therapists have a tendency to conduct themselves as if they belong to a secret society" (p. 179): "the relevant umbrella organisation" told Sands that her ex-analyst couldn't meet with her "for insurance reasons", because she had made a complaint (p. 181)—despite Sands having emphasized that that she "had no wish to take him to court and the last thing I wanted was money" (*ibid.*). Sands had to turn to the professional literature for confirmation that things can indeed "go wrong" in therapy (*ibid.*). One can only speculate about the motivations for such quasi-Kafka-esque secrecy—therapists' (understandable?) fear of costly and potentially humiliating litigation?; professional organizations' spin-driven desire to minimize bad publicity at a time when they are assiduously seeking statutory regulation of the field? ...

Sands remains impressively and maturely non-litigious about the whole situation: for as she states, "If accountability is reduced to the villains-and-victims mentality of the insurance broker, then therapy will not move forward. Legislation and formal contracts can undermine the very principles one is trying to safeguard—those of partnership and, ultimately, understanding and agreement" (pp. 185–186)—*therapy bureaucracies and policy-makers please take note!* ... Sands' deep desire is for a human rather than a legalized resolution of conflict—"When therapy has been the opposite of therapeutic, the client needs and deserves an apology, and informed and balanced feedback" (p. 184).

The unresolved conflict between the author and the UKCP continues fascinatingly to unravel in the pages of the journal *Self and Society*.

Features of good-enough therapy

When I worked with [my second therapist], I did not feel unequal or less powerful. Two people can meet as equals in a relationship which is asymmetrical, if they meet first and foremost as two people. [p. 27]

One theme that recurs at several points—paralleling the views of Peter Lomas and David Smail—is how an authentic, unpretentious *ordinariness* can be a highly effective antidote to the rarefied preciousness that can characterize therapy at its worst. Thus, we read that "In my experience, good therapy feels not unlike a normal conversation ... 'normal conversations' about everyday things ... can have an important role to play" (p. 10)—rather than always being interpreted as "a defence" or "resistance". "In my second experience of therapy ... it was an adult relationship with a real, receptive person" (p. 76)—in contrast to her first therapist, with whom she "sometimes felt he did not speak to me as if I was a normal human being" (p. 33). For Sands, "When therapy distorts the ordinary, we ... perpetuate a feeling of illegitimacy. ... [I]t is necessary to cherish the ordinary enough to leave it alone" (pp. 187, 153).

Sands also alludes to *flexibility*. In terms of appointments, "It should be possible to strike a sensible balance between flexibility and consistency" (p. 15)—a principle which, some might argue, might profitably be far more widely applied. Her second therapist was happy to meet at increasingly infrequent intervals (p. 16). Moreover, rather than the roles of "therapist" and "client" being immutably fixed and immobile, Sands evokes a more fluid, postmodern approach to therapy—for a therapeutic journey of freedom "involves the client being able to act both as a person and a client, and the therapist being able to act both as a person and a therapist" (p. 157).

Sands also wants a therapist who is willing to discuss the dangers of therapy (p. 175). She wants laughter and joy as well as pain (p. 202); a therapist who believes in mystery and enchantment rather than psychopathology (p. 197); a therapy which "salvage[s] the sacred and honour[s] our sacredness" (p. 195). She wants a therapy which recognizes that "we are more than a simple reductionist equation of cause and effect. If psychotherapy is to be an honourable profession, it must honour and nurture our essentialness ..., the unanalysable what-you-are-made-of" (*ibid.*). At its best, therapy is for her "a celebration of the richness and dynamism of the psyche", recognizing "the greatest gift of all—our shared humanity" (pp. 194, 149).

In advocating a deeply human(e), creative approach to therapy, Sands' description offers us—if we, as a "profession", are able to hear it—an invaluable cautionary reminder about what can happen when a practitioner- and therapy-centred ideology threatens to obscure the source of what is truly healing within a genuinely helping encounter.

Discussion

What about therapy's shadow? [p. 112]

To what extent are Sands' arguments generalizable to therapy *in general*? She maintains, for example, that psychotherapy *qua psychotherapy* "can promote a dissolving of the adult's boundary between fantasy and reality, and cause similar confusion and turmoil" (p. 81). However, to say that turmoil (for example) *can* occur within therapy is not *necessarily* the same as saying that it is "psychotherapy" *in and of itself* that causes such malaise. This is a critical—and complex—area of concern that surely requires urgent attention in the field. It might be, for example, that certain approaches to therapy are more likely to precipitate such effects; or that a certain type of "personality" (therapist, client—or both) might, for whatever reason(s), precipitate it.

One possible argument might be that, because therapy in general tends to focus on, and disproportionately accentuate, "the negative" in human experience, this in turn can "cause our existing fears [for example] to *appear* more rather than less substantial, and throw in a few extra ones for good measure" (p. 90, my emphasis). Or cast in the discourse of the present book, *the subjective experience of clients in therapy may take on a distorted one-sidedness that matches the artificial bias towards the negative of the typical therapeutic regime of truth.* And if, then, clients in therapy experience such distorted subjectivity as an intrinsic aspect of their "*true*" identity rather than as, in some sense, a distorted artefact of the artificial therapy setting, this could easily *create* and precipitate (for example) crises of identity, and even sanity, that simply were not present or active before the client entered therapy. On this scenario, it could then plausibly be claimed that it is therapy *qua therapy* that has (unnecessarily?) "materially generated" client disturbance.

Regarding *therapy's contradictions*: Sands found her analyst's impersonal manner incongruous within what is "a highly personal setting" (p. 12). Moreover, therapy is at once "relatively formal" *and* "unusually intimate"—and to Sands, "the two seemed at times to be impossibly incompatible" (p. 21). Another contradiction is that the ethical therapist's task is effectively *to put herself out of a job!*—i.e. to help clients (presumably as effectively *and efficiently* as possible) *not* to require further therapy. Put bluntly, where private therapists commonly need their clients in order to pay the mortgage and feed the family, *just what less-than-conscious forces might surreptitiously feed into our therapeutic approaches that might—albeit unwittingly—render therapy grossly inefficient for the paying client, and self-serving for the practitioner?* (Note that I am not needing to invoke some kind of crude conspiracy theory here—merely suggesting that therapists' collective survival needs may well have all kinds of scarcely visible, unintended effects in terms of therapeutic practices and their associated theoretical rationales; and given all we know about unconscious group processes, it would be very surprising if there *weren't* such effects.) The "endings question", and how therapists routinely make such a precious, fetishized drama out of endings, might well constitute one example of the way in which therapeutic practice is unwittingly colonized by the therapist's own needful agenda rather than that of the client.

Further, because "the therapist is ... so dependent on the client ...—is ... dependent on their need for his help, the very thing which he works towards eliminating" (p. 123), might therapy not typically be setting up *an institutionalized co-dependency relationship* from which, once established, it often becomes very difficult for either client or therapist to extricate themselves?—albeit for different dependency reasons, of course. *These again are highly prescient and challenging questions that, I contend, the nascent therapy "profession" simply cannot ignore any longer.*

Overall, *FfT* is certainly not a partisan or partial "therapy-bashing" exercise (as a book such as this one could so easily have become)—and in this sense Sands is continuing the admirable tradition first initiated by the late Ann France in her excellent book *Consuming Psychotherapy* (see Chapter 7). However, a strong advocate of the beneficence of therapy might object that the analysis offered in *FfT* and in this chapter is heavily biased against therapy. I do not pretend to have offered a balanced view of therapy in my "reading" of *FfT*; rather, I see *FfT* as providing *some kind of necessary counterweight to the heavy preponderance of largely uncritical therapist- and profession-centred literature that dominates the therapy field.* For as Sands herself correctly points out, "the literature on therapy ... often fails to demonstrate a consideration of the client's perspective" (p. 191). Lest there be any ambiguity, let me state quite categorically that I am personally convinced of the efficacy and beneficence of a great deal of therapy; but I am equally convinced by the importance of the arguments and challenges in *FfT*—and in this book—and the urgent need for therapy in general to face and respond to them fearlessly and without trimming, if therapeutic practice is to continue to mature rather than degenerate into a self-serving, self-perpetuating "regime of profession-centred truth".

Perhaps both client *and* therapist are subject to therapy's constraining regime of truth—albeit in different ways, and clearly with different effects. It seems to me that what is required is a sincere, whole-hearted attempt by both therapists and clients to place themselves in the shoes of the other (*Verstehen*)—and to carry an awareness of the *inherent impossibility* (Winnicott) of the relational enterprise in which they are co-creatively engaged. Notice that what I provocatively call therapy's "inherent impossibility" does not necessarily entail that therapy can't work—indeed, *perhaps the benefits that can result derive specifically from each side's honourable struggle with this very impossibility.*

Conclusions

Sometimes therapy becomes part of the problem instead of offering some solutions. [p. 171]

In her Introduction Sands states that her book is "about how it feels to be on the receiving end of therapy" (p. viii). My overriding impression of *FfT* is that it is veritably overflowing with intelligent, "dispassionately passionate" insight into the process of therapy. At one point, Sands offers a list of questions that any practising or aspiring therapist should surely ask themselves—for example, "Why do you spend all day being anonymous ...?; Do you enjoy being in a position of power? ... What about your need for control? ... Why do you wish to have intense relationships, closeted behind a closed door, in return for money? ... What makes you want to analyse another, to play the role of parent, to be of such importance to those who come your way?" (p. 112). Do I hear a collective "oouucchh!" from "the profession"? ...—surely a very appropriate response to such astute, uncomfortable questions.

I contend that, far from being dismissive (which *will* no doubt happen if therapists are too defended and self-interested to hear what she has to say), we should be extremely grateful to Anna Sands for having opened a revealing portal on to our constructed professional selves—and showing therapists that we have *at least* as much to learn from our clients as they from us.

I would argue that the extent to which *FfT* is embraced as a core text for therapy and counselling trainings will strongly indicate whether psychotherapy and counselling are yet sufficiently open or mature to deserve their increasingly sought-after status of recognized, legitimate "professions".

To date in this book, I have relentlessly deconstructed what I see as the often deleterious effects of therapy's tacitly taken-for-granted regime of therapeutic truth. After such a deconstruction, what might be left of therapy as a culturally legitimate, enabling, and empowering healing practice to aid people in their "difficulties of living"? In the remainder of this book, I begin the process of outlining what such a "postmodern" therapeutic praxis might look like. I begin this exploration with a close look at one extraordinary practitioner whose work and writings I see as in many ways prefiguring the current postmodern turn in therapy—namely, the contemporary and sometime friend of Sigmund Freud, Georg Groddeck.

Note

1. For the sake of succinctness and non-repetition, this chapter on Anna Sands' *Falling for Therapy* is considerably abbreviated from the original version (House, 2001e)—a copy of which can be sent by the author on request, via e-mail attachment—contact richardahouse@hotmail.com

PART III
A NEW PARADIGM,
POST-PROFESSIONAL ERA?

Consider:

> "... we are shifting from a physical to a *metaphysical* vision of reality—from matter to energy, from materialism to mentalism, from fragmentation to wholeness, from an inert universe to a conscious, evolving universe. We are moving beyond the rational mind ..."
>
> Edwards, 1992: 197, her emphasis

> "All paths end in metaphysics"
>
> Durrell, 1948: 397

CHAPTER NINE

Precursor of post-modernity: the phenomenon of Georg Groddeck[1]

"The age does need its Groddecks, and will continue to need them"

Lawrence Durrell, 1948: 384

Introduction

We know or seek to know what we can get by learning. Groddeck sees and knows without making this detour. [Simmel, quoted in Schacht, 1977: 8]

The foregoing epigraph from Georg Simmel is fascinating not least because it challenges our conventional, Western, culture-bound assumptions about what constitutes (valid) "knowledge" in human experience. Our whole world-view is in large part uncritically preoccupied with and dominated by "objectivity", experimental verification or "proof", linear–causal reasoning, Aristotelian logic, and all the other leitmotivs of the Western scientific *Zeitgeist*. We are deeply challenged by any suggestion that there might be qualitatively different, more creative, and at least as "valid" ways of "knowing" that the modern technocratic mentality is scarcely able to imagine, differing so radically as they do from that mentality's narrowly positivistic ontological framework. Perhaps this explains, at least in part, why pioneering counter-cultural figures like Georg Groddeck, Goethe, and Rudolf Steiner have been so criminally neglected in the Western "history of ideas".

In this the first chapter of Part III, I begin my foray into the "New Paradigm" world by examining the ideas and healing practice of the German healer-cum-analyst-cum-philosopher-cum-artist/art critic, Georg Groddeck, as a means of illustrating the woeful limitations of the existing paradigm that dominates our therapeutic culture, and of giving a glimpse of the kind of world-view that a New Paradigm promises. I believe that many of the difficulties with therapy as outlined in Parts I and II of this book stem from a dramatically incongruent (and typically implicit) adherence to fear-driven old-paradigm thinking—which cannot but severely limit the creativity and potential that any therapeutic experience could, and perhaps should, offer.

When I first came across the writings of Georg Groddeck in the early 1990s, I was greatly excited by his ideas, and not least because they coincided so closely with my own evolving thinking about healing, holism, and the nature of the therapeutic process. I felt as if I'd found a philosophical soul-mate; and I found it quite extraordinary that, having done some 4–5 years of training in counselling and psychotherapy, I had never even heard his name mentioned before I happened upon his seminal book *The Meaning of Illness* (1977) in the course of a library literature search about illness and disease. And yet in our rationality- and intellectually-dominated age of scientific reasoning, empiricist epistemologies, and mechanistic–technocratic ways of seeing the world, perhaps the notable neglect of Groddeck's work should come as no surprise.

Georg Groddeck the man, 1866–1934

We understand man better when we see the whole in each of his parts. [Groddeck, quoted in Durrell, 1948: 403]

Groddeck was a German physician practising around the turn of the century, who shared his physician-father's scepticism about so-called "medical science". He spent nearly all of his adult life in the German town of Baden-Baden, where he practised medicine, and specialising in particular on "treating" terminally ill patients. He did not feel any strong patriotic identifications (Homer, 1988: 10; cf. Krishnamurti's views on nationalism—Krishnamurti Foundation Trust, 1992: 351–354), which was both exceptional and remarkable for anyone living in Germany in this turbulent era of European history. He once said that there are Germans, Frenchmen—and Groddecks!—and "he always felt different and had no need for group identification" (Homer, 1988: 10). His father was also a physician, and Groddeck's mentor was Bismarck's unorthodox physician Ernst Schweninger.

Significantly, and like his contemporary Otto Rank, Groddeck began as a poet and a writer, and only in middle life did he turn to physicianship and "healing" (Durrell, 1948: 396). In an editorial in the BAC journal *Counselling*, editor Judith Longman wrote of "the sensibility of the mystic or the poet" perhaps being at least as effective in practitionership as the performance of the "practitioner-scientist" (Longman, 1998)—which view points clearly to the woeful limitations, and even wrong-headedness, of trying to make the therapeutic experience cohere with the world-view of modern empirical science (cf. Chapter 10, below). For Groddeck, the healer or therapist was definitely *an artist* rather than a scientist, "who has, by the surrender of his ego to the flux of the It, become the agent and translator of the extra-causal forces that rule us" (Durrell, 1948: 399). I return to Groddeck's interesting insights on "science" later in the chapter—and also to his notion of the "It", just mentioned.

Groddeck—physician, healer ... and analyst

People have described [Groddeck] as a physician who burst like a storm into the soul of men, penetrating into the depths where all life is one, all boundaries are broken down, and body and mind are fused together. [Boss, in Groddeck, 1951: 23]

According to Groddeck's translator, V. M. E. Collins (in Groddeck, 1951: 5–6), he became known in both Germany and England "as a masterful physician who had astonishing success with patients suffering from chronic symptoms long since abandoned as non-curable by others". Groddeck held the view that disease and ill-health were the result of "the patient's whole manner of living and attitude to life", and he strongly maintained that it was the patient–doctor relationship that was more important than any other factor in the treatment of illness and disease (*ibid.*). To the person-centred, humanistic therapist this may all sound very familiar, but such ideas were far from commonplace in Groddeck's time, and we can now see his form of "patient-centred medicine" to be decades ahead of its time—certainly as far as modern Western medicine is concerned. Homer stresses Groddeck's non-directiveness: "In his non-directive way, Groddeck departed from many of the early psychoanalysts, and resembles, among others, Carl Rogers, Rollo May, and George Weinberg" (Homer, 1988: 33).

It is also somewhat counterintuitive and seemingly paradoxical that one who believed the causes of sickness and disease to be intrinsically unknowable in any "scientific" sense (Durrell, 1948: 387) could have been such an inspired and successful healer. And needless to say, I do not consider it to be a coincidence that someone who quite explicitly stated that "on the outset of diseases. ... I know nothing ... [and] about their cure. ... I know just nothing at all" (quoted in *ibid.*: 395) was by all accounts such an exceptionally effective healer.

It was with the discovery of Freud's ideas and the growing discipline of psychoanalysis that Groddeck was able to find confirmation, between 1910 and 1918, of his developing ideas about the influence of unconscious symbolism in producing illness and disease symptoms; and in 1917 he published a pamphlet called "Mental Determination of Organic Disease"—again, prefiguring by many decades recent advances in the science of psychoneuro-immunology (e.g. Lyon, 1993) and related fields. Collins is very definite in maintaining that the course of Groddeck's theories about disease and healing would have been the same whether or not Freud and Freudian psychoanalysis had existed (Groddeck, 1951: 9). Indeed, as early as 1888 Groddeck was concerned with the role of unconscious forces in organic disease (*ibid.*: 26); and it is no surprise that Groddeck is often regarded as the father of psychosomatic medicine. Like Jung, his concept of the unconscious was far wider than that of Freud, and he constantly tested his theory on its most difficult and challenging terrain, that of chronic and mainly organic disease—in a way that philosopher of science Karl Popper (e.g. 1963) would doubtless have approved of.

As Durrell (1948: 388) points out, Groddeck was "using Freud for ends far greater than Freud himself could ever perceive". He departed radically from Freud both in terms of the forces assumed to produce health and illness, and also on the very nature of causality itself (an issue I discuss later in this chapter). In reading Groddeck's biographies (Grossman & Grossman, 1965; Homer, 1988), the running tension between Freud's own scientific–materialist world-view and that of Groddeck is continually erupting to the surface in their fascinating (and often intimate) correspondence (most of which is reproduced in Groddeck, 1977). In 1922, for example, Freud wrote to Groddeck, "I do not share your Panpsychism, *which amounts almost to mysticism* ... I believe you too-early despised reason and science" (quoted in Grossman & Grossman, 1965: 123–124, my emphasis). Yet despite their differences, "Freud's genius was able to understand and tolerate the very different genius of Groddeck" (Schacht, 1977: 27)—which represents a very powerful endorsement, given Freud's notorious intolerance of anyone who did not agree with his theoretical formulations. Groddeck's biographer Homer notes, however, that Groddeck was at pains to avoid "fractious disputes" with Freud (Homer, 1988: 23).

We may speculate that perhaps Freud saw in Groddeck the spiritual part of himself which he had so systematically denied in the course of rendering his new "science" of psychoanalysis legitimate within, and acceptable to, the scientific-materialist culture of his day. It is both fascinating and highly revealing that Freud's sometimes sycophantically loyal admirer and biographer Ernest Jones, who was at the time complaining about untrained "wild" analysts setting themselves up as analysts (Grossman & Grossman, 1965: 62), saw Groddeck as "an amusing oddity"! (*ibid*.: 93).

It will be useful to quote Collins on Groddeck's approach, written over 50 years ago now, as it could word-for-word be taken as a present-day description of humanistic person-centred therapy:

he learned to feel himself into the patient's situation and to look at life through his eyes. By this self-immolation, this submerging of himself in the mind of another, he was able ... to touch some key to the forces of life, and to cure many who had been ill so long that they came to him in despair rather than in hope.... [He became] the great-hearted friend to his patients, the unjudging commentator, the ever-ready helper. [Groddeck, 1951: 9–10]

Collins quotes Groddeck himself as saying, "If you really want to be my follower, look at life for yourself and tell the world honestly what you see" (*ibid.*: 10). And Robb states that for Groddeck, moral judgements were absent (*ibid.*: 14).

Yet Groddeck also believed in the *psychodynamics* of healing, and he is quite explicit about this—which makes him possibly the first theorist to show how a fundamentally humanistic approach to helping the distressed and the sick, combined with a psychodynamic understanding, is one key to effective healing. Thus, Groddeck himself writes in rather orthodox analytic fashion, "Any sick person who needs help must come under the influence of the transference as part of the cure ... he [the patient] will unconsciously act the child and put the doctor in the place of the father or mother" (*ibid.*: 189); and it is the handling of the resistance to the transference which constitutes "the alpha and omega of the healing art, no matter what the disease" (*ibid.*: 191; cf. Stein, 1985a). Groddeck prefigures Karl Menninger's views, expressed many years later (Menninger, 1963: Chapter 15), on the role of faith (and other so-called non-specific "intangibles" or subtleties) in treatment: "where it [faith] is lacking the doctor can be of little use, whatever resources may be at his disposal ..." (1951: 266).

A famous patient of Groddeck's, Keyserling, in his 1934 obituary, wrote: "He [Groddeck] took the view that the doctor really knows nothing, and of himself can do nothing ..., for *his very presence* can provoke to action the patient's own powers of healing" (*ibid.*: 12, my emphasis). Orbach (1994: 5) writes that "language has for many of us a way of hiding our feelings from ourselves, and a way of not disclosing them to others" (practitioners who believe that therapeutic change is necessarily a predominantly verbal, conscious, cognitive process, please note); and how fitting is such an insight in illuminating Groddeck's extraordinary success as a healer—for it appears that "the real essence of Groddeck's treatment was his silent presence. One could be with him when he asked no questions at all, and be more responsive than when under treatment by the cleverest of psychoanalysts" (Groddeck, 1951: 12). Here is Groddeck himself: "Silence may be strangling of a word but it is none the less expressive of meaning" (*ibid*.: 207).

I have argued elsewhere (House, 1996f) that it is essentially love that facilitates the client's healing (a point made at different times in different ways by, among others, Rueben Fine, Peter Lomas, Carl Rogers, Anthony Storr, and Donald Winnicott); so it should come as no surprise that "Groddeck was one of the few men who fittingly and inevitably called forth love, friendship and reverence in all who were able to know him" (Morris Robb, quoted in Groddeck, 1951: 14). According to his translator, Collins, "The fate of his patients concerned him far more than that of his theories" (*ibid*.: 28)—which could certainly not be said of Freud! (cf. House, 1999b). Groddeck himself put it thus: "Without the arrow of Eros no wound can heal, no operation succeed ..." (1951: 189); and as remarked earlier, Groddeck fully immersed himself in his patients' worlds, rather than relying on mere intellectual or theoretical awareness of "the facts" of the case. And—"professionalizers" and regulators please note!—for Robb, "it is impossible to schematise such a [healing] process, and *to talk of training anyone else to achieve its results is absurd*, yet some approximation to a character of this sort is *the only* basis on which psychotherapeutic power can be built" (*ibid*.: 15, my emphases).

Groddeck was also very much a "wounded healer" (to use Jung's term): his parents, play-mate sister, and brothers all died when he was still young—losses which "by some strange alchemy ... were transmuted into a fuller understanding of life, death, and grief" (*ibid*.). Perhaps it was, at least in part, because of his profound insight and "knowing" about pain and suffering that he became a threatening figure to many: to quote Kollerstrom, "Some are offended and hurry away lest he should reveal to them their own hidden sores" (*ibid*.: 20).

Here, then, may reside another reason why Groddeck's extraordinary contributions have been so comparatively ignored: for just as Otto Rank's challenge to Freudian orthodoxy, with his views on the trauma of birth, was systematically "frozen out" in the 1920s (and since) due to the unconscious and commonly unassimilable terror that his theoretical breakthrough represented (Wasdell, 1990), just so, Groddeck's capacity quite spontaneously to go straight to the core of a person's distress would have been extremely threatening and even dangerous for those as yet unable to contain the full reality of their own woundedness and the rawness of their primitive (including prenatal) developmental histories. Furthermore, "People were ... so much absorbed in sorting out the emotions he evoked in them that for a long time they were not in a state to appreciate his words exactly" (1951: 20). Collins wrote about half a century ago that Groddeck's ideas "were indeed so strange and unexpected, *so contrary to the crass materialism of his own generation*, that it may be years before his contribution to medical science is fully understood" (*ibid*.: 28, my emphasis). Sadly, perhaps in this sense little has really changed in the past 50 years.

For Groddeck, "*any* sort of treatment, scientific or old wive's poultice, may turn out to be right for the patient, since the outcome of medical or other treatment is not determined by the means prescribed but by what the patient's It likes to make of the prescription" (*ibid*.: 78–79, his emphasis; see p. 186, below, for a description of Groddeck's "It"). In an obituary to Groddeck, Robb revealingly wrote: "he seemed to be a part of nature, and his writings as natural as buds and flowers. Maybe this is the reason why he is taking such slow root in our culture and civilisation *which looks askance at anything not canned, labelled and patented*" (*ibid*.: 17, my emphasis).

In my own work as a counsellor working in general medical practice, I am constantly brought up against the indissoluble interdependencies of mind, body, soul, and spirit, philosophical questions of what a "person" actually consists in, and what precisely constitutes illness, disease, and health. Groddeck's philosophy quite fundamentally challenges the notions that it is valid and appropriate to "medicalize" ill-health or discomfort, that the human body is "nothing but a machine assembled from many parts" (Kollerstrom, quoted in *ibid*.: 18), that it is somehow possible to "treat" a person's body, or mind, or "faulty" thinking separately from the whole person. Broadly speaking Groddeck's approach was "the treatment of the whole organism irrespective of whether the symptoms appeared to be physical or not" (*ibid*.: 19). His philosophy, then, is the perfect antidote to the mechanistic, mind/body-split dualism of Descartes which has arguably had such a profound and deleterious effect on Western thinking for centuries.

No doubt Groddeck would have been highly critical of modern-day cognitive-behavioural approaches to therapy, because of their implicit anti-holistic ontology of the person, whereby rationality and thinking tend to be artificially split off and treated as relatively isolatable and autonomous from the rest of the person. Here is Groddeck: "up till now every step forward in technique has been paid for in increasing blindness to human life" (*ibid*.: 205–206).

Thankfully it is even starting to be recognized within science itself that "thinking" and "the emotional" form an indissolubly interdependent unity (Damasio, 1994; Goleman, 1996; cf. my discussion in Chapter 10), and that it is quite invalid to consider one level of human "beingness" while ignoring, or attempting to "hold constant", the other. A few Western philosophers have even managed to throw off the baggage of rationality-dominated analytic philosophy to reach much the same conclusion (Solomon, 1976; Oakley, 1992). Perhaps this is what Groddeck was alluding to when he wrote that "we are dishonest and misuse language when we speak of 'pure' thought" (1951: 104). On this view, then, our belief systems and ways of thinking are inextricably implicated and rooted in our emotional histories, and human experience is always and necessarily *embodied* (Johnson, 1987; Damasio, 1994). Echoing the views of Rudolf Steiner, for Groddeck, "thinking" is a concept far wider in scope than is typically assumed in our mechanistic materialist world-view: "In the assumption that one thinks only with the brain is to be found the origin of a thousand and one absurdities" (1951: 76). Thus, for example, "long before the brain comes into existence the It of man is already active and 'thinking' without the brain" (Groddeck, quoted in Durrell, 1948: 393)— echoes here again of Rudolf Steiner's philosophy and James Hillman's recently articulated "acorn theory" (Hillman, 1996).

Groddeck's approach to healing greatly illuminates current debates about the relative efficacy of differing approaches or "schools" in therapy. Here is Groddeck himself: "having found that all roads lead to Rome I do not consider it vastly important which road one takes, so long as one is willing to go slowly and is not too eager for wealth or recognition" (1951: 85). It is highly revealing to apply this thinking to the efficacy debate, for Groddeck's argument here is entirely consistent with the oft-repeated research finding that all forms of counselling and psychotherapy tend to yield very similar success rates (e.g. Bohart & Tallman, 1996). Following Groddeck, it is also clear that perhaps most of the current efficacy debate is based upon the quite false premise that it is the nature of the particular approach or technique(s) used by the practitioner which determine outcome. Seen from Groddeck's perspective, such a view is grossly naïve and just plain wrong: rather, clients-patients will "use" (in the Winnicottian sense) whatever form of help is available (from high-tech medicine at one extreme to (for example) shamanistic and spiritual healing practices at the other) in order to secure their own healing (cf. Frank & Frank, 1991). (Incidentally, this argument also accounts for what is, to many, the surprising finding that, to quote Richard Mowbray, *"there is no clear evidence that professionally trained psychotherapists are in general more effective than paraprofessionals"*— Mowbray, 1995: 118, his emphasis; and that, "Sadly, the correlation between training and effectiveness as a therapist is low"—Aveline, 1990: 321; see also Russell, 1981.)

As soon as we accept this Groddeckian view of change, then, our attention quite naturally shifts to the question of what are the barriers and blocks to clients' self-healing, rather than to the wild goose-chase of trying to determine in a so-called "scientific" sense which treatment modalities are the most efficacious when "applied to" the client-patient. Once again, then, the genius of Groddeck's insight effectively short-circuits, and makes redundant and largely irrelevant, a whole swathe literature on efficacy in the field of therapy. Psychodynamically speaking, that wrong-headed debate in the literature does, in fact, depict very clearly a distorting preoccupation with ego, control, and instrumentalist reasoning, the artificial splitting of object from subject via objectifying a process which is irreducibly (inter)subjective (cf. Chapter 10), the splitting of quality from quantity, and so on—issues to which I will have cause to return later.

Groddeck, object relations, and the transpersonal

Few people realise the meaning of that utter calm which transcends both joy and pain ..., that opening of a heaven without fear and without desire. It is no other than a union with Infinite Nature, a being at one with the creative universe, a surrender and dissolution of the barriers of personality so that the part, the ego, becomes merged with the whole. [Groddeck, 1951: 49]

Those who knew Groddeck personally, and those who write about him, testify to his quite natural affinity with the transpersonal dimension of human experience. There is a very Jungian—not to mention object-relational—flavour to his view that "everything contains its opposite within itself. ... One cannot even begin to understand life unless one realises that all its phenomena are conditioned by their opposites, that love is impossible without hatred, contempt without respect, fear without hope, loyalty without treachery" (*ibid*.: 90). In the early chapters of his *Book of the It*, Groddeck suggests that mother-hate and mother-love must be coupled together; and in his view "the intensity of the extremes of love and hate ... dominate the way the It conceptualizes all objects" (Homer, 1988: 26; see p. 186, below, for a discussion of Groddeck's "It"). Thus writes Boss (1951: 23): "he was always conscious of being at the mercy of forces greater than the self he knew"; and Robb describes how, in his writing, Groddeck would surrender himself to becoming "an impersonal instrument performing a task which is imperiously demanded of him, when he loses himself to find a greater self" (*ibid*.: 16). (In my Introduction I describe a similar process that I experienced in the writing of this book.)

In fundamental respects this remarkable man also prefigured by some years the articulation and development of psychoanalytic object relations theory, for he believed that "man creates the world in his own image, that all his inventions and activities, his science, art, finance, literature, vocabulary, industries and philosophies are in a special sense symbolic of his own nature and primitive experience" (Collins, in *ibid*.: 25). And Groddeck himself wrote that "human thought and action are the inevitable consequence of unconscious symbolisation, that mankind is animated by the symbol" (*ibid*.: 89). Echoing closely Rudolf Steiner's educational philosophy, Groddeck further writes that

in those first few hours ... and weeks of life ... the child is still accepting all that he sees as part of his own body, symbolising everything in terms of his own body. ... We ourselves never wholly abandon [such symbolisation] either in our conscious or our unconscious minds. ... Man's unconscious dependence upon symbolism in his everyday affairs ... has hardly been guessed at as yet, still less explored. [*ibid.*: 92, 152; cf., for example, Segal, 1985]

Groddeck on the limitations of the scientific mentality

Every observation is necessarily one-sided, every opinion a falsification. The act of observing disintegrates a whole into different fields of observation. ... [Groddeck, quoted in Durrell, 1948: 402]

Homer (1988: 9) points out that Groddeck had little time for the methodological canons and limiting jargon used in much of the research of his time, and that he himself was criticized (surprise surprise ...) for not being "scientific". Yet the ontology that emerges from his writings suggests that, far from being concerned by such a charge, he would almost certainly have taken it as a compliment! Certainly, and as I mentioned in my Introduction, Groddeck gravitated much more towards a kind of Bergsonian vitalism (Mullarky, 1999) than he did towards conventional scientific epistemologies (Homer, 1988: 12).

For Groddeck, there is something *intrinsically unknowable* (certainly in terms of *conventional* "knowing") about life and human-beingness—which view he formulated in his idea of "the It" (which Freud himself actually "borrowed" from Groddeck in his coining of the term "the id"). As Collins writes, Groddeck held the view that by their very nature, the unconscious forces operating in human behaviour will remain obscure and uncapturable in scientific terminology (in Groddeck, 1951: 40); and here is Groddeck himself: "The sum total of an individual human being, physical, mental, and spiritual. ... I conceive of as a self unknown and for ever unknowable, and I call this the It ..." (*ibid.*: 73). For Groddeck, the It was not a thing-in-itself, but merely a way of seeing—very reminiscent of the Tao concept (Durrell, 1948: 392). This constitutes a truly challenging and sobering perspective for those who make a fetish of "the rational" and the conscious in human experience.

Elsewhere, Groddeck refers to "the tyranny of conscious thought" (1951: 103). For him, the tyranny of the thinking ego "has left us without a faith in anything greater than ourselves, and is in large measure responsible for those troubles which are threatening our very existence today" (*ibid.*: 106; cf. House, 1996i). As Durrell (1948: 386) has it, "to Groddeck the ego appeared as a contemptible mask fathered on us by the intellect", with "an ideological scaffolding which the ego has run around itself" (p. 389). Many decades later we find Jill Hall writing that "Rational thought is not the most fitting mode with which to know the universe in its richness and fullness, and thus not a fitting mode with which to know ourselves" (Hall, 1993: 4; cf. Hart *et al.*, 1997). For Groddeck, then, it was not medical science and the application of objective, disembodied skills or techniques that helped people in distress or dis(-)ease, but rather, "that place of utter sincerity and selflessness where to be human is enough" (Collins, in Groddeck, 1951: 29). These are indeed the kinds of "intangibles" that are *an intrinsic accompaniment* of growth and healing which, among others, Karl Menninger (e.g. 1963) in medicine, and Rudolf Steiner (e.g. 1995, 1996) and Max van Manen (1986) within educational pedagogy, have emphasized so strongly. The danger is, of course, that *the very act* of endeavouring to make therapy "respectable" according to the canons of orthodox empiricist science will effectively destroy precisely that which is most effective in healing and therapeutic change. And Groddeck was clearly all too aware of this danger. In this book I argue passionately that *it is necessary to challenge the very foundations of modernity and its associated world-view* if these grave dangers are to be avoided (cf. Chapters 10 and 11).

According to Groddeck, the fundamental error that the scientific enterprise makes is to assume that its practices are not subject to the same unconscious forces that are operating in all other domains of existence and experience. Groddeck strongly believed that "the unconscious forces at work in human behaviour are too obscure—and by their very nature will probably always remain so—to be confined in strictly scientific terminology" (Collins, in Groddeck, 1951: 40). Thus, science was just another expression of fantasy that has no legitimate right to the pre-eminence that it so arrogantly proclaims: for the I is an illusion/delusion of the It, and can therefore never form the basis of sound, "objective" knowledge or truth about the world or human existence. Yet "we always proceed as if the I is sovereign" (Homer, 1988: 21)—which, for Groddeck, it most certainly isn't. As Homer puts it, "we might get at truth and being if we drop much of the pretense of the I and learn the rules of the It ..., [but] we never completely get around the problem of truth residing with the It and not the I" (*ibid.*: 18, 21).

Here is the prominent neurologist Antonio Damasio (1994) expressing similar scepticism about the modern scientific project in his important book *Descartes' Error*: "I am sceptical of science's presumption of objectivity and definitiveness. ... Perhaps the complexity of the human mind is such that the solution to the problem can never be known because of our inherent limitations. Perhaps we should not even talk about a problem at all, and speak instead of a mystery ..." (1994: xviii). As Collins so beautifully puts it, Groddeck never forgot "picture, poem and song whilst working for the relief of the sick and the sorrow-laden" (Groddeck, 1951: 31).

Some 70 years after Groddeck, Hall writes further that

> the time has come to go beyond causal thinking. ... If material existence is far too intricate and subtle a phenomenon to be understood through a cause/effect mode of thought, then surely we must let go the attempt to approach the human psyche from such a standpoint. When we come to try to understand the psyche causal thinking is not only inadequate but is even positively dangerous. [Hall, 1993: 2, 7]

Yet nearly a century ago, Groddeck was writing that "because we live we are bound to believe that ... there are such things as causes and effects ..., whereas *we really know nothing about the connection between one event and another*" (Groddeck, 1951: 77, my emphasis; cf. David Hume's famous "problem of induction"). In our ego-bound and control-oriented way, furthermore, we delude ourselves in believing that we are masters of nature and of ourselves —a view which "is assuredly false", but which it is necessary in our day-to-day lives to assume to be true (*ibid.*). The essential quality of man, according to Groddeck, is "his overestimation of himself" (*ibid.*: 78)—otherwise we will experience ourselves as impotent (or "victims", to use Hall's terminology). Yet at this stage in the evolution of human consciousness, the ego is enormously reluctant even to countenance the view that "everything important happens outside our knowledge and control" (*ibid.*).

For Groddeck, then, the scientific approach to reality is fundamentally alienating of our true nature. Many decades ago now, Groddeck wrote that "the more [man] struggles after exactitude in charting the world outside himself, the more deeply does he sink into his bondage to the ego" (*ibid*.: 105). For Groddeck, language is necessarily "cut off from its symbolic expression, and ... we must [therefore] go to the unconscious for evidence that the symbol is still operative in the depth of human nature" (*ibid*.: 199). And "Through psychoanalysis we have come to understand that the symbol is vital, *that it is life itself*" (*ibid*.: 267, my emphasis).

There can be little doubt that if Groddeck were alive today, he would have no truck whatsoever with the current fashion of cognitive-behavioural approaches to therapy: for as well as his disparagingly referring to "the tyranny of conscious thought", he writes a bit later that "There is little doubt that we Europeans have had enough to do with thinking" (*ibid*.: 104); and "Our brains are being overtaxed by the continual effort to suppress our real nature—primitive, purposeful ...—in favour of what we take to be the real, the objective" (p. 106). Yet in what is a truly postmodern tone, for Groddeck we can never *in principle* fully, or even approximately, know the real: thus, he refers to "the arrogance which refuses to recognise the inevitable limitations of human knowledge" (*ibid*.); and while "presumably the Real exists, ... never for one moment can we come into contact with it" (p. 91).

Groddeck on Goethean science

> It is with the heart that one rightly sees; what is essential is invisible to the eye. [Antoine de Saint-Exupéry, quoted in Goleman, 1996: 3]

Groddeck shared with the sage and modern Initiate Rudolf Steiner (1968, 1988) an extensive knowledge of and respect for Goethe's approach to science, prefiguring by almost a century the recent New Paradigm upsurge of interest in Goethean science (Bortoft, 1996; Naydler, 1996). It is interesting and significant that Groddeck invoked the term "God Nature", which he took from Goethe (Schacht, 1977: 11). Over 90 years ago Groddeck prophetically wrote with quite remarkable foresight that

> Goethe was greater as a scientist than as a poet. We can foresee now that in centuries to come people will rightly say that he was one of

the greatest thinkers of all times. He showed science a new approach, namely the approach of *seeing the part in the whole*, of taking the apparent whole as a symbol of the universe, of seeing the whole world symbolised in a flower, an animal, a pebble, the human eye, the sun; and to construct the world from this flower, this pebble, that is to create it anew and *to investigate things not by analysing but by placing them in the context of the whole*. He opened up this approach to science *which will achieve undreamed-of results* in fields which have so far been untested and unknown, for *hardly have we started on this approach*. [Groddeck, 1977: 252, my emphases]

It is little wonder that Groddeck was drawn to Goethe's holistic and inspirational vision of the scientific method, for by all accounts he possessed those artistic, intuitive, indefinable (and therefore unmeasurable and unaccreditable!) qualities of being that are regarded as central in a New Paradigm, transpersonal view of effective practitionership.

Groddeck was also very interested in the phenomenon of perception. He was fascinated by what we might call the "psychodynamics of seeing", and wrote several fascinating papers on long- and short-sightedness. He believed that visual problems resulted from efforts of "the It" to repress the sight of that which was painful; and for Groddeck the eyes were the most commonly used organ for expressing emotional difficulties (Grossman & Grossman, 1965: 97). The final lectures he gave before his death in 1934 were on seeing, and his 1932 manuscript is enthrallingly titled "Vision, the world of the eye, and seeing without an eye" (Schacht, 1977: 19). Groddeck himself observed that "The ancients thought of the poet as blind; and it makes sense that his eyes have to look inwards" (quoted in Schacht, 1977: 19).

Groddeck was aware of the human capacity to combine rational understanding with "an almost mystical experience of inner vision" (*ibid.*), and he thus identified two ways of seeing: the outside-inwards seeing of "normal" vision, and the inside-outwards way of the "dreamer" and the visionary—and even a clairvoyant like Rudolf Steiner, perhaps. Old-paradigm positivist ontologies are preoccupied with the former, and typically assume a so-called Correspondence Theory of Truth (Rorty, 1979; see Chapter 10) such that the act of seeing accurately captures an "objective" reality assumed to exist independently of the observer's perception of it.

New Paradigm perspectives, by contrast, tend towards the inside-outwards way of seeing of a Goethe, a Blake, a Steiner, or a Krishnamurti—amounting to what Heron (1996: 163–169) calls a *Congruence* Theory of Truth, in which the observer and the observed are not assumed to be completely independent of one another (cf. Krishnamurti, 1970: 79–82; 1992: 363–366), and in which the observer in some very real sense participates in (Skolimowski, 1994) and creates the reality she is apprehending.

As Durrell (1948: 392) puts it, "With Groddeck we learn the mystery of participation with the world of which we are a part, and from which our ego has attempted to amputate us". For Groddeck, "truth" was always ambivalent (*ibid*.: 400): we are "lived by" a symbolic process which it is intrinsically impossible to express in language—as Durrell puts it, "the symbol cannot be spoken. It lives and *we are lived by it*" (398, his emphasis). We might say that Groddeck championed a pluralistic notion of "truth": for as Homer puts it, "We have a plural, conflictive view of the universe. For Groddeck, this richness of and openness to experience is truth" (Homer, 1988: 35). By contrast, and as touched upon earlier, "the I simplifies reality at the expense of truth to enable us to act ... the I tries to simplify, or repress ..., the many and opposing views of the universe and clashes with the It's truth" (*ibid*.).

I return to these crucial questions about the status of "truth" in Chapter 10.

Groddeck on psychosomatic medicine and human consciousness

... we are trying to recover the earlier conception of a unit, the body-mind, and make it the foundation of our theory and action. [Groddeck, quoted in Durrell, 1948: 402]

For Groddeck, there are no random events in human experience, but rather, a deep and normally unconscious meaning waiting to be discovered. Thus, "it is my custom to ask a patient who has slipped and broken his arm, 'What was your idea in breaking your arm?' ... I have never failed to get a useful reply to such questions ... we can always find both an inward and an outward cause for any event in life" (Groddeck, 1951: 81)—although "For the most part ... these internal causes are not known to the conscious mind" (*ibid.*: 82). Because conventional medicine typically fetishizes and objectifies "outward causes" and ignores the deep subjectivities of "inward causes", Groddeck sees no harm in selectively emphasizing the latter as a counterweight to the mechanistic excesses of orthodox "scientific", *bits-of-person*-centred medicine. Thus, "man creates his own illnesses for definite purposes, using the outer world merely as an instrument, finding there an inexhaustible supply of material which he can use for this purpose" (*ibid.*: 81).

In an early letter to Freud we find Groddeck writing that "the distinction between body and mind is only verbal and not essential ... body and mind are one unit" (quoted in Schacht, 1977: 9). And many years later we find Edwards (1992: 221) writing that "we perhaps need to move beyond the Cartesian model of having 'mind specialists' for 'mind problems' and 'body specialists' for 'body problems'" (cf. House, 1996d).

Many decades ago, Groddeck was writing about the psychological or mental concomitants of cancer, thus again anticipating recent developments in psycho-oncology (Holland & Rowland, 1989): "it is a little surprising to find a disease so important to our age as cancer left almost entirely uninvestigated on the mental side. My own experience in cases of cancer leads me to associate it with the personal attitude of the sufferer towards motherhood" (1951: 160); and Groddeck explicitly advocated psychotherapy for cancer patients (*ibid.*: 166). More generally, he viewed the experience of guilt, and associated self-punishment and the desire for a clean slate, as a major psychological influence upon disease (*ibid.*: 161). Again, such a view dovetails neatly with Hall's argument, controversial to many, that ultimately and at some very fundamental level, we all have responsibility for what happens to us— whether we actually experience such responsibility or not (Hall, 1993).

Recent developments in the study of human consciousness have begun to question the previously taken-for-granted view that consciousness is exclusively a product of post-natal human development and a function of the brain alone (see, for example, Hall, 1993; Wasdell, 1990), with even some "postmodern" scientists beginning to talk in terms of so-called "cellular consciousness"; yet once again, Groddeck got there many decades earlier: "I go as far as to believe there is some sort of individual consciousness even in the embryo, yes, even in the fertilised ovule, and for that matter in the unfertilised one too ... that every single separate cell has this consciousness of individuality, every tissue, every organic system" (Groddeck, 1951: 83).

Groddeck on "the (wise) child within"

... the child knows far better how to live than does the adult. [*ibid*.: 208]

Groddeck writes eloquently and with great wisdom about the importance of the child inside all of us. Central to his thinking was the idea that we should return to being child-like but not child*ish*— for the child is open and receptive to ideas and not saturated with judgements, prejudices and fears (and he implies that judging others can lead to guilt and illness) (Homer, 1988: 29–30). Thus, Groddeck writes that "The essential life of any man depends upon the degree to which he has been able to remain childlike, infantile, in spite of the blunting influences of adult life" (Groddeck, 1951: 203).

This all sounds very similar to Donald Winnicott's notion of "the capacity to play" (Winnicott, 1971), for whom playing was the basis for "the whole of man's experiential existence" (1971: 75). Later, Groddeck writes that "his childish nature remains with man and rules him till the end of his life" (Groddeck, 1951: 207), and that "[the child] can still live in fullness of spirit because he has not come under the domination of the ego which distorts life" (*ibid*.: 208). And in an enchanting statement on power that quite fundamentally challenges the human "power-over" dynamics of hierarchical organization (and not least, those of therapy's own professional bureaucracies), Groddeck writes that "The greatest monarch in the world is the infant. *Whoever desires power*—and which of us does not?—*should go to little children and let himself be trained by them*" (*ibid*.: 218–219, my emphasis: echoes here of the philosophy underlying Steiner Waldorf educational pedagogy—Steiner, 1995, 1996). And on individuation, too, Groddeck anticipates many who have written on the subject since: "life may indeed be regarded as one long process of getting free from the mother, beginning at the moment of conception" (1951: 214).

Groddeck—the unaccreditable, "wild" analyst

I cannot send a prospectus of my small clinic. ... There is no prospectus. My charges are adjusted to the means of my patients ... I have not forgotten during my life as a doctor that *man's true profession is to become a human being*. [Groddeck at age 64, quoted in Schacht, 1977: 1, my emphasis]

That Groddeck was a mystical–spiritual practitioner with a transpersonal ontology relatively unencumbered by the fetters of modernist thinking can hardly be doubted:

I have searched for a way leading into my untrodden, the pathless. I knew that I was moving close to the boundaries of mysticism, if not already standing in the very thick of it. ... I do not see the borders between things, only their running into one another. ... Systematic heads need for their value people of my kind. [Groddeck, quoted in Grossman & Grossman, 1965: 114–115]

William Inman also wrote of Groddeck as possessing "the reverence of a mystic for the forces which carry man along the path of life" (*ibid.*: 155).

Certainly, in today's climate of therapy professionalization and compulsive regulation-mindedness, the maverick genius of Groddeck (who "cured" so many "incurables"—Simmel, quoted in *ibid.*: 166) would surely never have been registered or accredited. As Homer (1988: 10) has written, describing Groddeck's view, "... all attempts at systematization are pretences of the I to sovereignty over the It". In a truly deconstructive spirit which, I hope, also typifies this book, Groddeck consistently refused to follow conventional orthodoxies just for the sake of it, and was a free thinker apparently relatively unconditioned by the modernist cultural milieu in which he lived. As Homer (*ibid.*: 34) puts it, for Groddeck "adherence to a rigid set of structures and careful theory of process can inhibit the strategies for curing".

In a quotation which, one hopes, might make disturbing reading for those who would statutorily regulate the practice of therapy, Groddeck "owed his training to no-one but himself", "hat[ed] anything that savour[ed] of official action", and despised "those worn-out medical dogmas, which, with *professional egotism*, made the physician instead of the patient the centre of the medical picture" (Grossman & Grossman, 1965: 167, my emphasis). Groddeck would no doubt have shared Krishnamurti's deep scepticism about the value of organizations and institutions (Krishnamurti Foundation Trust, 1992: 381–382)—not least because of the way in which they usurp the intrinsic and natural authority of the individual.

I close this penultimate section with a highly revealing quotation from Lawrence Durrell (1948: 397): "[Groddeck] was determined that his work should not settle and rigidify into a barren canon of law: that his writings should not become molehills for industrious systematizers, who might pay only lip-service to his theories, respecting the letter of his work at the expense of the spirit".

I hope that Groddeck might have approved of the presentation of his philosophy which I have attempted in this chapter.

Conclusion: beyond the mechanistic Zeitgeist

It is absurd to suppose that one can ever understand life, but luckily one does not need to understand in order to be able to live or help others who want to live. [Groddeck, 1951: 84]

In these disquieting days of high-tech medicine (curing the patient rather than assisting the client to heal), accreditation- and registration-mindedness, preoccupation with audit, so-called "scientific" evaluation and cost–effectiveness, and pressures towards ever-more rationality-dominated therapeutic approaches, we would do well to pause and consider the profound wisdom and deep learning that can be gained from assimilating the quintessentially human/e/istic philosophy of Georg Groddeck. His writings are at once inspired, brilliantly creative, occasionally bewildering—like the best poetry, sometimes capturing in his soulful prose that which is normally impossible to articulate in human language. For those struggling with Groddeck's often extraordinary prose, Homer makes the important point that Groddeck's writing method stays as true as possible to his notion of the It: that is, and especially in his *Book of the It* and *The World of Man*, Groddeck attempts to speak through the language of his It. And it follows, of course, that anyone expecting these "It"-writings to make perfectly coherent "I"-sense are in for a rather rude awakening!

Robb describes his writings thus: they "are so much a part of himself, free, spontaneous. ... They carry something of the man himself, who has breathed his very spirit into the written word. They make a long moment of inspiration" (Groddeck, 1951: 16). And here again is Groddeck's translator, Collins: "he was pre-eminently the artist rather than the scientist ... [he] has the artist's vision which penetrates the veils we call reality, and the deep truths that he reveals are often only to be expressed in paradox" (*ibid*.: 28, 29). Again, Donald Winnicott would surely have heartily approved!

That the brilliantly insightful, thought-provoking, and deeply challenging ideas of Groddeck have been so neglected is a testimony to the mechanistic *Zeitgeist* of modernity and materialism which still seem to be in the ascendant some 75 years after Groddeck, despite the signs for all to see that the objectifying mechanistic "scientific" world-view and its cultural accompaniments are everywhere falling apart (Barratt, 1993)—from the level of quantum physics (e.g. Bohm, 1980), through the human psyche and consciousness and forms of human social organization, and into the realms of astrophysics (e.g. Davies, 1983). When the current modernist, scientistic paradigm is eventually transcended, which it most surely will be, it is only then, perhaps, that the works of visionaries like Georg Groddeck, Goethe, and Rudolf Steiner will receive the quite central recognition as landmarks in the evolution of human consciousness which they so richly deserve.

For those of us who profoundly believe that effective therapeutic practice is 95% (or more!) inspiration and intuition, and 5% theoretical perspiration, Georg Groddeck is a greatly neglected figure in the history of healing and therapy. Therapists of each and every hew could do much worse than return to Groddeck for their inspiration and re-affirmation of their values and practice—and I hope that this chapter has given readers a taste of the feast of wisdom and insight that awaits anyone who takes the step into Groddeck's inspirational world.

This chapter has served as a backdrop for my more systematic elucidation of New Paradigm philosophy which follows in Chapter 10, and in which I relate that philosophy more specifically to some issues of central relevance to the psychotherapeutic project.

Note: The published works of Georg Groddeck

The Book of the It, Vision, London, 1950 (orig. 1927).
The Unknown Self, Vision, London, 1951 (orig. 1930).
Exploring the Unconscious, Vision, London, 1949 (orig. 1933).
The World of Man, Vision, London, 1951 (orig. 1934).
The Meaning of Illness: Selected Psychoanalytic Writings (incl. his correspondence with Freud), Hogarth Press, London, 1977.

Coda: Another precursor of postmodern, New Paradigm philosophy: J. Krishnamurti

The reader will have noticed my liberal quoting of the Indian spiritual philosopher Jiddu Krishnamurti ("K") in this book, and will not be surprised when I say that I see K as another early harbinger of New Paradigm, post-professional philosophy. The relevance of K's teachings to the therapy world deserve a major study in their own right (House, in preparation); here, I will simply draw upon a few of his many talks to present a "composite" quotation illustrating his incisive, New Paradigm views on therapy and the analytical process:

> ... don't accept anything from psychologists ... discard the authority of psychological specialists ... artificial division in consciousness is brought by psychologists ... psychologists are emphasising individual suffering ... [they] have not solved any of our problems ... *[they] have told you what you are* [my emphasis; cf. my Chapter 2]; analysis has no value ... the past is conditioned by the analyser ... analysis is part of conditioning ... thought has separated itself as the analyser ... awareness does not lead to analysis ... there is no clarity in analysis ... [it] is a process of fragmentation ... [it] cannot free us from conflict; that very division in analysis creates conflict ... analysis does not free the mind (from hurt) ... [it] prevents observation ... [it] is a dead process,

observation is not [cf. Goethean science—RH] ... analysis is postponement ... [it] doesn't teach anything ... [it] uses the old instrument of thought ... analysis destroys urgency ... understand yourself, not through analysis ... [it] prevents you being responsible for yourself ... depending on analysis is the essence of neuroticism ... [we must] break away from the tradition of analysis. [compiled from Krishnamurti's talks, 1968–1985; Krishnamurti Foundation Trust, 1992: 423–424, 65–66]

Note

1. Shorter versions of this chapter are House, 1996a and 1997a.

CHAPTER TEN

The "New Paradigm" challenge: intimations of a post-professional era

"It may be that psychotherapy is oriented toward conquering soul rather than entering into soul wisdom. ... Some eighty years later, this method [of the 'talking cure'] has multiplied endlessly, and without questioning the kind of knowing involved"

Sardello, 1990: 7

"The answer to human life is not to be found within the limits of human life"

C. G. Jung, quoted in Lorimer, 1990: 220

Modernity and postmodernity: incommensurable paradigms?

... the society which recognises only objective reality is a barren desert ... [Stan Gooch, quoted in Edwards, 1992: 195]

A veritable cacophony of voices from a range of sources has recently been lamenting the loss of "the soul" within modernity. To take just a few examples: Barrett (1987) has bemoaned the loss of "the soul" in modernist discourse, and how this loss seriously compromises our ability to form an adequate understanding of "mind". More specifically in relation to therapy, Edwards (1992) has made a similar plea for what we might call the "re-enchantment" of therapy through soul (cf. Rowan, 2001; Sardello, 1992, 2001), which seems to have been increasingly lost in the era of didactic professionalization and its associated modernist ideology (cf. Berman, 1981; Griffin, 1988). Sardello, informed *inter alia* by the anthroposophical world-view of Rudolf Steiner, has challenged the whole basis of conventional therapy (1990) in invoking the concept of caring for "the soul of the world" (Sardello, 1992). And in his recent book *The Soul's Code*, Jungian iconoclast James Hillman (1996) has developed a compelling, so-called "acorn theory" of human development that challenges many of the fundamental assumptions of the conventional modernist world-view, embracing as he does notions of destiny and karma that offer quite new ways of understanding childhood difficulties and family influence, character and desire, freedom and "calling".

Within Western analytic philosophy, typically a bastion of rationalism and materialism, there have been substantial murmurings positing a quite different view (e.g. Pylkkanen, 1989; Robinson, 1982; and the essays in Smythies & Beloff, 1989). And finally, even within science itself there have been signs of growing unease with the project of modernity, with the recent upsurge of interest in Goethean science (e.g. Bortoft, 1996; Naydler, 1996; Chapter 9, this book), the burgeoning growth of the world-wide Scientific and Medical Network, and a whole range of studies challenging scientific orthodoxy from a variety of quasi postmodern standpoints (e.g. Brown, 1998; Capra, 1997; Clarke, 1996; Griffin, 1988; Laszlo, 1996; and the essays in Lorimer, 1998).

Before the advent of modernity, the phenomena of nature were accounted for teleologically with reference to their purpose, and not merely their physical or mechanical causes (Lorimer, 1990: 227, 255): "nature was explained as animated, alive, having not yet succumbed to the deadening influence of mechanical philosophy" (p. 228). The 17th century heralded an ontological shift from a concern with connections within the whole to a focusing on the mechanisms of separate parts: the metaphor of the organism was replaced by that of the clock, knowledge of the working of which can best be discovered by taking it apart (*ibid.*: 230). Accompanying this shift in world-view was a different definition of truth—an objectivist so-called "correspondence" theory which assumes that the scientific method accurately describes a world that exists independently of our perception of it—and, moreover, which is unaffected by our perception of it (Rorty, 1979). The scientific world-view claims to explain all phenomena as "by-products of matter and physical forces", and any kind of dualism of soul or body is disdainfully scorned as "unscientific" and mystical (*ibid.*: 246, 248).

As will become clear in what follows, recent developments in the fields of physics (e.g. Bohm, 1980; Clarke, 1996) and biology (e.g. Goodwin, 1994, 1997; Sheldrake, 1981) are beginning to cohere into a so-called New Paradigm world-view which is challenging quite fundamentally the old-paradigm consensus of positivist, objectivist science. Yet the fear aroused by, and the resistance to, revolutionary ideas can be enormous (Clarke, 1997): William James commented that "in admitting a new body of experience, we instinctively seek to disturb as little as possible the pre-existing stock of ideas" (quoted in leaflet for conference cited in Clarke, 1997).

The questions raised by the New Paradigm, explicitly and unashamedly spiritual world-view are absolutely central to the philosophy and authenticity of psychotherapy and counselling. Put differently, whether or not one subscribes to a New Paradigm world-view will fundamentally influence one's approach to therapeutic practice, one's philosophy of the person, and how one conceives of the therapeutic change process—not to mention, of course, one's attitude towards institutional professionalization and its associated ideologies and practices.

Within the therapy field, the so-called transpersonal approach tends to be partitioned off and neatly categorized as just one of many alternative therapeutic approaches—with little or no recognition of the fact that working transpersonally, with spirit or soul, can't just be picked up and used or not as the mood or fashion takes one, but rather, necessitates a fundamentally different world-view which is philosophically incompatible with alternative approaches rooted in the old-paradigm philosophy of Galilean science (cf. Clarkson, 2002). The view, as John Rowan for example has argued (1992: 165), that the whole field of therapy can somehow be treated as one unified profession, in which the differences between distinct approaches are less important than are the commonalities that unify them, ignores the fundamental ideological incompatibilities in world-view between different approaches. Jutta Gassner (personal communication) has referred to her own counselling work not as a profession, nor even as a career or a vocation, but as a calling (cf. House, forthcoming).

This terminology is absolutely crucial: the term "calling" immediately conveys a transpersonal or spiritual dimension which, from this perspective, is an indissoluble aspect of therapeutic work—and is one which so easily becomes submerged and lost under the deadening effects of credentialization, career-mindedness, and one-sided materialism. Many (spiritual) healers do not on principle charge a commercial fee for their healing work; and one can see how practitioners working within a New Paradigm worldview can experience the commercialization and commodification sweeping the therapy world as alienating and quite incongruous with their value system. From within the anthroposophically inspired world-wide Camphill Community movement, which is at the leading edge of global community-building initiatives, we find Karl König expressing views which should surely make every professional therapist pause for deep reflection: for within the Communities (which care for disabled people):

> none of our co-workers receive a wage or salary. . . . No professional person can be paid for his services. As soon as it is paid [for] it is no longer a service! Wages . . . create a barrier between the one who receives and the one who pays. To give and to take is a matter of mutual human relationship; the true relationship goes as soon as money intervenes . . . paid love is no love; paid help has nothing to do with help. [König, 1990: 33; orig. 1965]

In this view, then, the whole edifice of professionalization, concerned as it inevitably is with status, hierarchy, career development, material aggrandizement, and accreditation-mindedness, is firmly rooted within an old-paradigm philosophy which privileges conscious, rational knowledge, causal–linear ways of reasoning and knowing, measurement and controllability, guarantees of allegedly measurable competencies, and all the other leitmotivs of the modernist scientific world-view. If we accept Jung's view that we cannot hope to find the answers to life from within the limitations of conscious, rational human experience, then it follows that human-made structures of professionalization cannot begin to touch or help to throw light upon that which really matters in the realms of human potential. As Krishnamurti resoundingly stated, "If you [organise a belief], it becomes dead, crystallised" (quoted in House, 1997g: 31). (I will return to Krishnamurti's highly relevant contributions to what I call "post-professional" thinking later in this chapter.)

In the remainder of this chapter I focus on a selection of themes which illustrate the incommensurability between old and New Paradigm approaches to some of the central concerns of the therapeutic experience. In the course of the discussion I hope to demonstrate both the inadequacy of the conventional old-paradigm perspective and the potential that New Paradigm philosophy promises for heralding a post-professional era in the unfolding development of human consciousness.

Theory, academic "knowledge", and the spirit of learning: paradigms in conflict

Reason itself destroys the humanity it first made possible. [Ken Wilber, quoted in Lorimer, 1996a: 77]

This is not the place to discuss the spectacle of a so-called "profession" in which a series of very different and often mutually incompatible bodies of therapeutic theory sit together very uneasily (e.g. Dryden & Feltham, 1992; Erwin, 1997). Rather, I am concerned here with the status and place of academic theory in general within the field. I have already discussed the role and place of theory in therapeutic work (see Chapter 2): this is an issue which has received grossly inadequate discussion in the field; and the limited attention which it has received has typically been superficial and uncritically (and unconsciously) based on old-paradigm ontologies. As Schaef (1992: 248–249) argues, "the role of theory is often harmful to psychotherapy and it is one of the aspects of psychotherapy that is rarely challenged ... theories often limit and control the perceptions of therapists ... more often than not ..., theory tends to interfere with awareness and healing".

Within the professions in general, however, theoretical expertise is routinely assumed to be an indispensable prerequisite if the professional is to discharge her or his task competently and successfully (cf. Mair, 1992). Yet in New Paradigm philosophy, by contrast, the role of theory is quite fundamentally challenged (cf. Polkinghorne, 1990).

In a little-known paper written 15 years ago, Ian Craib (1987) had some very incisive and revealing things to say about the psychodynamics of theory:

> Problems occur when theoretical work becomes primarily an expression of individual psyches ... rather than an attempt to grasp the nature of the world. ... When I engage in theory, I am deploying a range of defences and projections. ... I am bringing into play or even acting out a range of phantasies and displaced early experiences (p. 35). ... The holding on to total monocausal explanations and assumptions seems to me to manifest something like infantile omnipotence. ... [The use of complicated languages] has to do with making the world safe and bringing it under control, a phantasized omnipotence. The dangerous complication of language is elevated into the comparatively safe complication of language (p. 47). ... Theory provides a means of establishing ... an infantile omnipotence which protects itself by ... a denial of real complexities, ambiguities and contradictions. ... There has been a quantitative increase in this type of theory over the past decades and ... *this can be seen as a symptom of a cultural malaise.* [p. 52, my emphasis]

The prevalence of what Craib calls "theoretical narcissism" means that "an organic link with a wider reality is severed" (p. 53). Craib calls for a modification of the original omnipotence, such that "the desire to know everything can be coupled with a realization that such knowledge is impossible ..." (p. 54). T. S. Eliot's famous dictum that human beings can't stand too much reality is surely very relevant to what Craib is saying here—put bluntly, that theory is normally used as a substitute for, and a defence against, the existential "terror" of being fully in the here and now of immediate lived experience (many parallels again here with Krishnamurti's challenging philosophy).

Somewhat predictably, however, the analyst Craib crucially stops short of undermining the theoretical *Weltanschauung* altogether:

"we need some intellectual security—we cannot simply surrender all ideas and somehow give ourselves up to the contradictions and complexities of the words" (p. 55). But others are more courageous —or foolhardy, depending on your point of view. The philosophies of Buddhism, diverse mystical traditions (notably including Wilfred Bion [Symington & Symington, 1996] and Michael Eigen, 1998), and Goethean science (to name but three tendencies) are highly sceptical about there being any role for theory in knowing and apprehending the world. In their collective view it is through direct experiential engagement with the world that we come to "know" it in a full sense that by far transcends the limiting confines of propositional– conceptual knowledge (cf. Heron, 1996).

In similar vein, the spiritual philosopher J. Krishnamurti repeatedly stressed that as long as we superimpose the template of thought and belief on to the world, we will inevitably only see what we expect to see, and that which coincides with our previous conditioning (cf. McDougall, 1995): "You will always experience what you believe and nothing else. And this invalidates your experience. . . . Belief conditions its own supposed proof" (quoted in House, 1997g: 35). There are surely very profound implications in all this for the proper place of theory in the activity of therapy and counselling.

It is unarguable that the field of therapy training is becoming increasingly "academicized", for training is now set "firmly at post-graduate level" (van Deurzen, 1997: 3). From a spiritual, New Paradigm perspective, however, the increasing emphasis being accorded to academic work on training courses is at the very least highly dubious. The increase in the academic component of trainings cannot be explained away as some kind of random event that is unrelated to professionalization. Rather, the academicization of training is an inevitable accompaniment of the attempt to make the therapy field into "a Profession": for as Mowbray (1995: 29) points out, the knowledge base of the professions is typically highly theoretical and academic, with access usually depending on the possession of an academic degree. Mowbray (ibid.: Chapter 14) has strongly—and to my mind convincingly—challenged the belief that academic study is a necessary prerequisite for attaining competence as a therapeutic practitioner. He quotes Roberta Russell (1981), who concluded after a major literature review that "Studies all indicate that long years of academic training are not a prerequisite for competence" (*ibid.*: 115). While the post-graduatization of the therapy field has developed at a breathtaking pace (House, 2001c), with the UKCP promoting increased academic content in training, we find Mowbray writing that "The over-intellectual focus ... may actually be counterproductive as a prerequisite for working in this area" (*ibid.*: 117).

In a different context, it is interesting that the journalist Melanie Phillips (1996) has highlighted a wider, society-level trend towards increasingly inappropriate academic "degree-*itis*", and a concomitant decline in more craft-based, apprenticeship-oriented, vocational types of training. The apprenticeship model is arguably far more appropriate for practitioner development in the therapy field than are increasingly academicized (post-)graduate-level trainings (for detailed arguments see Gladstone, 1997; House, 2001c; see also the recent debate within the Universities Psychotherapy and Counselling Association Newsletter—House, 2001f and Lohman, 2001). Perhaps the therapy world is subject to wider cultural forces with which it is uncritically colluding; and perhaps we are headed in the same direction as the United States—which, according to Art Bohart (Professor of Psychology at the State University of California at Dominguez Hills), would be a disaster: for as he wrote in a personal communication, "I'm sorry to hear about the fight over licensure in Great Britain. ... The battle, of course, is over here, and we are busy becoming more and more medical-like, rapidly losing our human souls. ... But we are a 'Profession'".

Although Mowbray does not present it as such, this is quintessentially old "versus" New Paradigm terrain—for the increasing intellectual focus in training represents, in a very real sense, a retreat and retrenchment into old paradigm ways of knowing and being. Nor should we find this regressive development particularly surprising, for the whole accreditation bandwagon has brought enormous and often uncontainable fear in its wake (cf. Wasdell, 1992; Shohet, 1997)—and it is well known how so-called "regressive acting-out" behaviour is the normal concomitant of a fear-saturated environment, at both individual *and* psychosocial, cultural levels (Wasdell, 1990, 1992).

The educational philosophies of the renowned spiritual teachers Jiddu Krishnamurti (known colloquially as "K") and Rudolf Steiner are relevant to this discussion. Sardello has emphasized the importance of education in a New Paradigm perspective: "the endeavor to bring about a true spiritual psychology belongs to the realm of education rather than psychotherapy. ... There is nothing whatsoever within the human being that would call forth from the processes of life such a particular cultivation of life as what is called psychotherapy" (Sardello, 1990: 23).

Both K and Steiner had a great deal to say about education (Krishnamurti, 1955, 1994; Steiner, 1995, 1996), and the way in which an over-intellectual, technical, programmatic educational environment does profound damage to the developing psyche of the child that is scarcely understandable within the ideology and discourse of modernity. Those readers familiar with the theory and practice of Steiner Waldorf education will know that one of its central features is that the child's early learning should be oriented towards artistic, intuitive, creative ways of knowing-through-being (or what Heron refers to as "presentational ways of making sense"—1996: 33), and that it is positively harmful to the child if its learning environment is over-intellectualized too soon (House, 2000a, 2001d). In this view, the sobering reality is that the vast majority of us have been subjected to a damaging over-intellectual early educational environment; so it is a supreme irony that professional developments in the therapy field (the latter, of course, claiming to heal the damage *of childhood experience*!) is moving in the same direction—i.e. towards measurable, assessable academic values, and, concomitantly, away from being-values (*ibid.*).

There are also fascinating and highly illuminating parallels between Krishnamurti's educational philosophy and the therapy training process. For Krishnamurti the essential factor in education was the relationship between teacher and pupil, "which it was impossible to create *by following a method*" (Hunter, 1988: 99, my emphasis). Generally, Krishnamurti felt there to be an overemphasis on technique, the intellect, and efficiency, and an underemphasis on emotional and spiritual awareness (*ibid.*: 113). For K, "the very institutions which claim to educate are in fact doing the opposite: by overemphasising the intellect they are preventing the awakening of true intelligence" (*ibid.*: 114); and there should be no system of punishment and reward-seeking and no imposition of ideology (*ibid.*: 123; cf. Feltham's incisive critique of the conventional wisdom of single-orientation "core-theoretical" therapy trainings—Feltham, 1997a).

Here is K himself: "[The Krishnamurti schools] are to be concerned with the cultivation of the total human being. These centres of education must help the student and the educator to flower naturally ... *not merely a mechanical process oriented to a career, to some kind of profession* (Krishnamurti, 1981: 7–8, my emphasis). Later, he writes of "a free inquiry into ourselves without the barrier of one who knows and the one who doesn't" (*ibid.*: 100): for K, "pupil and teacher are essentially equal partners in an open dialogue" (Hunter, 1988: 155). Krishnamurti was, of course, quite dismissive of hierarchy and authority as principles of being and relating.

For Krishnamurti, then, it was a fundamental error for the educational process to embrace current societal old-paradigm values and organizational principles: he asked, "is this what education is meant for, that you should willingly or unwillingly fit into this mad structure called society?" (Krishnamurti, 1974: 11; cf. Brian Thorne's view of therapy and counselling being fundamentally subversive activities—Thorne, 1997). For Krishnamurti (as well as for Rudolf Steiner with his so-called Three-fold Social Order—House, 2000c), schools should be small and, above all, *independent of any centralized authority structures*; for if freedom and independence were missing in a school, it would inevitably become an institution for the perpetuation of the cultural conditioning of which he was so critical (Hunter, 1988: 156).

In sum, "Krishnamurti was concerned to provide the basis for growth and transformation, but without imposing a detailed system of beliefs or behaviours" (*ibid.*: 312, my emphasis; cf. Feltham, 1997a). And he could hardly have been clearer about the damaging and constraining nature of old-paradigm, over-intellectual, despiritualized orientations to life: "we have been educated in a most absurd way. ... A lot of information is poured into our heads and we develop a very small part of the brain which will help us to earn a livelihood. The rest of the brain is neglected" (Krishnamurti, 1978: 260).

Thus, not only is the rationale for current trends in the therapy training field fundamentally undermined by the insights of Krishnamurti and Steiner, but just how it is remotely possible to measure and accredit qualities or "being-orientations" which are crucially "intangible" and intrinsically beyond intellectual, rational, old-paradigm ways of knowing is open to very severe doubt (cf. my Chapter 9 on Groddeck). Park (1992: 8) quotes a psychoanalyst in private conversation, thus: "What people say or write theoretically often has a marginal connection with what they say when describing what they actually do in a session". And we can take such embarrassment even further—for whether what therapists describe as "what they do" is a remotely representative description of what actually does happen in a therapy session is *also* open to very severe doubt! Such an uncomfortable view has been forcefully expressed by Spinelli (1996); and here too is Sardello (1990: 13): "... the psychotherapist has not the faintest notion of what he is dealing with nor of how very simplistic even the most complex of psychological theories really are because of the failure to recognize the reality of the spiritual worlds".

The ontology of "thinking" and "feeling"

it is only when the insidious distinction [between passion and reason] begins to disintegrate that the ideal of "self-esteem", "wisdom", and classical 'harmony of the soul' will begin to make any sense for us. [Solomon, 1976: 66]

Another manifestation of New Paradigm philosophy's relevance occurs in the realms of thinking and feeling. Typically, theory in the fields of counselling, psychotherapy, and psychoanalysis embraces quite uncritically the artificial analytic distinction between thinking and feeling: indeed, one of the central features distinguishing different schools is the relative emphasis each places on thinking and feeling. Yet New Paradigm philosophy fundamentally questions this too-often taken-for-granted conceptualization of human experience.

The late philosopher-scientist David Bohm held a very different view—a definition of thought which "brings to the fore the fact that the intellectual, emotional, sensuous, and physical responses of the memory are all aspects of one indissoluble process ..." (Cayer, 1997: 43; see also Bohm, 1994). In his illuminating Foreword to David

Bohm's book *Thought as a System*, Lee Nichol summarizes Bohm's radical position on thought, which is well worth quoting at some length:

> The essential relevance of Bohm's redefinition of thought is the proposal that body, emotion, intellect, reflex and artifact are now understood as *one unbroken field of mutually informing thought*. All of these components interpenetrate one another to such an extent, that we are compelled to see thought as a system—concrete as well as abstract, active as well as passive, collective as well as individual. ... Bohm rejects the notion that our thinking processes neutrally report on what is "out there" in an objective world. ... Once we make the ... false assumption that thought and knowledge are only reporting on [reality], we are committed to a view that does not take into account the complex, unbroken processes that underlie the world as we experience it. ... Thought ... is ... inclusive of *feelings*, in the form of latent emotional experiences. ... Our traditional world view, in an attempt to maintain a simple, orderly image of cause and effect, does not take into account [the] subtler aspects of thought's activity. [Nichol, in Bohm 1994: ix–xi, original emphases]

For Bohm, a systemic fault pervades the whole system of thought, because thought itself creates problems which thought then tries to solve, while continuing in so doing to create the problems! (there are clear signs in this formulation too of the fascinating published "dialogues" that Bohm co-created with his sometime friend Krishnamurti). For Bohm, and quite contrary to our everyday "folk" experience, there is no separate entity creating and observing thought (cf. the title of Buddhist Mark Epstein's book, *Thoughts without a Thinker*, 1996); and by failing to recognize its participation in this process, thought itself is responsible for the deception. All images of the self are seen by Bohm as representing something other than the image: the true nature of a person is essentially unknown and unknowable in propositional-conceptual terms, and conceptual ways of knowing alone are inadequate for exploring self-experience. Here is Bohm himself:

> whatever is behind the mind ... is a vast stream; and on the surface are ripples which are thought ... what we "see" is a self; but what we actually have is a whole lot of thoughts going on in consciousness ... the attempt to treat the self as an object is just

not going to mean anything. ... You say "I" and "me", and "myself". ... But that use of language will give rise to representations which we are liable to mistake for actuality ... whatever the self is its essence is unknown but constantly revealing itself. [Bohm, 1994: 172–173 *passim*]

Spiritual, holistic, New Paradigm views of human experience, then, challenge quite fundamentally all of our everyday assumptions about the role of so-called "thinking" and "emotion" in experience generally—and, by extension, in the therapeutic change process itself. Clearly, what is currently being called forth in the light of New Paradigm philosophy is *a root and branch deconstruction of the everyday conventions of human experience*, with the prospect of a quite revolutionary shift in human consciousness which threatens to leave in tatters current therapeutic ontologies, of which didactic professionalization—with its associated ideologies of hierarchy, privileged expertise, rigidly individualized helping modalities, and the like—is but one manifestation. As soon as we begin to problematize rationality and thinking as valid and appropriate ways of being, then immediately many of the leitmotivs of didactic professionalization are thrown into question—not least the arrogant "ego"-driven attempt to measure, predict, and somehow guarantee the effectiveness of the therapeutic experience, or the competence of practitioners (cf. House, 1996b). As Goethe wrote most poignantly, "number and measurement in all their baldness destroy form and banish the spirit of living contemplation" (quoted in Lorimer, 1996b: 60).

It might be objected that the New Paradigm critique of current therapeutic approaches amounts to little more than the flattening of a straw man. I offer the following prebuttal to this possible criticism by quoting the following excerpts from the prestigious, recently founded journal, the *International Journal of Psychotherapy (IJP)* in order pre-emptively to field such a charge. The *IJP* is the official journal and flagship of the European Association for Psychotherapy (EAP). The principles to which the journal and the EAP subscribe are set out in their grand-sounding "Strasbourg Declaration", from which I now quote: "Psychotherapy is *an independent scientific discipline*. ... Training ... takes place at an advanced, qualified, and *scientific level*" (European Psychotherapy Association, 1996, my emphases).

In the first issue of the journal, the President of the EAP, Heiner Bartuska, approvingly cites the Austrian law on psychotherapy, which regulates "the scientific analysis of the specific methods" ...; and a bit later, "It is the duty of the EAP to ensure that all scientific psychotherapeutic methods achieve adequate opportunity to achieve the European Certificate. ... The idea of the EAP is to establish this new regulation on psychotherapy within Europe as an independent scientific discipline" (Bartuska, 1996; 108–109 *passim*). And here is former UKCP Chair, Emmy van Deurzen, again in the same issue:

> [We have] ... to be able to train people to intervene in this dimension with some amount of purposeful certainty. ... We have to transform what used to be a craft or an art based on moral and religious principles *into a scientifically based accountable professional expertise.* ... We need to ... articulate precisely what the principles of human connectedness are and how psychotherapists intervene in them. ... We can no longer rely on prescriptive notions of faith, on beliefs or intuitive convictions; those were part of our heritage ... in a *prescientific* ... era ... we need to externalise such principles, describing and scrutinising them, so that we can work with them in a conscious and deliberate manner. [1996: 17–18 *passim*, my emphases]

What is quite clearly and unambiguously demonstrated here is what, in the light of the foregoing critique of old-paradigm world-views, amounts to a grossly naïve pretension that psychotherapy become a valid science. Such a pretension reveals a thorough-going ignorance of the current highly precarious status of the positivist–materialist world-view of conventional science, and of the (to my mind) devastating New Paradigm and postmodernist critiques to which the old scientific paradigm is increasingly being subjected (cf. House, 1997d). Yet of course, in order to render the field viably and respectably professionalizable, the ideology of scientific "expertise" (cf. Mair, 1992) must needs be embraced by those who wish didactically to professionalize the field of therapy.

Thankfully, a number of prominent practitioners are beginning to challenge the spurious "scientification" of therapy: for example, the first declaration of the recent Campaign for Effective Therapy (2002) initiative initiated by Nick Totton, and to which I subscribe, states that: "Psychotherapy is not an assemblage of expert techniques, but a rich encounter between people. It is a craft and art rather than a science" (Campaign for Effective Therapy, 2002).

New Paradigm perspectives on intersubjectivity

reality is to be found within relationships, not within concepts. [Clarke, 1996: 41]

... the new paradigm allows for transformation to occur through *dynamic interaction* of energy fields (or people) rather than via the mechanical *cause and effect* action of one particle (or person) on another. [Edwards, 1992: 202, her emphases]

In the therapy field it is arguably in the realm of intersubjectivity where New Paradigm and spiritual perspectives are most relevant. For Whitbeck, "Dualistic ontologies based on the opposition of self and other generate two related views of the person and of ethics: the patriarchal and that of individualism" (quoted in Schaef, 1992: 207). And existential philosopher Robert Solomon also has some interesting things to say about intersubjectivity and status:

it is generally the case that equal status will be as much of a presupposition of intersubjectivity as shared experiences and interests ... the sense of "we" that is so essential to the intersubjective emotions exists in at best an unstable compromise with interpersonal conflicts over status. ... The contrast of intersubjectivity is defensiveness. ... Emotions which take the other to be superior are inevitably emotions of defensiveness. [Solomon, 1976: 215–216]

Now this is bad news indeed for the practitioner who is wedded to their expert professional status (cf. Mair, 1992), yet who at the same time believes that intersubjectivity is a crucial aspect of a successful therapeutic relationship. For if Solomon is anything like right, then it seems that a practitioner's clinging to an expert professional status might actually be antithetical to the co-created intimacy that is arguably central to a successful therapeutic experience (e.g. Schaef, 1992).

Smithson (1997) has talked of the "Kairos Point" as being the point at which our inner subjective experience meets with the outer external world, and at which the real is somehow created. In social terms we can call this "intersubjectivity" (Crossley, 1996)—i.e. the view that relationship is created by two or more interpenetrating subjectivities, and is crucially indissoluble into its component parts (i.e. your subjectivity and my subjectivity; transference and countertransference, and so on), because the very act of analytical decomposition destroys the Gestalt of the relational whole, and the relational whole simply cannot be successfully apprehended and understood by artificially dividing it into parts. Here is Crossley (p. 173): "intersubjectivity is the key to understanding human life ... it is irreducible and sui generis, a generative principle of our identities. ... And *it is something we cannot step out of*. No amount of methodological procedure ... can negate this or even bracket it out. We are intersubjects ..." (my emphasis).

Thus, relational intersubjectivity (which is of course a key feature of all relationships, including therapeutic relationships) is intrinsically unmeasurable, ineffable, and beyond rationalist under-standing from within the conventional world-view of positivist science, which typically splits subject from object, observer from observed, self from other. In turn this situation has profound implications for therapy research—for apart from a quite limited number of phenomenologically informed "process" studies, the vast corpus of therapy research is squarely trapped within the naïve realism of positivist science, attempting as it does to describe and explain the therapeutic process by decomposing, analysing, atomizing, manipulating, predicting, and controlling what is an indissoluble intersubjective unity quite beyond first- and third-person ways of description and explanation.

In sum, with the exception of, perhaps, a limited number of therapeutic approaches which privilege existential-phenomenologi-cal ontologies (Laing, 1961; Spinelli, 1994: Part 5), it is quite clear that the very way we think about therapy and the therapeutic process is essentially trapped within the constraints of an increas-ingly discredited old paradigm of Galilean science (see, for example, Griffin, 1988; Weber, 1986; Pylkkanen, 1989; Schaef, 1992; Skoli-mowski, 1974; Bortoft, 1996; Clarke, 1996; DiCarlo, 1996; Heron, 1996; Woodhouse, 1996; Lorimer, 1998). Moreover, the essentially quantitative, measurement- and control-oriented approaches of formal top-down accreditation and licensing procedures are themselves, of course, thoroughly immersed in and imbued with the assumptions of this outmoded world-view.

In stark contrast, the Independent Practitioners Network (see Chapter 12) is struggling to pioneer alternative forms of validation (i.e. practitioner development through real, "live", ongoing inter-subjective encounter and experience) which are far more in tune with New Paradigm philosophy. John Heron's rich notion of the "self-generating culture" (see Heron, 1997) describes very well the core values of a participative, New Paradigm epistemology for human relations development and community-building which quite explicitly transcends the old-paradigm "power-over" dynamics of "dominator-hierarchical" values (to use Ken Wilber's term—see Kalisch, 1996a,b), and instead privileges "power-with", co-operative, and participative approaches to practitioner and human develop-ment more generally.

It is of course no coincidence that Heron (in common with all the other New Paradigm writers cited earlier) places spirituality at the centre of his philosophy (see also Heron, 1998): for an explicitly spiritual dimension is not only allowable or defendable, but is actually essential if we are to make sense of a world which the old paradigm is increasingly failing to describe or explain remotely adequately. Here is Heron, echoing the experiential truth enunciated by mystics over millennia: "there is a distinction but no separation between personal being and presented being, the imaginer and the imagined, the conceiver and the conceived, the doer and the done within" (Heron, 1996: 105, my emphasis). What Heron has done in his seminal book *Co-operative Inquiry* is to illustrate thoroughly and methodically how the spiritual values of new-paradigm philosophy can be operationalized through a grounded, mature, and enlight-ened participative methodology (cf. Skolimowski, 1994)—so it is no longer adequate for the apologists for the old-paradigm *status quo* to shrug their shoulders and maintain that "There is no alternative" to current conventional approaches to understanding the intersubjec-tive therapeutic process.

Fundamental paradigm shifts require, *inter alia*, a relative undefendedness and openness to the new, to uncertainty, to the "chaotic" (Goodwin, 1997)—and concomitantly, it is of course fear of the unknown which tends to paralyse, fix, and lead to profession-centred retrenchment in the face of a world where our very ontologies of what exists are suddenly being problematized in quite fundamental ways (Clarke, 1997). We can respond openly and creatively to these developments, or we can "act out" from our fear of the unknown, desperately striving to buttress the old, increasingly redundant world-view of positivistic science.

The eminently wise sage and precursor of New Paradigm philosophy, J. Krishnamurti, bequeathed some highly relevant teachings about human organizations: "Truth cannot be organised, nor should any organisation be formed to lead or coerce people along any particular path" (1929 Speech, quoted in Suares, 1953); and for the likes of Krishnamurti and Ivan Illich (1977a, 1978), man's urge continually to institutionalize is fundamentally misguided and immature, not least because it is frankly naïve to expect more institutionalization and systematization to promote healthy change when those very processes are themselves inevitably cast in the image of the old-paradigm values and assumptions from which they have emerged (cf. House, 1999d).

I will close this section with a composite quotation from Krishnamurti's talks (given between 1972 and 1981), which offers insights into (inter)relationship which are highly germane to the foregoing discussion, and to New Paradigm perspectives on relational subjectivity more generally:

> ... the individual is the root of conflict in relationship ... the fact in relationship is division—me and you ... the self is the cause of difficulty in relationship ... our relationship is based on images ... [which] become an impediment in relationships ... relationship is based on thought and therefore limited ... when thought interferes relationship becomes mechanistic ... relationship without registration is entirely different. [compiled from Krishnamurti Foundation Trust, 1992: 432–437]

The further reaches (or death throes?) of modernity: NVQs

> Men develop a capacity for mastering the universe and a compulsive preoccupation with what can be predicted, possessed, piled up and counted in order to deny the strength of their early physical and emotional link with the mother. [Maguire, 1995: 60]

... why this constant measurement? ... why caught in measurement? ... truth cannot be measured ... measurement brings
fragmentation ... the moment you measure you are insufficient ...
[there can be] no change as long as there is a continuation of
measurement ... where there is measurement there is no spirituality
... when there is no measurement, you see the whole of
consciousness. [compiled from Krishnamurti's talks, 1972–83;
Krishnamurti Foundation Trust 1992: 331–332]

To take just one example of the professionalization process, in New
Paradigm terms the attempt to introduce NVQs into the therapy
field in the late 1990s was patently absurd, and was caught squarely
within the old-paradigm, ego-driven delusion that it is somehow
possible to measure competence in the field of human (therapeutic)
relationship. NVQs are based on the assumption that it is possible to
measure what a practitioner does, and then award them a
qualification at a specific NVQ level for that achievement. As
Rowan points out (1996a: 42), both the BAC and the UKCP seemed
at the time to have bought into and embraced the NVQ ideology.

It is clear that such an approach stems from the old-paradigm
ideology of control—that is, the view that it is not only possible but
fitting and appropriate to attempt to control and somehow
guarantee the safety of the therapeutic process which, according
to New Paradigm thinking, is necessarily outwith the ambit of
conscious programmatic control or linear–causal understanding. I
have already deconstructed the notion of "safety" in Chapter 4: and
as I have written elsewhere, "if with clients who have been
fundamentally betrayed in love we dare to work at the depth they
require for their own healing, then it is inevitable that we will
sometimes have to work at the very edge of our capacity to hold the
'frame' ", (House, 1996f: 25); and "When one works at great depth
with clients, such work is often risky and dangerous, and goes close
to the edge of tolerance and holding" (House, 1995b: 37).

It comes as no surprise, of course, that the idea of NVQs comes
from cognitive–behavioural roots (Rowan, 1996: 43), which
approach is quintessentially located within an old-paradigm
assumptive ontology. Little wonder, too, that NVQs have nothing
whatsoever to say about the transpersonal or the spiritual (on
reflection perhaps we should be grateful for small mercies!); and
that Rowan (a former supporter of the NVQ idea) should conclude

that NVQs "cannot be of much relevance to humanistic practitioners. ... In my opinion, the NVQ for humanistic practitioners is a dead duck" (*ibid*.: 44).

In the light of all this, it is little surprise that even from within the realms of psychoanalytic orthodoxy we read Joyce McDougall writing as follows (and quoted favourably elsewhere in this book):

> The question of a paradigm shift with regard to our metapsychology merits a full exploration ... there is the ever-present risk that our ... analysands may employ much of their analytic process in an attempt to confirm their analysts' theoretical expectations! ... It would be presumptuous to imagine that it is our theories that bring about psychic change and symptomatic cure! ... *Is not our leading perversion ... the belief that we hold the key to the truth*? [1995: 236, 234, her emphasis]

The recent New Paradigm literature cited earlier certainly has one central and recurring characteristic in common: namely, that an explicitly spiritual dimension is not only allowable or defendable, but is actually essential if we are to make sense of a world which the old paradigm fails to describe or explain remotely adequately—a one-sidedly materialistic paradigm, moreover, which is presiding over the systematic ecological destruction of our planet (House, 1999d). The Scientific and Medical Network, based in the UK, is a relatively informal and substantial global body of scientists, doctors, psychologists, engineers, philosophers, therapists, and other professionals who hold in common a highly critical attitude to old-paradigm science, and who seek to deepen our understanding of the world through intuitive-spiritual as well as rational insight. Some of the most cutting-edge philosophizing and research from a New Paradigm perspective is being undertaken by Network members.

Conclusion

> When the scientists focused more of their attention on [the] irregularities [in nature] they formulated the theory of relativity and quantum physics, and things never looked the same again. Something of the sort is needed in the field of psychotherapy. [Kotowicz, 1993: 151]

I do not claim any particular originality for the ideas on which this chapter has been based; rather, this book represents just one branch of a growing lineage of New Paradigm thinking in the therapy world (e.g. Hillman, 1975, 1996; Sardello, 1990, 1992; Edwards, 1992; Schaef, 1992; Clarkson, 2002)—although the particular application of deconstructive analysis to profession-centred therapy's regime of truth in Part II is, I believe, a new departure in elucidating the implications of these radical ideas. Edwards (1992), for example, writes eloquently and, to my mind, convincingly about the need for a New Paradigm in psychotherapy and psychology:

> Science has claimed a monopoly on truth, seeing the scientific method as the only valid path towards knowledge ... as recent products of their culture, modern psychology and psychotherapy were built upon the shifting sands of Cartesian–Newtonian assumptions—with devastating consequences; ... [and] many therapists are still clinging to the scientific tradition ... and refusing to open their eyes ... the old paradigm gave birth to a positivist, materialist psychology which values objectivity, rationality and empiricism. ... The mechanistic, reductionist, determinist assumptions of the Cartesian–Newtonian world view are endemic in psychology and psychotherapy. ... Orthodox psychotherapy reinforces the "meaninglessness" of life, and the limited, rational self ... I long for psychology to be rescued from the blind alley of Cartesian–Newtonian science. [Edwards, 1992: 194–211 *passim*]

I believe the most interesting (and important) question to be just how soon the full implications of New Paradigm philosophy will be embraced by the therapy world; for even a cursory glance at the recent didactic professionalization of the field is sufficient to see how tenaciously the ideology of an old-paradigm modernity is still very much "alive and kicking"—even (and perhaps *especially*) in its death throes (Barratt, 1993). For from a New Paradigm, spiritual perspective, surely the very energy of professionalization, together with its associated ideologies and practices, is fundamentally antithetical to the kinds of New Paradigm, spiritual values which are now gaining increasing ground as the inadequacies and threadbare nature of the old world-view become increasingly exposed (e.g. Polkinghorne, 1990; Barratt, 1993).

Yet as many commentators have pointed out, entrenched

conventional belief systems and world-views (archetypally or emotionally rooted in distress as they often are) are notoriously impervious to even the most coherent, penetrating challenge (Edwards, 1992; Clarke, 1997)—as the economist J. K. Galbraith put it, "Faced with having to change our beliefs [particularly where livelihoods are involved!—RH] or prove that there is no need to do so, most of us get busy on the proof" (quoted in Edwards, 1992: 220–221). Whether or not the therapy field is "ready to receive the interpretation" (to use its own discourse on itself) offered in this book is an open question; but I repeat my challenge to the reader to allow the arguments to "resonate in their soul" (as in a Bohmian Dialogue), rather than jumping to pre-emptive defensive conclusions.

In both this and the previous chapter, I hope to have illustrated convincingly that the kinds of qualities that are really decisive in therapy work are crucially beyond rationalist discourse and scientific specification and measurement. And any professionalizing world-view that assumes otherwise is not only fundamentally barking up the wrong tree, but—far worse that this—it threatens to do untold damage to those very ineffable, intangible processes that are so foundational to creative and effective practitionership.

Certainly, it will come as no surprise to the reader who has reached this far in the book that in my view, increased commercialization, commodification, and all the other leitmotivs of the didactic professionalization process most certainly will not significantly figure in any New Paradigm, modernity-transcending vision for the future trajectory of the field. I will close with Edwards again: "Professionalization of helping—which goes hand in hand with scientific detachment—is an unfortunate legacy of the old world-view, and inevitably empowers the professionals rather than the clients" (1992: 199).

PART IV
WHITHER "POST-PROFESSIONAL" THERAPY?

Consider:

> "[Therapy] can touch the human heart and promote freedom;
> but it can just as likely mechanize, enslave and drive a person
> crazy ... there is a hidden potential for enslavement in every
> therapeutic situation, no matter what the school. ...
> [Therapy's] contradictions tend to be as serious as those of
> the market [economy], and there is no use in pretending
> them away"

> Kovel, 1976: 19, 292, 300

> "I'm not interested in everyone being in therapy. What I am
> interested in is how what we've understood about emotional
> life and about damage, and cruelty and hurt, how we might
> incorporate that understanding into the national curriculum,
> day care centres, child rearing practices, schools. All of that,
> how that might be imbued with a completely different
> sensibility"

> Orbach, 1996: 32

> "The question of whether psychotherapy, in its current form,
> should exist at all within the new holistic paradigm is
> certainly one to be seriously considered"

> Edwards, 1992: 201

CHAPTER ELEVEN

Reflections on profession-centred therapy

I n this book I have been concerned to lay bear some of the self-serving effects of individualized therapy's regime of truth. As a consequence I have not addressed the political and socio–cultural correlates of therapy's individualizing ideology—which have been penetratingly and revealingly detailed by several recent commentators (e.g. Cloud, 1998; Cushman, 1995; House, 1999b; Pilgrim, 1997; Smail, 1996). These social and cultural aspects of the therapy *Zeitgeist* must surely constitute a crucial aspect of any comprehensive critique of "therapeutic rhetoric" (Cloud, 1998), and the arguably deleterious cultural consequences of therapy's increasingly pervasive "treatment technology", manifesting in "late-modern" Western society. As Cloud has it, "Psychotherapy is a politically contradictory phenomenon that sometimes helps suffering people even as it can reinscribe individuals into the very social relations that produced their 'illnesses'" (Cloud, 1998: xv). I have also made no attempt to locate "therapy" culturally and historically as just one transitory "moment" in the so-called "evolution of human consciousness" (e.g. Crook, 1980; Neumann, 1954; Steiner, 1966)—though I believe that such an analysis would be of inestimable value if only someone had the overarching vision and insight of a Steiner or a Jung to carry it off.

In these discussions I will set out under a series of headings the main points to emerge from this study, and the radical counter-intuitive conclusions to which its arguments lead on a number of issues that are central to the whole project of therapy. For ease of reference the headings are as follows:

- The question of professionalization and "scientification"
- The limitations of theory and the core theoretical model
- "Informed consent", abuse, and efficacy
- What kind of therapy for a post-professional era?
- General practice counselling—nascent postmodern therapy?
- What kind of organizational arrangements (if any) in a post-professional era?
- So who would be a therapist?
- Objections and prebuttals

The question of professionalization and "scientification"

Licensing does not protect the public. Licensing does not exclude incompetents. Licensing does not encourage innovation. It stultifies ... [Will Schutz, 1979; quoted in Mowbray, 1995: 213]

I should like to propose a new name for psychotherapy. ... The [aims] of such a change in terminology are immense ...—namely, resurrecting the human soul from the therapeutic grave in which our technological age has buried it, and preserving the dignity and discipline of art from modern man's insatiable passion for professionalism. [Szasz, 1978: 208]

A central concern in this book has been that of the professionalization of therapy. As will have become clear, I am highly critical of what I call "didactic" professionalization—an institutional, dominator–hierarchical process which so easily becomes antithetical to the individual empowerment and responsibility-taking of practitioners. With regard to professional ethics (see Chapter 4), for the philosopher Beyerstein, "[The question] 'what ought I to do?' is not equivalent to the question, 'What is the consensus of my colleagues about what to do?'. What makes [a given action] right has nothing to do with the numbers of people who take it to be so" (1993: 422). Thus is the very legitimacy of and reliance upon institutional, centralized codes of ethics thrown into severe question (cf. House, 1997b).

The conventional pro-professionalization view is well expressed by Sills:

> I think accreditation in Britain is improving enormously. ... Until recently clients were not protected against incompetence or wrong treatment. ... I hope that ultimately [regulation] will become part of the law. ... Generally speaking ... I think the UKCP, the BPS, the BAC and other organisations are really taking standards seriously now. It's ethics that's the most important. [Sills, 1996: 72, 73]

No one would disagree, of course, that ethics are important; the question is how best *to be with* ethical questions. Not least of the considerable ironies of this pro-professionalization position is that, following the arguments in this book, an institutional preoccupation with codes of ethics itself can easily create precisely the opposite of its intention—that is, unethical, damaging effects throughout the whole field of therapy, through its *de facto* institutional entrench-ment and the ossification of what can become intrinsically abusive therapeutic practice.

Contrast Sills's view with that expressed by House and Totton (1997b: 1), that the institutional professionalization of the therapy field "would be a disaster"—a somewhat counterintuitive conclu-sion which is by no means reached merely, or even primarily, because of the many reasons so ably articulated by Mowbray (1995) (stifled creativity and innovation, an increasing preponderance of "defensive" psychotherapy, restricted entry to the field, and so on). (The reader is also referred to the devastating critique of professionalization in Hogan [1979], an exhaustive American study which is—unsurprisingly—never referred to by the apologists for professionalization.) What I have argued in this book goes much further, and is far more fundamental than this: namely, that the fetishization and institutional sedimentation of therapy's profes-sion-centred conventions actively threatens to create an increasingly abusive therapeutic environment, thereby rendering therapy far more likely to enmesh clients in its thrall—curtailing rather than enhancing client freedom in the process. And putting this argument together with Mowbray's analysis, then the professionalization process, far from being beneficent for clients (as the "official" rhetoric has it), may well itself be intrinsically abusive, and be doing net harm to the field as whole (cf. Hogan, 1979).

I have also attempted to make an ambitious link between didactic professionalization in the therapy field and the old-paradigm values and practices of modernity. In my view the link is a crucial yet greatly neglected one—for while there do exist extensive *and quite separate* critiques of professionalization and modernity, only very rarely are the two phenomena seen as being inextricably interrelated. One notable exception is Schaef in her excellent and much neglected book *Beyond Therapy, Beyond Science*:

> Historically, we have always seen that when an old cultural paradigm is dying and on the verge of collapse, there is a tendency to become more rigid in the old paradigm, *to set up progressively stricter controls*, and to try to kill off new ideas and dissenters through the use of the regulatory and legal arms of the culture. ...
> *As the old paradigm is being challenged professionally, politically, and economically, the arm of regulation and control gets stronger and stronger.* [Schaef, 1992: 226, my emphases]

I maintain that those aspiring to human potential development should as far as possible step outside of the conditionings of modernity, and locate their helping practices within an historical, consciousness-evolutionary context, rather than ossifying them into ever tighter "regimes of institutionalized truth" which are, if anything, antithetical to rather than facilitative of human potential development. Such a fully articulated understanding would need to encompass both the more spiritually inclined work of writers like Erich Neumann and Rudolf Steiner (referred to above) and also the post-structuralist, Foucauldian analyses of Nikolas Rose in his important work on modern "regimes of the self" and the construction of subjectivity (e.g. 1989, 1996, 1997; see also Parker, 1997a and my Chapter 2).

I agree with Henriques *et al.*, then, that "The pressures that assert the need for professionalization will tend also to reassert the more traditional practices of psychology: the development of regulative tools ... and the concomitant emphasis on its respectability as a science" (1984: 6). One only has to read the recent grandiose pronouncements of the new European Association for Psychotherapy (see pp. 211–212) to see the veracity and pertinence of this point nearly 20 years after it was written.

Finally, it is this lethal cocktail—comprising the ideology of modernity, the fear-driven dominator–hierarchical attempt to police the therapy field, and the considerable vested interests (both material and power-related) infusing in the whole process—that in my view make the ongoing deconstruction of therapy's most hallowed and taken-for-granted assumptions absolutely crucial if we are to avoid creating a self-serving, sometimes abusive, *therapist*-centred practice. Schaef again puts the point wonderfully well:

> Are psychologists ... open to ask, Is the unspoken worldview that underlies the assumptions in the way I practice my profession perhaps, unwittingly, contributing to the very problems that I am committed to help solve? If we are not open to struggling with this question and articulating our assumptions, we are, indeed, part of the problem. [Schaef, 1992: 227]

In my view, the perspective offered both by Anne Schaef and in this book makes the case for therapy being ongoingly deconstructive both compelling and, ultimately, irresistible.

The limitations of theory and the "core theoretical model"

> Theories are not innocent, value-free constructs, but are often themselves defenses against, or attempts to get rid of, the very phenomena that is their subject matter. [Davis, 1989: 274]

> ... the new paradigm cannot be approached theoretically. The very nature of the paradigm is that it is a participatory paradigm. [Schaef, 1992: 287]

Earlier in this book I have discussed what is arguably the intrinsic defensiveness, and even abusiveness, of profession-centred theory (see particularly Chapter 2), which in turn I link closely with the ideology of modernity and old-paradigm ways of thinking about, controlling, and even plundering our world. Such empirical or positivist ways of knowing, rooted as they are in a naïvely untenable correspondence theory of truth, are, I believe, inherently limited and limiting, and are beginning to give way to far more holistic, participative, tacit–intuitive, and even spiritual–clairvoyant ways of knowing. Notable examples of this emerging trend are the recent upsurge of interest in Goethean science (see Chapters 9–10), and the burgeoning international growth of the Scientific and Medical Network, a global grouping of scientific scholars, researchers, and clinicians (including Nobel prize-winners and numerous university professors) who challenge and reject the one-sidedly materialist assumptions of modern science, and are working and writing in the exciting field of New Paradigm thinking. As I have written elsewhere (House, 1999d), the integration of postmodern thinking with the ideas of, for example, David Bohm, Krishnamurti, Lacan, and Heidegger (to name but four) offers very considerable possibilities for developing a truly coherent, participative, and humane philosophy of living and life for a new millennium.

Within the therapy field there has in recent years been a quite passionate debate about the centrality or otherwise of what is called the "core theoretical model" (or CTM), particularly in relation to practitioner training (Feltham, 1997a; Wheeler, 1998). As Corbett has it (echoing the arguments of Masson, 1992a), "it has been common for senior analysts to teach the kind of orthodoxy that is expected which essentially repeats the party line" (Corbett, 1995; quoted in Feltham, 1997a: 122); and apart from those trainings which have an explicitly "integrative" orientation, it seems that such parochial "theoretical hegemony" is the rule rather than the exception within the therapy training field. This situation leads to an inevitable tension, if not radical incoherence, at the core of most therapy training—for "the common aim of psychotherapy—autonomy—is belied by the reality of training institutes which demand conformity from trainees, and by psychotherapy which either mystifies clients or subtly converts them to belief in the tenets of the particular approach" (Feltham, 1997a: 122).

Feltham provides an excellent illustration of the kind of mad-making training "double-think" that often occurs (driven in turn by the incoherence of the il-logic of modernity)—with the surface rhetoric of "freedom of thought" being underlain by the iron fist of theoretical authoritarianism. Thus, he quotes the rationale given in 1941 for Karen Horney's demotion within the New York Psycho-analytic Institute:

REFLECTIONS ON PROFESSION-CENTRED THERAPY   229

The Educational Committee is fully in favour of free unhampered discussion of all points of view existing in psychoanalysis. Such discussions are possible and most fruitful only if preparatory analyses and preliminary, theoretical fundamentals are such as not to prejudice the student in advance to the basic principles of psychoanalysis. [S. Quinn, quoted in Feltham, 1997a: 119]

This will sound all too familiar to anyone who has read Masson's book *Final Analysis: The Making and Unmaking of a Psychoanalyst*. The reader might object that this tendency is confined to psychoanalysis alone; but I contend (and Feltham seems to concur) that in *any* system that is dominated (implicitly or otherwise) by dominator-hierarchical values, such theoretical authoritarianism is essentially inevitable—though of course in many cases the *rhetoric* of "freedom of expression" and "autonomy" may camouflage the underlying coercion far more successfully and subtly than in the New York Institute! Nor should we be surprised by this, for any regime of truth (whether it be the "local" regime of a particular school, or the meta-regime of "therapy-in-general") will have to demand such conformity—surreptitiously or otherwise.

Under such circumstances, moreover, and taking into account the transference and "deference" dynamics triggered in any training milieu, it is very difficult to see how there can be any degree of space for thinking outside of the presuppositions that are conditioned into newly training practitioners being schooled into one of therapy's many "local" regimes of truth. A close analysis of the exchange between Feltham and Wheeler provides a wonderful example of profession-centred therapy's regime of truth (discussed in Chapters 2), and its seeming need to reproduce itself—not unlike Louis Althusser's "ideological state apparatus" (Althusser, 1971; see also House, 1984). The notion of "schooling into a regime of truth", or the inculcation of an ideology, is strongly suggested when considering the rationale typically offered in favour of a CTM, and which is described thus by Feltham:

Failure to embrace one model in depth results in practitioners who are confused, lacking in rigour, and whose knowledge base is thin. Trainees ... must learn and hone the practical and clinical attitudes, skills and techniques associated with a particular approach if they are to become competent practitioners. ... They cannot achieve ...

maturity without first having had a thorough grounding in a coherent model. ... [P]ractitioners should hold strong theoretical positions. [Feltham, 1997a: 118]

Within the world-view of modernity, theory is typically clung on to as representing some kind of "objective truth", promoting methods which are, thereby, assumed to be pretty much infallible: as Burman (1997b: 126) has it, mainstream psychotherapy is—or pretends to be—a quintessentially rational, modernist enterprise which "rehearses the modern condition of western split subjectivity wedded to singular truths and linear histories". From a critical postmodern stance, perhaps the profession's determination to promulgate CTMs has far more to do with colluding with the anxiety-driven needs for control and certainty than it does a sober and appropriate engagement with the uncomfortable reality of intersubjective relationship (cf. Chapter 10). Feltham again:

we appear to insist on core counselling models without even knowing what we mean. ... All therapeutic models are partly fictions. ... Many of us cling to an ideological object, such as a particular ... psychotherapy, which we cherish and can never let go of. Arguably, all such ideologies act as opiates and *their true function is to infuse us with a reassuring but defensive sense of certainty and direction* in an unpredictable and frightening world. [1997a: 120, 123–124 *passim*, my emphasis]

On this view, then, perhaps the psychodynamics (or emotional drivenness) of "theory" (Craib, 1987) is at least as important in therapy's preoccupation with theoretical models and rationales as is any pretension to therapeutic "objectivity" or "scientificity". I am certainly not arguing that it is somehow wrong, unhealthy, or unnecessary to need comfort in a frightening world; but I am arguing that it can hardly lead to very effective or authentic therapeutic practitionership to have what is an emotionally driven security need so successfully camouflaged and obfuscated by a garb of illusory objectivity that not even practitioners themselves seem aware of it. This is one area, then, in which the postmodern, New Paradigm critique of the modernist world-view seems to me to become absolutely essential—uncomfortable as it may be for those unwilling to relinquish their comforting "ideological object". Or for those with a vested interest in perpetuating the theoretical fictions that dominate contemporary profession-centred therapy. Or for those who believe that "a first training must treat (adult) trainees as babies to be spoon-fed traditional material (however stodgy or toxic)" (Feltham, 1997a: 125).

I agree wholeheartedly with Feltham (1997a: 121), in common with the considerable literature that highlights the essential role of "non-specificity" in therapy efficacy (e.g. Shepherd & Sartorius, 1989), that "Individual clinical giftedness, so overlooked as a factor in therapy, may well be more significant than any pedagogic theory". Feltham goes on to remark upon how often he finds that "generalized theory" fails to fit his experience of "real individuals", and that untrained carers or minimally trained practitioners sometimes seem far more "human and insightful" than some "highly trained practitioners ... steeped in one or another core theoretical model" (1997a: 124). Feltham's perception is certainly in tune with a great deal of research pointing to a conclusion that is deeply uncomfortable for the professional therapy "expert"—that lightly trained paraprofessionals appear to effect outcomes at least as effective as trained therapy practitioners (see, for example, Bohart & Tallman, 1996; House, 1996j).

In her revealing attempt to respond to Feltham's withering critique of the CTM, Wheeler (1998) makes a valiant but ultimately unconvincing attempt to shore up the crumbling edifice of the theory-dominated modernist project of profession-centred therapy. Below I reproduce a major extract from Wheeler's paper, *substituting my term "regime of truth" for her term "(core theoretical) model"*—which I think will make my point with little need for further elaboration:

> ... I believe that counsellor training courses should define and then adhere to a **regime of truth** that influences all aspects of training. ...
> The **regime of truth** should be reflected in all aspects of the course, from theory to skills training, methods of and criteria for assessment [another aspect of the modernist project in therapy, incidentally—RH], supervision and personal development. ... [T]he **regime of truth** should be reflected ... in the way the course is structured, assessed, taught and administered. ... In other words, the **regime of truth** is evident throughout the course, providing coherence and internal consistency. ... Students need clarity ..., which a **regime of truth** provides. ... [I]t will be easier to recruit staff to teach a course that has a well-known and well documented **regime of truth** [note

the incursion of a "rationale of convenience" here—RH]. ... Students need a comprehensive and digestible **regime of truth** that provides a foundation for their practice. ... The [training] journey ... cannot include too many deviations or the ultimate destination will not be reached. ... *[I]t is helpful to see counsellor training as akin to the process of growing up.* ... Children like to know where they are and what is expected of them. Parents ... can provide a template for thinking about and managing life. ... Parents adhere to their values and beliefs and pass them on to their children. ... *This seems like a helpful metaphor for counsellor training.* [Wheeler, 1998: 134–138 *passim*, my emphases and **"replacements"**]

Quite apart from the spurious incursion of the infantilizing ideology of analytic theory in this account, it is also highly revealing that Wheeler's paper is liberally smattered with "demands", "shoulds", and "musts"—again betraying the hierarchical and authoritarian values that necessarily accompany any system purveying a "regime of truth" masquerading as a "core theoretical model".

For Edwards (1992: 197), "We are reaching beyond our human potential towards our spiritual potential. And to avoid becoming anachronistic and irrelevant, psychotherapy must rapidly follow suit". And if she is anything like right (which I believe she is), then the field's whole approach to the place of theory will, I believe, have to be quite fundamentally problematized and then recast in ways far more consonant with New Paradigm thinking, and, concomitantly, away from the philosophically incoherent and profoundly damaging world-view of modernity (Barratt, 1993; Polkinghorne, 1990).

Informed consent, abuse, and efficacy

The situational difficulty for all clients is that this first encounter is inscrutable ... there is a discrepancy of knowledge between the two parties about what therapy is as a process, ritual or stylised conversation. [Pilgrim, 1997: 117]

The therapist as gaoler is an engaging if somewhat sinister metaphor. Is this really the nature of the power exerted by the analyst ...? Is this really what is going on in a thousand private practices up and down the land ...? [Thorne, 1999: 7]

I will not rehearse here the detailed arguments of earlier chapters which set out the diverse ways in which I believe the prevailing profession-centred form taken by individualized therapy can become routinely, surreptitiously—and unconsciously—abusive. I will merely mention the question of "informed consent" (see Chapters 6–8), for I believe this to be a much neglected yet absolutely core issue in the inherently self-serving and sometimes mesmerizing regime of truth that profession-centred therapy tends to set up. It will be clear from the earlier discussion (e.g. of Hinshelwood's & Alexander's work—Chapters 2 and 6 respectively) that I believe it to be extremely problematic if not impossible for there to exist anything remotely approaching informed client consent in therapy. And this situation can only be exacerbated in an oversupplied practitioner market in which therapists wishing to make a living compete fiercely for a given client base (Clark, 2002), and therefore have a survival-driven vested interest in clients succumbing to the entanglements of profession-centred therapy and its common tendency to encourage long-term therapy via the dynamics of dependency and attachment (cf. my discussion of "material generation" at the close of Chapter 3).

Pilgrim (1997: 134) has similar concerns: in his experience, therapists very rarely inform clients at the start of therapy that the experience can sometimes be harmful, with there never being any guarantee that a given therapy will not be harmful. This concern, moreover, is quite apart from the fact that therapists probably never tell their new clients that it is impossible for either client or therapist to give informed consent to therapy at the beginning, or that therapy may well trigger deep attachment dynamics which might make it very difficult for the client to choose to leave the therapy once they are engaged in it (cf. the experience of Rosie Alexander, Chapter 6). In my experience these are extremely thorny and quintessentially ethical issues which (unsurprisingly!) receive little or no attention whatsoever in the therapy institutions' allegedly comprehensive Codes of Ethics. And at worst, they threaten to leave the therapy world with the unedifying choice of either risking the kinds of intrinsic abuse exhaustively outlined in earlier chapters, or else rendering itself a truly "impossible profession" to which very few clients will choose to come once they are fully and frankly informed of its possible dangers. Later, I set out the parameters which a non-abusive, post-professional form of therapy might follow, which would explicitly attempt to avoid some of these ethical abuses.

I only read Pilgrim's important book after having written the bulk of this text, yet he makes many points which closely echo the arguments developed in this book—not least about the nature of what I call profession-centred therapy's regime of truth. Thus, he writes:

> [P]sychotherapy [has] a peculiar setting with unexpected rules (compared to everyday life). ... The territorial control which therapists avidly seek over the boundaries of their work with clients confirms this tendency to construct contexts which are isolated and artificial. ... Clients ... walk into a framed context which has been constructed in advance by therapists. ... The setting and type of conversation warranted or disallowed is under the control of the therapist. ... [A] central feature of indoctrination is that the total control that the persuader exerts deliberately engenders an emotional state in the target, which can disorientate them about their existing way of construing the world. [There is an] anxious pedantry which surrounds questions of boundaries. ... [S]etting is important not because of its therapeutic *role* but because it provides a constraint on, and opportunity for, the *existence* of therapy as a social practice. Consequently, a reliance on the psychotherapeutic discourse to illuminate the importance of the setting will lead to a partial and reductionist account. [Pilgrim, 1997: 33, ix, 97–98, 99, 102, his emphases]

It does appear that therapy's honey-moon may now be largely over, and that an increasing number of critical commentators are beginning to pose deeply searching and uncomfortable questions about the whole therapeutic project and its assumptive base, the open and honest consideration of which can only surely lead to better, less self-serving practices in the therapeutic realm.

Finally, it is worth mentioning here that the analyses in Chapters 6–8 provide, I believe, a very important insight into the dangers of profession-centred therapy's coercing regime from the client's point of view. In Chapter 4 I argued that the accurate or meaningful specification of efficacy within therapy outcome research is quite probably impossible—not least because the very way in which such an assessment is typically formulated is stuck firmly within the "objectivist" positivist paradigm and naïve foundationalism of modernity. And even if we accept, as argued in Chapter 5, that honestly reported subjective experience also provides by no means an infallible account of the therapeutic experience, it does not follow from this that the client's subjective experience has nothing of value to tell us. Indeed, I believe that such experience gives us a unique and privileged insight into the machinations that profession-centred individual therapy can wreak on the unsuspecting client—and we should be deeply grateful to Alexander, France, and Sands for providing us with such an extensive record of their deeply distressing therapeutic experiences. I hope that my detailed analyses of those experiences in all their immediacy and rawness have helped to throw light on and substantiate my more abstract discussion of profession-centred therapy's regime of truth in Chapters 2–4 inclusive.

In my final chapter I will consider some more substantive elaborations of what therapy in a mature "post-professional" era might look like.

CHAPTER TWELVE

Elaborations on the "post-professional" era

What kind of therapy for a post-professional era?

Gotta find some therapy; this treatment takes too long. [from the song "Twenty-four hours" by Joy Division, 1980]

... psychotherapy does exist, whether or not it functions effectively. The question is not whether to ignore it, but how to conduct it so that it really is therapeutic, and does not exacerbate problems, or merely fail to relieve them. [France, 1988: 240]

Psychotherapists ... must make a paradigm shift, themselves ... and that will not be psychotherapy as we know it ... I do believe that psychotherapists can recover from their enmeshment in a paradigm that does not work for us, and as we do, our work will be completely different. [Schaef, 1992: 307]

C learly, given my choice of the Rollo May epigraph to introduce this book (p. xvii), I too look towards a society in which individualized, professional therapy is simply not needed. Yet until we reach such a position, perhaps the best we can do is to embrace quite explicitly and self-consciously a deconstructive therapeutic practice (House, 1999b; Parker, 1999), and hope and trust that the new millennium will bring new cultural forms for supporting people with their difficulties of living. Clearly such an approach requires striking a delicate and sensitive balance between fearless critique, on the one hand, and offering constructive suggestions as to the specific nature that a less self-serving and abusive therapy might take, on the other. As Kovel (1976: 326) has it, "The actuality of neurotic suffering in today's society is such that the therapies cannot be turned aside. This need not detract from the goal of abolishing the need for the service of therapists".

I would describe a processually deconstructive therapy (*which is not one*, as Luce Iragaray might have said—1985) as having a goodly proportion of the following distinguishing characteristics (some of which do, of course, overlap with each other).

Framework and resources for a "post-profession-centred", deconstructive-critical therapy

✓ *nought*, it would achieve a "state" (or, better, way of being) in which all theoretical or classificatory devices such as the one I am about to present would be redundant and transcended;

✓ *first*, it would essentially eschew preconceived theoretical frameworks—having an inclusive, pluralistic approach to diverse, "local" "knowledges" which values (for example) intuitive, spiritual, and feminist "knowing" at least as highly as rational-empirical knowledge (Gunew, 1990; Edwards, 1992; T. Hart, 1998; Hart *et al.*, 1997; House, 1996g; Polanyi, 1958; Schaef, 1992); and would follow Wilfred Bion's suggestion that, as far as possible, the therapist enter the consulting room free of memory, desire, or understanding (Smith, 1984: 215; Symington & Symington, 1996: Chapter 14);

✓ *second*, it will tend to embrace a postmodernist, deconstructionist epistemology (e.g. Anderson, 1997; Barratt, 1993; DiNicola, 1993; Finlay, 1989; House, 1997a, 1999e; Kvale, 1992; Lax, 1992; Levin, 1987; Lowenthal, 1996; Parker, 1999; Parker *et al.*, 1995; Polkinghorne, 1990; White, 1991), rather than the essentially positivistic, modernist agenda that dominates so much of the therapy world (e.g. Erwin, 1997) and the psychology discipline more generally (Parker, 1998b);

✓ *third* and relatedly, it will tend to gravitate towards a so-called

New Paradigm, spiritual, transpersonal, or even mystical ontology which recognizes the ultimately ineffable nature of human life and existence (e.g. Bergin, 1988; Clarkson, 2002; Claxton, 1986; Eigen, 1998; Garrett, 1998; Hillman, 1996; Hitter, 1997; House, 1997a and Chapter 9, this book; Nelson, 1994; Richards & Bergin, 1997; Schaef, 1992; Thorne, 1998; Valle, 1998; Watson, 1998; see also the *Journal of Transpersonal Psychology*), eschewing the overtly egotistical individualism that professional therapy typically embraces and encourages (e.g. Cloud, 1998; Dawes, 1994); recognizing that healing practices from every culture and epoch are of value (Bromberg, 1975; Frank, 1973; Kiev, 1964; Torrey, 1986); that therapy and healing might well be commensurable practices (Boyer, 1983; West, 1997); and that we should be open to locating and contextualizing the therapy phenomenon within the broader evolution of human consciousness (see Chapter 11);

✓ *fourth*, it would tend to be essentially hermeneutical (Messer *et al.*, 1988; Richardson & Fowers, 1997; Sass & Woolfolk, 1988), with a phenomenological/existential focus (e.g. Cohn, 1997; Pollio *et al.*, 1998; Spinelli, 1994; Valle, 1998; Valle & Halling, 1989);

✓ *fifth*, it will accommodate seminal critical, post-structuralist perspectives on the so-called "invention" of contemporary subjectivity and the hegemony or "regime" of the (modern) self (Nikolas Rose) which increasingly holds sway in Western culture (e.g. Cushman, 1990, 1991, 1995; Mauss, 1979; Parker, 1997a; Rose, 1989, 1992, 1996, 1997)—and couched within the wider question of the evolution of human consciousness and the Western mind (Crook, 1980; Tarnas, 1991);

✓ *sixth*, it will tend to pay more attention than conventionally to the interface and cross-fertilization between psychology and philosophy (e.g. Carruthers & Boucher, 1998; Craib, 1986; Faulconer & Williams, 1990; Howard, 2000; Martin, 1998; Miller, 1992; O'Donohue & Kitchener, 1996; Polkinghorne, 1990; Russell, 1987; Toulmin, 1981; see also the excellent journals, the *Journal of Consciousness Studies* and the *Journal for the Society of Existential Analysis*, and the recent development of "philosophical counselling"—Howard, 2000). Under this category I include the fundamental question of "victimhood" (Hall, 1993; Schaef,

1992), and the tension between environmental determinist and responsibility-taking conceptions of human experience (Dawes, 1994; cf. my Chapter 4);

✓ *seventh*, it will tend to have a de-profession-centred, devolved structure along the lines of the "self-generating practitioner community" concept outlined by Heron (1997), the nearest current equivalent of which is the Independent Practitioners Network (Totton, 1997a); and a non-institutional, responsibility-embracing, and participative approach to ethical conduct (Bates & House, in preparation; Brown, 1997; House, 1997b; see also Chapter 4);

✓ *eighth*, it will tend to sympathize with the project of critical and feminist psychological perspectives (e.g. respectively [critical], Brown, 1973; Burman & Parker, 1998; Fox and Prilleltensky, 1997; Hare-Mustin & Marecek, 1990; Heather, 1976; Hillman, 1975; Ingleby, 1981; Kovel, 1988; Newman, 1991; Radical Therapist Collective, 1974; Sarason, 1981; Tolman & Maiers, 1991; and [feminist] Brown, 1994a,b; Gartrel, 1994; Joy, 1993; Lerman & Porter, 1990; Rave & Larsen, 1995; Seu & Heenan, 1998; Wilkinson, 1997);

✓ *ninth*, it will typically challenge the "myth of normality" (Buck, 1992), and reject the ideologically driven language of "abnormality" (Buck, 1990; Freides, 1960; House, 1997e, 2001b; Prilleltensky, 1994b), or any kind of medical-model focus (tacit or otherwise) on so-called "psychopathology" (Halling & Nill, 1989; Levin, 1987; Lowson, 1994; Pallone, 1986; Parker *et al.*, 1995);

✓ *tenth*, it will tend to problematize, and certainly not take for granted, the ideology of "developmentalism" in developmental psychology (Bradley, 1989, 1993; Broughton, 1987; Burman, 1994, 1997a; Morss, 1990, 1996; Russell, 1987; Walkerdine, 1984, 1993);

✓ *eleventh*, it would advocate and achieve a radical transparency, openness, and "power-with" way-of-being with clients (as in the Person-Centred tradition—Mearns & Thorne, 1988; Rogers, 1951), minimizing the exploitative power dynamics that so saturate the conventions of profession-centred therapy (cf. Chapter 2);

✓ *twelfth*, it will be ordinary and quite specifically non-mystifying in terms of both theoretical affectation and procedural minutiae, with a "friendship" rather than a clinical focus (cf. Lomas, 1981; Hobson, 1985; Howe, 1993; Smail, 1987, 1996), and eschewing pretensions to therapist "expertise" (Dawes, 1994; Mair, 1992);

✓ *thirteenth*, its focus will tend to be more on taking care (Smail, 1987) than on a medical, "assessment–diagnosis–cure" model (e.g. Boyle, 1996; Levy, 1992)—in other words, it will privilege human love over technique or clinical "treatment" ideologies (Edwards, 1992; Fine, 1985; House, 1996f, h; Lasky & Silverman, 1988);

✓ *fourteenth*, it would lay stress on "play" ("Psychotherapy has to do with two people playing together"—Winnicott, 1971: 44), "the dance", and creativity, rather than the "deficit" ideologies of "psychopathology" and "(ab)normality" (cf. point 9, above)— a move well characterized by anthroposophist Georg Kühlewind in his phrase "from normal to healthy" (Kühlewind, 1988);

✓ *fifteenth*, it will more likely embrace a (social) constructionist rather than a positivist/objectivist framework (e.g. Gergen, 1985; Krause, 1998; McNamee & Gergen, 1992; Nightingale & Cromby, 1999; Parker, 1998a); and it will tend towards being conversational, narrative, story-focused, and dialogical (Epston, 1997; Freedman & Combs, 1996; Friedman, 1992, 1998; Gergen & Gergen, 1988; Gilligan & Prince, 1993; Heard, 1993; Hermans & Kempen, 1993; Hycner, 1991; Mair, 1989; Monk *et al.*, 1997; Riikonen & Smith, 1997; Sampson, 1993; van Deurzen-Smith, 1992; White & Epston, 1990; Williams, 1999; but for a critique, see Rose, 1996: 177–182);

✓ *sixteenth*, and relatedly, it will tend to privilege notions of the indissolubly co-creative intersubjectivity of human relationship in its therapeutic ontology (e.g. Braten, 1999; Cohn, 1997; Crossley, 1996; House, 2000b; Josselson, 1996; Mitchell, 1988; Natterson & Friedman, 1995; Stolorow *et al.*, 1987; cf. Chapter 10), rather than an intra-psychic, subject/object, observer/observed ontology;

✓ *seventeenth*, it would tend to be time-limited or of relatively short duration (e.g. Alexander & French, 1946; Coren, 1996; Feltham, 1997b; Strupp & Binder, 1984; Thorne, 1994), thereby minimizing the possibility of (though not completely—see Alexander, 1995; Maroda, 1991) infantilizing dependency issues being triggered and exploited within the emotional cauldron of the profession-centred therapy milieu—and yet being able to stay true to Person-Centred, humanistic values (House, 1997c; Thorne, 1994, 1999);

✓ *eighteenth*, it will tend to be flexible rather than rigidly and obsessively "boundaried" in nature (Alexander, 1971; Brown, 1994a,b; Hermansson, 1997; Lazarus, 1994a; Mahrer, 1996), both in terms of working contracts and periodicity of meeting;

✓ *nineteenth*, it will consider the so-called "extra-therapeutic" dimension—the social, the cultural, and the political—at least as much as it does the intra-psychic, with its associated individualistic ideology (e.g. Albee, 1990; Cloud, 1998; Cushman, 1995; Danziger, 1990; Gergen, 1990; Kurtz, 1992; Pilgrim, 1992, 1997; Prilleltensky, 1994a; Ryan, 1971; Samuels, 1993, 2001; Smail, 1996; Totton, 2000) (see also point 8, above)—and including a greater engagement with community psychology (Heller & Monahan, 1977; Levine & Perkins, 1987; Prilleltensky & Nelson, 1997; Sarason, 1982; Tolan *et al.*, 1990);

✓ and *twentieth* and finally, it would tend to have an open view about the nature of "change" (Douglas, 1997; House, 1996f; Smail, 1996), and would by no means slavishly follow the old-paradigm (and professionally self-serving) view that therapeutic change necessarily has to be a long-winded and painful process (e.g. Edwards, 1992; Krishnamurti, 1973; Schaef, 1992; Thorne, 1999).

Clearly this brief sketch cannot remotely do justice to the form that an explicitly post-professional deconstructive therapy might take (cf., for example, Barratt, 1993; Kvale, 1992; Lax, 1992; Lowenthal, 1996; McNamee & Gergen, 1992; Riikonen & Smith, 1997): the articulation of that task has already been started in Parker's important recent anthology (Parker, 1999, reviewed at House, 1999e), and no doubt it will be picked up and developed in different forums and in diverse ways in the coming years. There are, of course, precedents within the history of therapy for principled and coherent challenges to the received norms of therapeutic practice, even within psychoanalysis itself (see, for example, the innovative writings and practice of Franz Alexander, Sandor Ferenczi, Jacques Lacan, and Donald Winnicott—see Totton, 2000).

However, no matter how assiduously we might strive to create a non-self-serving therapeutic culture that is maturely post-professional, and which responds to the concerns expressed in this book, at least some of the contradictions nestling at the very heart of the therapeutic project will surely remain. Pilgrim (1997), for example, asks rhetorically:

> some family therapists operating now self-consciously within a post-structuralist framework have sought to remove the trappings of expertise in order to create a therapeutic context of ordinariness. But can their designation as paid therapists ever close the gap between the parties and dissolve disciplinary power? [p. 34]

General practice counselling—nascent postmodern therapy?

> ... a postmodern perspective has something to contribute to understanding the complexity of counselling in general practice. [Miller-Pietroni, 1999: 17]

> I am sure that short-term counselling for specific problems usually does help. The dangers are more likely to concern long-term or in-depth therapy of a more analytic nature. [France, 1988: 239]

It may surprise many readers when I suggest that the burgeoning phenomenon of general practice counselling might be a fertile area for developing a more deconstructive approach to therapy (cf. Miller-Pietroni, 1999). Of the 21 characteristics outlined above, the key points of 17, 18, and 19 are certainly central to and naturally embraced in the GP setting. In my own practice I have found it eminently possible to incorporate many of the other characteristics outlined above (House, 1997c, 1999c). Certainly, it is a setting where I find that by far the majority of clients come without any preconceptions about therapy and the "rules" of how to be "a good profession-centred therapy client" (House, 1997c)—and as a result they often enter into a co-creative dialogic relationship with enthusiasm, ease, and a minimum of mystification—a meeting which naturally seems to embrace many of the characteristics listed above.

A case in point is the phenomenon of *flexibility* (see the essays in

Lees, 1999—most notably, Smith, 1999). Lees (1997) advocates a Winnicottian-style flexibility for the GP therapeutic framework in which the practitioner is exquisitely sensitive and responsive to the dialectical "dance" between flexibility and firmness—rather than pre-emptively assuming (à la Robert Langs and "communicative psychotherapy"—Smith, 1991; Hoag, 1992) that firm, "holding" boundaries are essential (cf. Chapter 3). In fact, in advocating such flexibility, Lees, along with Hermansson (1997), House (1999c), and Smith (1999), is following a long lineage in the therapy field, stretching back, for example, to the highly innovative work of Sandor Ferenczi (Masson, 1988, Chapter 3; Stanton, 1991), and the radical technical innovations of Franz Alexander (Alexander, 1971), who questioned the assumption that prolonged "treatment" was a necessary precondition for therapeutic change to occur, and that rigid therapeutic boundaries were necessary. Ann France (1988) is very revealing on flexibility:

> Some of the problems [of combining a professional framework with a personal relationship] arise because the traditional concepts governing the professional framework are often interpreted too rigidly, and inhibit the expression of the personal relationship. ... My own experience of psychotherapy ... suggested that there was room for far more flexibility in the practice, and that this did not prove harmful. [p. 240, 241]

Another important feature of the GP setting that is potentially subversive of profession-centred therapy's regime of truth is its bypassing of the arguably alienating commodity form of therapy (Kovel, 1976: Chapter 16). Within the British National Health Service, counselling is free at the point of delivery, and is effectively paid for by the community as a whole (and, incidentally, at rates well below prevailing market levels for individual counselling), rather than being fully inserted into the sphere of capitalist market exchange and the often alienating social relations that accompany it (Kovel, 1976; Ollman, 1971). Counselling in general practice is therefore one of the few settings in which counselling is not unduly contaminated by the alienating forces of commodity exchange. This has a number of crucial implications—not least the fact that because there is a seemingly inexhaustible supply of clients (certainly in my own and my colleagues' experience), the counsellor does not have a vested material interest in needing a given client to return again and again. This in turn takes a great deal of anxiety away for the counsellor, and leaves the client comparatively free of profession-centred enthralment, and freer to "do their work" without the burdening preoccupation of what we might call the "I'm-paying-the-practitioner's-mortgage" syndrome—the feeling that the practitioner is personally reliant for her or his livelihood on the client's continuing clienthood.

In addition, it is precisely because the GP setting is a medical setting that it offers an excellent opportunity for practitioners to explore ways of transcending simplistic mind/body dualism, and of working holistically and creatively with so-called "psychosomatic" symptoms (e.g. Erskine & Judd, 1994; House, 1996e; McDougall, 1989; Stein, 1985b; Taylor, 1987, 1992; Taylor *et al.*, 1997; Totton, 1998; Wilson & Mintz, 1989; Winnicott, 1975). My strong hunch is that there is almost certainly a significant amount of highly innovative, path-breaking therapeutic work being done in GP settings up and down the country, and that such innovations will in time diffuse into the therapy field more generally in quite unforeseeable ways (House, 1999c). Some specialist medical writers have even suggested that the general practice setting is one in which postmodernist deconstructionist views can sit quite comfortably (e.g. McWhinney, 1996).

It is indeed ironic that this wonderfully innovative crucible for pioneering new, creatively "postmodern" therapy forms is under continual threat from the forces of modernity that demand so-called "scientifically validated" cognitive–behavioural therapy, "cost–effectiveness", measurability, and all the other totems of the mechanistic and increasingly all-pervasive accountability culture (see Fahy & Wessely, 1993; House, 1996b,f).

What kind of organizational arrangements (if any) in a post-professional era?—the IPN as a self-generating practitioner community

Trainers and theoreticians dissatisfied with the prescriptive positions of existing professional bodies might risk launching themselves as independent commentators, critics and creators of new therapeutic cultures and methods, thus challenging the assumption that the only alternatives to traditional models are flimsy, illegitimate hybrids. [Feltham, 1997a: 125]

... relationship without registration is entirely different. [Jiddu Krishnamurti—Krishnamurti Foundation Trust, 1992: 437]

Colin Feltham's challenge to the discontented within the therapy field captures well the spirit and drive behind the founding of the Independent Practitioners Network (IPN) in the UK in 1994. The editors of the anthology *Implausible Professions* (House & Totton, 1997), both active participants in the Network, collected together a number of papers which directly address the future of "psycho-practice" in a "post-professional era" (Illich, 1977a). The IPN, in which I have personally been involved since its founding conference in November 1994, is a Network which attempts to respond openly and creatively to at least some of the concerns raised in this book. Totton (1997a) succinctly describes the "new model of account-ability" that the IPN represents; and Heron (1997) and House (1997b) set out in detail the form that what Heron calls a "self-generating practitioner community" might plausibly take in a post-professional world.

Briefly, I see the IPN as a response to the mounting disquiet in the therapy field with the soulless and incongruous values charac-terizing the didactic professionalization process. The Network was founded at an inaugural national conference held at the (appro-priately named) Open Centre in London in November 1994, growing out of a proposal made by Em Edmondson and Nick Totton for a radically different approach to therapist accountability, as the registration bandwagon was beginning to gather ominous momen-tum in the therapy world. Before long the Network had become a steadily growing alternative to the institutional, dominator–hierarchical model (Kalisch, 1996a) promulgated by the therapy bureaucracies, with several hundred participating therapists of richly diverse orientation in practitioner-groups all over Britain. A tentative proposal towards introducing an *international* dimension to the IPN accountability framework has even been advanced (Jutta Gassner, personal communication).

The Network has no formal hierarchical power structure, and no executive making centralized decisions about what qualifications are necessary or acceptable for effective practitionership. Administration is facilitated in an open, participative way at meetings which anyone can attend. Relatedly, no individual can speak for the Network, as there exists no power structure that could confer such authority on any one individual. It can also be seen from this description that the Network has a group, communitarian ideology, rather than the "privatized", individualizing focus which I have challenged in this book.

To quote directly from the Network's collectively written advertising leaflet: the IPN

> makes no distinction between more or less qualified, or "registered" members, as we recognise that there are many routes to being a good practitioner. ... We specifically favour a richly pluralistic and multi-skilled ecology [of therapeutic practice]. ... We are committed to defending freedom of practice and creating a culture of openness and challenge. The Network grows out of the belief that no organisation has the right or the ability to decide who should practise therapy, facilitation or equivalent skills.

The Network is therefore a form of "self-generating practitioner community" in which participatory ethics (Brown, 1997; House, 1997b) (requiring responsibility-taking by all involved) are privileged over didactic, responsibility-eschewing institutional Codes of Ethics (cf. Chapter 4). The only unit of Network membership is a *practitioner group* of at least five members, all of whom stand by each others' work through regular face-to-face engagement in ongoing peer-group experience via self and peer assessment (SAPA) and accreditation. (The rigorous SAPA procedure developed by the *"Leonard Piper"* IPN Group, of which I have been a participating member for seven years, is set out in detail in Lamont & Spencer, 1997.) Each and every practitioner therefore has a built-in and intrinsic interest in the quality of their colleagues' therapeutic work. And it is of central importance that the Network's self-regulating participative system of validation and accountability has been quite explicitly fashioned so as to be consistent with the core values of pluralistic therapeutic practice.

To become a full "member-group", each practitioner-group must develop and establish organic links with two other groups, such that the two link-groups feel able to "stand by" their work.

There has been a great deal of discussion within the Network as to the precise meaning and procedural implications of "standing by"—a debate which will no doubt continue to unfold and deepen as the Network matures. The overall Network structure is therefore horizontal rather than vertical or hierarchical—rendering it far more in tune with recent progressive developments in organization theory than the hierarchical therapy bureaucracies.

The Network stands for an approach to difficulties or complaints which encourages the willingness to own "mistakes" in an atmosphere of non-defensive openness (Totton, 1997b), and thereby seeks to transcend the regressive "victimhood", "blaming" dynamics (Hall, 1993) that dominate conventional punitive, shame-inducing and victimhood-reinforcing complaints procedures.

There are regular weekend National Gatherings (about three a year), open to anyone to attend, together with occasional Regional Gatherings. It is interesting to note that the values underpinning the IPN do seem to have much in common with the Person-Centred and community-building philosophy of Carl Rogers (Rogers, undated), as Gassner (1999) has very clearly articulated. Overall, the IPN is founded in the values of creative pluralism (House & Totton, 1997a; Samuels, 1997), an unambitious modesty, and the celebration of growth and human potential development, rather than in those of infantilizing hoop-jumping, "power-over" hierarchy, and a preoccupation with "psychopathology".

I would personally like to see a significant client/user dimension to the Network, as it is currently still exclusively practitioner-driven; but as is the way of the Network, the responsibility to make this happen is left with me and others with a similar view to pursue, if I/we have the energy and commitment to follow it through. It would be wrong to imply that the Network's strugglings with the intricate and subtle dialectic between radical individualism and communitarian values has not been variously challenging, frustrating, and even exhausting (e.g. House, 2002b). Yet these "birth pangs" are arguably a *necessary* and unavoidable process with which *any* human grouping struggling towards a mature, operational *social community ethic and praxis* must struggle. The extraordinary subtlety and complexity of what is at stake in all this is beautifully summed up by Rudolf Steiner in his "Motto of the Social Ethic", given to Edith Maryon in 1920 (and cited in Lipsker, 1990):

The healthy social life is found when in the mirror of each human soul the whole community finds its reflection, and when in the community the virtue of each one is living. [p. 60]

It is certainly no coincidence that there are many interesting philosophical and procedural commonalities between the IPN, and the worldwide Steiner Waldorf educational (Steiner, 1995, 1996) and Camphill Community movements (Griffiths, 1995; König, 1990; Lievegoed, 1991), founded as they are in the anthroposophical principles deriving from Steiner's work.

Possible objections to Therapy Beyond Modernity— and their "prebuttals"

I have not enjoyed the personal criticisms directed against my person that have greeted my books ... [but] whether they are true or false is irrelevant to the criticisms I bring to bear. ... [Masson, 1992b: 23]

Jeffrey Masson's powerful critiques of therapy (e.g. 1988, 1992a,b) have, I believe, left him open to the kind of disreputable counter-attack typified by Holmes (1992: 29, 32, 34–35), and disapprovingly referred to by Spinelli (1995: 154), because he arguably fails to produce the kind of painstaking analysis that would be needed to sustain and buttress his radical assertion, backed by many a suggestive anecdote, that there is something inherently abusive about the whole therapeutic project. As he himself writes, "my critics can always claim ... that no matter how many individual examples of corruption among psychotherapists I can provide, this does not necessarily reflect on the discipline of psychotherapy as a whole" (1992b: 13–14). Whether or not my own attempt to supply some of those missing arguments increases or reduces the likelihood of such attacks upon myself by "the profession" remains to be seen. What I have tried to do is to shift the argument away from the abusive therap*ist per se*, and towards the view that the very form taken by an individualized, privatized therapy at the very least threatens to possess inherent tendencies towards client/patient abuse.

Clearly the ideas and arguments formulated in this book are at least in part a product of my own personal experiences of therapy and counselling—as client, trainee, (individual and group) practitioner, supervisor, trainer, writer, and IPN participant. And I cannot deny (and have no wish to) that I fall within the ambit of Kennard and Small's statement that "many psychotherapists ... feel let down that [therapy] doesn't have all the answers" (1997: 161). But as Masson (quoted above) has clearly expressed, the veracity or otherwise of the arguments and challenges in this book is logically quite independent of any emotionally driven origin they may have in my own personal disillusionment with the project of profession-centred therapy. Moreover, that my arguments possess an emotionally driven dimension is, I believe, inevitable—for in my view *any* position we take or belief system to which we adhere—including both "pro" and "anti" therapy viewpoints—have crucial emotional roots; and this book will have more than served its purpose if it leads those with strong views about therapy professionalization, "pro" or "anti", to examine more deeply and undefendedly their own particular belief systems, foundational assumptions, and therapeutic praxis. I agree wholeheartedly with Krause (1998, my emphasis), that:

> It is ... necessary that the therapist examines her own position within a field of producers of knowledge and in particular becomes aware of the social, historical and professional origins of her own assumptions about issues *which generally ... seem natural and beyond questioning* and which yet are crucial to her professional project.

It may be as well to reiterate what I have *not* tried to do in this book. First, I have not attempted to locate the cultural phenomenon of "therapy" within an evolutionary or an historical context (e.g. in terms of the decline of organized religion and "community", and the concomitant rise of "ego", individualism, narcissism, and the technocratic mentality of modern science). Nor have I attempted to account for therapy as clinical practice in a quasi-Marxist, "historical materialist" analysis of "late capitalism" (e.g. exposing the alienating commodity form of capitalist social exchange relations, and the "fetishizing" social–relational effects of such on the private-exchange relationship of therapy itself—Ollman, 1971). Such analyses are, I believe, of crucial importance in helping us to locate ourselves far more accurately and knowingly in terms of the meaning and wider relevance of individualized therapy as cultural healing practice at this point in the evolution of consciousness. I intend to examine these complex questions in depth in future writings.

Neither should the arguments developed above necessarily be seen as applying to "therapy-*in-general*" (not that I believe there is any such valid ontological category anyway!). Thus, I personally know several therapists who work in ways that coincide with many of the 21 post-professional criteria I outlined above, and who in the process do everything they can *not* to collude with and encourage the profession-centred tendencies inscribed within the profession-centred form as outlined in Chapters 3 and 4. Yet I also know practitioners who in my judgement do very little if anything to respond to the potential abusiveness of profession-centred therapy's regime of truth; and my strong hunch (based admittedly on personal anecdotal experience) is that the latter type of practitioner may substantially outnumber the former. And hence, the strong need I have felt to write this book.

My main concern, then, has been with private-sector, individualized (one-to-one) psychotherapy and counselling. This is not to say, of course, that at least some of my concerns might not be applicable to therapy in settings other than private practice, or that other, potentially less problematic forms of therapy are not subject to their own particular, "local" regimes of truth (for example, time-limited therapy, group therapy, and family therapy). It is for others more conversant with these other modalities than myself to assess the degree to which either the substance of my critique, or the methodology I have adopted in developing it, might be useful in their own particular fields.

Of course, thinking about therapy within a "regime of truth" perspective can itself all too easily become another regime of truth!—which of course I wish to avoid, lest I be hoist by my own critical petard. What I have tried to do in this book, then, is to offer a perspective on contemporary one-to-one, profession-centred therapy: a way of trying to think about and understand this peculiar cultural phenomenon (just how peculiar I don't think we begin to realize as it has become so commonplace and culture-saturating—Parker, 1997a), which has rapidly diffused throughout Western culture in recent times. I hope the perspective I have offered may be useful and illuminating for those—both practitioners and clients—who might have uncritically taken "therapy" to be some kind of universal, unchallengeable "given" of modern culture. Certainly, whether what I have written proves to have any credence will surely depend upon whether it finds a resonance within the evolving culture of therapy and the history of ideas, and not on whether it is in some sense "objectively" accurate in any naïve "correspondence-theory-of-truth" sense.

I concur with the Derridean view that it is a fundamental error of the (ironically named) "Enlightenment" project to expect humanly built systems of Truth to lead to reliable and complete accounts of the real. And as a consequence I do not claim anything more than a "local" "truth" for the foregoing analysis. Nor from within my own world-view can I claim any more than this with any coherence or authenticity. And as stated at the outset, I do not believe that views such as those set out in this book are anyone's personally owned property or creation, but rather, they have somehow been "channelled" through me from the culture—or from we know not where ...

Returning to deconstruction: I certainly believe that it is critical that the process of deconstruction itself be open to a healthy dose of deconstruction from time to time—being non-defensively open to itself being deconstructed, as part of the ongoing "evolution" (if such it be) of human consciousness. This in turn leads me on to consider the postmodern position I have explicitly adopted in this book, and the criticisms to which such a position might plausibly be subjected. Clearly, this is not a philosophy text, so I cannot at this late juncture even begin to engage with the extant critiques that exist of the postmodernist, New Paradigm world-view. [Perhaps I should say "world-views" (plural); for there certainly does not exist some monolithic, universalizing New Paradigm perspective, for such would be directly contrary to the pluralistic ontology that postmodernism posits as a healthy antidote to the universalizing colonization of modern thought that modernity and scientism represent—Tarnas, 1991]. Thus, in recent years there have been a number of studies which have strongly challenged the postmodernist world-view (e.g. Brodribb, 1992; Erwin, 1997; Greenwood, 1994; Held, 1995; O'Neill, 1995; Parker, 1998c; Pilgrim, 1997: 30–32)— quite apart from the frequent doses of ideological scientism to which we are regularly exposed by the "popular" media apologists for modernity and technocratic science—Professors Colin Blakemore, Richard Dawkins, Stephen Pinker, and Lewis Wolpert come to mind.

I have read a number of critiques of postmodernist thinking, and I must say I find none of them remotely convincing at the level of epistemology and ontology; for while they sometimes successfully point up some epistemological difficulties within the postmodernist world-view, it seems to me that the glaring incoherency that New Paradigm thinking highlights in the modernist *Weltanschauung* is of far greater substance (House, 1999a, d). Clearly I can only assert this personal viewpoint in this context; it remains for philosophers and other profound thinkers to grapple with these complex questions in their respective contributions to the development of human understanding. I believe that the therapy field is, however, in a quite unique position to contribute to this "battle of ideas", given its potential for integrating "head and heart", or intellectual–analytical knowledge on the one hand, and "soul-wisdom" (Rowan, 2001; Sardello, 2001), "emotional intelligence", or intuitive/spiritual knowing on the other. I hope that my lengthy discussions in Chapters 9 and 10 has set out a clear vision of what a coherent New Paradigm world-view might begin to look like, as the modernist agenda becomes increasingly discredited both philosophically (Barratt, 1993; Polkinghorne, 1990) and ecologically (House, 1996i; 1999d).

One possible objection to a postmodernist approach is graphically described by Feltham (1997a: 124), who argues that those drawn to a deconstructivist-type approach might conceivably be

> pathologically avoiding belonging to any group, casting themselves romantically as outsiders, heroic and lonely defenders of unpalatable truths. They may simply be manifesting a naughty child/ rebellious adolescent archetype, or a negative transference toward theory. The tendency towards nihilism, cynicism, arrogance and empty relativity is obvious in this approach.

I will have to leave it to the reader to decide whether my analysis deserves any or all of these charges; but I repeat the point made earlier—that even if it were true that I had some or all of these motivations, it would not *ipso facto* render my case against profession-centred therapy fallacious—for the veracity or otherwise of my arguments has no necessary connection with any personal motivations I may have, conscious or unconscious, in formulating them.

Certainly some of the most challenging and exciting new work in the postmodern field is coming from therapist and philosopher Eugene Gendlin (1997) (of "focusing" fame), who is seeking ways of taking language beyond postmodernism—as Levin puts it, beyond a postmodernism which is either "caught inside unfinished conceptual structures or lost outside them in utter indeterminacy" (Levin, 1997a: 1). Perhaps the very dichotomy between realist and constructionist epistemologies itself needs to be problematized. Certainly, I believe that the therapy field must needs engage with these profound philosophical questions (see Howard, 2000 for a laudable recent example) if it is not to become increasingly moribund and irrelevant in the face of such important cutting-edge developments in human understanding (see Levin's important edited anthology on language and postmodernism—Levin, 1997b).

One charge to which I must plead "guilty" is that the way in which I have written this book is very much in "old-paradigm" style—intellectual, academic, analytical, rational. ... Yet if it is anything like right that "It is not possible to use the techniques and philosophies of the mechanistic paradigm to heal the effects and devastations of that paradigm" (Schaef, 1992: 307)—or that "you can't use the brain to go beyond the brain"—then what I have been able to do in this book is inevitably highly circumscribed. And while it may to some degree be legitimate to demonstrate how the old modernist paradigm's most cherished values and procedures are self-refuting from within its own discourse, one must always remain alert to the seductive strength of the old paradigm—and to how easy it is to delude ourselves that we've transcended it when we're still deeply caught up in it (House, 1996k).

Riikonen and Smith, in their book *Re-Imagining Therapy*, are alert to this difficulty: "Will this book be a systematic, single-voiced text which argues against single-voiced texts? Will it present yet another set of well ordered truths as it argues against well ordered truths?" (1997: 7). The authors clearly realized that if their "re-imagining" of therapy was to have substance and credibility, then it was important that they transcend the traditional language and style of modernist "therapy", which they achieved by "speak[ing] differently, metaphorically, even strangely. ... We have to use different styles. ... We have to exaggerate and use wrong words (and lose at least some of our academic respectability" (*ibid.*). Schaef says something similar: "Writing *about* a new paradigm truly requires writing *in* a new paradigm" (1992: 4, her emphases).

Alas, I have not been nearly as brave as this in the current book; rather, I have set myself the more limited task of challenging conventional profession-centred therapy from within the (for me) safe and comfortable terrain of rational academic discourse. Yet perhaps "[the] notion of epistemic collapse does not imply that we can yet think and speak outside of the epistemic constitution of modern thought" (Barratt, 1993: 208). I just hope that what I have been able to write has some value, notwithstanding these constraints. And perhaps the conventional written-word form is by no means the best or most appropriate medium for the emergence of a new paradigm; as Brian Swimme said of Nobel prize-winner Barbara McClintock, "She does not theorize about a new paradigm. She does her work as it unfolds and by so doing demonstrates a new scientific paradigm" (quoted in Schaef, 1992: 327). There are echoes here of the great healer-cum-analyst Georg Groddeck (see Chapter 9), as well as of arguably the last century's greatest philosopher Ludwig Wittgenstein.

It is also important to stress that I have not written this book in the spirit of criticizing other therapists' practice while excluding myself from the critique. For *I am as implicated as any other therapist in being a purveyor of the regime of truth I have tried to describe and deconstruct in this book*. But equally, I have recently reached a point where my increasing awareness of, and discomfort with, contemporary individualized therapy's self-serving regime has led me to challenge and seek to transcend the assumptions and practices of conventional profession-centred therapy—and I hope this book has made a significant contribution to that process. Rather like Anne Schaef, I too see myself as a "recovering professional psychotherapist" (Schaef, 1992: 4, 9, 84, 136, 193–194, 255); and she sums up my own position very well in describing her own important book, *Beyond Therapy, Beyond Science*, thus: "Because I have been and continue to be part of the problem, I begun to see clearly that this book cannot be a book about what *they* are doing wrong. It must be a book about what *I* can no longer do ..." (8–9, her emphases).

In 1990 David Kalisch wrote that "The behaviour of 'the profession' is the next piece of resistance that needs looking at"— and further, in 1996, "Developments over the last six years have simply heightened my misgivings about that behaviour" (1996b: 46). I do not want to "psychopathologize" the therapy field, not only because I am myself a part of it, but more importantly because such a pathologizing world-view is, I believe, not only epistemologically unsustainable (House, 1997e; Parker *et al.*, 1995), but can easily amount to little more than *ad hominem* abuse which obscures far more than it reveals. Yet I do hope that before launching the counter-attack—or heading for the bunkers—therapy practitioners will feel able to consider closely and relatively undefendedly the challenges I have mounted to profession-centred therapy in this book—challenges which, I hope, have been constructive rather than destructive, and whose careful consideration can, in my view, only lead to *less* self-serving and *more* enabling therapeutic practices in our increasingly rapidly changing and unsettling world.

It now remains to offer a brief conclusion.

Conclusion:
who, then, would be a therapist?

"... with the increasing professionalization of counselling, postmodernism provides a useful way of exploring such questions as: ... To what extent does the other (client, patient ...) ... become only part of a supporting cast in a drama set up to preserve the counsellor's privilege and protect the counsellor's approach? ... Can the postmodern counsellor stop counselling from reverting to a technique orientated mechanism of professional vested interests, and instead find a better way for all of us to put the other first?"

Lowenthal, 1996: 373

So who would be a therapist? ...

For each person with a "need to help" there probably exists a unique constellation of underlying motives and aims ... there appears to be a broad consensus that ... *a major determinant for becoming a therapist involves the conscious and/or unconscious wish to resolve one's own emotional conflicts.* [Sussman, 1992: 13, 34, my emphasis]

257

My hunch is that, notwithstanding the force of argument developed in this book, there will continue to be a veritable stampede of people wanting to enter the therapy world as practitioners—certainly if the wildly proliferating number of training courses that have mushroomed since the early 1990s is anything to go by. And one has only to read Sussman's excellent book *A Curious Calling: Unconscious Motivations for Practicing Psychotherapy* (1992), to see clearly why this should be so. For in our individualistic, narcissistic culture (Lasch, 1979), therapy has so easily become a "profession" or activity upon which people can "project" or "act out" (to use the language of therapeutic discourse) all manner of personal difficulties, within a carefully structured, culturally sanctioned environment that confers "permission" and respectability upon their behaviour. Like the little boy entering the city I have fingered the "Emperor's-clothes-ness" of modern therapy in pretty uncompromising terms—not least to provide some kind of counterweight to the uncritical treatment that therapy receives from the vast swathe of proliferating (and predominantly profession-centred) therapy literature.

Following Cushman (1995), perhaps the increasing cultural ascendancy of "the therapeutic" parallels deeper processes in the evolution of individualized consciousness and ego/self-hood, of which the vast majority of us are unaware ... and yet which it may be crucial to identify and understand if we are to fashion a therapy which is facilitative of a healthy human evolution, rather than it being just one more ideological trapping of late modernity (Barratt, 1993). Under these circumstances, I want to ask: *Just who would want to be a therapist?* Certainly, I find myself gradually relinquishing my erstwhile chosen occupation of counsellor and therapist, and in recent years there have been signs of others leaving the therapy field because they no longer feel able to work as therapists with authenticity. Anne Schaef, in a book that should surely be on every therapist's reading list, describes in graphic detail her own personal journey through the therapy "profession", and into a "post-therapy" way of helping people with their problems of living (she revealingly refers to herself as a "recovering psychotherapist"—1992: 193–194). And Robert Sardello, drawing upon the anthroposophical vision of Rudolf Steiner and the latter's early lectures (1912–21) criticizing the newly developed practice of psychoanalysis, has similarly left the world of psychotherapy for what he calls "adult education into soul-wisdom" and "spiritual psychology":

> [Steiner's lectures] ... force us to confront the inadequate knowledge used in founding psychoanalysis and psychotherapy as a method of soul work. Now, some eighty years later, this method has multiplied endlessly, and without questioning the kind of knowing involved. ... [B]y sequestering it in a private room, *therapy removes soul from the world*. ... [F]eeling and will are not ... a purely individual matter. Symptoms ... do not belong to the individual but *to the culture as a whole*. ... Psychotherapy is an abstraction, culturally sanctioned in a world of materialist abstractions. ... Cultural forms are needed for the cure; psychotherapy cannot do the job and seems to me a deviation contributing to the destruction of culture. ... The conclusions are not easy to confront. They have led me, a practicing psychotherapist, to the necessity of relinquishing this practice. [Sardello, 1990: 7, 14, 24, 25, 29, my emphases]

A conclusion which is not one ...

> The Post-Professional Ethos will hopefully result in a social panorama more colourful and diverse than all the cultures of past and present taken together. [Illich, 1977a: 39]

I agree wholeheartedly with Kovel when he writes that "We cannot ... conceive of the health of the individual apart from that of the social whole in which he [*sic*] is embedded" (1976: 33); and while it might have been true in 1976 that "there is as yet no therapy that takes more than faltering steps down this path" (*ibid.*), the work of erstwhile therapists like Georg Groddeck, James Hillman, Robert Sardello, and Anne Schaef inspires in me the hope that there are at least signs of a qualitatively different kind of post-professional, New Paradigm therapeutic practice beginning to emerge. In future writings I hope to address these questions full on—that is, both the cultural embeddedness of therapy, and therapy's appropriateness or otherwise for the "difficulties of living" it aspires to address in its individualized form; whether it is in principle possible to envision and construct a form of explicit therapeutic practice that is appropriate for our difficulties of living; and if not, what kinds of support and enablement are potentially available within postmodern culture.

The following quotation from Colin Feltham captures well the spirit in which this book has been written:

> As still relatively young and status-hungry professions, counselling and psychotherapy are probably in no mood for any radical revision of their theories and practices. This is regrettable, since not only do they thereby defend untenable orthodoxies but unwittingly and oppressively place an obstacle in the path of real enquiry and growth. [Feltham, 1997a: 126]

If this book contributes to loosening up or displacing the "obstacle to enquiry and growth" (to quote Feltham) which I believe the pernicious professionalization process and its handmaiden, mechanistic modernity, entail, then it will have more than served its purpose.

It feels fitting to leave the last word to the late Ann France, with a memorable quotation which eloquently captures much of the spirit in which I have written this book, and the core of its most central concerns:

> The stress in psychotherapeutic theory and practice needs, I think, to shift from the idea that this is a treatment meted out by a specialist to a sick person, who has no right to question it, to the attitude that this is a co-operative venture between two equals, with the same goal of effectively enhancing the life of the consulter, and freeing him or her from the temporary bond created with the therapist. [France, 1988: 243]

Afterword

David Smail

rofessional psychotherapy of the kind so comprehensively
taken apart in these pages has from its inception sought
authorization for its practice. Right from the beginning it has
shuttled between three possible sources of authority: science, magic,
and the dogmatic assertions of supposedly "charismatic" founders
of various therapeutic "schools". Freud, for example, made use at
different stages of his career of all three, but with a very distinct
emphasis throughout on his own brand of science.

So long as it is making *any* kind of claim to alleviate suffering, it
is not, I think, surprising that psychotherapy should feel the need to
attach itself to one or other of these "regimes of truth". Indeed, I
think it has to. And, twist and turn as it may, the "New Paradigm"
embracing "postmodernist deconstruction", etc., cannot convincingly deny that it is attempting to establish itself as just such
another regime.

For the practices of therapy and counselling have to be *justified*.
Take, for example, the typical sufferer who approaches his or her
general practice counsellor in search of relief. There are a number of
questions that such a person may ask: "can you help me?"; "how?";
"will I feel better?". In other words, "what evidence is there that

your practice is going to do me any good?". "Old paradigm" or not, these questions have a legitimacy that is not, easily and in good faith, to be side-stepped.

The problem with "evidence-based practice" is not that it is the unreasonable demand of a moribund world-view, but simply that the way it has been put forward is deeply dishonest and in the worst possible faith. For the "evidence-based practitioners" continue to practise *despite the fact that there is no evidence* worthy of the name for what they do. This does indeed lay bare the corruption and failure of the scientific paradigm such that it becomes, in this field, a depleted parody of itself, but it does not, I believe, invalidate the paradigm itself: science has achieved too much so easily to be dismissed. The scientific method, freed so far as possible from the takeovers of power and the rigid orthodoxies that they try to impose, is the best hope we have of penetrating the darkness that surrounds us.

It could be argued that the "New Paradigm" is in essence a way of shaking off the constraints of the old such that therapy and counselling can continue to be professionally practised unimpeded by "old-fashioned" requirements of reason. That is to say, if the uncomfortable demand for evidence *of the kind practitioners need* reveals that there is none, an obvious "way forward" is to discredit the whole notion of evidence so that they may continue, with less cognitive dissonance, to be remunerated for their undertaking. We are, in other words, involved here in a struggle for legitimacy.

However, there is, I believe, a more radical option. This is to recognize that, however desirable, essential, even inescapable, the whole notion of therapy may seem, and however compelling the subjective experience of those who, whether as clients or practitioners, take part in it, it is in fact not a particularly useful or effective way of tackling the kinds of distress that bring sufferers to the clinic. Much of the argument of this book seems to me to point in this direction. What might be the consequences of such a conclusion?

First, we need to re-evaluate the extremely simplistic scientistic assumptions, so ably criticised by Richard House and those he cites, that we have come to adopt in this field. If, as they seem to, psychotherapy and counselling fail to provide an adequate account of how human beings function and what causes and ameliorates their suffering, then we need to consider other accounts. I do not believe that the scientific locker has yet been emptied in this respect: we have hardly begun to consider, for example, the possibility that it is not *people* who suffer "pathology" so much as the spatio–temporal *environments* they occupy (see Smail, 2001). The implications of any such approach tend to be political more than therapeutic, which is no doubt partly why we have fought so shy of them.

Second—and again this emerges very strongly from Richard House's text—we need to re-engage with issues that scientistic psychology has failed to address at all satisfactorily. Principal among these is the nature, indeed the mystery, of human subjectivity; that is to say, the ways in which our mortal existence comes to be experienced by us, and what that experience may signify. I do not myself believe that in order to do this we have to invent a new paradigm or invoke mysticism or other spiritual disciplines (I have nothing against these: I just do not see them as appropriate tools of psychological investigation). Our subjectivity arises out of our interaction as embodied beings with a material and social world. Again, apart from at the margins of the discipline, we have hardly begun to think seriously about and investigate the issues that follow from this.

There are other questions which present themselves to those who have an interest in this field: what makes some human relationships healing and others noxious? What conditions further the former and minimize the latter? We don't know the answers to such questions, but I don't feel that we have yet exhausted the possibilities. The answers we may find, moreover, won't necessarily have implications for the practice of therapy and counselling, and indeed they may well suggest that such practices have little relevance at all.

I do not by any of this want to suggest that those of us practising therapy and counselling should cease to do so. I do think, though, that the authority for our so doing has to be revised. It may turn out that we do indeed have to abandon science as a justification, and if so we may be thrown back on no other grounding for our activities than our personal status as human beings. In this way psychotherapy becomes a calling or vocation

(Paul Gordon, 1999, presents a persuasive case for this), but, I fear, a vocation that has no theology. Perhaps, in other words, we will have to do without *any* authority beyond ourselves.

REFERENCES

Adler, G. (Ed.) (1976). *C. G. Jung Letters, Volume II*. R. F. C. Hull (Trans.). London: Routledge & Kegan Paul.

Albee, G. W. (1990). The futility of psychotherapy. *Journal of Mind and Behavior*, 11(3–4): 369–384.

Alcoff, L. M. (1996). *Real Knowing: New Versions of the Coherence Theory*. Ithaca, NY: Cornell University Press.

Alexander, F. (1971). The principle of flexibility. In: H. H. Barton (Ed.), *Brief Therapies* (pp. 28–41). New York: Behavioral Publications.

Alexander, F., & French, T. M. (1946). *Psychoanalytic Therapy: Principles and Applications*. New York: Ronald Press.

Alexander, R. (1995). *Folie à Deux: An Experience of One-to-One Therapy*. London: Free Association Books.

Alexander, R. (1996). Author's corrections (letter). *Counselling News*, September, p. 16.

Alexander, R. (1998a). Life stories. *The Times Magazine*, September 26th, pp. 90–91.

Alexander, R. (1998b). Letter to the editor. *The Times Magazine*, October 24th, p. 95.

Alexander, R. (1998c). Mind games. *The Times Magazine*, November 28th, p. 113.

Alexander, R. (1999). Web site correspondence ("Emotional and Verbal

Abuse in Psychotherapy and Psychoanalysis"). Available at: www.home.aone.net.au/psychotherapy, 15th January.

Althusser, L. (1971). Ideology and ideological state apparatus (notes towards an investigation). In his *Lenin and Philosophy* (pp. 123–173). London: New Left Books.

Alvarez, A. (Ed.) (1962). *The New Poetry*. Harmondsworth: Penguin.

Anderson, H. (1997). *Conversation, Language, and Possibilities: A Postmodern Approach to Therapy*. New York: Basic Books.

Anderson, H., & Goolishian, H. (1992). The client is the expert: a not-knowing approach to therapy. In: S. McNamee & K. J. Gergen (Eds.), *Therapy as Social Construction* (pp. 25–39). London: Sage.

Austad, C. S. (1996). *Is Long-Term Psychotherapy Unethical? Toward a Social Ethic in an Era of Managed Care*. San Francisco: Jossey-Bass.

Austin, K. M., Moline, M. E., & Williams, G. T. (1990). *Confronting Malpractice: Legal and Ethical Dilemmas in Psychotherapy*. Newbury Park, CA: Sage.

Aveline, M. (1990). The training and supervision of individual therapists. In: W. Dryden (Ed.), *Individual Therapy: A Handbook* (pp. 313–339). Buckingham: Open University Press.

Barratt, B. B. (1993). *Psychoanalysis and the Postmodern Impulse: Knowing and Being since Freud's Psychology*. Baltimore: Johns Hopkins University Press.

Barrett, W. (1987). *Death of the Soul: From Descartes to the Computer*. Oxford: Oxford University Press [orig. 1986].

Bartuska, H. (1996). Updates from members of the executive of the European Psychotherapy Association. *International Journal of Psychotherapy*, 1(1): 107–109.

Baruss, I. (1996). *Authentic Knowing: The Convergence of Science and Spiritual Aspiration*. West Lafayette: Purdue University Press.

Bates, Y., & House, R. (Eds.) (in preparation). *Ethically Challenged Professions: Enabling Therapy Beyond Modernity*. Ross-on-Wye: PCCS Books.

Bates, Y., & Sands, A. (2002). An interview with Anna Sands, Parts 1 and 2. *Ipnosis: An Independent Journal for Practitioners*, 6(Summer): 4–6; 7(Autumn): 18–19.

Bergin, A. E. (1988). Three contributions to a spiritual perspective to counseling, psychotherapy, and behavior change. *Counseling and Values*, 33: 21–31.

Berman, M. (1981). *The Reenchantment of the World*. Ithaca: Cornell University Press.

Beyerstein, O. (1993). The functions and limitations of professional codes of ethics. In: E. R. Winkler & J. R. Coombs (Eds.), *Applied Ethics: A Reader* (pp. 416–425). Oxford: Blackwell,.

Bion, W. R. (1987). Making the best of a bad job. In his *Clinical Seminars and Four Papers*. Abingdon: Fleetwood Press [orig. 1979].

Bird, C. (1998). Review of Moline *et al.*'s *Documenting Psychotherapy*. *Counselling*, 9(3): 235.

Blackham, H. J. (Ed.) (1974). *Ethical Standards in Counselling*. London: Bedford Square Press.

Bohart, A. C., & Tallman, K. (1996). The active client: therapy as self-help. *Journal of Humanistic Psychology*, 36(3): 7–30.

Bohm, D. (1980). *Wholeness and the Implicate Order*. London: Routledge & Kegan Paul.

Bohm, D. (1994). *Thought as a System*. London: Routledge.

Bohm, D., & Edwards, M. (1991). *Changing Consciousness: Exploring the Hidden Source of the Social, Political, and Environmental Crises Facing Our World*. New York: HarperSanFrancisco.

Bollas, C. (1992). *Being a Character: Psychoanalysis and Self-Experience*. New York: Hill and Wang.

Bond, T. (1993). *Standards and Ethics for Counselling in Action*. London: Sage.

Bortoft, H. (1996). *The Wholeness of Nature: Goethe's Way of Science*. Edinburgh: Floris Books.

Borys, D. S. (1994). Maintaining therapeutic boundaries: the motive is therapeutic effectiveness, not defensive practice. *Ethics and Behavior*, 4(3): 267–273.

Boss, Dr (1951). Georg Walther Groddeck 1866–1934. In: G. Groddeck, *The World of Man* (pp. 21–23). London: Vision.

Bowie, H. (1991). *Lacan*. London: Fontana Press.

Boyer, L. B. (1983). Approaching cross-cultural therapy. *Journal of Psychoanalytic Anthropology*, 6(3): 237–245.

Boyle, M. (1996). Schizophrenia: the fallacy of diagnosis. *Changes*, 14(1): 5–13.

Bracken, P., & Thomas, P. (1998). Limits to therapy. *Open Mind*, 93: 17.

Bradley, B. S. (1989). *Visions of Infancy: A Critical Introduction to Child Psychology*. Cambridge: Polity Press.

Bradley, B. S. (1993). Introduction: The future of developmental theory. *Theory and Psychology*, 3(4): 403–414.

Braten, S. (Ed.) (1999). *Intersubjective Communication and Emotion in Early Ontogeny*. Cambridge: Cambridge University Press.

Brodribb, S. (1992). *Nothing Mat(t)ers: A Feminist Critique of Postmodernism*. Melbourne: Spinifex Press.

Bromberg, W. (1975). *From Shaman to Psychotherapist: A History of the Treatment of the Mentally Ill*. Chicago: Henry Regenry.

Broughton, J. M. (Ed.) (1987). *Critical Theories of Psychological Development*. New York: Plenum Press.

Brown, A. (1998). The soul is coming back into science. *The Independent* newspaper, April 4th.

Brown, J., & Mowbray, R. (1990). Whither the human potential movement? *Self and Society, 18*(4): 32–35 [reprinted as Appendix A in Mowbray, 1995].

Brown, J., & Mowbray, R. (1994). Primal integration. In: D. Jones (Ed.), *Innovative Therapy: A Handbook* (pp. 13–27). Buckingham: Open University Press.

Brown, L. S. (1989). Beyond thou shalt not: thinking about ethics in the lesbian therapy community. *Women and Therapy, 8*(1–2): 13–25.

Brown, L. S. (1994a). Boundaries in feminist therapy: a conceptual formulation. *Women and Therapy, 15*(1): 29–38.

Brown, L. S. (1994b). Concrete boundaries and the problem of literal-mindedness: a response to Lazarus. *Ethics and Behavior, 4*(3): 275–281.

Brown, L. S. (1994c). *Subversive Dialogues: Theory in Feminist Therapy*. New York: Basic Books.

Brown, L. S. (1997). Ethics in psychology: *cui bono*? In: D. Fox & I. Prilleltensky (Eds.), *Critical Psychology: An Introduction* (pp. 51–67). London: Sage.

Brown, P. (Ed.) (1973). *Radical Psychology*. London: Tavistock Publications.

Buck, L. (1990). Abnormality, normality and health. *Psychotherapy, 27*(2): 187–194.

Buck, L. A. (1992). The myth of normality. *Social Behavior and Personality, 20*: 251–252.

Buckley, P., Karasu, T. B., & Charles, E. (1981). Psychotherapists view their personal therapy. *Psychotherapy: Theory, Research, and Practice, 18*: 299–305.

Burman, E. (1994). *Deconstructing Developmental Psychology*. London: Routledge.

Burman, E. (1997a). Developmental psychology and its discontents. In: D. Fox & I. Prilleltensky (Eds.), *Critical Psychology: An Introduction* (pp. 134–149). London: Sage.

Burman, E. (1997b). False memories, true hopes and the angelic: revenge of the postmodern in therapy. *New Formation, 30*: 122–134.

Burman, E. (Ed.) (1998). *Deconstructing Feminist Psychology*. London: Sage.

Burman, E., & Parker, I. (1998). What is critical psychology?: an interview. *Gecko*, 2: 51–61.

Burman, E., & others (1996a). *Psychology Discourse Practice: From Regulation to Resistance*. London: Taylor & Francis.

Burman, E., & others (1996b). *Challenging Women: Psychology's Exclusions, Feminist Possibilities*. Buckingham: Open University Press.

Burton, A. (1975). Therapists' satisfactions. *American Journal of Psychoanalysis*, 35: 115–122.

Campaign for Effective Therapy (2002). Contact Nick Totton at 86 Burley Wood Crescent, Leeds LS4 2QL. ntotton@cs.com

Caplan, P. J., & Hall-McCorquodale, I. (1985). Mother-blaming in major clinical journals. *American Journal of Orthopsychiatry*, 55(3): 345–353.

Capra, F. (1997). *The Web of Life: A New Synthesis of Mind and Matter*. London: Flamingo/HarperCollins.

Carruthers, P., & Boucher, J. (1998). *Language and Thought: Interdisciplinary Themes*. Cambridge: Cambridge University Press.

Casement, P. (1985). *On Learning from the Patient*. London: Tavistock/Routledge.

Cayer, M. (1997). Bohm's dialogue and action science: two different approaches. *Journal of Humanistic Psychology*, 37(2): 41–66.

Charles-Edwards, D., Dryden, W., & Woolfe, R. (1989). Professional issues in counselling. In: W. Dryden, D. Charles-Edwards, & R. Woolfe (Eds.), *Handbook of Counselling in Britain* (pp. 401–423). London: Routledge.

Clark, J. (Ed.) (2002). *Freelance Counselling and Psychotherapy: Competition and Collusion*. Hove: Brunner-Routledge.

Clarke, A. M., & Clarke, A. D. B. (1976). *Early Experience: Myth and Evidence*. London: Open Books.

Clarke, C. J. S. (1996). *Reality through the Looking-Glass: Science and Awareness in the Postmodern World*. Edinburgh: Floris Books.

Clarke, C. J. S. (1997). Superstition or liberation? Heretical ideas and the physical sciences. Paper presented at the Scientific and Medical Network Conference on "Science, Heresy and the Challenge of Revolutionary Ideas", London, May.

Clarkson, P. (1995). *The Therapeutic Relationship in Psychoanalysis, Counselling, Psychology and Psychotherapy*. London: Whurr.

Clarkson, P. (2002). *The Transpersonal Relationship in Psychotherapy: The Hidden Dimension of Spirituality*. London: Whurr.

Claxton, G. (Ed.) (1986). *Beyond Therapy: The Impact of Eastern Religions on Psychological Theory and Practice*. London: Wisdom [reprinted by Prism Press, Bridport, 1996].

Cloud, D. L. (1998). *Control and Consolation in American Culture and Politics: Rhetoric of Therapy*. Thousand Oaks, CA: Sage.

Cohen, D. B. (1999). *Stranger in the Nest: Do Parents Really Shape Their Child's Personality, Intelligence or Character?* Chichester: John Wiley.

Cohn, H. W. (1997). *Existential Thought and Therapeutic Practice: An Introduction to Existential Psychotherapy*. London: Sage.

Corbett, L. (1995). Supervision and the mentor archetype. In: P. Kugler (Ed.), *Jungian Perspectives on Clinical Supervision*. Einsiedeln, Switzerland: Daimon.

Coren, A. (1996). Brief therapy—base metal or pure gold? *Psychodynamic Counselling*, 2: 22–38.

Corsaro, W. A. (1997). *The Sociology of Childhood*. London: Sage.

Coyne, J. (1982). Undressing the fashionable mind. *Family Process*, 21: 391–396.

Craib, I. (1986). Freud and philosophy. *Free Associations*, 4: 64–79.

Craib, I. (1987). The psychodynamics of theory. *Free Associations*, 10: 32–56.

Crisp, A. H. (1966). "Transference", "symptom emergence", and "social repercussion". *British Journal of Medical Psychology*, 39: 179–196.

Crook, J. H. (1980). *The Evolution of Human Consciousness*. Oxford: Oxford University Press.

Crossley, N. (1996). *Intersubjectivity: The Fabric of Social Becoming*. London: Sage.

Cushman, P. (1990). Why the self is empty. *American Psychologist*, 45: 599–611.

Cushman, P. (1991). Ideology obscured: political uses of the self in Daniel Stern's infant. *American Psychologist*, 46(3): 206–219.

Cushman, P. (1995). *Constructing the Self, Constructing America: A Cultural History of Psychotherapy*. Reading, MA: Addison-Wesley.

Damasio, A. (1994). *Descartes' Error: Emotion, Reason and the Human Brain*. New York: Avon Books.

Danziger, K. (1990). *Constructing the Subject: Historical Origins of Psychological Research*. Cambridge: Cambridge University Press.

Dartington, A. (1995). Very brief psychodynamic counselling with young people. *Psychodynamic Counselling*, 1(2): 253–261.

Davies, P. (1983). *God and the New Physics*. London: Dent.

Davis, W. A. (1989). *Inwardness and Existence: Subjectivity in/and Hegel,*

Heidegger, Marx, and Freud. Madison, WI: University of Wisconsin Press.

Davis, L. (1996). Rosie in Horrorland (review of Alexander, 1995). *Counselling News*, March 30th.

Davis, M., & Wallbridge, D. (1987). *Boundary and Space: An Introduction to the Work of D. W. Winnicott*. New York: Brunner/Mazel [orig. 1981].

Dawes, R. M. (1994). *House of Cards: Psychology and Psychotherapy Built on Myth*. New York: Free Press.

Derrida, J. (1974). *Of Grammatology*. Baltimore: Johns Hopkins University Press.

de Zulueta, F. (1993). *From Pain to Violence: The Roots of Human Destructiveness*. London: Whurr.

DiCarlo, R. E. (Ed.) (1996). *Towards a New World View: Conversations at the Leading Edge*. Edinburgh: Floris Books.

DiNicola, V. F. (1993). The postmodern language of therapy: at the nexus of culture and family. *Journal of Systemic Therapies*, 12: 49–62.

Dinnage, R. (1988). *One to One: Experiences of Psychotherapy*. London: Viking.

Dixon, H. (1998). Letter to the Editor. *The Times Magazine*, October 10th, p. 103.

Dixon, N. (1981). *Preconscious Processing*. Chichester: John Wiley.

Douglas, T. (1998). *Change, Intervention and Consequence: An Exploration of the Process of Intended Change*. London: Free Association Books.

Dreier, O. (1998). Client perspectives and uses of psychotherapy. *European Journal of Psychotherapy, Counselling and Health*, 1(2): 295–310.

Dryden, W., & Feltham, C. (1992). Concluding comments. In: W. Dryden & C. Feltham (Eds.), *Psychotherapy and Its Discontents* (pp. 254–265). Buckingham: Open University Press.

Durrell, L. (1948). Studies in genius, VI: Groddeck. *Horizon*, 17: 384–403 [reprinted in Groddeck's *The Book of the It*. London: Vision, 1950].

Edwards, G. (1992). Does psychotherapy need a soul? In: W. Dryden & C. Feltham (Eds.), *Psychotherapy and Its Discontents* (pp. 194–224). Buckingham: Open University Press.

Eigen, M. (1998). *The Psychoanalytic Mystic*. London: Free Association Books.

Embleton Tudor, L., & Tudor, K. (1994). The personal and the political: power, authority and influence in psychotherapy. In: P. Clarkson & M. Pokorny (Eds.), *The Handbook of Psychotherapy* (pp. 384–402). London: Routledge.

Epstein, M. (1996). *Thoughts without a Thinker: Psychotherapy from a Buddhist Perspective*. London: Duckworth.

Epstein, W. M. (1995). *The Illusion of Psychotherapy*. New Brunswick: Transaction Publishers.

Epston, D. (Ed.) (1997). *Narrative Therapy: The Archaeology of Hope*. San Francisco: Jossey-Bass.

Erikson, E. H. (1964). *Insight and Responsibility: Lectures in the Ethical Implications of Psychoanalytic Insight*. New York: Norton.

Erskine, A., & Judd, D. (Eds.) (1994). *The Imaginative Body: Psychodynamic Therapy in Health Care*. London: Whurr.

Erwin, E. (1997). *Philosophy and Psychotherapy*. London: Sage.

European Association for Psychotherapy (1996). *International Journal of Psychotherapy*, Carfax Publ. Available at: http://www.carfax.co.uk/ijp-ad.htm

Eyer, D. E. (1992). *Mother–Infant Bonding: A Scientific Fiction?* New Haven: Yale University Press.

Fahy, T., & Wessely, S. (1993). Should purchasers pay for psychotherapy? *British Medical Journal, 307*: 576–577.

Fairbairn, G. (1987). Responsibility, respect for persons and psychological change. In: G. & S. Fairbairn (Eds.), *Psychology, Ethics and Change* (pp. 244–271). London: Routledge & Kegan Paul.

Falconar, A. E. I. (1997). *How To Use Your Nous*. Maughold, Isle of Man: Non-Aristotelian Publishing.

Faulconer, J. E., & Williams, R. N. (Eds.) (1990). *Reconsidering Psychology: Perspectives from Continental Philosophy*. Pittsburgh, PA: Duquesne University Press.

Feltham, C. (1997a). Challenging the core theoretical model. In: R. House & N. Totton (Eds.), *Implausible Professions* (pp. 117–128). Ross-on-Wye: PCCS Books [reprinted from *Counselling, 8*(2): 121–125, 1997].

Feltham, C. (1997b). *Time-Limited Counselling*. London: Sage.

Ferrell, R. (1996). *Passion in Theory: Conceptions of Freud and Lacan*. London: Routledge.

Fine, R. (1985). *The Meaning of Love in Human Experience*. New York: John Wiley.

Finlay, M. (1989). Post-modernizing psychoanalysis/psychoanalysing postmodernity. *Free Associations, 16*: 43–80.

Fischer, F. (1990). *Technocracy and the Politics of Expertise*. Newbury Park, CA: Sage.

Fox, D., & Prilleltensky, I. (Eds.) (1997). *Critical Psychology: An Introduction*. London: Sage.

France, A. (1988). *Consuming Psychotherapy*. London: Free Association Books.

Frank, J. D. (1964). Foreword. In: A. Kiev (Ed.), *Magic, Faith, and Healing: Studies in Primitive Psychiatry Today* (pp. vii–xiv). New York: Free Press.

Frank, J. D. (1973). *Persuasion and Healing*. Baltimore: Johns Hopkins University Press.

Frank, J. D., & Frank, J. B. (1991). *Persuasion and Healing: A Comparative Study of Psychotherapy* (3rd ed.). Baltimore: Johns Hopkins University Press.

Freedman, J., & Combs, G. (1996). *Narrative Therapy: The Social Construction of Preferred Realities*. New York: Norton.

Freides, D. (1960). Toward the elimination of the concept of normality. *Journal of Consulting Psychology*, 24(2): 128–133.

Friedman, M. S. (1992). *Dialogue and the Human Image: Beyond Humanistic Psychology*. Newbury Park, CA: Sage.

Friedman, M. S. (1998). Buber's philosophy as the basis for dialogical psychotherapy and contextual therapy. *Journal of Humanistic Psychology*, 38(1): 25–40.

Friedson, E. (1984). Are professions necessary? In T. L. Haskell (Ed.), *The Authority of Experts* (pp. 3–27). Bloomington: Indiana University Press.

Frischer, D. (1977). *Les Analyses Parlent*. Paris: Stock.

Fromm, E. (1949). *Man for Himself: An Inquiry into the Psychology of Ethics*. London: Routledge & Kegan Paul [1971 ed.].

Frosh, S. (1987). *The Politics of Psychoanalysis: An Introduction to Freudian and Post-Freudian Theory*. New Haven: Yale University Press.

Gale, D. (1996). Humanistic psychology. In: B. Mullan (Ed.), *Therapists on Therapy* (pp. 1–18). London: Free Association Books.

Garrett, C. (1998). *Beyond Anorexia: Narrative, Spirituality and Recovery*. Cambridge: Cambridge University Press.

Gartrell, N. K. (Ed.) (1994). *Bringing Ethics Alive: Feminist Ethics in Psychotherapy Practice*. New York: Haworth.

Gassner, J. (1999). The Independent Practitioners Network and the person-centred approach. Seminar held at the Norwich Centre, January (mimeo).

Gendlin, E. (1997). How philosophy cannot appeal to existence, and how it can. In: D. M. Levin (Ed.), *Language Beyond Postmodernism: Saying and Thinking in Gendlin's Philosophy* (pp. 3–14). Evanston, IL: Northwestern University Press.

Genosko, G. (1998). *Undisciplined Theory*. London: Sage.

Gergen, K. J. (1985). The social constructionist movement in modern psychology. *American Psychologist, 40*: 266–275.

Gergen, K. J. (1990). Therapeutic professions and the diffusion of deficit. *Journal of Mind and Behavior, 11*: 353–368.

Gergen, K. J., & Gergen, M. (1988). Narrative and the self as relationship. In: L. Berkowitz (Ed.), *Advances in Experimental and Social Psychology* (pp. 17–56). New York: Academic Press.

Gergen, K. J., & McNamee, S. (1997). Foreword to E. Riikonen & G. M. Smith, *Re-Imagining Therapy: Living Conversations and Relational Knowing* (pp. vii–ix). London: Sage.

Gilligan, S., & Prince, R. (Eds.) (1993). *Therapeutic Conversations*. New York: Norton.

Giovacchini, P. L. (1990). Regression, reconstruction, and resolution: containment and holding. In: P. L. Giovacchini (Ed.), *Tactics and Techniques in Psychoanalytic Therapy: III. The Implications of Winnicott's Contributions* (pp. 226–264). Northvale, NJ: Jason Aronson.

Gladstone, G. (1997). The making of a therapist and the corruption of the training market. In: R. House & N. Totton (Eds.), *Implausible Professions* (pp. 171–185). Ross-on-Wye: PCCS Books.

Gladwell, M. (1998). Do parents matter? *The New Yorker*, August 17th, pp. 54–64.

Goleman, D. (1996). *Emotional Intelligence: Why It Can Matter More than IQ*. London: Bloomsbury [orig. 1995].

Goodwin, B. (1994). *How the Leopard Changed Its Spots: The Evolution of Complexity*. London: Weidenfeld & Nicolson.

Goodwin, B. (1997). Challenges to Darwinian orthodoxy. Paper presented at the Scientific and Medical Network conference on "Science, Heresy and the Challenge of Revolutionary Ideas", London, May.

Gordon, P. (1999). *Face to Face. Therapy as Ethics*. London: Constable.

Gray, A. (1994). *An Introduction to the Therapeutic Frame*. London: Routledge.

Greenwood, J. D. (1994). *Realism, Identity and Emotion: Reclaiming Social Psychology*. London: Sage.

Griffin, D. R. (Ed.) (1988). *The Reenchantment of Science: Postmodern Proposals*. Albany, NY: University of New York Press.

Griffiths, V. (1995). Care in the community? A short history of the Camphill movement. In: C. Coates & others (Eds.), *Diggers and Dreamers 96/97* (pp. 85–89). Winslow: D & D Publications.

Groddeck, G. (1950). *The Book of the It*. London: Vision (orig. 1927).

Groddeck, G. (1951). *The World of Man*. London: Vision [orig. 1934].

Groddeck, G. (1977). *The Meaning of Illness: Selected Psychoanalytic Writings*. London: Hogarth Press.

Grossman, C. K., & Grossman, S. (1965). *The Wild Analyst: The Life and Work of Georg Groddeck*. London: Barrie & Rockliff.

Guggenbühl-Craig, A. (1971). *Power in the Helping Professions*. Dallas: Spring Publications.

Guidano, V. F. (1987). *Complexity of the Self: A Developmental Approach to Psychopathology and Therapy*. New York: Guilford Press.

Gunew, S. (Ed.) (1990). *Feminist Knowledge: Critique and Construct*. London: Routledge.

Guntrip, H. (1975). My experience of analysis with Fairbairn and Winnicott. *International Review of Psycho-Analysis*, 2: 145–156.

Guy, J. D. (1987). *The Private Life of the Psychotherapist*. Chichester: Wiley.

Habermas, J. (1978). *Communication and the Evolution of Human Society*. London: Heinemann.

Habermas, J. (1982). *The Theory of Communicative Action*. London: Heinemann.

Hadley, S. W., & Strupp, H. H. (1976). Contemporary views of negative effects in psychotherapy. *Archives of General Psychiatry*, 33: 1291–1302.

Haley, J. (1976). *Problem-Solving Therapy*. San Francisco: Jossey-Bass.

Hall, J. (1988). The source of victimhood (public lecture given at the University of East Anglia). Norwich: The Norwich Collective, December (mimeo).

Hall, J. (1993). *The Reluctant Adult: An Exploration of Choice*. Bridport: Prism Press.

Halling, S., & Nill, J. D. (1989). Demystifying psychopathology: understanding disturbed persons. In: R. S. Valle & S. Halling (Eds.), *Existential–Phenomenological Perspectives in Psychology: Exploring the Breadth of Human Experience* (pp. 179–192). New York: Plenum Press.

Handley, N. (1995). The concept of transference: a critique. *British Journal of Psychotherapy*, 12(1): 49–59.

Hare-Mustin, R. T., & Marecek, J. (Eds.) (1990). *Making a Difference: Psychology and the Construction of Gender*. New Haven: Yale University Press.

Harré, R. (1983). *Personal Being*. Oxford: Basil Blackwell.

Hart, N. (1998). Discourses of power within the therapeutic relationship. Paper presented at the BAC Research Conference, Birmingham (mimeo).

Hart, T. (1995). Ethical choice in a postmodern world: cognition, consciousness and contact. In: M. J. LaFountain (Ed.), *Postmodern Ethics* (pp. 131–158). Carrollton, GA: West Georgia College [Studies in the Social Sciences, Vol. 33].

Hart, T. (1998). A dialectic of knowing: integrating the intuitive and the analytic. *Encounter: Education for Meaning and Social Justice*, 11(3): 5–16.

Hart, T., Nelson, P., & Puhakka, K. (Eds.) (1997). *Spiritual Knowing: Alternative Epistemic Perspectives*. Carrollton, GA: State University of West Georgia [Studies in Social Sciences, Vol. 34].

Havens, L. (1989). *A Safe Place: Laying the Groundwork for Psychotherapy*. Cambridge, MA: Harvard University Press.

Hawkins, A. J., & Dollahite, D. C. (Eds.) (1997). *Generative Fathering: Beyond Deficit Perspectives*. London: Sage.

Heard, W. G. (1993). *The Healing Between: A Clinical Guide to Dialogical Psychotherapy*. San Francisco: Jossey-Bass.

Heather, N. (1976). *Radical Perspectives in Psychology*. London: Methuen.

Held, B. S. (1995). *Back to Reality: A Critique of Postmodern Theory in Psychotherapy*. New York: W. W. Norton.

Heller, K., & Monahan, J. (1977). *Psychology and Community Change*. Homewood, IL: Dorsey.

Henriques, J., Hollway, W., Urwin, C., Venn, C., & Walkerdine, V. (1984). *Changing the Subject: Psychology, Social Regulation and Subjectivity*. London: Methuen.

Herman, N. (1985). *My Kleinian Home*. London: Quartet Books.

Hermans, H., & Kempen, H. (1993). *The Dialogic Self: Meaning as Movement*. New York: Academic Press.

Hermansson, G. (1997). Boundaries and boundary management in counselling: the never-ending story. *British Journal of Guidance and Counselling*, 25(2): 133–146.

Heron, J. (1990). The politics of transference. *Self and Society*, 18(1): 17–23 [reprinted as Chapter I.1 in R. House & N. Totton (Eds.), *Implausible Professions*, 1997, pp. 11–18].

Heron, J. (1996). *Co-operative Inquiry: Research into the Human Condition*. London: Sage.

Heron, J. (1997). A self-generating practitioner community. In: R. House & N. Totton (Eds.), *Implausible Professions* (pp. 241–254). Ross-on-Wye: PCCS Books.

Heron, J. (1998). *Sacred Science: Person-Centred Inquiry into the Spiritual and the Subtle*. Ross-on-Wye: PCCS Books.

Heyward, C. (1994). *When Boundaries Betray Us: Beyond Illusions of What Is Ethical in Therapy and in Life*. New York: HarperSanFrancisco.

Hillman, J. (1975). *Re-Visioning Psychology*. New York: Harper & Row.

Hillman, J. (1996). *The Soul's Code: In Search of Character and Calling*. London: Bantam [1997 ed.].

Hinshelwood, R. D. (1997). *Therapy or Coercion? Does Psychoanalysis Differ from Brainwashing?* London: Karnac Books.

Hitter, G. T. (1997). *Freud's Innuendo and Jamshid's Cup: The Postmodern Quest for Self in the Shadow of the Newtonian World*. Bristol, WI: PsyQuest Books.

Hoag, L. (1992). Psychotherapy in the general practice surgery: considerations of the frame. *British Journal of Psychotherapy, 8*(4): 417–429.

Hobson, R. F. (1985). *Forms of Feeling: The Heart of Psychotherapy*. London: Tavistock.

Hogan, D. (1979). *The Regulation of Psychotherapists*, 4 vols. Cambridge, Mass.: Ballinger.

Holland, J. C., & Rowland, J. H. (Eds.) (1989). *Handbook of Psychooncology: Psychological Care for the Patient with Cancer*. Oxford: Oxford University Press.

Holmes, J. (1992). Response to Masson. In: W. Dryden and C. Feltham (Eds.), *Psychotherapy and Its Discontents* (pp. 29–36). Buckingham: Open University Press.

Holt, E. B. (1915). *The Freudian Wish and Its Place in Ethics*. London: Fisher Unwin.

Homer, F. D. (1988). *The Interpretation of Illness*. West Lafayette, IN: Purdue University Press.

Horner, T. M. (1985). The psychic life of the young infant: review and critique of the psychoanalytic concepts of symbiosis and infantile omnipotence. *American Journal of Orthopsychiatry, 55*(3): 324–344.

House, R. (1984). "The Geography of Public Finance in the UK: Conventional and Radical Formulations". Unpublished Ph.D. thesis, School of Environmental Sciences, University of East Anglia, Norwich.

House, R. (1995a). The dynamics of power. *Counselling News, 20*: 24–25.

House, R. (1995b). Legislating against abuse of clients in therapy: a cautionary view. *Self and Society, 23*(2): 34–39.

House, R. (1996a). The genius of Georg Groddeck, precursor of humanistic-dynamic counselling—an appreciation (mimeo).

House, R. (1996b). "Audit-mindedness" in counselling: some under-lying dynamics. *British Journal of Guidance and Counselling*, 24(2): 277–283 [reprinted as Chapter I.6 in R. House & N. Totton (Eds.), *Implausible Professions*, 1997, pp. 63–70].

House, R. (1996c). In: the wake of "Watchdog". *Counselling*, 7(2): 115–116.

House, R. (1996d). Object relations and the body. *Energy and Character: Journal of Biosynthesis*, 27(2): 31–44.

House, R. (1996e). General Practice counselling: a plea for ideological engagement. *Counselling*, 7(1): 40–44.

House, R. (1996f). Love, intimacy and therapeutic change. *Self and Society*, 24(1): 21–26.

House, R. (1996g). What is truth? [Letter to the Editor]. *Counselling*, 7(3): 190–191.

House, R. (1996h). On healing, being, love … and "empathy scores" [Letter to the Editor]. *The Therapist*, 3(3): 46–47.

House, R. (1996i). "Psychoenvironmentalism": a psychodynamic para-digm for environmentalism. *International Minds*, 6(3): 8–11.

House, R. (1996j). The professionalization of counselling: a coherent "case against"? *Counselling Psychology Quarterly*, 9(4): 343–358.

House, R. (1996k). Conference Report: Beyond the Brain, Cambridge, August 1995. *Self and Society*, 23(6): 30–31.

House, R. (1997a). Therapy in New Paradigm perspective: the phenomenon of Georg Groddeck. In: R. House & N. Totton (Eds.), *Implausible Professions* (pp. 225–240). Ross-on-Wye: PCCS Books.

House, R. (1997b). Participatory ethics in a self-generating practitioner community. In: R. House & N. Totton (Eds.), *Implausible Professions* (pp. 321–334). Ross-on-Wye: PCCS Books.

House, R. (1997c). An approach to time-limited humanistic-dynamic counselling. *British Journal of Guidance and Counselling*, 25(2): 251–262.

House, R. (1997d). The dynamics of professionalisation: a personal view of counselling research. *Counselling*, 8(3): 200–204 [reprinted as Chapter I/5 in R. House & N. Totton (Eds.), *Implausible Professions*, 1997, pp. 51–62].

House, R. (1997e). The unmasking of the pathologising mentality [review article of Parker *et al.*, 1995]. *Asylum: Magazine for Democratic Psychiatry*, 10(1): 37–40.

House, R. (1997f). Training: a guarantee of competence? In: R. House & N. Totton (Eds.), *Implausible Professions* (pp. 99–108). Ross-on-Wye: PCCS Books.

House, R. (1997g). From professionalisation to a post-therapy era. *Self and Society*, 25(2): 31–35.

House, R. (1999a). Holistic perspectives in science [review article]. *Steiner Education*, 33(1): 41–42.

House, R. (1999b). Limits to professional therapy: deconstructing a professional ideology. *British Journal of Guidance and Counselling*, 27(3): 377–392.

House, R. (1999c). The culture of general practice and the therapeutic frame. In: J. Lees (Ed.), *Clinical Counselling in Primary Care* (pp. 19–42). London: Routledge.

House, R. (1999d). The psychology of self, society and ecological survival [Review Feature of Caroline New's *Agency, Health and Social Survival*]. *European Journal of Psychotherapy, Counselling and Health*, 2(1): 103–117.

House, R. (1999e). Deconstruction, post-(?)-modernism and the future of psychotherapy. *Psychotherapy Review*, 1(7): 322–332

House, R. (1999f). The place of psychotherapy and counselling in a healthy European social order: a commentary on Tantam and van Deurzen. *European Journal of Psychotherapy, Counselling and Health*, 2(2): 237–244.

House, R. (2000a). Psychology and early years learning: affirming the wisdom of Waldorf. *Steiner Education*, 34(2): 10–16.

House, R. (2000b). Steiner's elusive twelfth sense: some explorations inspired by ego-sense. *New View*, 17: 41–44.

House, R. (2000c). But what about childhood? Increasing state control erodes autonomy in British early years learning. *Steiner Education*, 34(1): 5–8.

House, R. (2001a). The statutory regulation of psychotherapy: still time to think again ... *The Psychotherapist*, 17(Autumn): 12–17.

House, R. (2001b). Psychopathology, psychosis and the kundalini: postmodern perspectives on unusual subjective experience. In: I. Clarke (Ed.), *Psychosis and Spirituality: Exploring the New Frontier* (pp. 107–125). London: Whurr.

House, R. (2001c). Psychotherapy professionalization: the post-graduate dimension and the legitimacy of statutory regulation. *British Journal of Psychotherapy*, 17(3): 382–390 [reprinted in *Ipnosis: An Independent Journal for Practitioners*, 5 & 7, 2002].

House, R. (2001d). Loving to learn: protecting a natural impulse in a technocratic age. *Natural Parent*, May–June: 38–40 [extended version in *Paths to Learning* (USA), Spring 2002: 32–36].

House, R. (2001e). Extended book review: Therapy on the couch?—a client scrutinizes the therapy phenomenon. *European Journal of Psychotherapy, Counselling and Health*, 4(1): 123–136.

House, R. (2001f). What is so bad about the academicization of training?: a response to Frans Lohman. *Universities Psychotherapy and Counselling Association Newsletter*, 7: 12–13.

House, R. (2002a). Ahead of his time: Carl Rogers on "professionalism", 1973. *Ipnosis: An Independent Journal for Practitioners*, 6: 21–23.

House, R. (2002b). The individualism/communitarian dialectic and the IPN: a critique of Talbot. *Ipnosis: An Independent Journal for Practitioners, 8* (forthcoming).

House, R. (forthcoming). From "encounter" to "calling": one practitioner's journey through and beyond professionalisation. In his *With an Independent Voice: Critical Essays on Psychotherapy and Counselling*.

House, R. (in preparation). *Krishnamurti and the End(s) of Psychotherapy.*

House, R., & Totton, N. (Eds.) (1997a). *Implausible Professions: Arguments for Pluralism and Autonomy in Psychotherapy and Counselling.* Ross-on-Wye: PCCS Books.

House, R., & Totton, N. (1997b). Introduction. In: R. House & N. Totton (Eds.), *Implausible Professions* (pp. 1–10). Ross-on-Wye: PCCS Books.

Howard, A. (1996). *Challenges to Counselling and Psychotherapy.* Basingstoke: Macmillan.

Howard, A. (2000). *Philosophy for Counselling and Psychotherapy: Pythagoras to Postmodernism.* Basingstoke: Macmillan.

Howard, G. S., Nance, D. W., & Myers, P. (1987). *Adaptive Counselling and Therapy.* San Francisco: Jossey-Bass.

Howarth, I. (1989). Psychotherapy: who benefits? *The Psychologist*, 2(4): 149–152.

Howe, D. (1993). *On Being a Client: Understanding the Process of Counselling and Psychotherapy.* London: Sage.

Hugill, B. (1998). Analysts in trauma over identity crisis. *Observer* newspaper, March 22nd.

Hunter, A. (1988). *Seeds of Truth: J. Krishnamurti as Religious Teacher and Educator.* University of Leeds: unpublished Ph.D. thesis.

Hycner, R. H. (1991). *Between Person and Person: Toward a Dialogical Psychotherapy.* Highland, NY: Center for Gestalt Development.

Illich, I. (1977a). Disabling professions. In: I. Illich & others (Eds.), *Disabling Professions* (pp. 11–39). London: Marion Boyars.

Illich, I. (1977b). *Limits to Medicine.* Harmondsworth: Penguin.

Illich, I. (1978). *Towards a History of Needs.* New York: Pantheon Books.

Ingleby, D. (Ed.) (1981). *Critical Psychiatry: The Politics of Mental Health*. Harmondsworth: Penguin.

Ingleby, D. (1984). The ambivalence of psychoanalysis. *Radical Science*, 15: 39–71.

Irigaray, L. (1985). *This Sex Which is Not One*. Ithaca, NY: Cornell University Press [orig. in French, 1977].

Jayran, S. (1992). The passion of therapy: healer and lover. *Self and Society*, 20(2): 18–23.

Johnson, M. (1987). *The Body in the Mind: The Bodily Basis of Meaning, Imagination, and Reason*. Chicago: Chicago University Press.

Josselson, R. (1996). *The Space Between Us: Exploring the Dimensions of Human Relationships*. London: Sage.

Joy, M. (1993). Feminism and the self. *Theory and Psychology*, 3(3): 275–302.

Joy Division (1980). *Closer* album. Manchester: Factory Records.

Kalisch, D. (1990). Professionalisation: a rebel view. *Self and Society*, 18(1): 24–29.

Kalisch, D. (1996a). Letter to the Editor. *Self and Society*, 24(2): 38–39.

Kalisch, D. (1996b). Registration: who is asking the right questions? [Letter to the Editor]. *The Therapist*, 3(3): 46.

Kassan, L. D. (1999). *Second Opinions: Sixty Psychotherapy Patients Evaluate Their Therapists*. Northvale, NJ: Jason Aronson.

Katherine, A. (1991). *Boundaries: Where You End and I Begin*. New York: Simon & Schuster.

Katz, M. (1997). *On Playing a Poor Hand Well*. New York: Norton.

Karnac Books (1998). *Psychoanalysis and Related Subjects* (Book Catalogue). London: Karnac Books.

Kendall, T., & Crossley, N. (1996). Governing love: on the tactical control of countertransference in the psychoanalytic community. *Economy and Society*, 25(2): 178–194.

Kennard, D., & Small, N. (1997). Commentary: Cold comfort. In: D. Kennard & N. Small (Eds.), *Living Together* (pp. 160–163). London: Quartet Books.

Kiev, A. (1964). Implications for the future. In: A. Kiev (Ed.), *Magic, Faith, and Healing: Studies in Primitive Psychiatry Today* (pp. 454–464). New York: Free Press.

Kimball, P. (1988). Journalism: art, craft or profession? In: A. Flores (Ed.), *Professional Ideals* (pp. 135–146). Belmont, CA: Wadsworth.

King, P., & Steiner, R. (Eds.) (1990). *The Freud–Klein Controversies, 1941–45*. London: Routledge.

Kivlighan, D. M. (1989). Changes in counselor intentions and response modes and in client reactions and session evaluations after training. *Journal of Counseling Psychology*, 36: 471–476.

Knight, T. (2001). Psychiatric Delusional Disorder Discovered. *Asylum: The Magazine for Democratic Psychiatry*, 13(1): 19.

König, K. (1990). The three essentials of Camphill. In: C. M. Pietzner (Ed.), *A Candle on the Hill: Images of Camphill Life* (pp. 29–34). Edinburgh: Floris Books.

Kotowicz, Z. (1993). Tradition, violence and psychotherapy. In: L. Spurling (Ed.), *From the Words of My Mouth: Tradition in Psychotherapy* (pp. 132–157). London: Routledge.

Kovel, J. (1976). *A Complete Guide to Therapy: From Psychoanalysis to Behavior Modification*. New York: Pantheon Books [1978 Penguin ed. quoted].

Kovel, J. (1988). *The Radical Spirit: Essays on Psychoanalysis and Society*. London: Free Association Books.

Krause, I.-B. (1998). *Therapy across Culture*. London: Sage.

Krishnamurti, J. (1955). *Education and the Significance of Life*. London: Gollancz [orig. 1953].

Krishnamurti, J. (1969). *Freedom from the Known*. London: Gollancz.

Krishnamurti, J. (1973). *The Awakening of Intelligence*. New York: HarperSanFrancisco [1987 ed.].

Krishnamurti, J. (1974). *Krishnamurti on Education*. Madras: Krishnamurti Foundation Trust.

Krishnamurti, J. (1978). *Beginnings of Learning*. Harmondsworth: Penguin [orig. 1975].

Krishnamurti, J. (1981). *Letters to the Schools, Volume 1*. India: Mirananda.

Krishnamurti, J. (1993). *On Mind and Thought*. New York: HarperSanFrancisco.

Krishnamurti, J. (1994). *On Learning and Knowledge*. New York: HarperSanFrancisco.

Krishnamurti Foundation Trust (1992). *The Krishnamurti Index: Audio and Video Recordings, 1965–1986*. Brockwood Park, Hants: KFT.

Kühlewind, G. (1988). *From Normal to Healthy: Paths to the Liberation of Consciousness*. Hudson, NY: Lindisfarne Press.

Kurtz, S. (1989). *The Art of Unknowing: Dimensions of Openness in Analytic Therapy*. Northvale, NJ: Jason Aronson.

Kurtz, S. N. (1992). *All Mothers Are One: Hindu India and the Cultural Reshaping of Psychoanalysis*. New York: Columbia University Press.

Kvale, S. (Ed.) (1992). *Psychology and Postmodernism*. London: Sage.

Lacan, J. (1965). *Écrits*. Paris: Seuil.

LaFountain, M. J. (Ed.) (1995). *Postmodern Ethics*. Carrollton, GA: West Georgia College [Studies in Social Sciences Vol. XXXIII].

Laing, R. D. (1961). *The Self and Others*. London: Tavistock [2nd ed., *Self and Others*. Harmondsworth: Penguin, 1969].

Lamont, J., & Spencer, A. (1997). Self and peer assessment: a personal story. In: R. House & N. Totton (Eds.), *Implausible Professions* (pp. 295–303). Ross-on-Wye: PCCS Books.

Laplanche, J. (1989). *New Foundations for Psychoanalysis*. Oxford: Blackwell.

Lasch, C. (1979). *The Culture of Narcissism*. New York: Norton.

Lasky, J. F., & Silverman, H. W. (Eds.) (1988). *Love: Psychoanalytic Perspectives*. New York: New York University Press.

Laszlo, E. (1996). *The Whispering Pond: A Personal Guide to the Emerging Vision of Science*. Shaftsbury: Element Books.

Lax, W. D. (1992). Postmodern thinking in a clinical practice. In: S. McNamee and K. J. Gergen (Eds.), *Therapy as Social Construction* (pp. 69–85). London: Sage.

Lazarus, A. A. (1994a). How certain boundaries and ethics diminish therapeutic effectiveness. *Ethics and Behavior*, 4(3): 255–261.

Lazarus, A. A. (1994b). The illusion of therapist's power and the patient's fragility: my rejoinder. *Ethics and Behavior*, 4(3): 299–306.

Lees, J. (1997). An approach to counselling in GP surgeries. *Psychodynamic Counselling*, 3(1): 33–48.

Lees, J. (Ed.) (1999). *Clinical Counselling in Primary Care*. London: Routledge.

Legg, C. (1998). Psychology for therapists. *The Therapist*, 5(3): 10–15.

Lemma-Wright, A. (1995). *Invitation to Psychodynamic Psychology*. London: Whurr.

Lerman, H., & Porter, N. (Eds.) (1990). *Feminist Ethics in Psychotherapy*. New York: Springer.

Lerner, M. (1986). *Surplus Powerlessness: The Psychodynamics of Everyday Life and the Psychology of Individual and Social Transformation*. New Jersey: Humanities Press.

Levin, D. M. (Ed.) (1987). *Pathologies of the Modern Self: Postmodern Studies on Narcissism, Schizophrenia, and Depression*. New York: New York University Press.

Levin, D. M. (1997a). Introduction. In: Levin (Ed.), *Language Beyond Postmodernism* (pp. 1–2). Evanston, IL: Northwestern University Press.

Levin, D. M. (Ed.) (1997b). *Language Beyond Postmodernism: Saying and Thinking in Gendlin's Philosophy*. Evanston, IL: Northwestern University Press.

Levine, M., & Perkins, D. V. (1987). *Principles of Community Psychology*. Oxford: Oxford University Press.

Levy, D. A. (1992). A proposed category for the DSM: Pervasive Labeling Disorder. *Journal of Humanistic Psychology*, 32(1): 121–125.

Lievegoed, B. (1991). *Developing Communities*. Stroud: Hawthorn Press.

Lipsker, B. (1990). Three pillars. In: C. M. Pietzner (Ed.), *A Candle on the Hill: Images of Camphill Life* (pp. 59–60). Edinburgh: Floris Books.

Little, M. I. (1985). Winnicott working in areas where psychotic anxieties predominate—a personal record. *Free Associations*, 3: 9–42.

Little, M. I. (1990). *Psychotic Anxieties and Containment: A Personal Record of an Analysis with Winnicott*. London: Karnac.

Llewelyn, S. P. (1988). Psychological therapy as viewed by clients and therapists. *British Journal of Clinical Psychology*, 27: 223–237.

Lohman, F. (2001). What is so bad about the academicization of training?: a reply to Richard House. *Universities Psychotherapy and Counselling Association Newsletter*, 6: 11–12.

Lomas, P. (1981). *The Case for a Personal Psychotherapy*. Oxford: Oxford University Press.

Lomas, P. (1987). *The Limits of Interpretation: What's Wrong with Psychoanalysis*. Harmondsworth: Penguin.

Longman, J. (1998). Editorial. *Counselling*, 9(2): 82.

Lorimer, D. (1990). *Whole in One: The Near-death Experience and the Ethic of Interconnectedness*. London: Arkana/Penguin.

Lorimer, D. (1996a). Book Review of Ken Wilber's *Sex, Ecology, Spirituality. Network: Scientific and Medical Network Review*, 61: 76–78.

Lorimer, D. (1996b). Book Review of Naydler 1996. *Network: Scientific and Medical Network Review*, 62: 59–60.

Lorimer, D. (Ed.) (1998). *The Spirit of Science: From Experiment to Experience*. Edinburgh: Floris Books.

Lowenthal, D. (1996). The postmodern counsellor: some implications for practice, theory, research and professionalism. *Counselling Psychology Quarterly*, 9(4): 373–381.

Lowson, D. (1994). Understanding Professional Thought Disorder: a guide for service users and a challenge to professionals. *Asylum: Magazine for a Democratic Psychiatry*, 8(2): 29–30.

Lutyens, M. (1990). *The Life and Death of Krishnamurti*. London: Rider.

Lyon, M. L. (1993). Psychoneuroimmunology: the problem of the situatedness of illness and the conceptualization of healing. *Culture, Medicine and Society*, 17(1): 77–97.

McCord, J. (1978). A thirty year follow up of treatment effects. *American Psychologist*, *33* (March): 284–289.

McDougall, J. (1989). *Theatres of the Body: A Psychoanalytic Approach to Psychosomatic Illness*. London: Free Association Books.

McDougall, J. (1995). *The Many Faces of Eros: A Psychoanalytic Exploration of Human Sexuality*. London: Free Association Books.

McLeod, J. (1990). The client's experience of counselling and psychotherapy: a review of the research literature. In: D. Mearns & W. Dryden (Eds.), *Experiences of Counselling in Action* (pp. 1–19). London: Sage.

McMahon, G. (1998). News Editorial. *Counselling*, *9*(2): 89.

McNamee, S., & Gergen, K. J. (Eds.) (1992). *Therapy as Social Construction*. London: Sage.

McWhinney, I. R. (1996). The importance of being different. *British Journal of General Practice*, *46* (July): 433–436.

Maguire, M. (1995). *Men, Women, Passion and Power: Gender Issues in Psychotherapy*. London: Routledge.

Mahrer, A. R. (1996). *The Complete Guide to Experiential Psychotherapy*. New York: Wiley.

Main, T. F. (1975). Some psychodynamics of large groups. In: L. Kreeger (Ed.), *The Large Group*. London: Constable.

Mair, K. (1992). The myth of therapist expertise. In: W. Dryden & C. Feltham (Eds.), *Psychotherapy and its Discontents* (pp. 135–60). Buckingham: Open University Press [reprinted in abridged form as Chapter II.1 in R. House & N. Totton (Eds.), *Implausible Professions*, 1997, pp. 87–98].

Mair, M. (1989). *Between Psychology and Psychotherapy: A Poetics of Experience*. London: Routledge.

Malcolm, J. (1980). *Psychoanalysis: The Impossible Profession*. New York: Viking.

Maroda, K. J. (1991). *The Power of Countertransference: Innovations in Analytic Technique*. Chichester: John Wiley.

Martin, B. (Ed.) (1996). *Confronting the Experts*. New York: State University of New York Press.

Martin, R. (1998). *Self-Concern: An Experiential Approach to What Matters in Survival*. Cambridge: Cambridge University Press.

Masson, J. (1988). *Against Therapy: Emotional Tyranny and the Myth of Psychological Healing*. New York: Atheneum; London: Fontana [1990 ed. quoted].

Masson, J. (1992a). *Final Analysis: The Making and Unmaking of a Psychoanalyst*. London: Fontana [orig. Addison-Wesley, 1990].

Masson, J. (1992b). The tyranny of psychotherapy. In: W. Dryden & C. Feltham (Eds.), *Psychotherapy and its Discontents* (pp. 7–29, 36–40). Buckingham: Open University Press.

Mauss, M. (1979). The category of the person. In his *Psychology and Sociology: Essays* (pp. 57–94). London: Routledge & Kegan Paul.

May, R. (1987). Therapy in our day. In: J. K. Zeig (Ed.), *The Evolution of Psychotherapy* (pp. 212–219). New York: Brunner/Mazel.

Mayer, J. E., & Timms, N. (1970). *The Client Speaks: Working Class Impressions of Casework*. London: Routledge & Kegan Paul.

Mays, D. T., & Franks, C. M. (Eds.) (1985). *Negative Outcome in Psychotherapy and What To Do about It*. New York: Springer.

Mearns, D., & Thorne, B. (1988). *Person-Centred Counselling in Action*. London: Sage.

Menninger, K. (1963). *The Vital Balance: The Life Process in Mental Health and Illness*. New York: Viking Press.

Messer, S. B., Sass, L. A., & Woolfolk, R. L. (Eds.) (1988). *Hermeneutics and Psychological Theory: Interpretive Perspectives on Personality, Psychotherapy, and Psychopathology*. New Brunswick: Rutgers University Press.

Miller, A. (1987). *The Drama of Being a Child*. London: Virago.

Miller, R. B. (Ed.) (1992). *The Restoration of Dialogue: Readings in the Philosophy of Clinical Psychology*. Washington, DC: American Psychological Association.

Miller, S. D., Duncan, B. L., & Hubble, M. A. (1997). *Escape from Babel: Toward a Unifying Language for Psychotherapy Practice*. New York: W. W. Norton.

Miller, T., & McHoul, A. (1998). *Popular Culture and Everyday Life*. London: Sage.

Miller-Pietroni, M. (1999). The postmodern context of counselling in General Practice. In: J. Lees (Ed.), *Clinical Counselling in Primary Care* (pp. 6–18). London: Routledge.

Mitchell, S. A. (1988). *Relational Concepts in Psychoanalysis*. Cambridge, MA: Harvard University Press.

Mohr, D. C. (1995). Negative outcome in psychotherapy: a critical review. *Clinical Psychology*, 2: 1–27.

Monk, G., Winslade, J., Crocket, J., & Epston, D. (Eds.) (1997). *Narrative Therapy in Practice: The Archaeology of Hope*. San Francisco: Jossey-Bass.

Mowbray, R. (1995). *The Case Against Psychotherapy Registration: A Conservation Issue for the Human Potential Movement*. London: Trans Marginal Press.

Mowbray, R. (1997). Too vulnerable to choose? In: R. House & N. Totton (Eds.), *Implausible Professions* (pp. 33–44). Ross-on-Wye: PCCS Books.

Morss, J. R. (1990). *The Biologising of Childhood: Developmental Psychology and the Darwinian Myth*. Hove: Lawrence Erlbaum.

Morss, J. R. (1996). *Growing Critical: Alternatives to Developmental Psychology*. London: Routledge.

Moser, T. (1977). *Years of Apprenticeship on the Couch*. Urizen Books.

Mullarky, J. (Ed.) (1999). *The New Bergson*. Manchester: Manchester University Press.

Natterson, J. M., & Friedman, R. J. (1995). *A Primer of Clinical Inter-Subjectivity*. Northvale, NJ: Jason Aronson.

Naydler, J. (Ed.) (1996). *Goethe on Science*. Edinburgh: Floris Books.

Nelson, J. E. (1994). *Healing the Split: Integrating Spirit into Our Understanding of the Mentally Ill* [revised ed.]. Albany, NY: State University of New York Press.

Neumann, E. (1954). *The Origins and History of Consciousness*. New York: Pantheon Books [orig. 1949].

Newman, F. (1991). *The Myth of Psychology*. New York: Castillo International.

Nightingale, G., & Cromby, J. (Eds.) (1999). *Psychology and Social Constructionism: A Critical Analysis of Theory and Practice*. Buckingham: Open University Press.

Nisbett, R. E., & Ross, L. (1980). *Human Inference: Strategies and Shortcomings in Social Judgment*. Englewood Cliffs, NJ: Prentice-Hall.

Oakley, C. (1998). The perniciousness of professionalisation. *European Journal of Psychotherapy, Counselling and Health*, 1(2): 311–318.

Oakley, J. (1992). *Morality and the Emotions*. London: Routledge.

O'Donohue, W., & Kitchener, R. F. (Eds.) (1996). *The Philosophy of Psychology*. London: Sage.

Oldfield, S. (1983). *The Counselling Relationship: A Study of the Client's Experience*. London: Routledge & Kegan Paul.

Ollman, B. (1971). *Alienation: Marx's Conception of Man in Capitalist Society*. Cambridge: Cambridge University Press.

O'Neill, J. (1995). *The Poverty of Postmodernism*. London: Routledge.

Orbach, S. (1994). *What's Really Going on Here?* London: Virago.

Orbach, S. (1996). Psychoanalysis. In: B. Mullen (Ed.), *Therapists on Therapy* (pp. 19–36). London: Free Association Books.

Owen, I. R. (1997). Boundaries in the practice of humanistic counselling. *British Journal of Guidance and Counselling*, 25(2): 163–174.

Owens, G. (1987). Radical behaviourism and the ethics of clinical psychology. In: G. & S. Fairbairn (Eds.), *Psychology, Ethics and*

Change (pp. 91–114). London: Routledge & Kegan Paul.

Pallone, N. J. (1986). *On the Social Utility of Psychopathology: A Deviant Majority and Its Keepers?* New Brunswick, NJ: Transaction Books.

Palmer Barnes, F. (1998). *Complaints and Grievances in Psychotherapy: A Handbook of Ethical Practice.* London: Routledge.

Park, J. (1992). *Shrinks: The Analysts Analysed.* London: Bloomsbury.

Parker, I. (1996). Postmodernism and its discontents: therapeutic discourse. *British Journal of Psychotherapy,* 12(4): 447–460.

Parker, I. (1997a). *Psychoanalytic Culture: Psychoanalytic Discourse in Western Society.* London: Sage.

Parker, I. (1997b). Discourse analysis and psychoanalysis. *British Journal of Social Psychology,* 36: 479–496.

Parker, I. (Ed.) (1998a). *Social Constructionism, Discourse and Realism.* London: Sage.

Parker, I. (1998b). Qualitative data and the subjectivity of "objective" facts. In: D. Dorling & S. Simpson (Eds.), *Statistics in Society: The Arithmetic of Politics* (pp. 83–88). London: Arnold.

Parker, I. (1998c). Constructing and deconstructing psychotherapeutic discourse. *European Journal of Psychotherapy, Counselling and Health,* 1(1): 65–78.

Parker, I. (1998d). Against postmodernism: psychology in cultural context. *Theory and Psychology,* 8(5): 601–627.

Parker, I. (Ed.) (1999). *Deconstructing Psychotherapy.* London: Sage.

Parker, I. (2001). What is wrong with the discourse of the university in psychotherapy training? *European Journal of Psychotherapy, Counselling and Health,* 4(1): 27–43.

Parker, I., & Spears, R. (Eds.) (1996). *Psychology and Society: Radical Theory and Practice.* London: Pluto Press.

Parker, I., Georgaca, E., Harper, D., McLaughlin, T., & Stowell-Smith, M. (1995). *Deconstructing Psychopathology.* London: Sage.

Payton, C. R. (1994). Implications of the 1992 Ethics Code for Diverse Groups. *Professional Psychology: Research and Practice,* 25: 317–320.

Perkin, H. (1996). *The Third Revolution.* London: Routledge.

Perris, C., & Arrindell, W. A. (Eds.) (1994). *Parenting and Psychopathology.* Chichester: Wiley.

Phillips, M. (1996). When education fuels the class war. *The Observer* newspaper, May 26th (Review, p. 5).

Pilgrim, D. (1992). Psychotherapy and political evasions. In: W. Dryden & C. Feltham (Eds.), *Psychotherapy and Its Discontents* (pp. 225–253). Buckingham: Open University Press.

Pilgrim, D. (1997). *Psychotherapy and Society*. London: Sage.

Pokorny, M. R. (1998). Alchemy, daydreams and fictions: psychotherapy in Britain today. *International Journal of Psychotherapy*, 3(3): 265–266.

Polanyi, M. (1958). *Personal Knowledge: Towards a Post-Critical Philosophy*. Chicago: Chicago University Press.

Polkinghorne, D. (1990). Psychology after philosophy. In: J. E. Faulconer & R. N. Williams (Eds.), *Reconsidering Psychology* (pp. 92–115). Pittsburgh, PA: Duquesne University Press.

Pollio, H. R., Henley, T. B., & Thompson, C. J. (1998). *The Phenomenology of Everyday Life: Empirical Investigations of Human Experience*. Cambridge: Cambridge University Press.

Pope, K. (1990). Therapist–patient sexual involvement: a review of the research. *Clinical Psychology Review*, 10: 477–490.

Pope, K. S., & Vasquez, M. J. T. (1991). *Ethics in Psychotherapy and Counseling: A Practical Guide for Psychologists*. San Francisco: Jossey-Bass.

Popper, K. R. (1963). *Conjectures and Refutations*. London: Routledge & Kegan Paul.

Postle, D. (1998). Gold into lead: the annexation of psychotherapy in the UK. *International Journal of Psychotherapy*, 3(1): 53–83.

Postle, D. (1999). Review of Palmer Barnes, 1998. *Counselling News*, 6(January): 32.

Prilleltensky, I. (1994a). *The Morals and Politics of Psychology: Psychological Discourse and the Status Quo*. Albany, NY: State University of New York Press.

Prilleltensky, I. (1994b). The politics of abnormal psychology: past, present and future. *Political Psychology*, 11(4): 767–785.

Prilleltensky, I., & Nelson, G. (1997). Community psychology: reclaiming social justice. In: D. Fox & I. Prilleltensky (Eds.), *Critical Psychology* (pp. 166–184). London: Sage.

Pylkkanen, P. (Ed.) (1989). *The Search for Meaning: The New Spirit in Science and Philosophy*. Wellingborough: Crucible/Aquarian Press.

Rachman, S. J., & Wilson, G. T. (1981). *The Effects of Psychological Therapy* (2nd ed.). Oxford: Pergamon Press.

Radical Therapist Collective (1974). *The Radical Therapist*. Harmondsworth: Penguin.

Rank, O. (1934). *The Trauma of Birth*. New York: Warner Torch Books.

Rave, E. J., & Larsen, C. L. (Eds.) (1995). *Ethical Decision-Making in Therapy: Feminist Perspectives*. New York: Guilford.

Richards, P. S., & Bergin, A. E. (1997). *A Spiritual Strategy for Counseling and Psychotherapy*. Washington, DC: American Psychological Association.

Richardson, F. C., & Fowers, B. J. (1997). Critical theory, postmodernism, and hermeneutics: insights for critical psychology. In: D. Fox & I. Prilleltensky (Eds.), *Critical Psychology* (pp. 265–283). London: Sage.

Riikonen, E., & Smith, G. M. (1997). *Re-Imagining Therapy: Living Conversations and Relational Knowing*. London: Sage.

Riviere, J. (1987). A character trait of Freud. In: J. D. Sutherland (Ed.), *Psychoanalysis and Contemporary Thought*. London: Maresfield Reprint/Karnac Books [orig. 1958].

Robinson, H. (1982). *Matter and Sense*. Cambridge: Cambridge University Press.

Rogers, C. R. (1951). *Client-Centered Therapy: Its Current Practice, Implications, and Theory*. Boston: Houghton Mifflin.

Rogers, C. R. (1973). Some new challenges to the helping professions. *American Psychologist*, 28(5): 379–387 [reprinted in H. Kirschenbaum & V. L. Henderson (Eds.), *The Carl Rogers Reader* (pp. 357–375). London: Constable, 1990].

Rogers, C. R. (undated). Building Person-Centred communities: the implications for the future (mimeo).

Rorty, R. (1979). *Philosophy and the Mirror of Nature*. Princeton, NJ: Princeton University Press.

Rose, N. (1989). *Governing the Soul: The Shaping of the Private Self*. London: Routledge.

Rose, N. (1992). Engineering the human soul: analysing psychological expertise. *Science in Context*, 5(2): 351–369.

Rose, N. (1996). *Inventing Our Selves: Psychology, Power and Personhood*. Cambridge: Cambridge University Press.

Rose, N. (1997). "Power in therapy: Techne and Ethos". Paper presented at the Universities Psychotherapy Association Annual Conference, Power and Influence in Psychotherapy, 14–15 November 1997, Brunei Gallery, School of Oriental and African Studies, University of London. Reproduced at the Academy for the Study of Psychoanalytic Arts web site, available at: http://www.academyanalyticarts.org/ rose2.html; to appear in Y. Bates & R. House (Eds.). (forthcoming/in preparation), *Ethically Challenged Professions: Enabling Therapy Beyond Modernity*. Ross-on-Wye: PCCS Books.

Roth, A., & Fonagy, P. (1996). *What Works for Whom?: A Critical Review of Psychotherapy Research*. New York: Guilford Press.

Rowan, G. (2001). Soul in psychotherapy: an individual account. *Ipnosis: An Independent Journal for Practitioners*, 2(Summer): 18–19.

Rowan, J. (1988). Review of France (1988). *Self and Society*, 26(6): 275–277.

Rowan, J. (1992). Response (to Mair, 1992). In: W. Dryden & C. Feltham (Eds.), *Psychotherapy and its Discontents* (pp. 160–166). London: Sage.

Rowan, J. (1996a). Humanistic NVQs? *Self and Society*, 24(4): 42–44.

Rowan, J. (1996b). Love is not enough (letter). *Counselling*, 7(1): 12.

Rowe, D. (1990). Foreword to J. Masson's *Against Therapy* (pp. 7–23). London: Fontana.

Rudnytsky, P. L. (1991). *The Psychoanalytic Vocation: Rank, Winnicott, and the Legacy of Freud*. New Haven: Yale University Press.

Russell, J. (Ed.) (1987). *Philosophical Perspectives on Developmental Psychology*. Oxford: Blackwell.

Russell, R. (1981). *Report on Effective Psychotherapy: Legislative Testimony*. New York: R. R. Latin Associates.

Rutter, P. (1989). *Sex in the Forbidden Zone*. Los Angeles: Jeremy Tarcher. [1992 ed. quoted.]

Ryan, W. (1971). *Blaming the Victim*. New York: Pantheon Books.

Sachs, J. S. (1983). Negative factors in brief psychotherapy: an empirical assessment. *Journal of Consulting and Clinical Psychology*, 51: 557–564.

Sampson, E. E. (1993). *Celebrating the Other: A Dialogic Account of Human Nature*. New York: Harvester Wheatsheaf.

Samuels, A. (1993). *The Political Psyche*. London: Routledge.

Samuels, A. (1997). Pluralism and psychotherapy: what is good training? In R. House & N. Totton (Eds.), *Implausible Professions* (pp. 199–214). Ross-on-Wye: PCCS Books.

Samuels, A. (2001). *Politics on the Couch: Citizenship and the Internal Life*. London: Profile Books.

Sandler, J., Dare, C., & Holder, A. (1992). *The Patient and the Analyst*. London: Maresfield Reprints/Karnac Books [orig. 1973].

Sands, A. (2000). *Falling for Therapy: Psychotherapy from a Client's Point of View*. London: Macmillan.

Sarason, S. B. (1981). *Psychology Misdirected*. New York: Free Press.

Sarason, S. B. (1982). *Psychology and Social Action*. New York: Praeger.

Sardello, R. (1990). Introduction. In: R. Steiner (Ed.), *Psychoanalysis and Spiritual Psychology: Five Lectures, 1912–21* (pp. 1–29). Hudson, NY: Anthroposophic Press.

Sardello, R. (1992). *Facing the World with Soul: The Reimagination of Modern Life*. Hudson, NY: Lindisfarne Press.

292   REFERENCES

Sardello, R. (2001). *Love and the World: A Guide to Conscious Soul Practice*. Great Barrington, MA: Lindisfarne Books.

Sass, L. A., & Woolfolk, R. L. (1988). Psychoanalysis and the hermeneutic turn: a critique of narrative truth and historical truth. *Journal of the American Psychoanalytic Association, 36*: 429–454.

Schacht, L. (1977). Introduction. In: G. Groddeck (Ed.), *The Meaning of Illness* (pp. 1–30). London: Hogarth Press.

Schaef, A. W. (1992). *Beyond Therapy, Beyond Science: A New Model for Healing the Whole Person*. New York: HarperSanFrancisco.

Schneiderman, S. (1983). *Lacan: The Death of an Intellectual Hero*. Cambridge, MA: Harvard University Press.

Schon, D. A. (1992). The crisis of professional knowledge and the pursuit of an epistemology of practice. *Journal on Interprofessional Care, 6*(1): 49–63.

Schutz, W. (1979). *Profound Simplicity*. USA: Joy Press.

Segal, J. (1985). *Phantasy in Everyday Life: A Psychoanalytic Approach to Understanding Ourselves*. Harmondsworth: Penguin.

Seligman, P. (1998a). Letter to the Editor. *The Times Magazine*, October 10th, p. 103.

Seligman, P. (1998b). Letter to the Editor. *The Times Magazine*, November 7th, p. 95.

Seu, I. B., & Heenan, M. C. (Eds.) (1998). *Feminism and Psychotherapy: Reflections on Contemporary Theories and Practices*. London: Sage.

Sheldrake, R. (1981). *A New Science of Life*. London: Blond & Briggs.

Shepherd, M., & Sartorius, N. (Eds.) (1989). *Non-Specific Aspects of Treatment*. Toronto: Hans Huber.

Shlien, J. M. (1984). A countertheory of transference. In: R. F. Lavant & J. M. Shlien (Eds.), *Client-Centered Therapy and the Person-Centered Approach: New Directions in Theory, Research and Practice* (pp. 153–181). New York: Praeger.

Shohet, R. (1997). Reflections on fear and love in accreditation. In: R. House & N. Totton (Eds.), *Implausible Professions* (pp. 45–50). Ross-on-Wye: PCCS Books.

Sills, C. (1996). Transactional analysis. In: B. Mullen (Ed.), *Therapists on Therapy* (pp. 57–75). London: Free Association Books.

Sivyer, J. (1997). Review of Alexander (1995). *Self and Society, 24*(6): 49–50.

Skolimowski, H. (1994). *The Participatory Mind: A New Theory of Knowledge and the Universe*. London: Penguin/Arkana.

Smail, D. (1983). Psychotherapy and psychology. In: D. Pilgrim (Ed.), *Psychology and Psychotherapy: Current Trends and Issues* (pp. 7–20).

London: Routledge & Kegan Paul.

Smail, D. (1987). *Taking Care: An Alternative to Therapy*. London: Dent.

Smail, D. (1996). *How to Survive Without Psychotherapy*. London: Constable.

Smail, D. (2001). *The Nature of Unhappiness*. London: Robinson.

Smith, D. L. (1984). On the psychoanalytic listening process. *Self and Society*, 12(4): 213–216.

Smith, D. L. (1991). *Hidden Conversations: An Introduction to Communicative Psychotherapy*. London: Routledge.

Smith, J. (1999). Holding the dance: a flexible approach to boundaries in General Practice. In: J. Lees (Ed.), *Clinical Counselling in Primary Care* (pp. 43–60). London: Routledge.

Smithson, A. (1997). *The Kairos Point: The Marriage of Mind and Matter*. Shaftsbury: Element Books.

Smythies, J. R., & Beloff, J. (Eds.) (1989). *The Case for Dualism*. Charlottesville: University Press of Virginia.

Solomon, R. C. (1976). *The Passions: Emotions and the Meaning of Life*. Indianapolis: Hackett [1993 ed.].

Spinelli, E. (1994). *Demystifying Therapy*. London: Constable.

Spinelli, E. (1995). Afterword. In: R. Alexander, *Folie à Deux* (pp. 153–165). London: Free Association Books.

Spinelli, E. (1996). Do therapists know what they're doing? In: I. James & S. Palmer (Eds.), *Professional Therapeutic Titles: Myths and Realities* (pp. 55–61). Leicester: British Psychological Society [Occasional Paper 2].

Spinelli, E. (2001). *The Mirror and the Hammer: Challenging Orthodoxies in Psychotherapeutic Thought*. London: Continuum.

Spinelli, E., & Longman, J. (1998). Counselling and the abuse of power. *Counselling*, 9(3): 181–184.

Stanton, M. (1991). *Sandor Ferenczi: Reconsidering Active Intervention*. Northvale, NJ: Jason Aronson.

Stein, H. (1985a). What is therapeutic in clinical relationships? *Family Medicine*, 17(5): 188–194.

Stein, H. F. (1985b). *The Psychodynamics of Medical Practice: Unconscious Factors in Patient Care*. Berkeley, Calif.: University of California Press.

Steiner, G. (1978). Has truth a future? *The Listener*, January 12th: 42–46.

Steiner, R. (1966). *The Evolution of Consciousness as Revealed Through Initiation-Knowledge*. London: Rudolf Steiner Press [orig. 1926].

Steiner, R. (1968). *A Theory of Knowledge Based on Goethe's World Conception*. New York: Anthroposophic Press.

Steiner, R. (1973). *The Riddles of Philosophy*. Spring Valley, NY: Anthroposophic Press [orig. in German, 1914].

Steiner, R. (1988). *Goethean Science*. Spring Valley, NY: Mercury Press.

Steiner, R. (1995). *The Kingdom of Childhood: Introductory Talks on Waldorf Education*. Hudson, NY: Anthroposophic Press.

Steiner, R. (1996). *The Child's Changing Consciousness and Waldorf Education*. Hudson, NY: Anthroposophic Press.

Stolorow, R., Brandchaft, B., & Atwood, G. (1987). *Psychoanalytic Treatment: An Intersubjective Approach*. Hillsdale, NJ: Analytic Press.

Strasser, F., & Strasser, A. (1997). *Existential Time-Limited Therapy: The Wheel of Existence*. Chichester: John Wiley.

Strupp, H. H., & Binder, J. L. (1984). *Psychotherapy in a New Key: A Guide to Time-Limited Dynamic Psychotherapy*. New York: Basic Books.

Strupp, H. H., Fox, P., & Lessler, V. (1969). *Patients View Their Psychotherapy*. Baltimore: Johns Hopkins University Press.

Strupp, H. H., Hadley, S. W., & Gomes-Schwartz, B. (1977). *Psychotherapy for Better or Worse: The Problem of Negative Effects*. New York: Jason Aronson.

Suares, C. (1953). *Krishnamurti and the Unity of Man*. Bombay: Chetana [1971 ed.].

Sussman, M. B. (1992). *A Curious Calling: Unconscious Motivations for Practicing Psychotherapy*. Northvale, NJ: Jason Aronson.

Sutherland, S. (1987). *Breakdown: A Personal Crisis and a Mental Dilemma* (2nd ed.). London: Weidenfeld & Nicolson [orig. 1976].

Sutherland, S. (1992). What goes wrong in the care and treatment of the mentally ill? In W. Dryden & C. Feltham (Eds.), *Psychotherapy and its Discontents* (pp. 169–186, 190–193). Buckingham: Open University Press.

Symington, J., & Symington, N. (1996). *The Clinical Thinking of Wilfred Bion*. London: Routledge.

Szasz, T. (1963). The concept of transference. *International Journal of Psycho-Analysis, 44*: 432–443.

Szasz, T. (1978). *The Myth of Psychotherapy*. New York: Syracuse University Press.

Tarnas, R. (1991). *The Passion of the Western Mind: Understanding the Ideas that Have Shaped Our World View*. New York: Ballantine.

Taylor, G. J. (1987). *Psychosomatic Medicine and Contemporary Psychoanalysis*. Madison, CT: International Universities Press.

Taylor, G. J. (1992). Psychoanalysis and psychosomatics: a synthesis. *Journal of the American Academy of Psychoanalysis, 20*(2): 251–275.

Taylor, G. J., Bagby, R. M., & Parker, J. D. A. (1997). *Disorders of Affect*

Regulation: Alexithymia in Medical and Psychiatric Illness. Cambridge: Cambridge University Press.

Taylor, S. E. (1989). *Positive Illusions: Creative Self-Deception and the Healthy Mind.* New York: Basic Books.

Taylor, S. E., & Brown, J. D. (1988). Illusion and well-being: a social psychological perspective on mental health. *Psychological Bulletin,* 103(2): 193–210.

Tennyson, W. W., & Strom, S. M. (1986). Beyond professional standards: developing responsibleness. *Journal of Counseling and Development,* 64(5): 298–302.

Thorne, B. (1994). Brief companionship. In: D. Mearns, *Developing Person-Centred Counselling* (pp. 60–64). London: Sage,

Thorne, B. (1997). The accountable therapist: standards, experts and poisoning the well. In: R. House & N. Totton (Eds.), *Implausible Professions* (pp. 141–50). Ross-on-Wye: PCCS Books [reprinted from *Self and Society,* 23(4), 1995].

Thorne, B. (1998). *Person-Centred Counselling and Christian Spirituality: The Secular and the Holy.* London: Whurr.

Thorne, B. (1999). The move towards brief therapy: its dangers and its challenges. *Counselling,* 10(1): 7–11.

Tolan, P., Keys, C., Chertok, F., & Jason, L. (Eds.) (1990). *Researching Community Psychology.* Washington, DC: American Psychological Association.

Tolman, C. W., & Maiers, W. (Eds.) (1991). *Critical Psychology: Contributions to an Historical Science of the Subject.* Cambridge: Cambridge University Press.

Torrey, E. F. (1986). *Witchdoctors and Psychiatrists: The Common Roots of Psychotherapy and Its Future.* New York: Harper & Row.

Totton, N. (1997a). The Independent Practitioners Network. In: R. House & N. Totton (Eds.), *Implausible Professions* (pp. 287–293). Ross-on-Wye: PCCS Books.

Totton, N. (1997b). Learning by mistake: client–practitioner conflict in a self-regulated network. In: R. House & N. Totton (Eds.), *Implausible Professions* (pp. 315–320). Ross-on-Wye: PCCS Books.

Totton, N. (1998). *The Water in the Glass: Mind and Body in Psychoanalysis.* London: Rebus Books.

Totton, N. (2000) *Psychotherapy and Politics.* London: Sage.

Toulmin, S. (1981). Epistemology and developmental psychology. In: E. S. Gollin (Ed.), *Developmental Plasticity: Behavioral and Biological Aspects of Variations in Development* (pp. 253–268). New York: Academic Press.

Valle, R. S. (Ed.) (1998). *Phenomenological Inquiry in Psychology: Existential and Transpersonal Dimensions*. New York: Plenum Press.

Valle, R. S., & Halling, S. (Eds.). (1989). *Existential-Phenomenological Perspectives in Psychology: Exploring the Breadth of Human Experience*. New York: Plenum Press.

van Deurzen-Smith, E. (1992). Dialogue as therapy. *Journal of the Society for Existential Analysis*, 3: 15–23.

van Deurzen-Smith, E. (1996). The future of psychotherapy in Europe. *International Journal of Psychotherapy*, 1(1): 15–21.

van Deurzen-Smith, E. (1997). Counselling: registration—what it will mean to you the counsellor. Paper presented at the 5th Counselling in Primary Care Conference. London: St George's Hospital Medical School (mimeo).

van Manen, M. (1986). *The Tone of Teaching*. Richmond Hill, Ontario: Scholastic/TAB Publications.

Van Sweden, R. C. (1995). *Regression to Dependence: A Second Opportunity for Ego Integration and Developmental Progression*. Northvale, NJ: Jason Aronson.

Walkerdine, V. (1984). Developmental psychology and the child-centred pedagogy: the insertion of Piaget into early education. In: J. Henriques *et al.* (Eds.), *Changing the Subject: Psychology, Social Regulation and Subjectivity* (pp. 153–197). London: Methuen.

Walkerdine, V. (1993). Beyond developmentalism? *Theory and Psychology*, 3(4): 451–469.

Walsch, N. D. (1995). *Conversations with God, Book 1: An Uncommon Dialogue*. London: Hodder & Stoughton.

Wasdell, D. (1990). *The Roots of the Common Unconscious*. London: Unit for Research into Changing Institutions [Meridian Monograph 1].

Wasdell, D. (1992). In the shadow of accreditation. *Self and Society*, 20(1): 3–14.

Watson, G. (1998). *The Resonance of Emptiness: A Buddhist Inspiration for Contemporary Psychotherapy*. Curzon Press.

Webb, S. B. (1997). Training for maintaining appropriate boundaries in counselling. *British Journal of Guidance and Counselling*, 25(2): 175–188.

Weber, R. (Ed.) (1986). *Dialogues with Scientists and Sages: The Search for Unity*. London: Routledge & Kegan Paul [Arkana/Penguin, 1990].

West, W. (1997). Integrating counselling, psychotherapy and healing: an inquiry into counsellors and psychotherapists whose work includes healing. *British Journal of Guidance and Counselling*, 25(3): 291–311.

Wheeler, S. (1998). Challenging the core theoretical model: a reply to Colin Feltham. *Counselling, 9*(2): 134–138.

Whitbeck, C. (1983). A different reality: feminist ontology. In: C. Gould (Ed.), *Beyond Domination*. MD: Rowman & Allenheld.

White, M. (1991). Deconstruction and therapy. *Dulwich Centre Newsletter, 3*: 21–40; also in S. Gilligan & R. Price (Eds.), *Therapeutic Conversations* (pp. 22–61). New York: Norton.

White, M., & Epston, D. (1990). *Narrative Means to Therapeutic Ends*. Adelaide: Dulwich Centre Publications.

Wilkinson, S. (1997). Feminist psychology. In: D. Fox & I. Prilleltensky (Eds.), *Critical Psychology* (pp. 247–264). London: Sage.

Williams, P. (1999). Telling tales: the elusive power of stories. *The Therapist, 6*(1): 18–23.

Wilson, C. P., & Mintz, I. L. (Eds.) (1989). *Psychosomatic Symptoms: Psychodynamic Treatment of the Underlying Personality Disorder*. Northvale, NJ: Jason Aronson.

Winnicott, D. W. (1971). *Playing and Reality*. Harmondsworth: Penguin.

Winnicott, D. W. (1975). Mind and its relation to the psyche-soma. In his *Through Paediatrics to Psychoanalysis* (pp. 243–254). London: Hogarth.

Woodhouse, M. B. (1996). *Paradigm Wars: Worldviews for a New Age*. Berkeley, CA: Frog Ltd.

Woolfolk, R. L., & Richardson, F. C. (1984). Behavior therapy and the ideology of modernity. *American Psychologist, 39*(7): 777–786.

Critical perspectives on/within therapy

Introduction

T his bibliography is intended as a resource for those wishing to pursue the considerable literature offering critical and postmodern perspectives on therapy, particularly profession-centred therapy—and, to some extent, psychology more generally. Please note that I have generally NOT duplicated references already quoted and listed in the main-text References, except where this was unavoidable. Note also that "critical" is interpreted broadly to include critiques from both "the left" *and* "the right" (to use those increasingly oversimplistic terms). I would be particularly interested in receiving and including literature from *non*-UK sources on therapy professionalization, regulation etc., and also critical press reports on therapy and counselling.

I would like to acknowledge Richard Mowbray's book *The Case Against Psychotherapy Registration*, the excellent bibliography of which I have drawn upon in helping to compile the following bibliographic resource.

The bibliography is as comprehensive as I have been able to make it, but I will inevitably have missed important references.

I would like to encourage readers to send me relevant references (especially international material) which I have missed (send c/o the publisher, or to richardahouse@hotmail.com), so that any future editions of the book can be appropriately updated. References to works from 2000 onwards would be especially welcome. All contributors to the bibliography will be acknowledged in any future edition(s). Thank you.

Adams, M. (1998). Review of Smail's *How to Survive without Psychotherapy*. *Counselling*, 9(4): 320.

Agel, J. (1972). *The Radical Therapist*. New York: Ballantine.

Albee, G. W. (1986). Toward a just society: lessons from observations on the primary prevention of psychopathology. *American Psychologist*, 41: 891–898.

Alberding, B., Lauver, P., & Patnoe, J. (1993). Counselor awareness of the consequences of certification and licensure. *Journal of Counseling and Development*, 72(Sept.): 33–38.

Anon. (1996a). Is the UKCP floundering? [editorial]. *The Therapist*, 3(3): 3.

Anon. (1996b). A personal experience of accreditation. *Pin: Newsletter for the IPN*, 6(December): 7.

Anon. (1998). When therapists fail their clients (by Fiona and Emily). *Self and Society*, 26(1): 5–12.

Anon. (2001a). Alderdice rolled by government: report on the demise of the Psychotherapy Bill. *Ipnosis: An Independent Journal for Practitioners*, 2: 4–5.

Anon. (2001b). IPN News: The human face of government—Richardson meets IPN. *Ipnosis: An Independent Journal for Practitioners*, 4: 26–27.

Anon. (2001c). Petrūska Clarkson attacks UKCP complaints procedures. *Ipnosis: An Independent Journal for Practitioners*, 1: 7–8.

Anon. (2001d). Responses to Tantam and van Deurzen's Eurotherapy. *Ipnosis: An Independent Journal for Practitioners*, 1: 14–15.

Anon. (2002). The difficulties of working without hierarchy. *Ipnosis: An Independent Journal for Practitioners*, 5(Spring): 25.

Anon ("Alex"). (2002). Alice's adventures in psychoanalysis: or a survival guide for first-time users of psychotherapy. *Ipnosis: An Independent Journal for Practitioners*, 5(Spring): 4–6.

Bannister, D. (1983). The internal politics of psychotherapy. In: D. Pilgrim (Ed.), *Psychology and Psychotherapy: Current Trends and Issues* (pp. 139–150). London: Routledge & Kegan Paul.

Banton, R., Clifford, P., Frosh, S., Lousada, J., & Rosenthall, J. (1985). *The Politics of Mental Health*. Basingstoke: Macmillan.

Bates, Y. (2002). Listening to our clients. *Ipnosis: An Independent Journal for Practitioners*, 5(Spring): 3.

Bennett, C. (1994). Lend me your ears: mind games: What's the point of counselling? *Guardian* newspaper, May 5th, pp. 2–3, 14.

Berman, J. S., & Norton, N. C. (1985). Does professional training make a therapist more effective? *Psychological Bulletin*, 94(2): 401–407.

Blomfield, V. (1997). Practitioner development through self-direction: the South West London College Counselling Courses. In: R. House & N. Totton (Eds.), *Implausible Professions* (pp. 255–270). Ross-on-Wye: PCCS Books.

Bowden, M. (1996–7). The registration debate: vested interests. *Human Potential, Winter*: 12–13.

Bradley, B., & Selby, J. (1997). Therapy, consciousness raising, and revolution. In: I. Parker & R. Spears (Eds.), *Psychology and Society: Radical Theory and Practice* (pp. 209–219). London: Pluto Press.

Brown, J. (1996). Reply—Personal opinions are not enough. *The Therapist*, 3(3): 45–47.

Brown, J., & Mowbray, R. (1994). No they don't! (on UKCP and NVQs). *Self and Society*, 22(5): 11–12.

Bunting, M. (1994). Unsuitable cases for treatment? *Guardian* newspaper, February 23rd, p. 18.

Button, J. (1995). Review of Mowbray's *Case* (1995). *Self and Society*, 2(4): 52–54.

Campbell, T. W. (1992). Therapeutic relationships and iatrogenic outcomes: the blame-and-change maneuver in psychotherapy. *Psychotherapy*, 29(3): 474–480.

Cannon, C., & Hatfield, S. (1992). Some thoughts after the 2nd National Conference on the Dynamics of Accreditation, Cambridge, June 1992. *Self and Society*, 20(4): 28–34.

Carroll, M. (1998). Review of House & Totton (Eds.), *Implausible Professions*. *Counselling News, March*: 30.

Claxton, G. (1996). Therapy and beyond: concluding thoughts. In: G. Claxton (Ed.), *Beyond Therapy: The Impact of Eastern Religions on Psychological Theory and Practice* (2nd ed.) (pp. 311–325, 352). Sturminster Newton: Prism Press.

Clement, C. (1987). *The Weary Sons of Freud*. London: Verso [orig. 1978].

Cohen, C. I. (1986). Marxism and psychotherapy. *Science and Society*, 50(1): 4–24.

Cohen, D. (Ed.) (1990). Challenging the therapeutic state: critical perspectives on psychiatry and the mental health system. Special Issue of *Journal of Mind and Behavior*, 11(3–4).

Cohen, D. (Ed.) (1994). Challenging the therapeutic state, part two: further disquisitions on the mental health system [Special Issue]. *Journal of Mind and Behavior*, 15(1–2).

Collins, G. (1988). *Can You Trust Counselling? 31 Key Questions Answered*. Leicester: Inter-Varsity Press.

Collis, W. (1998). Review of House & Totton (Eds.), *Implausible Professions*. *International Journal of Psychotherapy*, 3(2): 188–191.

Corrigan, P., & Leonard, P. (1978). Individual consciousness and ideology. In their *Social Work Practice under Capitalism: A Marxist Approach* (pp. 107–123). London: Macmillan.

Coulson, C. J. (1998a). Is supervision becoming a scam? *Association of Humanistic Psychology Practitioners Newsletter*, 4(October): 1–4.

Coulson, C. J. (1998b). Review of House & Totton (Eds.), *Implausible Professions*. *Self and Society*, 26(1): 47–48.

Crews, F. (1986). *Skeptical Engagements*. Oxford: Oxford University Press.

Crews, F. (1996a). *The Memory Wars: Freud's Legacy in Dispute*. London: Granta.

Crews, F. (1996b). The verdict on Freud. *Psychological Science*, 7(2): 63–68.

Crews, F. (1998). *The Unauthorized Freud*. New York: Viking.

Crichton, J. (1995). Wise counsel? *Changes*, 13: 60–63.

Danish, S. J., & Smyer, M. A. (1981). The unintended consequences of requiring a license to help. *American Psychologist*, 36: 13–21.

Davies, J. (1997). Experiences of Self and Peer Accreditation: assessment tension on a university-based counselling training course. In: R. House & N. Totton (Eds.), *Implausible Professions* (pp. 281–286). Ross-on-Wye: PCCS Books.

Dickson, A. (2002). Exploring the world of counselling. *Ipnosis: An Independent Journal for Practitioners*, 5(Spring): 10–11.

Dineen, T. (1996). *Manufacturing Victims: How the Psychology Business Wants To Keep You Dependent for Life*. Canada: R. Davies Multimedia Publishing [London: Constable, 1998].

Eales, M. (1997). Experiences of self and peer accreditation: developing self-determination: the Institute for the Development of Human Potential. In: R. House & N. Totton (Eds.), *Implausible Professions* (pp. 271–275). Ross-on-Wye: PCCS Books.

Efran, J. S. (1992). Constructionist therapy: sense and nonsense. In: S. McNamee & K. J. Gergen (Eds.), *Therapy as Social Construction* (pp. 200–217). London: Sage.

Eisold, K. (1994). The intolerance of diversity in psychoanalytic institutes. *International Journal of Psycho-Analysis, 75*: 795.

Ellis, A., & Yeager, J. (1989). *Why Some Therapies Don't Work: The Dangers of Transpersonal Psychology*. Buffalo, NY: Prometheus Books.

Epstein, W. M. (1999). The ineffectiveness of psychotherapy. In: C. Feltham (Ed.), *Controversies in Psychotherapy and Counselling* (pp. 64–73). London: Sage.

Erwin, E. (1996). The value of psychoanalytic therapy: a question of standards. In: W. O'Donohue & R. F. Kitchener (Eds.), *The Philosophy of Psychology* (pp. 291–303). London: Sage.

Eysenck, H. (1992). The outcome problem in psychotherapy. In: W. Dryden & C. Feltham (Eds.), *Psychotherapy and Its Discontents* (pp. 100–124). Buckingham: Open University Press.

Feltham, C. (Ed.) (1999a). *Controversies in Psychotherapy and Counselling*. London: Sage.

Feltham, C. (1999b). Against and beyond core theoretical models. In: C. Feltham (Ed.), *Controversies in Psychotherapy and Counselling* (pp. 182–193). London: Sage.

Finell, J. S. (1985). Narcissistic problems in analysts. *International Journal of Psycho-Analysis, 66*: 433–445.

Fletcher, D. (1997). Counselling "Does More Harm Than Good". *Daily Telegraph*, September 27th.

Foucault, M. (1967). *Madness and Civilisation: A History of Insanity in the Age of Reason*. London: Tavistock [orig. 1961].

Foucault, M. (1988). The political technologies of individuals. In: L. Martin, H. Gutman, & P. Hutton (Eds.), *Technologies of the Self: A Seminar with Michel Foucault*. Amherst: University of Massachusetts Press.

Frosh, S. (1997). *For and Against Psychoanalysis*. London: Routledge.

Gale, D. (1999). The limitations of boundaries. In: C. Feltham (Ed.), *Controversies in Psychotherapy and Counselling* (pp. 124–131). London: Sage.

Gellner, E. (1985). *The Psychoanalytic Movement*. London: Paladin.

Gladstone, G. (1995a). On NVQs and psychotherapy within the spectacle. *Pin: Newsletter for the IPN*, 2(September): 6–7.

Gladstone, G. (1995b). Conference afterthoughts. *Self and Society, 22*(6): 11–17.

Gladstone, G. (1996). On PCSR and the conservative profession. *Pin: Newsletter for the IPN*, 4(March): 14.

Greenberg, S. (Ed.) (1999). *Mindfield: Therapy on the Couch: A Shrinking Future?* London: Camden Press.

Gross, M. L. (1978). *The Psychological Society: A Critical Analysis of Psychiatry, Psychotherapy, Psychoanalysis and the Psychological Revolution*. New York: Random House.

Gross, S. J. (1977). Professional disclosure: alternative to licensing. *Personnel and Guidance Journal, 55*: 586–588.

Gross, S. J. (1978). The myth of professional licensing. *American Psychologist, 33*: 1009–1016.

Grünbaum, A. (1984). *The Foundations of Psychoanalysis: A Philosophical Critique*. Berkeley: University of California Press.

Grünbaum, A. (1996). Is psychoanalysis viable? In W. O'Donohue & R. F. Kitchener (Eds.), *The Philosophy of Psychology* (pp. 281–290). London: Sage.

Guardian newspaper. (1994). The values and dangers of counselling [four Letters to the Editor]. May 10th.

Hall, J. (1991). Letter to the Editor on Accreditation. *Self and Society, 19*(5): 58–59.

Hall, M. (1997). Stepping off the "Board-Game": A new practitioner's view of accreditation. In: R. House & N. Totton (Eds.), *Implausible Professions* (pp. 305–314). Ross-on-Wye: PCCS Books.

Hancock, A. (1998). Accreditation: who needs it? *Pin: Newsletter for the IPN, 11*(March): 8–9.

Hare-Mustin, R. T. (1994). Discourses in the mirrored room: a postmodern analysis of therapy. *Family Process, 33*: 19–35.

Hare-Mustin, R. T., & Marecek, J. (1997). Abnormal and clinical psychology: the politics of madness. In: D. Fox & I. Prilleltensky (Eds.), *Critical Psychology: An Introduction* (pp. 104–120). London: Sage.

Harris, M., (1994). *Magic in the Surgery: Counselling and the NHS—a Licensed State Friendship Service*. London: Social Affairs Unit [Research Report 20].

Hatfield, S., & Cannon, C. (1997). Uncovering the mirror: our evolving personal relationship with accreditation. In: R. House & N. Totton (Eds.), *Implausible Professions* (pp. 187–198). Ross-on-Wye: PCCS Books.

Hawkes, N. (1997). Study counsels caution on a cure-all for life's ills. *The Times*, August 19th, p. 7.

Hayes, C. (1997). My understanding of IPN. *Pin: Newsletter for the IPN*, 9(September): 4–5.

Hayes, C., & McMillan, M. (1997). Experiences of self and peer accreditation: the Diploma in Counselling at the University of East Anglia. In: R. House & N. Totton (Eds.), *Implausible Professions* (pp. 275–281). Ross-on-Wye: PCCS Books.

Heaton, J. M. (1993). Scepticism and psychotherapy: a Wittgensteinian approach. In: L. Spurling (Ed.), *From the Words of My Mouth: Tradition in Psychotherapy*. London: Routledge.

Hermans, H. J. M., Kempen, H. J. G., & van Loon, R. J. P. (1992). The dialogical self: beyond individualism and rationalism. *American Psychologist*, 47(1): 23–33.

Highfield, R. & others (1998). Psychology a fake science that abuses public, says expert [being Ian Parker—RH]. *Daily Telegraph*, September 12th.

Hillman, J. (1995). *Kinds of Power: A Guide to Its Intelligent Uses*. New York: Currency Doubleday.

Hillman, J., & Ventura, M. (1992). *We've Had a Hundred Years of Psychotherapy and the World's Getting Worse*. New York: HarperCollins.

Hincksman, B. (1998). Review of House & Totton (Eds.), *Implausible Professions*. *Counselling*, 9(3): 231–232.

Hinshelwood, R. D. (1997). Convergences with psychoanalysis. In: I. Parker & R. Spears (Eds.), *Psychology and Society: Radical Theory and Practice* (pp. 93–104). London: Pluto Press.

Hogan, D. B. (1980). The impact of professional certification on counseling psychology. *Counseling Psychologist*, 9: 29–43.

Hogan, D. B. (1999). The US regulation example. In: S. Greenberg (Ed.), *Mindfield* ... London: Camden Press.

Holzkamp-Osterkamp, U. (1991). Action potence, education and psychotherapy. In: C. W. Tolman & W. Maiers (Eds.), *Critical Psychology: Contributions to an Historical Science of the Subject* (pp. 134–159). Cambridge: Cambridge University Press.

House, R. (1992). A tale of two conferences: organisational form and accreditation ethos. *Self and Society*, 20(4): 35–37.

House, R. (1995a). Review of Mowbray 1995. *Clinical Psychology Forum*, December: 43–44 [also in *Changes*, 14(1): 85–87, 1996].

House, R. (1995b). Letter on professionalisation. *Self and Society*, 23(5): 49.

House, R. (1995c). The dynamics of power: why Mowbray is right about professionalisation. *Counselling News*, 20(Dec.): 24–25.

House, R. (1995c). Review of Hall's *Reluctant Adult*. *Self and Society*, 23(1): 52–53.

House, R. (1996a). Letter [Response to Tantam on professionalisation]. *Self and Society*, 24(3): 54–55.

House, R. (1996b). To the point [Critique of BBC's "Watchdog" Programme]. *Counselling News*, 22(June): 3–4.

House, R. (1996c). Professional versus vocational training in counsellor development. Mimeo [included in House, 2001c—see References].

House, R. (1996d). "Diagnosing" the growth of counselling: responses to Raj Persaud. *Counselling*, 7(4): 276.

House, R. (1996–7). The registration debate: an illusion of policing. *Human Potential, Winter*: 13.

House, R. (1997a). Correspondence: Registering concern about professionalisation. *British Journal of Guidance and Counselling*, 25(1): 107–110.

House, R. (1997b). A professionalised fetish can be made of supervision. *The Therapist*, 4(4): 23 [published "anonymously"].

House, R. (1997c). Review of Parker *et al.*'s *Deconstructing Psychopathology*. *Self and Society*, 25(1): 58.

House, R. (1997d). Participative New Paradigm methodology [review article of Heron's *Co-operative Inquiry*]. *Network: The Scientific and Medical Network Review*, 65(Dec.): 57–58.

House, R. (1998a). Rival registers? (Letter). *Counselling*, 9(1): 3.

House, R. (1998b). Letter to the Editor [on Rowan's reviews of Smail]. *Self and Society*, 26(5): 43.

House, R. (1998c). Review of James and Palmer, *Professional Therapeutic Titles*. *British Journal of Guidance and Counselling*, 26(1): 128–129.

House, R. (1998d). Review of Erwin's *Philosophy and Psychotherapy*. *Counselling*, 9(1): 55–56.

House, R. (1998e). Review of Parker's *Psychoanalytic Culture*. *Counselling*, 9(2): 139.

House, R. (1999a). Letter to the Editor [on Pokorny's Response to Postle]. *International Journal of Psychotherapy*, 4(2): 263–264.

House, R. (1999b). The Independent Practitioners Network: therapist accountability with heart. Mimeo [available at: richardahouse@hotmail.com].

House, R. (2001). Transforming commodifed supervision into peer support. *Ipnosis: An Independent Journal for Practitioners*, 4(Winter): 4–5.

House, R., & Hall, J. (1991). Peer accreditation: within a humanistic framework? *Self and Society*, 19(2): 33–36.

House, R., & Totton, N. (Eds.) (1997a). *Implausible Professions: Arguments for Pluralism and Autonomy in Psychotherapy and Counselling*. Ross-on-Wye: PCCS Books.

House, R., & Totton, N. (1997b). Conclusion. In: R. House & N. Totton (Eds.), *Implausible Professions* (pp. 335–337). Ross-on-Wye: PCCS Books.

Howard, A. (1987). Psychotherapy: just a status symbol? *OpenMind*, *28*: 9.

Howard, A. (1988). The necessities and absurdities of accredited helping. *Counselling*, *64*: 19–22.

Howard, A. (1990). Counselling plc. *Counselling*, *1*(1): 15–16.

Howard, A. (1992). What, and why, are we accrediting? *Counselling*, *3*(3): 171–173.

Howard, A. (1993). A fairy story (a light-hearted look at the helping professions). *The Psychologist*, *6*: 268–270.

Howard, A. (1998). Roads to professionalisation: dare we travel the "integrity route?". *British Journal of Guidance and Counselling*, *26*(2): 303–309.

Howard, A. (1999a). Can you rely on registered counselling? *LM Magazine*.

Howard, A. (1999b). Psychotherapy and counselling as unproven, overblown and unconvincing. In: C. Feltham (Ed.), *Controversies in Psychotherapy and Counselling* (pp. 269–277). London: Sage.

Ibanez, T., & Iniguez, L. (Ed.) (1997). *Critical Social Psychology*. London: Sage.

Ingleby, D. (Ed.) (1981). *Critical Psychiatry: The Politics of Mental Health*. Harmondsworth: Penguin.

Ingleby, D. (1984). The ambivalence of psychoanalysis. *Free Associations* [Pilot Issue; *Radical Science, 15*]: 39–71.

Ingleby, D. (1985). Psychology and ideology. In: J. Broughton (Ed.), *Critical Developmental Theory*. New York: Plenum.

Jacobs, D. H. (1994). Environmental failure–oppression is the only cause of psychopathology. *Journal of Mind and Behavior*, *15*(1–2): 1–18.

Jacobson, N. (1995). The overselling of therapy. *Family Therapy Networker*, *19*(2): 41–47.

Johnson, R. E. (1971). *Existential Man: The Challenge of Psychotherapy*. New York: Pergamon Press.

Jones, A. (1991). Formal training is antithetical to the spirit of psychotherapy: A review and commentary. *Counselling Psychology Quarterly*, *4*(1): 65–73.

Jung, A. R. (1987). Alternatives to psychotherapy. *Issues in Radical Therapy, 17*(4): 30–33, 54–55.

Kalisch, D. (1992). The living tradition and the division of the spoils: professionalisation again. *Self and Society, 18*(4): 36–37.

Kalisch, D. (1998). Review of House & Totton (Eds.), *Implausible Professions. Self and Society, 26*(1): 46–47.

Kaye, J. (1999). Toward a non-regulative praxis. In: I. Parker (Ed.), *Deconstructing Psychotherapy* (pp. 19–38). London: Sage.

Kearney, A. (1996). *Counselling, Class and Politics: Undeclared Influences in Therapy*. Manchester: PCCS Books.

Kernberg, O. (1996). Thirty methods to destroy creativity of psycho-analytic candidates. Available at: http://ijpa.org/kernberg.exe

Kilpatrick, W. K. (1983). *Psychological Seduction: The Failure of Modern Psychology*. Nashville: Nelson.

Kilpatrick, W. K. (1985). *The Emperor's New Clothes: The Naked Truth about Psychology*. Westchester, IL: Crossway.

King-Spooner, S. (1995). Psychotherapy and the white dodo. *Changes, 13*: 45–51.

Kittrie, N. N. (1971). *The Right To Be Different: Deviance and Enforced Therapy*. Baltimore: Johns Hopkins University Press.

Kovel, J. (1981). *The Age of Desire: Reflections of a Radical Psychoanalyst*. New York: Pantheon Books.

Kovel, J. (1988a). *The Radical Spirit: Essays on Psychoanalysis and Society*. London: Free Association Books.

Kovel, J. (1988b). Therapy in late capitalism. In his *The Radical Spirit: Essays on Psychoanalysis and Society* (pp. 121–146). London: Free Association Books.

Kovel, J. (1988c). Values, interests and psychotherapy. In his *The Radical Spirit: Essays on Psychoanalysis and Society* (pp. 147–160). London: Free Association Books.

Kovel, J. (1988d). The Marxist view of man and psychoanalysis. In his *The Radical Spirit: Essays on Psychoanalysis and Society* (pp. 167–188). London: Free Association Books.

Kvale, S. (1985). Skinner's Radical Behaviorism and behavior therapy— an outline for a Marxist critique. *Revista Mexicana del Analisis de la Conducta, 11*: 239–253.

Lamont, J. (1995). Review of Mowbray's *Case Against Psychotherapy Registration. Gestalt South West, 21*: 18–19.

Larner, G. (1999). Derrida and the deconstruction of power as context and topic in therapy. In: I. Parker (Ed.), *Deconstructing Psychotherapy* (pp. 39–53). London: Sage.

Larsen, K. S. (Ed.) (1986). *Dialectics and Ideology in Psychology*. Norwood, NJ: Ablex.

Lather, P. (1992). Postmodernism and the human sciences. In: S. Kvale (Ed.), *Psychology and Postmodernism* (pp. 88–109). London: Sage.

Laungani, P. (1995). Can psychotherapies seriously damage your health? *Counselling, 6*(2): 110–115.

Levy, D. A. (1991). How to be a good psychotherapy patient. *Journal of Polymorphous Perversity, 8*(1): 17–19.

Lichtman, R. (1982). *The Production of Desire: The Integration of Psychoanalysis into Marxist Theory*. New York: Free Press.

Lomas, P. (1997). The teaching of psychotherapy. In: R. House & N. Totton (Eds.), *Implausible Professions* (pp. 215–224). Ross-on-Wye: PCCS Books.

Lonie, I. (1991a). The burning fiery furnace: psychotherapy research— scientific method or scientific trial? *Australian Journal of Psychotherapy, 10*(2).

Lowe, R. (1999). Between the "no longer" and the "not yet": postmodernism as a context for critical therapeutic work. In: I. Parker (Ed.), *Deconstructing Psychotherapy* (pp. 71–85). London: Sage.

Macaskill, A. (1999). Personal therapy as a training requirement: the lack of supporting evidence. In: C. Feltham (Ed.), *Controversies in Psychotherapy and Counselling* (pp. 142–154). London: Sage.

Maclean Matheson, S., & Sylvester, R. (1994). Letter to the Editor [on accreditation]. *Self and Society, 21*(6): 46.

Madsen, P. (1992). Postmodernism and late capitalism: on terms and realities. In: S. Kvale (Ed.), *Psychology and Postmodernism* (pp. 209–223). London: Sage.

Makay, J. (1980). Psychotherapy as rhetoric for secular grace. *Central States Speech Journal, 31*: 184–196.

Malleson, J., & Booth, A. (1997). On the couch: therapists under analysis [Letters to the Editor]. *Guardian* newspaper, January 16th.

Marshall, R. (1988). The role of ideology in the individualization of distress. *Psychologist: Bull. Brit Psychol. Soc., 2*: 67–69.

Martin, L., Gutman, H., & Hutton, P. (Eds.) (1988). *Technologies of the Self: A Seminar with Michel Foucault*. Amherst: University of Massachusetts Press.

Masson, J. (1984). *The Assault on Truth: Freud and Child Sexual Abuse*. New York: Farrar, Straus & Giroux.

Masson, J. (1994). The question of power in psychotherapy. *Journal of the Society for Existential Analysis, 5*: 24–36.

Masson, J. (1999). Still against therapy. In: S. Greenberg (Ed.), *Mindfield* ... London: Camden Press.

McHugh, P. (1994). Psychotherapy awry. *American Scholar*, 63(1): 17–30.

McKinstry, L. (1997). Today, Britain employs more counsellors than soldiers. Is self-obsession becoming our greatest enemy? *Daily Mail*, January 20th.

McLellan, B. (1995). *Beyond Psychoppression: a Feminist Alternative to Therapy*. Melbourne: Spinifex.

McLellan, J. (1999). Becoming an effective psychotherapist or counsellor: are training and supervision necessary? In C. Feltham (Ed.), *Controversies in Psychotherapy and Counselling* (pp. 164–173). London: Sage.

Minsky, T. (1987). Prisoners of psychotherapy. *New York magazine*, August 31st, pp. 34–40.

Mirowsky, J., & Ross, C. E. (1989). *Social Causes of Psychological Distress*. New York: Aldine de Gruyter.

Mithers, C. L. (1994). *Therapy Gone Mad*. Reading, MA: Addison-Wesley.

Montaut, M. (1998). Review Article of House & Totton (Eds.), *Implausible Professions* and Holmes & Lindley's *The Values of Psychotherapy*. *Inside Out* (Ireland), *Spring*: 35–42.

Morss, J. R. (1992). Making waves: deconstruction and developmental psychology. *Theory and Psychology*, 2(4): 445–465.

Mowbray, R. (1994). The Death of the Human Potential Movement? [Letter]. *Self and Society*, 22(2): 43.

Mowbray, R. (1995a). Psychotherapy—a suitable case for statutory treatment? *The Therapist*, 3(2): 8–9.

Mowbray, R. (1995b). Organic growth. *Counselling News*, 19(Sept.): 8–9.

Mowbray, R. (1996a). Case not proven. *Counselling News, September*: 12–13.

Mowbray, R. (1996b). Registration: the case against. *Human Potential*, 19(Autumn): 12–15.

Mowbray, R. (1996c). Letter to the Editor [on SAFAA]. *Self and Society*, 24(2): 42–43.

Mowbray, R. (1996d). Registering humanistic psychology and the case for a flat earth. *Self and Society*, 24(3): 22–26.

Mowbray, R. (1996e). Letter to the Editor. *Connections: Scotland's Voice of Alternative Health*, 28: 50.

Mowbray, R. (1996f). Case not proven. *Counselling News*, 23(Sept.): 12–13.

Mowbray, R. (1996g). Richard Mowbray replies to the UKCP. *The Therapist*, 3(4): 47–48.

Mowbray, R. (1996h). SAFAA is safer. *Self and Society*, 23(6): 16–19.

Mowbray, R. (1997). A case to answer: justifying the UK Register of Counsellors. *Counselling in Scotland* (Stirling: COSCA).

Mowbray, R. (1999). Professionalisation of therapy by registration is un-necessary, ill advised and damaging. In: C. Feltham (Ed.), *Controversies in Psychotherapy and Counselling* (pp. 206–216). London: Sage.

Murdin, L. (1995). What harm can it do? A discussion of the potential harm inherent in psychodynamic work. *Psychodynamic Counselling*, 1(3): 391–402.

Musgrave, A. (2002). Letter to the *Observer*. *Ipnosis: An Independent Journal for Practitioners*, 5(Spring): 12–15.

Myers, D. G. (1981). *The Inflated Self*. New York: Seabury.

Nature, Society, and Thought. (1995). Special Issue: Marx and Freud, 8(1).

New Age Journal. (1992). Is therapy turning us into children? *May–June*: 60–65, 136–141.

Newman, F., & Holzman, L. (1996). *Unscientific Psychology: A Cultural–Performatory Approach to Understanding Human Life*. Westport, CT: Praeger.

Newman, F., & Holzman, L. (1997). *The End of Knowing: A New Developmental Way of Learning*. London: Routledge.

Newton, T. (1999). Stress discourse and individualization. In: C. Feltham (Ed.), *Controversies in Psychotherapy and Counselling* (pp. 241–251). London: Sage.

North, M. (1972). *The Secular Priests*. London: Allen & Unwin.

Orbach, S. (1994). False therapy syndrome. *Guardian Weekend* Magazine, June 11th, p. 57.

Owen, I. R. (1995). Power, boundaries, intersubjectivity. *British Journal of Medical Psychology*, 68: 97–107.

Parker, I. (1996). Against Wittgenstein: materialist reflections on language in psychology. *Theory and Psychology*, 6(3): 363–384.

Parker, I. (1998). Review of House & Totton (Eds.), *Implausible Professions. European Journal of Psychotherapy, Counselling and Health*, 1(3): 477–479.

Parker, I. (1999a). Deconstructing diagnosis: psychopathological prac-tice. In: C. Feltham (Ed.), *Controversies in Psychotherapy and Counselling* (pp. 104–112). London: Sage.

Parker, I. (1999b). Deconstruction and psychotherapy. In: I. Parker (Ed.), *Deconstructing Psychotherapy* (pp. 1–18). London: Sage.

Pilgrim, D. (1990). British psychotherapy in context. In: W. Dryden (Ed.), *Individual Therapy: A Handbook*. Buckingham: Open University Press.

Pilgrim, D. (1991). Psychotherapy and the social blinkers. *The Psychologist*, 2: 52–55.

Pilgrim, D. (1993). Objections to private practice. In: W. Dryden (Ed.), *Questions and Answers on Counselling in Action* (pp. 156–160). London: Sage.

Piohtee, S. (2001). Ethics and close relatives. *Ipnosis: An Independent Journal for Practitioners*, 2: 6–7 (part 1); *Ipnosis: An Independent Journal for Practitioners*, 3: 22–23 (part 2).

Postle, S. (1994). The glacier reaches edge of town. *Self and Society*, 23(6): 7–11.

Postle, D. (Ed.) (1996-date). G.O.R.I.L.L.A. world wide web professionalisation archive. Available at: http://lpiper.demon.co.uk/ [see *Ipnosis: An Independent Journal for Practitioners*, 4: 23, 2001].

Postle, D. (1996). A self and peer assessment process for existing practitioners. *Pin: Newsletter for the IPN*, 4(March): 7–8.

Postle, D. (1996–7). The registration debate: Freezing psychotherapy. *Human Potential, Winter*: 12.

Postle, D. (1997a). Counselling in the UK: jungle, garden or monoculture? In R. House & N. Totton (Eds.), *Implausible Professions* (pp. 151–158). Ross-on-Wye: PCCS Books.

Postle, D. (1997b). A self and peer assessment process for existing practitioners. London: "Leonard Piper" IPN Group (mimeo).

Postle, D., & Anderson, J. (1990). Stealing the flame. *Self and Society*, 18(1): 13–15.

Prilleltensky, I. (1989). Psychology and the status quo. *American Psychologist*, 44: 795–802.

Prilleltensky, I. (1990). On the social and political implications of cognitive psychology. *Journal of Mind and Behavior*, 11: 127–136.

Prilleltensky, I. (1992). Humanistic psychology, human welfare and the social order. *Journal of Mind and Behavior*, 13: 315–328.

Prilleltensky, I. (1996). Human, moral, and political values for an emancipatory psychology. *The Humanistic Psychologist*, 24(3): 307–324.

Prilleltensky, I. (1997). Values, assumptions, and practices: assessing the moral implications of psychological discourse and action. *American Psychologist*, 52(5): 517–535.

Reeves, D. (1998). Face-to-face therapy (letter). *Counselling*, 9(2): 86–87.

Richards, B. (1984b). Schizoid states and the market. In: B. Richards (Ed.), *Capitalism and Infancy* (pp. 122–166). London, Free Association Books.

Richards, B. (1985). Psychoanalysis and the deconstruction of psychology. *Free Associations*, 1: 105–112.

Rieff, P. (1966). *The Triumph of the Therapeutic: Uses of Faith after Freud*. Chicago: University of Chicago Press.

Riikonen, E., & Vataja, S. (1999). Can (and should) we know how, where and when psychotherapy takes place? In I. Parker (Ed.), *Deconstructing Psychotherapy* (pp. 175–187). London: Sage.

Riley, D. (1978). Developmental psychology, biology and Marxism. *Ideology and Consciousness*, 4: 73–92.

Rosen, R. D. (1978). *Psychobabble*. London: Wildwood House.

Rowan, J. (1995). An open letter to Richard Mowbray. *Self and Society*, 23(4): 43–44.

Rowan, J. (1998). Review of House & Totton (Eds.), *Implausible Professions*. *Dialogue*, 3(July): 37.

Rowe, D. (1997a). The comforts of unreason. In: D. Kennard & N. Small (Eds.), *Living Together* (pp. 150–159). London: Quartet Books.

Rowe, D. (1997b). Why therapy does not work. *The Times*, January 3rd, p. 16.

Rusk, T. (1991). *Instead of Therapy: Help Yourself Change and Change the Help You're Getting*. Carson, CA: Hay House.

Salter, A. (1953). *The Case Against Psychoanalysis*. London: Medical Publications.

Sampson, E. E. (1981). Cognitive psychology as ideology. *American Psychologist*, 26: 730–743.

Samuels, A. (1997). Pluralism and psychotherapy: What is good training? In R. House & N. Totton (Eds.), *Implausible Professions* (pp. 199–214). Ross-on-Wye: PCCS Books.

Schneider, M. (1975). *Neurosis and Civilisation: A Marxist/Freudian Synthesis*. New York: Seabury Press.

Self and Society (1990). Special Issue: Accreditation. *18*(4).

Self and Society. (1994). Special Issue: Do Therapists Cure Clients? 22(5): 4–12.

Self and Society. (1998a). Special Issue: Co-Counselling. 25(6): 3–19.

Self and Society. (1998b). Special Issue: Emotional abuse in therapy. 26(1): 4–25.

Shohet, R. (1990). A group begins to tackle accreditation. *Self and Society*, *18*(1): 16.

Shohet, R. & others (1991). Peer group accreditation of psychotherapists. *Self and Society*, *19*(2): 31–32.

Sigman, A. (1995). *New, Approved?: Exposing the Misuse of Popular Psychology*. London: Simon & Schuster.

Simmons, M. (1996). Qualified success: are counsellors' registers a good thing? *Guardian* newspaper, September 4th.

Singer, M. T., & Lalich, J. (1996). *"Crazy" Therapies: What Are They? Do They Work?* San Francisco: Jossey-Bass.

Sivyer, J. (1998). Review of Pilgrim's *Psychotherapy and Society*. *Self and Society*, 26(4): 37–39.

Smail, D. (1987). Psychotherapy and "change": some ethical considerations. In: G. & S. Fairbairn (Eds.), *Psychology, Ethics and Change* (pp. 31–43). London: Routledge & Kegan Paul.

Smail, D. (1997). Psychotherapy and tragedy. In: R. House & N. Totton (Eds.), *Implausible Professions* (pp. 159–170). Ross-on-Wye: PCCS Books.

Smith, J. A., Harré, R., & Van Langenhove, L. (Eds.) (1995). *Rethinking Psychology*. London: Sage.

Spinelli, E. (1993). The Unconscious: an idea whose time has gone? *Journal of the Society for Existential Analysis*, 4: 19–47.

Spinelli, E. (1998). Personal therapy (letter). *Counselling*, 9(4): 259–260.

Steiner, C. M. (1987). The seven sources of power: an alternative to authority. *Transactional Analysis Journal*, 17(3): 102–104.

Steiner, R. (1946). *Psychoanalysis in the Light of Anthroposophy: Five Lectures (1912–21)*. New York: Anthroposophic Press.

Steiner, R. (1991). Methods and rationale of Freudian psychoanalysis (Sept. 13th, 1915). In his *Community Life, Inner Development, Sexuality and the Spiritual Teacher* (pp. 53–67). Hudson, NY: Anthroposophic Press.

Striano, J. (1988). *Can Psychotherapists Hurt You?* Santa Barbara: Professional Press.

Sylvester, R., & Maclean Matheson, S. (1992). The training and accreditation of psychotherapists and counsellors. *Self and Society*, 20(3): 26–29.

Szasz, T. S. (1961). *The Myth of Mental Illness: Foundations of a Theory of Personal Conduct*. New York: Harper & Row.

Szasz, T. S. (1971). *The Manufacture of Madness: A Comparative Study of the Inquisition and the Mental Health Movement*. London: Routledge & Kegan Paul [orig. 1970].

Szasz, T. (1974). *Ideology and Insanity: Essays on the Psychiatric Dehumanization of Man*. Harmondsworth: Penguin [orig. 1970].

Szasz, T. S. (1976). *Karl Kraus and the Soul-Doctors: A Pioneer Critic and His Criticism of Psychiatry and Psychoanalysis*. Baton Rouge: Louisiana State University Press.

Szasz, T. (1998). The healing word: its past, present, and future. *Journal of Humanistic Psychology*, 38(2): 8–20.

Talbot, J. (2001a). Psychotherapy is different. *Ipnosis: An Independent Journal for Practitioners*, 2: 14–15.

Talbot, J. (2001b). Conflict resolution. *Ipnosis: An Independent Journal for Practitioners*, 3: 20–21.

Taylor, A. (1992). It felt as if he had seduced me. *The Independent* newspaper, September 1st, p. 11.

Tennov, D. (1973). Feminism, psychotherapy and professionalism. *Journal of Contemporary Psychotherapy*, 5(2): 107–111.

Thorne, B. (1997a). Counselling and psychotherapy: the sickness and the prognosis. In: S. Palmer & V. Varma (Eds.), *The Future of Counselling and Psychotherapy* (pp. 153–166). London: Sage.

Thorne, B. (1997b). Spiritual responsibility in a secular profession. In: I. Horton & V. Varma (Eds.), *The Needs of Counsellors and Psychotherapists*. London: Sage.

Thorne, B., & Bates, Y. (2001a). Education, registration and professionalisation: an interview with Brian Thorne (part 1). *Ipnosis: An Independent Journal for Practitioners*, 1: 4–6.

Thorne, B., & Bates, Y. (2001b). The UKRC, IPN and collective accountability cultures: an interview with Brian Thorne (part 2). *Ipnosis: An Independent Journal for Practitioners*, 2: 24–25.

Thorne, B., & Bates, Y. (2001c). The future: an interview with Brian Thorne (part 3). *Ipnosis: An Independent Journal for Practitioners*, 3: 18–19.

Tolman, C. W. (1994). *Psychology, Society, and Subjectivity: An Introduction to German Critical Psychology*. London: Routledge.

Tolman, C. W., & Maiers, W. (Ed.) (1991). *Critical Psychology: Contributions to an Historical Science of the Subject*. Cambridge: Cambridge University Press.

Tomkins, G. (2001a). The fallacy of accreditation: part 1. *Ipnosis: An Independent Journal for Practitioners*, 3: 6–8.

Tomkins, G. (2001b). The fallacy of accreditation: part 2—The impact of the drive to accreditation and registration. *Ipnosis: An Independent Journal for Practitioners*, 4: 24–25.

Tomkins, G. (2002). The fallacy of accreditation: part 3—Re-ensouling psychotherapy as an alternative to accreditation. *Ipnosis: An Independent Journal for Practitioners*, 5(Spring): 22–24.

Torrey, E. F. (1992). *Freudian Fraud: The Malignant Effect of Freud's Theory on American Thought and Culture*. San Francisco: HarperCollins.

Totton, N. (1992). Therapists on the couch. *i to i*, July–Sept.

Totton, N. (1994). Letter to the Editor. *Self and Society*, 21(6): 47.

Totton, N. (1995a). Independent Therapists Network Founding Conference: a personal view. *Self and Society*, 22(6): 32–33.

Totton, N. (1995b). The Independent Therapists' Network. *Self and Society*, 23(3): 31–33.

Totton, N. (1997a). Inputs and outcomes: the medical model and professionalisation. In: R. House & N. Totton (Eds.), *Implausible Professions* (pp. 109–116). Ross-on-Wye: PCCS Books.

Totton, N. (1997b). Not just a job: psychotherapy as a spiritual and political practice. In: R. House & N. Totton (Eds.), *Implausible Professions* (pp. 129–140). Ross-on-Wye: PCCS Books.

Totton, N. (2001a). *Falling for Therapy* (review of Sands' *Falling for Therapy*). *Ipnosis: An Independent Journal for Practitioners*, 2: 21.

Totton, N. (2001b). Politics on the couch (review of Samuels' book). *Ipnosis: An Independent Journal for Practitioners*, 3: 25.

Trebilcock, M. J., & Shaul, J. (1982). Regulating the quality of psychotherapeutic services. In: D. N. Dewees (Ed.), *The Regulation of Quality: Products, Services, Workplaces, and the Environment*. Toronto: Butterworths.

Tudor, K. (1998). Review of House & Totton (Eds.), *Implausible Professions*. *Person-Centred Practice*, 6: 115–117.

Vale, H. (2001). A view from this end of the eyeglass. *Ipnosis: An Independent Journal for Practitioners*, 2: 22–23.

van Deurzen-Smith, E. (1994). Questioning the power of psychotherapy: is Jeffrey Masson onto something? *Journal of the Society for Existential Analysis*, 5: 36–44.

Vitz, P. C. (1977). *Psychology as Religion: The Cult of Self-Worship*. Grand Rapids, MI: Eerdmans.

Volosinov, V. N. (1976). *Freudianism: a Marxist Critique*. New York: Academic Press.

Wallach, M. A., & Wallach, L. (1983). *Psychology's Sanction of Selfishness: The Error of Egoism in Theory and Therapy*. San Francisco: W. H. Freeman.

Walter, N. (1995). Beyond therapy (Portrait of Alice Miller). *Guardian Weekend* Magazine, April 29th: 42–46.

Ward, M. (1998). Therapy as abuse. *Self and Society*, 26(1): 13–16.

Wasdell, D. (1991). *The Pre- and Peri-natal Ground of Capitalism and the Free Market Economy*. London: Unit for Research into Changing Institutions.

Watters, E., & Ofshe, R. (1999). *Therapy's Delusions: The Myth of the Unconscious and the Exploitation of Today's Walking Worried*. New York: Scribner.

Webster, M. (1991). Emotional abuse in therapy. *Australian and New Zealand Journal of Family Therapy*, 12(3): 137–145.

Webster, M. (1998). Emotional abuse in therapy. *Self and Society*, 26(1): 17–25.

Webster, R. (1995). *Why Freud Was Wrong: Sin, Science and Psycho-analysis*. London: HarperCollins.

Webster, R. (1996). Freud's labyrinth of error [interview]. *The Therapist*, 3(4): 24–32.

Weldon, F. (1997). Mind at the end of its tether. *Guardian* newspaper, January 11th.

Weldon, F. (1999). Mind at the end of its tether. In: C. Feltham (Ed.), *Controversies in Psychotherapy and Counselling* (pp. 287–293). London: Sage.

Wessely, S. (1996). The rise of counselling and the return of alienism. *British Medical Journal*, 313(20 July): 158–160.

Whan, M. (1987). On the nature of practice. *Spring*, pp. 77–86

Whan, M. (1999). Registering psychotherapy as an institutional neurosis: or, compounding the estrangement between soul and world. *European Journal of Psychotherapy, Counselling and Health*, 2(3): 309–323.

White, L. (1997). Speaking your mind. *Sunday Times Magazine*, January 5th: 37–42.

Wilkinson, H. (1999). Editorial: Psychotherapy, fascism and constitutional history. *International Journal of Psychotherapy*, 4(2): 117–125.

Willmot, J. (1995). Backlash against therapy [Review Article]. *Open Mind*, 73(Feb.–March): 22.

Wood, G. (1983). *The Myth of Neurosis: Overcoming the Illness Excuse*. London: Macmillan.

Young, C. (1992). Report of the Cambridge Conference (on the Dynamics of Accreditation). *Self and Society*, 20(4): 38–40.

Young, R. M. (1996). Psychodynamics of Psychoanalytic Organisations. Available at: http://www.shef.ac.uk/uni/academic/N-Q/psysc/staff/rmyoung/index.html

Young, R. M. (1997). Psychoanalysis and psychotherapy: the grand leading the bland. Paper presented to the University Psychotherapy Association Conference on "Power and Influence in Psychotherapy", November; reprinted in *The Review: Journal of the Universities Psychotherapy and Counselling Association*, 2: 66–83, 2001.

Zilbergeld, B. (1983). *The Shrinking of America: Myths of Psychological Change*. Boston: Little, Brown.

INDEX

DATE DUE
